Watriama and Co
Further Pacific Islands Portraits

Hugh Laracy

Watriama and Co

Further Pacific Islands Portraits

Hugh Laracy

E PRESS

Published by ANU E Press
The Australian National University
Canberra ACT 0200, Australia
Email: anuepress@anu.edu.au
This title is also available online at http://epress.anu.edu.au

---

National Library of Australia Cataloguing-in-Publication entry

Author: Laracy, Hugh, author.

Title: Watriama and Co : further Pacific Islands portraits / Hugh Laracy.

ISBN: 9781921666322 (paperback) 9781921666339 (ebook)

Subjects: Watriama, William Jacob, 1880?-1925.
Islands of the Pacific--History.

Dewey Number: 995.7

All rights reserved. No part of this publication may be reproduced, stored in a retrieval system or transmitted in any form or by any means, electronic, mechanical, photocopying or otherwise, without the prior permission of the publisher.

Cover design and layout by ANU E Press

This edition © 2013 ANU E Press

Contents

Preface ix

1. Pierre Chanel of Futuna (1803–1841): The making of a saint .. 1
2. The Sinclairs Of Pigeon Bay, or 'The Prehistory of the Robinsons of Ni'ihau': An essay in historiography, or 'tales their mother told them' 33
3. Insular Eminence: Cardinal Moran (1830–1911) and the Pacific islands 53
4. Constance Frederica Gordon-Cumming (1837–1924): Traveller, author, painter 69
5. Niels Peter Sorensen (1848–1935): The story of a criminal adventurer 93
6. John Strasburg (1856–1924): A plain sailor 111
7. Ernest Frederick Hughes Allen (1867–1924): South Seas trader 127
8. Beatrice Grimshaw (1870–1953): Pride and prejudice in Papua 141
9. W.J. Watriama (c. 1880–1925): Pretender and patriot, (or 'a blackman's defence of White Australia') 169
10. Lucy Evelyn Cheesman (1881–1969): Traveller, writer, scientist 187
11. Donald Gilbert Kennedy (1898–1967): An outsider in the Colonial Service 211
12. George Bogese (1904–1959): 'Just a bloody traitor'? 229
13. Hector MacQuarrie (1889–1973): Traveller, writer, friend of Vouza 243
14. Patrick O'Reilly (1900–1988): Bibliographer of the Pacific .. 257

Index 267

Dedicated to my grandchildren:
Daniel, Sebastian, Hugh, Nell, Maria and William

Preface

This book is the product of a long-sustained, yet desultorily applied, personal curiosity. Hence its somewhat random and eclectic composition. It is, in part at least, a harvest of uncoordinated enquiries in response to a plethora of diverse yet cognate stimuli. These include a plethora of tantalising gaps that have been left in the works of other writers on the history of the Pacific islands;[1] seductively intriguing entries in archival finding lists; and puzzlement about the authorship of books on which one might draw without appreciating their provenance. Such encounters prompted questions. Who were these people and where did they come from? What else did they do? What became of them when they passed beyond the range of the records in which one first encountered them, and what more might be said of them?

The responses evoked by such questions, though, have gone beyond building a set of personal profiles. They are also designed to illuminate and test the panoply of generalisations and abstractions, the identifying of processes and the thematic essaying that are the stock-in-trade of historical analysis and reconstruction. The individuals are not isolates. They are also able to be comprehended within categories which subsume singularity: be it indigenes, colonisers, settlers, missionaries, traders, administrators, writers, patriots and so on. The particular and the collective, like the concrete and the conceptual, are distinctive entities; but these figures can be seen as representative of people operating in the Pacific within the period ranging from the early nineteenth century to World War II. Those whose stories are told here may be seen as being complementary within a broad context of historical experience.

Thus, the Sinclairs of New Zealand, progenitors of the Robinsons of Hawai'i, were scarcely 'typical' of nineteenth century settlers in the Pacific. Yet they were part of—and their story helps illuminate it—a major migrant outflow from Europe that had profound implications in many parts of the world, not least for the Pacific islands and their indigenous inhabitants. The Pacific was a magnet for footloose Europeans of various kinds: missionaries (Pierre Chanel), merchants (Niels Sorensen, Ernest Allen, John Strasburg), writers (Constance Gordon-Cumming, Beatrice Grimshaw, Lucy Cheesman), colonial officials (Hector MacQuarrie, Donald Kennedy), and a stimulus for visionaries (Cardinal Moran) and scholars (Patrick O'Reilly). The native islanders, too, were an essential part of these enterprises: responding and resisting, becoming literate, acquiring

---

1   For a welcome exception to this comment, see Mike Butcher, '… *when the long trick's over*': *Donald Kennedy in the Pacific*, Kennington, Vic., 2012.

new tastes in consumer goods and asserting themselves (W.J. Watriama, George Bogese, Jacob Vouza) against what they found disagreeable. And, of course, having their futures profoundly shaped by these enterprises.

For the promiscuous inquisitiveness that generated these essays, musing about the Robinsons of Ni'ihau offers a case in point. It was an unanticipated by-product of a trip to Hawai'i to conduct research on World War II in the Solomon Islands. My immediate interest in the Robinsons was born not of their notorious reclusiveness, but by the attention directed to their island through its being terrorised by Shigemori Nishikaichi, a Japanese air force pilot who crash-landed there following the treacherous and (in hindsight) ill-advised raid on Pearl Harbor on the morning of Sunday 7 December 1941. That assault propelled the United States actively into the conflict; and, so led to the turning point of the conflict in the Pacific, the Guadalcanal landings on 7 August 1942.[2]

Awareness of the events that took place on Ni'ihau prompted the question 'who were these folk among whom Shigemori had landed'? It need not have, but it did. Similarly, puzzlement over the far from self-evident causal connection between the death of Pierre Chanel on Futuna in 1841 and his canonisation in 1954 led to the examination of a well-known Pacific incident in its more arcane European context. Even more puzzling, were references to a 'King of the Loyalty Islands' in the National Archives of Australia finding lists, when none of the many publications on Pacific kingdoms (a markedly Polynesian phenomenon) mentions such a being. But the misnomer did prompt a richly paper-generating investigation of William Jacob Watriama from that district in France's dependency of New Caledonia, in southern Melanesia. Possibly the essay of most adventitious—and convivial—provenance is that on E.F. Allen. Over lunch one day, Beverley Simmons, an Auckland friend with Samoan connections (her father, Gordon Bryant, had been employed there on the Reparations Estates established by the New Zealand regime which replaced the German one in 1914) commented that an acquaintance of hers, Tanumafili Allen, had written a family history. Then, work on the history of Tuvalu brought Donald Kennedy, who would later achieve fame in the Solomon Islands during World War II, more clearly into view. And the story of his Solomons career could not properly be told without that of that of his indigenous deuteragonist: hence the story of George Bogese. And so it went on. Who were those women whose works occasionally appeared in footnotes: Constance Gordon-Cumming, Beatrice Grimshaw, Evelyn Cheesman? (J.C. Beaglehole, for instance, usefully draws on the latter in his edition of Captain James Cook's account of the New Hebrides.[3]) If there is a deity revealing suitable subjects for closer scrutiny, he/she has been working steadily, unpredictably and resourcefully.

---

2   Blake Clark, *Remember Pearl Harbor*, Honolulu, 1987, pp. 193–214.
3   *The Journals of James Cook Captain*, Cambridge, 1969, vol. II, pp. 480, 490.

While the book may lack the inherent thematic unity of a monograph or of a single biography, the people presented herein may be deemed to constitute a 'company' in two significant senses, even if (despite the title) they do not fit together like Rudyard Kipling's *Stalky and Co*. In the first case, they may be taken as samples of the diverse range of influences that impacted on the Pacific and helped shape its future. Of course, the various island peoples already had well-established—and enduring—cultures and identities when Europeans began arriving off their shores, following Magellan's crossing of the ocean in 1520–1521. But there were marked regional differences and similarities. Hence, the convenient (if scarcely infallible) geographical arrangement of the Pacific into three broad ethno-cultural categories by Dumont d'Urville in 1832: Melanesia, Micronesia, Polynesia.[4] Among the many dates making European activity a significant part of indigenous Pacific history, one may (arbitrarily!) cite 1788, the foundation of Sydney; 1797, the arrival of the London Missionary Society missionaries in Tahiti; and, 1869, the completion of the American transcontinental railway, which magnified the relevance of shipping to and from the port of San Francisco to the Pacific.

Then there is the second sense of 'company'. In having their stories grouped within the same set of covers, the people presented herein are placed within an honourable historiographic tradition. The pattern was set by *Pacific Islands Portraits*, edited by J.W. Davidson and Deryck Scarr of The Australian National University, and published in 1970. That volume was a harvest of essays that served as a manifesto for the emerging discipline of Pacific history, of which Davidson was the founding professor.[5] From a political perspective, that discipline was designed to help make peoples who were moving from colonial subjection to being citizens of self-governing and independent states more comprehensible to the world at large, and to present them and their experiences on their own terms. Nine years later a complementary volume titled *More Pacific Islands Pacific Portraits* appeared, edited by Scarr; preceded in 1978 by a related, but more narrowly focused, collection of *Papua New Guinea Portraits: the expatriate experience*, edited by James Griffin. *Watriama and Co*, then, whatever its shortcomings, is of a noble lineage. One hopes that it will prove worthy of its precedents, and will help generate further inheritors of Davidson's inspiration.

Hugh Laracy

---

4   I.C. Campbell, *Worlds Apart: a history of the Pacific Islands*, Christchurch, 2003, pp. 15–33.
5   Niel Gunson, 'An Introduction to Pacific History', in Brij V. Lal (ed.), *Pacific Islands History: journeys and transformations*, Canberra, 1992, pp. 1–13; Donald Denoon, 'Pacific Island History at the Australian National University: the place and the people', *The Journal of Pacific History*, vol. 31, no. 2 (Dec. 1996), pp. 202–214.

1. Pierre Chanel of Futuna (1803–1841): The making of a saint

Apart from James Cook and William Bligh—and leaving aside the creative geniuses, Herman Melville, Robert Louis Stevenson and Paul Gauguin, whose lives and works find their main constituency of interest elsewhere—who is the most variously and extensively commemorated figure in the field of Pacific history? Nowhere, with the obvious exceptions of the small Polynesian islands of Wallis and Futuna, north of Tonga, is his name an ingrained commonplace. Yet, admittedly without the benefit of exhaustive comparative research, but after perusing bibliographies and consulting with mission historians, one may confidently assert that the likely answer is 'Pierre Chanel'.[1] A quiet-mannered Catholic missionary, Chanel, after a sojourn of three and a half years unrewarded by a tally of converts or, indeed, by any other conspicuous accomplishment, was murdered on Futuna in 1841. He was a singularly unlikely candidate for fame and his notability is entirely posthumous. Yet it has become deep-rooted, widespread, abundantly attested and, above all, remains current. Within the international Catholic community his *cultus* is particularly marked in those areas influenced by the sub-culture of the Society of Mary (Marist Fathers), of which there is none more so than the South Pacific.

The major biography of Chanel appeared in ten editions and in five languages between 1885 and 1935. Interest remains steady. Churches, educational establishments and mission ships have been dedicated to him in over a dozen countries.[2] People entering religious life have regularly adopted his name. A bibliography concerning him lists over 120 items and, in the 1990s alone, he inspired at least ten publications in three languages.[3] What follows is an attempt to trace and explain the process, by no means fortuitous, by which his memory has been secured and propagated. While finding expression in a multitude of local, ethnic and cultural particularities, that memory has also been incorporated into the transcendent Catholic metaculture. There, distinctions between the introduced and the indigenous are blurred if not obliterated; as,

---

1 Private communications from Ian Breward, Allan Davidson, John Garrett, Francis Hezel, David Hilliard. Davidson writes 'Chanel has an international profile that has continued to grow because of the saintifying process … [In contrast], the whole Protestant missionary world which exalted heroes like Williams, Patteson and [James] Chalmers has virtually died. [However], they still have considerable local significance—for example, Patteson in Melanesia, Williams in Samoa and Chalmers in the Cook Islands and Papua'.
2 For the spread and distribution of the Marists, see Francis Durning, *The Whole World Marist: a narrative of the expansion of the Society of Mary*, Wellington, 1983.
3 Hugh Laracy, 'Chanel—bibliography', unpublished TS in author's possession. His full surviving correspondence is included in the massive Marist compilation Charles Girard (ed.), *Lettres reçues d'Océanie, 1836–1854*, 10 vols, Rome, 2009.

for instance, when Monsignor Marcel Lefebvre, later famous as a schismatic archbishop, sealed a relic of Chanel in the foundation stone of a Marist college at Dakar in Senegal in West Africa in 1948.[4]

The nearest challenger for Chanel's place on the commemorative ranking table for the Pacific—and the pre-eminent figure within the ambit of English-speaking Protestantism there—is John Williams of the London Missionary Society. Besides spectacularly receiving Samoa for Christianity in 1830, Williams travelled extensively through the Pacific, including a visit to New Zealand, and in 1835 he published a widely read narrative of his evangelistic and exploratory exploits. Within five years of publication, 35,000 copies of this book were sold.[5] As a hero of the expanding frontier of British enterprise, Williams has even been likened to Cook. And, like Cook in Hawai'i in 1779, at Eromanga in the New Hebrides in 1839 he secured his own claim upon the attention both of contemporaries and of posterity by being killed in the course of his much-admired labours. It was no coincidence that the best known print of his death—contrasting noble innocence with brutish depravity—was made to echo John Webber's famous 'The Death of Captain Cook'. A putative coincidence of patriotism and religion was reflected in this tendentious conflation of images.[6] One eulogist, who understood publicity, commented,

> for popular effect, for the reputation of Mr. Williams, and for the purposes of history, he died in the proper manner, at the proper place, and at the proper time.[7]

That is, of course, a familiar phenomenon. Would the Easter Uprising of 1916 have contributed much to the Irish nationalist cause without the serial execution of its leaders? Blood sacrifice, or some other dramatic demise (such as death from leprosy), attracts attention and harnesses the loyalty and affection of those who sympathise with the victim's cause. Base misfortune is thus transmuted by the alchemy of adulation into golden martyrdom. So it also was with John Coleridge

---

4   The notion of 'metaculture' is discussed in Kenelm Burridge, *In the Way: a study of Christian missionary endeavours*, Vancouver, 1991. For a perceptive tragi-comic exploration of it, see Brian Moore's novel *Catholics*, London, 1972. Jean-Claude Marquis, *St Pierre Chanel, de l'Ain au Pacifique*, Bourg-en-Bresse, 1991, p. 83.

5   James J. Ellis, *John Williams: the martyr missionary of Polynesia*, Kilmarnock, n.d. [1890?], p. 127; Richard M. Moyle (ed.), *The Samoan Journals of John Williams*, Canberra, 1984, p. 14.

6   Since the late 1970s historians seem to have ben more interested in Cook's death than in his deeds. K.R. Howe, 'The Making of Cook's Death', *Journal of Pacific History*, vol. 31, no. 1 (1996), pp. 108–118; Bernard Smith, *European Vision and the South Pacific*, Sydney, 1984, pp. 318–321; Rudiger Joppien and Bernard Smith, *The Art of Captain Cook's Voyages*, Melbourne, 1987, vol. 3 (text), pp. 126–128. Basil Mathews' *John Williams the Shipbuilder* (London, 1915) is replete with references to Cook.

7   John Campbell, quoted in Gavan Daws, *A Dream of Islands:voyages of self-discovery in the South Seas*, Sydney, 1980, p. 67.

Patteson, the Old Etonian bishop killed at Nukapu near the Solomon Islands in 1871. The story of his death 'remains central in the traditions of Melanesian Anglicanism'.[8]

So, too, it was with Chanel. The ecclesiastical response to him, though, contrasts significantly with that towards Williams and Patteson. His memory has been more systematically sustained. For Chanel belonged to a Church that, beyond simply according him a hallowed place in its traditions, had the theological and institutional capacity—albeit exercised via labyrinthine procedures—to recognise martyrs (along with other models of heroic virtue) with canonical formality.[9] Second, he was a member of a religious congregation that had a special interest in seeing one of its own elevated to the highest level of veneration, namely sainthood. That goal was reached in 1954. To mark it, 22 publications appeared between 1953 and 1955 and dedications grew apace. In New Zealand alone by 2000 there were six parishes and five schools bearing his name, as well as a shrine at Russell (where his bones once rested for seven years) and the architecturally precious Futuna Chapel in Wellington.[10]

***

The son of a peasant farmer, Pierre-Louis-Marie Chanel was born in the parish of Cuet near Lyon in south-central France in 1803. From childhood he aspired to be a priest, and he was duly ordained for the diocese of Belley in 1827. Then, in 1831, he joined the incipient Society of Mary, a group of priests who, under their leader, Jean-Claude Colin, hoped to become an autonomous religious congregation; that is, independent of the bishop of a diocese. As with numerous other congregations, the matrix from which the Marists originated was the powerful, desperate, even millenarian, Catholic revival that developed in reaction to the persecutions and blasphemies unleashed on the Church by the French Revolution; and which continued spasmodically until being defused by the sacrificial bravery of the clergy in defence of *la patrie* during the war of 1914–1918. The Marists were part of a movement that, careless of hardships, aimed not only at rebuilding the Church in France, but also at reminding the nation of the honours and obligations that had historically bound it to Catholicism as *la fille ainée de l'eglise* ('the eldest daughter of the Church').[11] Interest in

---

8   David Hilliard, 'The Making of an Anglican Martyr', in Diana Wood (ed.), *Martyrs and Martyrologies*, Oxford, 1993, pp. 333–345.
9   Kenneth L. Woodward, *Making Saints: how the Catholic Church determines who becomes a saint and who doesn't, and why*, New York, 1990.
10 *New Zealand Catholic Directory* (annual), Wellington, 1996–2000. Chanel's bones were at Russell/Kororareka from 3 Feb. 1842 to early April 1849, and on 30 Mar. 1977. Lillian G. Keys, *Philip Viard: bishop of Wellington*, Christchurch, 1968, p. 35; J. Gorinsky, 'Peter Chanel's Body in Australia', *Harvest*, June 1954, pp. 8–9; K.J. Roach, 'The Journeyings of the Relics of St Peter Chanel' MS, 1979, Marist Archives, Wellington; Russell Walden, *Voices of Silence: New Zealand's chapel of Futuna*, Wellington, 1987.
11 That title was of later origin. The king of France was traditionally called *le fils annee de l'eglise* ('the eldest son of the Church'), but not the country. Use of the feminine form represented a transfer of what had been

foreign missions was conspicuous in this religious resurgence. Therefore, when the Vatican offered the Marists the islands of the western Pacific as a field of operation, Colin readily agreed in order to expedite approbation for his Society. This was granted on 29 April 1836.[12]

Chanel was in the first party of Marist missionaries, five priests and three coadjutor brothers, who left France on 24 December 1836, led by Bishop J.B. Pompallier. After reaching Tahiti, Pompallier turned south to New Zealand. *En route* he settled Pierre Bataillon and a brother at Wallis (or Uvea), and Chanel and Brother Marie-Nizier Delorme at Futuna, 150 kilometres to the west, with each pair under the protection of the leading chief of the island. On Futuna, this was at Poi, in the district of Tua, with 'king' Niuliki. Pompallier intended to return to Futuna within six months, but more than four years were to pass before he did so. Then, it was to collect Chanel's remains.[13]

From the outset, Chanel's task was difficult. Demonstrating the worldly wisdom shown by many Pacific islanders in their early dealings with Europeans, Niuliki heeded an adviser who urged 'I believe we would do well to keep these Whites on the island, their presence could be profitable to us'. But he evinced slight interest in their religion.[14] The reason is plain; while there might be advantages in tolerating missionaries, Niuliki was in no way dependent on them. There were other and more abundant sources of European metal goods and cloth available to him. Above all, he was already prospering politically. Since the early years of the century, whaling ships trading for food and water had visited regularly while, by the late 1830s, there was a resident trader on Futuna as well as several beachcombers.

A major consequence of these contacts was that the Futunans obtained firearms, which helped to enlarge the scale of indigenous warfare and to concentrate power into fewer but larger *blocs*. In June 1838, following the visit of the *Hudson*, Chanel wrote

---

the monarch's title to the nation, and developed in the wake of Pope Leo XIII's call in 1889 to the Catholics of France to 'rally' to the Republic.
12   See, generally, Ralph Gibson, *A Social History of French Catholicism, 1789–1914*, London, 1989; Ralph M. Wiltgen, *The Founding of the Roman Catholic Church in Oceania, 1825 to 1850*, Canberra, 1979, pp. 101–131. For the war service of the Catholic clergy, see [Henri Bordeaux], *La Preuve du Sang: livre d'or du clerge et des congregations, 1914–1922*, 2 vols, Paris, 1925 and 1930.
13   E.R. Simmons, *Pompallier: prince of bishops*, Auckland, 1984, pp. 24–28; Wiltgen, pp. 151–163. Useful first-hand accounts of the Marists' entry into the Pacific are contained in Willian Joseph Stuart and Anthony Ward, *Ever Your Poor Brother: Peter Chanel, surviving letters and Futuna journal*, Rome, 1991.
14   Quoted in Claude Nicolet, *Vie du Bienheureux Pierre-Louis-Marie Chanel: pretre mariste, premier martyr du l'Oceanie*, Lyon, 1935, p. 181 (trans H.L.).

> My poor islanders have bought from the captain only powder, muskets and shot. They burn with the wish to become *malo* (the 'victors') and anything that can make them terrible to their enemies is worthwhile.[15]

In fact, the Tua people were already *malo*—but they wished to consolidate their position. About the year 1800 they had been one of six or seven independent districts in Futuna, but, by about 1820, the contestants for supremacy had been reduced to two—Sigave in the West and Tua in the East. In the following years Tua enjoyed two notable victories over Sigave, reducing it to the status of *lava* (the 'defeated'), before being itself defeated in a third clash. Then, in a further encounter shortly before the missionaries arrived, Tua, under Niuliki, regained the title of *malo*. Finally, in the engagement of greatest importance, Niuliki defeated the Sigave again on 10 August 1839 when, in the last battle in the island's history, he killed their leader, Vanai, and affirmed his primacy over the whole island. In thus becoming 'king' without missionary assistance, Niuliki had no reason to transfer his (or his people's) spiritual loyalties away from the *atua* (traditional spirits) who had favoured his progress. Chanel commented:

> Our good king Niuliki, said to be the man into whom the greatest god in the island [Fakavelikele] descends, seems to have a great fear of what his islanders will say if he rejects a god he has so often told them is powerful and terrifying.[16]

Not that the Tua leader had not wavered. In June 1839, during a visit to Futuna, the formidable Bataillon from Wallis had persuaded Niuliki to allow him to burn a number of sacred objects in order to demonstrate the superior power of Jehovah. Great was said to be the general admiration when this was achieved without mishap, and Niuliki himself said he would be converted as soon as the whole island decided to become Catholic.[17] But then came the final victory over Sigave. Niuliki's renewed indifference was matched by his subjects' strengthened demands for 'signs and wonders' before yielding: they wanted to see Jehovah, to be cured of sickness, and to have a shelter built to protect Futuna from the wind.[18] That those who did accept baptism (even though *in extremis*) always died was no inducement for them to lower their price. In May 1839 Chanel had commented 'Twenty baptisms, four of which were adults and the rest children, and all in danger of death, make up the entire harvest I have reaped in eighteen months'. Nor did Pompallier's delayed return help

---

15 Chanel to Bataillon, 21 June 1838, in Claude Rozier (ed.), *Ecrits du Pere Pierre Chanel: missionaire mariste, 1803–1842*, Paris, 1960, p. 350 (trans H.L.). Also, Stuart and Ward, p. 166.
16 Chanel to Colin, 16 May 1840, in Stuart and Ward, p. 225; also, Rozier 1960, p. 285.
17 Chanel, Diary, 1 June 1839, in Stuart and Ward, p. 355; R.P. Mangeret, *Mgr Bataillon et les Missions de l'Oceanie Centrale*, Lyon and Paris, 1884, pp. 269–270; Joseph Ronzon, *Jean-Marie Delorme, Frere Marie-Nizier (1817–1874): essai de biographie du compagnon missionaire du Pere Chanel*, Saint-Martin-en-Haut, 1995, pp. 66–68.
18 Chanel, Diary, Feb. 1840, in Stuart and Ward, p. 409; also, Rozier (1960), pp. 486–487.

matters: 'Brother Marie-Nizier and I were made to look like liars, or like two abandoned men'. He even called for a French naval visit to help counter that bad impression.[19] Throughout Chanel's time on Futuna the only service Niuliki and his fellows consistently sought from the missionaries was a shave with a steel razor. That attraction flagged only once, and then only for three days, after the razor had been used by a Wallisian surgeon to operate on a man with a putrifying testicle. (The patient, named Manogi Tulia, died two days later).[20]

Relations took a further turn for the worse in November 1840. Niuliki, tolerant of Chanel's growing insistence on the falsity of traditional religious beliefs as his facility in the local language increased, turned strongly against the mission when he heard that, defying their chief, Lavelua Vaimua, the people of Wallis were turning towards Christianity. As Chanel commented, 'now that he is truly *malo,* he gives the impression of wanting to cling to Fakavelikele'.[21] Worse still for Niuliki, early in 1841 his eldest son, Meitala, emerged as the leader of a party of young men sympathetic to the missionaries. They were, apparently, impressed by what they had heard from Wallis of the promised benefits of the new religion. More particularly, though, it seems that Meitala, as his father's heir, was bound by taboo to refrain from eating yams until he himself had fathered a son. Meitala resented this prohibition and, after being reassured by the priest that the *atua* would not kill him, 'cooked a large oven full of yams' and ate his fill. On 18 April 1841 Chanel noted that Meitala had decided 'to embrace [our] religion'. With this 'new and important conquest' the crisis point had been reached. 'Maddened by the disobedience of his son and the insult [to] his gods', Niuliki ordered that the missionary be killed. On 28 April, therefore, a party of assassins led by his son-in-law, Musumusu, attacked Chanel in his house, speared him, then clubbed him to death. The other attackers were named Fikitika, Fuasea, Umutaouli and Ukuloa.[22]

***

The momentous aftermath of this event unfolded gradually. Delorme was not at Poi at the time of the attack, but, hearing of it soon afterwards from Meitala, he sought refuge among the Sigave. He stayed there until 11 May when, with Sigave connivance and to the chagrin of Niuliki, he and three other Europeans

---

19 Chanel to Colin, 16 May 1839, and Chanel to Bataillon, 7–21 Sept. 1939, in Stuart and Ward, pp. 171, 196; also, Rozier (1960), pp. 224, 251–252.
20 Stuart and Ward, pp. 236, 243, 282, 341, 347, 381, 389, 390, 395, 399, 423, 429, 430; operation, pp. 346.
21 Chanel to Bataillon, 19 Nov. 1840, in Stuart and Ward, p. 229.
22 Chanel, Journal, 18–19 April 1841, in Stuart and Ward, p. 431, and Rozier 1960 pp. 502–503; John Power Twyning, *Adventures in the South Seas*, London, 1850, quoted in Claude Rozier, *S. Pierre Chanel d'apres ceux qui l'ont connu*, Rome, 1991, pp. 77–78; Delorme to Pompallier, 1 May 1841, in Edward Clisby (trans. and ed.), 'Letters from Oceania: letters of the first Marist Brothers in Oceania, 1836–1850', private circulation, Auckland, 1993–1999; Frederic Angleviel, *Les Missions a Wallis at Futuna au XIXe Siecle*, Bordeaux, 1994, pp. 71–73. Servant, Proces Verbal, 3 Aug. 1845, in Rozier (1991).

managed to escape to the American whaler *William Hamilton*, which was bound for Wallis. From there news of Chanel's death was sent to Colin in France and to Pompallier, who was visiting the French settlers at Akaroa when word reached him on 4 November. Towards the end of that month, in his schooner *Sancta Maria*, accompanied by Fr Philip Viard, and escorted by the French warship *Allier* (Capt. Dubouzet), he set sail for Wallis, reaching there on 30 December.[23]

From Wallis, Viard, under naval escort and accompanied by Delorme and by Sam Keletaona, a Futunan well acquainted with Europeans, was despatched to Futuna to retrieve Chanel's remains and take them to New Zealand. He was greeted with a prudent mixture of remorse and fear. The Futunans, blaming Niuliki—who had since died—for the killing, begged forgiveness, and pleaded for another missionary to come among them. Seeing the *Allier* at hand and being mindful of the reprisals taken in October 1838 by Dumont d'Urville against the Fijians of Bau for attacking the French trader *Aimable Josephine*, they were also conspicuously relieved when the missionaries persuaded Dubouzet not to inflict similar vengeance upon them.[24] Soon after the departure of the two vessels Letavai, the wife of Meitala, composed a chant, 'which the women performed with a melancholy air and mournful keening', voicing their readiness for religious change:

> Pierre, alas!
> here he is no more!
> Chanel came to see,
> but, the sad news is
> he is dead on Futuna.
> Why? Was he a bad man?
> Pierre, alas!
> Marie [Nizier] has come to tell us New Zealand has embraced the Faith.
> Let us do the same
> lest we be left in the midst of the fire.
> Pierre, alas!
> here he is no more, alas![25]

Writing to Colin a month after the killing, Bataillon complained that had Pompallier visited his northern missions earlier, as he had promised—and as Chanel had expected—the missionary would still be alive. 'But then',

---

23 Delorme to Pompallier, 1 May 1841, 19 Dec. 1841; to Colin, 6 Oct. 1844; to Hermitage, 14 June 1846, in Clisby; Keys, pp. 32–35; Ronzon, pp. 91–112; Simmons, p. 61; Twyning, in Rozier (1991), pp. 77–78.
24 Chanel, Journal, 11 Dec. 1838, in Stuart and Ward, p. 315, and Rozier p. 398; Delorme to Colin, 6 Oct. 1844, in Clisby; Angleviel, pp. 74–76; Keys, p. 34; Helen Rosenman (trans. and ed.), Jules S-C Dumont D'Urville, *Two Voyages to the South Seas*, Melbourne, 1987, vol. II, pp. 367–369, 572–573.
25 Clisby, p. 179, note on Delorme to Colin, 24 May 1846. The source is a report by Servant, quoted in Rozier (1991), p. 140.

he continued, 'we would not have a martyr'.[26] Early in 1842, Viard, citing Tertullian's sanguine dictum regarding the Roman persecutions of the third century, declared that 'I have confidence that the blood of our confrère will soon be for the island the seed of Christians'.[27] That this trust was quickly fulfilled, even if for a variety of reasons that included fear along with hope of temporal wellbeing, ensured that the story of Chanel and Futuna would be exploited as a stimulus to piety by generations of preachers and hagiographers.[28] Fathers Servant and Roulleaux came up from New Zealand in June 1842 to collect the harvest; and, a year later, most of the 1,000 inhabitants of Futuna had been baptised.[29] In this there was, for those sympathetic to such an understanding, and susceptible to being inspired by it, dramatic proof of the intervention of divine providence. The number of people involved might be small, but the 100 per cent success rate pointed persuasively heavenwards. Killing and conversion were thus linked, in the non-verifiable logic of *faith* and *belief*, as cause and effect; there, on a plane of privileged perception, explanation merged with interpretation and, in defiance of orthodox reasoning, subsequence became consequence.[30] In 1860 Pompallier wrote:

> it appears that the special mission of Father Chanel was just to be that of the gentle lamb whose blood, united to that of Jesus Christ which takes away the sins of the world, has been spilled by the axe of the infidel and the savage for the benefit of the people of Futuna, who have all become edifying Christians.[31]

In 1845 Jean Faramond, the French consul in Sydney, had detected the same unworldly sentiment when farewelling a party of Marists heading for New Guinea. Referring to their leader, Bishop Jean-Baptiste Epalle, who had earlier worked in New Zealand, he wrote

> I was struck by the vagueness of his plans. I pointed out to him the dangers to which he was exposing himself in landing in the midst of savage people … . But I knew in advance that my warnings were useless, he placed himself at the mercy of Providence and regarded it as a culpable lack of confidence in divine power to arrange his voyage according to the ordinary rules of human prudence. I accompanied him to his ship

---

26   Letter, 31 May 1841, in Rozier (1991), p. 121 (trans. H.L.).
27   Quoted in Keys, p. 34. The original comment is in Tertullian, *Liber Apologeticus*, cap. L: 'Plures efficimur, quoties metimur a vobis: semen est sanguis Christianorum'.
28   There is an extensive literature on 'why Pacific Islanders became Christian'. The best introduction is John Garrett, *To Live Among the Stars: Christian origins in Oceania*, Suva, 1982.
29   Angleviel, p. 99; [Anon.], *Le Tres Reverend Pere Colin*, Lyon, 1896, vol. III, pp. 23–28. For Servant, see *Ecrits de Louis Catherin Servant*, Paris, 1996.
30   Church authorities versed in Scholastic philosophy were not prone to the fallacy of arguing *post hoc, ergo propter hoc* ('after this, therefore because of this').
31   Pompallier to Bourdin, 5 Aug. 1860, in Rozier (1991), p. 87 (trans. H.L.).

1. Pierre Chanel of Futuna (1803–1841): The making of a saint

.... . I was following him with Archbishop [Polding's] Vicar General [Abbott Gregory OSB] to whom I said 'There is a good missionary that we shall never see again. He will be dead with his companions before six months'. 'That would be a great happiness', he replied. 'It is the blood of martyrs which makes religion prosper. Look at Futuna, a missionary was sacrificed there and today the entire island is Catholic.[32]

As events proved, Faramond's misgivings were justified, and Gregory's expectation went unfulfilled. There was to be more blood-letting, but not another Futuna. As David Loades observes, 'the conversion of a victim into a martyr is the business of the apologist, and the success of the apologist depends ultimately upon the success of the cause'.[33]

***

Meanwhile, Chanel's death had also triggered an eager, expectant, response in France. He did not lack apologists and early steps towards his canonisation were soon being taken. In August 1842 formal enquiries regarding his character were initiated in the diocese of Belley. The following month Colin, who had already invoked the killing in arguing (successfully) for the creation of a new vicariate apostolic centred on Wallis and Futuna, with Bataillon as bishop, commissioned a biography of Chanel from his former close associate and friend, Antoine Bourdin. To better provide for the temporal needs of his missionaries, he also helped launch a religious and commercial shipping company, the Société francaise de l'Océanie, and established a mission supply centre in Sydney, but he remained a visionary pragmatist.[34] In 1845 Colin obtained a formal report on the events in Futuna from his subjects there and, in 1847, Bataillon obliged with another. Next, Colin ordered that Chanel's bones be repatriated. They left Auckland in April 1849, were held in Sydney for nine months, and were received in honour at the General House of the Society in Lyon in June 1850.[35] At about the same time, Bourdin presented the manuscript of his book, which was to be included in Chanel's dossier for consideration in Rome. But it was unsatisfactory. Colin, who was also a pragmatic visionary, found the draft to be

---

32 Faramond, despatch of 30 April 1846, Correspondence Commerciale, Sydney, t.1 (1842–1847), Archives Diplomatiques, Ministere des Affaires Etrangeres, Paris (trans. H.L.).
33 David Loades, 'Introduction', in Wood, p. xvi. See also Hugh Laracy, 'Roman Catholic "Martyrs" in the South Pacific, 1841–55', *Journal of Religious History*, vol. 9, no. 2 (1976), pp. 189–202; and *Marists and Melanesians: a history of Catholic missions in the Solomon Islands*, Canberra, 1976, pp. 11–31.
34 Garrett, p. 99; John Hosie, *Challenge: the Marists in colonial Australia*, Sydney, 1987, pp. 22–36; Wiltgen, pp. 299, 449–450.
35 Rozier (1991), pp. 141–167; Kevin Roach, 'The Journeyings of the Relics of St Peter Chanel', TS, 1979, Marist Archives, Wellington; and 'Saint and Martyr: the story of St Peter Chanel', *Marist Messenger*, May 1977, pp. 10–13; J. Gorinsky, 'Peter Chanel's body in Australia', *Harvest*, June 1954, pp. 8–9; Jean-Claude Marquis, *St Pierre Chanel: de l'Ain au Pacifique*, Bourg-en-Bresse, 1991, pp. 80–85.

inaccurate, overly reverential and unduly concerned with personalities, so he rejected it, and turned his attention to composing the definitive constitutions for his Society.[36]

With that, the Marist call for Chanel's elevation faded, but only temporarily, though not for the last time. It was resumed under a new superior-general, Julien Favre, who had succeeded Colin in 1854 and, following discussions with the Pope himself, by Bataillon during a visit to Rome in 1857.[37] Accordingly, in September 1857, the Vatican's Sacred Congregation of Rites accepted the Marist's application. It thereby awarded Chanel the title of Venerable and undertook to deal with his cause for canonisation according to the requirements of Canon Law (which, in the codified version in force from 1917 to 1983, contained 142 articles pertaining to that matter).[38]

To this same end, Bourdin was persuaded to revise his book. It was eventually published in 1867, running to 624 pages. But it was still flawed, as Delorme, the closest witness to what is the probably the most thoroughly investigated missionary death in Oceania, pointed out in a long and detailed letter to Colin.[39] So, in 1875, Rome requested a new biography. This was entrusted to Claude Nicolet, a Marist priest, who also took on the office of postulator in attempting to persuade professionally sceptical tribunals of the merits of Chanel's case. It was slow work, but efficacious. Chanel's writings were favourably reviewed in 1877; Nicolet's book appeared in 1885; and a decree of authentic martyrdom, certifying that Chanel had been killed *in odium fidei* ('in hatred of the Faith'), was issued in 1888. Then, on 17 November 1889 Pope Leo XIII affirmed that Chanel had lived an unimpeachable life and declared him Blessed, along with another French missionary, Jean-Gabriel Perboyre, a Vincentian, who had been killed in China in 1840.[40]

While the Beatification was an honour for Chanel it was also a singular accolade, a sign of coming of age, a warrant of fitness for the Society to which he had belonged. The Marists celebrated accordingly, encouraged by the spirit of display fostered by the Paris exhibition of 1889 and, more particularly, by the spirit of the *Ralliement*. This was a timely interlude of reduced tension in the endemic feud between church and state and was engendered by Pope Leo XIII's acceptance of the view that it would be better for French Catholics at last, 100

---

36   Rozier (1991), pp. 11–12.
37   Ibid. Mangeret, pp. 211–219. Bataillon brought a Wallisian, a Tongan and a Rotuman to Europe with him.
38   *Missions des Iles*, no. 55 (1954), p. 19.
39   Delorme to Colin, 7 Oct. 1867, in Rozier (1991), pp. 175–219.
40   For detailed chronologies of Chanel's life and of the progress of his Cause see Rozier (1960), pp. 21–30; Stuart and Ward, pp. 31–50; *Acta Societatis Mariae*, pp. 93–95.

years after the outbreak of the revolution, to recognise the Republic rather than endure permanent alienation from government by continuing to support the Royalists.[41]

During 1890, beginning at Belley and in the presence of Cardinal Richard, Archbishop of Paris, Chanel was honoured throughout France by a series of at least 20 *tridua*. These were three-day-long liturgical festivals of Masses, blessings, prayers, processions and sermons by distinguished preachers, and several were graced by the presence of the martyr's bones in their handsome reliquary. Other *tridua* were held in San Francisco and at Madawaska in Maine, where there were large French communities; in Sydney, in the presence of Cardinal Moran;[42] and also in Belgium, England and Spain. All these events were well-publicised and many generated sizable volumes of proceedings. That for Lyon, where Monseigneur d'Hulst, rector of the Institut Catholique[43] in Paris, preached, had 80 pages, and that for Saint-Brieuc, where Bishop Grimes of Christchurch was present, ran to 107 pages.[44] As well as providing both devotional occasions and nationally significant displays of religious triumphalism, the *triduum* series of 1890 also advertised on an unprecedented scale the existence and works of the hitherto obscure Marist congregation; indeed, they were its epiphany. As one report had it:

> Four years ago the Marists endured the sad privation of not being able to celebrate the fiftieth anniversary of the approbation of the Society. Alas, in our own France we were proscribed, in our chapels prayer had to be in silence so as not to be deemed seditious. How could we sing the canticle of gratitude, which requires *elan* as much as gratitude? Our divine mother sympathised with us, and let us wait but a little time for an even more memorable anniversary. She inspired the controllers of the churches to open their, for the moment respected, temples to us, and the vast surroundings of them were well suited to resounding with the zeal of the faithful. Thus we have had the jubilee year of our Martyr.[45]

Nor was that all. Between 1889 and 1892 the Marists kept the printing presses busy airing Chanel's name. Among various items published were a second edition of Nicolet's biography (with translations into Italian, Spanish and German), a 200-page abridgement (which would run to at least eight printings and several translations), a pamphlet 'Life' (which saw six editions by 1926), an oratorio and a verse drama in three acts. Furthermore, an elaborate reliquary

---

41 D.W. Brogan, *The Development of Modern France (1870–1939)*, London, 1953, pp. 257–267; Alexander Sedgwick, *The Ralliement in French Politics, 1890–1898*, Cambridge, 1965.
42 *Freeman's Journal*, 3 May 1890.
43 The leading centre of higher education for the French clergy.
44 Laracy, Chanel—bibliography.
45 Societe de Marie, *Compte rendu sommaire des solennites du triduum en l'honneur du bienheureux Pierre-Louis-Marie Chanel, 1889–1890*, Lyon, 1891, p. 4 (trans. H.L.).

was commissioned from a prominent Lyon silversmith to hold Chanel's remains. And, on Futuna itself, a hexagonal-shaped stone chapel was built on the very site of the martyrdom to house some relics deposited there amidst great ceremony by Bishop Armand Lamaze, Bataillon's successor, on his return from the celebrations in Europe. The first shrine on that spot, a leaf and bamboo structure, had been erected in 1844.[46]

Elsewhere, too—notably at Cuet, Chanel's birthplace—efforts were made to enshrine his memory permanently and prominently. There the enthusiasm of 1890 begot a project (abandoned in 1914) for building a basilica in his name; a weekly pilgrimage (which lasted until 1939), and was promoted by a monthly bulletin from 1920 to 1927); and a series of panegyrics extolling some feature of his life, work or character. These were preached, and later usually published, annually until 1940. Disruptive as it was, though, the impact of two wars on such observances did not expunge Cuet's claim to share in the glory of its famous son. In 1991, marking the sesquicentenary of his death, local church and civic authorities combined to set up a museum there dedicated to him, the *Musée Océanien et de Saint Pierre Chanel*.[47]

***

Rigorous as the path to beatification was, the way from there to canonisation was even more problematic. It required the occurrence of two events which, after close scientific investigation, had defied all explanation as natural phenomena and which might, therefore, *according to the assumptions of Faith*, reasonably be attributed to supernatural intervention. That is, two 'miracles' which could be used as evidence that the candidate for sainthood was ensconced in Heaven (however that supernatural realm might be conceived) and had the power to procure divine favours. The favours sought were to be unambiguous cures for some serious ailment, and the candidate needed also to have been invoked directly. The earliest claim for a miracle wrought through Chanel's intercession concerned a missionary nun who is said to have been cured of a strangulated hernia after praying at the scene of his death in 1858.[48] Others followed. In 1891 Nicolet issued a book recounting a dozen more cures and 'signal graces' from the same source. One involved a young soldier named Francois Vion-Dury who was blinded by fire in November 1889. Both his retinas were detached, so that no light rays were relayed to the optic nerves. Eye specialists declared his condition incurable. Yet, in August 1890, his sight was suddenly restored. Doctors agreed that there was no natural explanation for the cure. A similar case was that of Marie-Rosalie Monnier, a 33-year-old woman with an inoperable

---

46 Angleviel, p. 100; Clisby, p. 138; Ronzon, p. 122.
47 Louis Jannel et al., *Musee Oceanien et de Saint Pierre Chanel*, Cuet, 1991; Laracy, Chanel—bibliography; Marquis, pp. 85–87.
48 Mangeret, vol. II, pp. 330–333.

gastric ulcer, and who had suffered from tuberculosis for 15 years. She was on the point of death when, on 8 September 1904, after prayerfully invoking Chanel's assistance during a visit to the healing shrine at Lourdes, she was suddenly cured. The disease never returned, and she died at the age of 73.[49]

These two events were duly investigated in both diocesan and Vatican tribunals. In the latter they were several times scrutinised by a theologian acting as Defender of the Faith (the famous 'Devil's Advocate') and by a panel of medical specialists. These processes were inherently thorough rather than rapid. They were conducted within a system of thought that was doctrinally bound to allow the *possibility* of metaphysical agency in mundane affairs, but which, despite that, was not predisposed to recognising alleged instances of it. Explanations that needed to be located within a realm of subsistent mystery might be conceded, but not at all readily, as was shown in the case of Monnier's cure. That was submitted to the Vatican in 1911, to replace a cure that had been presented ahead of it, but which was rejected in 1906, only to prove diagnostically problematic itself. With that setback Chanel's cause was side-lined for four decades. Procrastination, though, also derived from the fact that during the term of the fifth superior-general, Ernest Rieu (1922–1947), the Marists became more interested in procuring the beatification of their founder, Colin, who was declared Venerable in 1908, than in advancing the cause of Chanel. That order of priority, however, was reversed by his successor, Alcyme Cyr, an American, and in January 1954, after renewed Marist pressure and reconsideration of the Monnier file, the Roman authorities formally recognised each of the nominated cures as miracles. Consequently, (but not inadvisedly, since 1954 was being celebrated as a 'Marian Year')[50] on 12 June 1954, in Rome, amidst spectacular ceremony, Chanel, along with four others, was canonised as a saint by infallible decree of Pope Pius XII, and was named as spiritual patron of Oceania.[51] In 1969 he was additionally honoured, and exposed to a vastly wider audience, when his feast day was added to the general liturgical calendar of the Catholic Church.[52]

A feature of the proceedings in Rome in 1954, which attracted an international Marist-organised group of about 2,000 pilgrims, was a procession through St Peter's square with a banner showing the martyr being received into glory. Such visual representations of the Greek practice of apotheosis, of transforming

---

49 [Claude Nicolet], *Quelques guerisons et graces signalees obtinues par l'intercession du Bx P.-L.-M. Chanel, pretre de la Societe de Marie et premier martyr d l'Oceanie*, Lyon, 1891; John Thornhill, 'The Seal of God', *Harvest*, June 1954, pp. 11–13; *Missions des Iles*, no. 55 (pp. 20–21).
50 A 'Marian Year' is one dedicated to honouring in a particular way Mary the mother of Jesus, a matter of special importance to the Society of Mary.
51 *Acta Societatis Mariae*, no. 14 (1954), pp. 93–95; Pius XII, *Litterae Decretales quibus Beato Petro Aloisio Chanel Martyri Sanctorum Honores Decernuntur*, Vatican, 1955. The others canonised with Chanel were Gaspard del Bufalo, Joseph Pignatelli, Dominic Savio and Maria Crocifissa di Rosa.
52 Stuart and Ward, p. 50.

heroes into gods, had been revived in the Baroque art of the seventeenth century. For the neo-classical heirs of the Enlightenment, it lasted until the late eighteenth century, long enough for Cook to be depicted ascending into the clouds clutching his sextant and escorted by the buxom spirits of Britannia and of Fame. But, in Catholic iconography, it found a more permanent home.[53] So, in his turn, Chanel was shown with two angels, rather more demure than Cook's physically exuberant escorts, while beneath the clouds a high, verdant island edged with a sweeping coast and bounded by blue sea represented his patronal fiefdom. To complete the formal rites, a solemn *triduum*, at which Archbishop Liston of Auckland preached, was held in the church of Saint Louis des Francais.

The mood of pious enthusiasm was sustained. There were more dedications, and publications proliferated: in 1954 Marists published seven 'lives' of Chanel, while in New Zealand in 1952, anticipating the need to celebrate, the noted composer Ernest Jenner had produced an English adaptation of J.M. Garin's 1889 oratorio. In 1960 a critical edition of Chanel's writings was published and, since 1954, another ten 'lives' have appeared, including one in Portuguese, published in Brazil in 1980. In 1991 the sesquicentenary of his death inspired not only more publishing, and a wave of liturgical celebrations, but begot the museum at Cuet.[54] Ironically, especially given a family connection to the saint, the odour of sanctity was rather less appealing to the French perfume house of Chanel. Also in 1991, fearing confusion with its own products Chanel threatened legal action against the Marists in New Zealand unless their Mission Estate winery in Hawkes Bay dropped the name Chanel from the label of its best chardonnay. Although the Chanel block grapes had been planted in 1911, and the vineyard established in 1851, the Marists capitulated. The intolerance of the *parfumerie* reminded one local cartoonist of the cowardly French military attack on the *Rainbow Warrior* in Auckland in 1985, but the law governing use of trade names prevailed. Sadly, the scarcely evocative name 'Jewelstone' was subsequently adopted, although the quality of the wine was unchanged.[55]

***

Meanwhile, the Futunans, too, had challenged the Marists, but for possession of Chanel's tangible remains. Mixing piety with political assertiveness, they

---

53 Bernard Smith, *Imagining the Pacific: in the wake of the Cook voyages*, Melbourne, 1992, pp. 233–235; and 'Cook's Posthumous Reputation', in Robin Fisher and Hugh Johnston, *Captain James Cook and his Times*, Vancouver, 1979, pp. 161–185; Gananath Obeyesekere, *The Apotheosis of Captain Cook: European mythmaking in the Pacific*, Princeton, 1992, p. 130.
54 *Acta Societatis Mariae*, no. 14 (1954); 'Jenner', in Claudia Orange (ed.), *Dictionary of New Zealand Biography*, vol. 4, p. 254; *Short Oratorio in Honour of Blessed Peter Chanel, S.M.*, Wellington, 1952; Laracy, Chanel—bibliography; Rozier (1960).
55 W.J. Symes, *The Life of St Peter Chanel: the Marist missionary martyr*, Bolton, 1963, p. 8; *Dominion Sunday Times*, 1 Dec. 1991; *National Business Review*, 13 Dec. 1991; John Dyson, *Sink the Rainbow: an enquiry into the 'Greenpeace Affair'*, London, 1986.

1. Pierre Chanel of Futuna (1803–1841): The making of a saint

wanted the bones of 'Petelo Sanele' *their* sainted martyr returned to Futuna. They argued that Chanel had, after all, given his life for them and, in the post-colonial ethos fostered by the Second Vatican Council, their claim was heard sympathetically. Already, in 1966, Pope Paul VI had converted the Pacific's mission vicariates, including that of Wallis and Futuna, into independent dioceses.

In 1977, therefore, at the request of the new indigenous bishop of the diocese, Mgr Lolesio Fuahea, the relics from Lyon were despatched to Oceania, in the care of Fr Claude Rozier, editor of the scholarly edition of Chanel's writings. Following a circuitous route through the region, and venerated at every stop, including New Zealand (where Whina Cooper, the cynosure of Maori leadership at the time, kept vigil at Te Unga Waka Marae in Auckland), the relics were eventually deposited in the sanctuary of Our Lady Queen of the Martyrs at Poi on 28 April. The last leg of the journey, from Wallis, was made aboard a French naval vessel, while a set of postage stamps had been issued by Wallis and Futuna to mark the occasion.[56] The Futunans, though—in customary Polynesian style—were not to be satisfied until they also possessed Chanel's skull, which had been taken to Rome in 1954. Accordingly, in 1987, on the 150th anniversary of the Marist's arrival in the Pacific, and a year after the opening of a handsome basilica dedicated to Chanel at Poi, that wish, too, was gratified. Poi has since become, though on a modest scale, a place of pilgrimage. That development, incidentally, had been foreshadowed as early as 1903 by Moran. He had recently been engaged in bitter sectarian arguments about the progress of religion in the Pacific islands, and planned to lead a tour party from Sydney to visit—and publicise—the Marist missions there, including Futuna, until a shipping strike scuttled the scheme.[57]

Despite the time, effort and money involved, the canonisation of Chanel did not bring about a decline in interest in saint-making among the Marists or within the Church of Oceania. Having crossed that reef, in 1955 the Marists returned to Colin's cause. To that end Jean Coste, a French scripture scholar, and Gaston Lessard, a Canadian, were appointed from their ranks to produce a definitive record of his life and thought and of the founding of the Society of Mary. Numerous publications followed, chiefly the magisterial four-volume work *Origines Maristes*.[58] But, during the 1980s, interest began to flag, especially in the 'non-Latin' provinces of the Society. While John Paul II, who became Pope

---

56 Noel Delaney, Provincial circular, no. 5/77, Marist Archives, Wellington; John Craddock, 'Patron Saint of the Pacific Comes Home', *Marist Messenger*, May 1977, pp. 8–10; Michael King, *Whina: a biography of Whina Cooper*, Auckland, 1983, pp. 232–233.
57 Oceania Marist Province, Newsletter 87/5; Marquis, pp. 80–85; *Missions des Iles*, no. 55 (1954), p. 15; Peter McMurrich, 'Not Angels, Nor Men Confirmed in Grace: the Society of Mary in Australia, 1892–1938', MA thesis, University of Sydney, 1988, pp. 82–84. Interview with Joachim Fernandez, Marist Superior-General (Rome, 1998). Fernandez had taken Chanel's skull back to Futuna in 1987.
58 Rome, 1960–1967.

in 1978, was an unusually zealous canoniser, white male founders of religious orders were already well represented among the saints, and the costs of advancing a cause were high, yet success uncertain.[59] Many Marists, accordingly, doubted the need to proceed further. Besides, they already had Chanel as a sanctified emblem. In 1993, therefore, the six-yearly General Chapter of the Society voted that while 'the cause of canonisation of Fr Colin remains open it should not be actively promoted at this time'.[60]

Notwithstanding the canonisation in April 1999 of Marcellin Champagnat, Colin's confrère and founder of the Marist teaching brothers, who are well known in Australia, New Zealand and the Pacific islands, successful candidates for sainthood are for the time being more likely to be found among those who spent themselves witnessing to the Church outside its traditional European heartlands.[61] For Oceania that list is already substantial. Blessed Mary MacKillop, co-founder of the Sisters of St Joseph of the Sacred Heart in Australia; Blessed Giovanni Mazzucconi, an Italian missionary martyred in New Guinea in 1855; and Blessed Peter ToRot, a Papua New Guinean, martyred by Japanese forces there in 1943, are obvious candidates.[62] Others, from New Zealand, who have been mentioned as possibilities include Suzanne Aubert, who founded the Daughters of Compassion; Emmet McHardy, a Marist missionary on Bougainville; and Francis Vernon Douglas, a Columban missionary killed by the Japanese in the Philippines in 1943.[63] Then, too, and above all, there is Damien de Veuster. The leper priest of Molokai in Hawai'i, and posthumous protégé of Robert Louis Stevenson, he has long had an international reputation and was canonised in 2009.[64] It cannot be known if any others of these will attain canonisation; and the list could well grow longer before Colin is again seriously considered. His

---

59 Between 1978 and 2005 Pope John Paul II made 482 Saints. *New Zealand Herald*, 4 April 2005. Justin Taylor sm, private communication.
60 1993 General Chapter, Statements and Decisions, no. 169 (Jago 7), p. 22, Archivio Padri Maristi, Rome. Interviews with Marist General Administration, Rome, 1998.
61 Alban Doyle, *The Story of the Marist Brothers in Australia, 1872–1972*, Sydney, 1972, pp. 147–168, 295–290, 297–310, 377–384, 597–604; Pat Gallagher, *The Marist Brothers in New Zealand, Fiji and Samoa, 1876–1976*, Tuakau, 1976; Keith B. Farrell, *Achievement from the Depth: a critical historical survey of the life of Marcellin Champagnat*, Sydney, 1984; *NZ Catholic*, 28 Mar. 1999.
62 William Modystack, *Mary MacKillop: a woman before her time*, Adelaide, 1982. Nicholas Maestrini, *Mazzucconi of Woodlark: priest and martyr*, Hong Kong and Detroit, 1983. Kaspar G. Vaninara, *Laip Stori Bilong Pita ToRot: Pita ToRot i katekis, sios lida, na martir*, Kokopo, n.d, and *Peter ToRot: catechist and martyr (1912–1945)*, Vunapope, 1993; Theo Aerts (ed.), *The Martyrs of Papua New Guinea:333 missionary lives lost during World War II*, Port Moresby, 1994, pp. 247–250.
63 Jessie, Munro, *The Story of Suzanne Aubert*, Auckland, 1996; 'McHardy', in Claudia Orange (ed.), *Dictionary of New Zealand Biography*, vol. 4 (1998), p. 311; Patricia Brooks, *With No Regrets: the story of Francis Vernon Douglas*, Quezon City, 1998.
64 Gavan Daws, *Holy Man: Father Damien of Molokai*, Honolulu, 1973, pp. 250–251; Richard Stewart, *Leper Priest of Molokai: the Father Damien story*, Honolulu, 2000, pp. 387–396.

name, though, should continue to be honoured as that of the spiritual mentor of Chanel and of the more than 1,700 Marists who, since 1836, have been assigned to the Pacific missions.[65]

And what became of Musumusu, who precipitated Chanel's rise to glory by killing him? He was baptised Maulisio in 1844, and died on 15 January 1846.[66] Fittingly, given his prominent part in the story, his grave, surmounted by a large white cross, is at Poi, in front of the basilica where Chanel's bones, like an Oceanic equivalent of the remains of, say, St Ambrose of Milan, hold the place of honour. More humbly, the relics offer an encouraging precedent to the Maori Catholics of northern New Zealand who, reclaiming a valued part—albeit of colonial provenance—of their own heritage, called for Bishop Pompallier's remains to be returned from France to the Hokianga, where he settled on 10 January 1838, after dropping Chanel at Futuna.[67]

Appendix

Chanel bibliography[68]

1867

Bourdin, [Antoine], *Vie du Venerable P.-M.-L. Chanel, pretre de la Societe de Marie, provicaire apostolique et premier martyr de l'Oceanie*, Paris/Lyon, Jacques Lecoffre, 624pp.

1884

Mangeret, Antoine, *Mgr Bataillon et les Missions de l'Oceanie Centrale*, Lyons, Vitte and Perrussel / Paris, J. Lecoffre, 2 vols, 415pp, 421pp. Re-published in one volume in 1895.

---

65   This is an approximate figure. It is based on a register held in the Archivio Padri Maristi, Rome, covering the period 1836–1959, which lists 740 Society of Mary missionaries and 505 Marist missionary sisters. The figures for subsequent decades, especially for the 1960s and 1970s, are considerable but can only be estimated. To reach the final estimate, about 200 Marist Brothers of the Schools are also included. For an account of the 'Marist family' see Craig Larkin, *A Certain Way: an exploration of Marist spirituality* (Rome, 1995).
66   Servant, Proces Verbal, 3 Aug. 1845, and Bataillon to Colin, Dec. 1847, in Rozier (1991), pp. 152, 189; Mangeret, pp. 128–131; Angleviel, p. 103.
67   *NZ Catholic*, 31 Jan., 14 Mar. 1999.
68   Compiled by Hugh Laracy, (13 April 1999, draft), University of Auckland, New Zealand.

1885

[Nicolet, Claude], *Vie du Venerable P.-M.-L. Chanel, pretre de la Societe de Marie et premier martyr de l'Oceanie*, Saint Breuc, L. Prud'Homme, 386pp. Refer later dates for other editions and translations: French—1890, 1893, 1907 (United States), 1923, 1935; Italian—1889; Spanish—1890; German—1891. Translations are from the 1890 edition.

1886

Martin, Abbe, *Vie du Venerable Pierre-Marie-Louis Chanel, pretre de la Societe de Marie et premier martyr de l'Oceanie*, Macon, Imprimerie Protat Freres, 62pp.

1889

Garin, J.M., *Oratorio-Cantate: en honneur du Bienheureux Pierre-Louis-Marie Chanel, mariste, premier martyr de l'Oceanie*, Paris, Rene Haton, 96pp. English adaptation: Jenner (1952).

Martin, Abbe, *Manuel de la devotion au bienheureux Pierre-Marie-Louis Chanel et preparation a la premiere communication*, Bourg, J.-M., Villefranche, 150pp.

Nicolet, [Claude], *Vie Abregee du Bienheureux Pierre-Louis-Marie Chanel: pretre de la Societe de Marie et premier martyr de l'Oceanie*, Lyon, Vitte and Perrussel, 194pp. This book went to at least eight, mostly undated, 'editions' (so styled on the title pages); they are, in fact, exact reprints of the original.

———, *Vita del B. Pietro Luigi Maria Chanel: sacerdote della Societa di Maria, primo martire dell' Oceania*, Roma, Tipografia Poliglotta, 375pp.

———, *Compendio della Vita del B. Pietro Luigi Maria Chanel: sacerdote della Societa di Maria, primo martire dell' Oceania*, Roma, Tipografia Poliglotta, 228pp. Also issued with a different cover and title and bearing a Marist imprint: *Il protomartire dell' Oceania, Beato pietro Luigi Chanel (1803–1841)*, Roma, Presso 'L'Araldo di Maria'. Translation of *Vie Abregee*.

[Pierre Janin], 'Un Pere Mariste missionaire', *Quatre Cantates pour les fetes de la beatification du Venerable Pierre L. M. Chanel, missionaire-mariste*, Saint-Louis, [Nouvelle Caledonie], Imprimerie Catholique, 20pp.

1890

[Anon], i. *Vie Admirable du Bienheureux Pierre-Louis-Marie Chanel, pretre mariste et premier martyr d'Oceanie*, Abbeville (Somme), Editions Charles Paillart, 32pp. First published early in 1890, this work appeared in five further editions. It announced that 'Le diocese de Belley et tous les sanctuaires confies aux religieux de la Societe de Marie se disposent a celebrer tour a tour, dans le cours de la presente annee 1890, des *triduums* (sic) solonnels'.

———, ii. *Short Life of the Blessed Peter Aloyius Mary Chanel, Marist priest and first martyr of Oceania*, Abbeville, Paillart, early 1890. Translation of i, above; identical format.

———, iii. *Petite vie illustree du Bienheureux Pierre-Louis-Marie Chanel,pretre Marist et premier Martyr de l'Oceanie*, Abbeville, Paillart, late 1890, 33pp.

———, iv. *Short Life of the Blessed Peter Aloysius Mary Chanel, Marist priest and first martyr of Oceania*, Sydney, [Society of Mary], 1923, 40pp. Same text as ii, above, but of larger format and with a commentary on J.M. Garin, '*Oratorio*' (1889).

———, v. *Leven van den Gelukzaligen: Petrus-Aloysius-Marie Chanel*, Abbeville, Paillart, [1924/5?], 36pp. In Dutch. Same format as iii, above, but with additional material regarding Marists in Holland.

———, vi. *Petite vie du Bienheureux Pierre-Louis-Marie Chanel, pretre Mariste et premiere martyr de l'Oceanie*, Abbeville, Paillart, 1927, 32pp, Slightly revised version of iii, above.

[Monfat, A.], *Lettre adressee aux RR. PP. Maristes par leur confreres, Fetes de la beatification du bienheureux Pierre-Louis-Marie Chanel, 17 Novembre 1889*, Lyon , Vitte et Perrussel, 45pp. An account of the journey to Rome and of the proceedings there.

Nicolet, [Claude], *Vie de Bienheureux P.-M.-L. Chanel, pretre de la Societe de Marie et premier martyr de l'Oceanie*, Lyon, Vitte, 557pp. 2nd edn. Translated into Italian (1889), Spanish (1890), German (1891).

———, *The Life of Blessed Peter Aloysius Mary Chanel; priest of the Society of Mary and proto-martyr of Oceania*, Dublin/London, M.H. Gill/Burns and Oates, 186pp. English translation of *Vie Abregee* (1889).

———, Rodriguez de Ureta, Antonia (trans), *Vida del Bienaventurado Pedro Luis Maria Chahel, sacerdote de la sociedad de Maria y primer martir de la Oceania, beatificado et 17 de noviembre de 1880 por Su Santidad El Papa Leon XIII*, Barcelona, Tipografia de la Casa Provincial de Caridad, 247pp. Spanish translation of *Vie Abregee*.

Tissot, R.P., et al., *Les Martyrs Jean-Gabriel Perboyre et P.-L.-Marie Chanel: souvenir du triduum de Saint-Jean*, Lyon, Oeuvre de la Propagation de la Foi,

32pp. Reprinted from *Les Missions Catholiques*, 22 eme annee, no. 1093 (16 Mai 1890), pp. 229-252, and from *Le Triduum de Lyon* (1890). Perboyre, of the Congregation de la Mission, was killed in China, 11 September 1840.

1890–1891 Triduum publications (principle items)

Relation des fetes religieuses celebrees a l'Institution Sainte Marie les 9, 10, et 11 mars 1890. En l'honneur de la Beatificationde P.-L.-M. Chanel, E. Pugnaire, La Seyne-sur-Mer, 1890, 13pp.

Triduum Solennel et Inauguration du pelerinage en l'honneur du Bienheureux Pierre-Louis-Marie Chanel, a Cuet, sa paroisse natale, les 26, 27 et 28 Avril 1890: petit guide de pelerin, Bourg, J.-M. Villefranche, 1890, 48pp.

Eglise Sainte-Marie, Toulon. Triduum solonnel en honneur du Bx P.-L.-M. Chanel, de la Societe de Marie, premier martyr de l'Oceanie, [9, 10, 11 Mai], Toulon, Th. Gaillac, 1890, 74pp.

Eglise Notre-Dame des Champs. Les fetes du triduum en l'honneur du Bx P.-L.-M. Chanel, les 20, 21 et 22 Mai 1890, Paris-Auteuil, Apprentis-orphelins-Roussel, 1890, 45pp.

'10 Juillet 1890 et le Triduum en l'honneur du Bienheureux Chanel', *Bulletinde l'Association des Anciens eleves de l'institution Sainte-Marie de Saint-Chamond*, no. 2, 1890, 16pp. A school reunion marked the last day of the triduum.

Recit des fetes solonnelles celebrees a l'Institution St-Joseph de Montlucon, en l'honneur du Bx P.-L.-M. Chanel de la Societe de Marie, Montlucon, A. Herbin, 1890, 62pp.

Recit des fetes solennelles celebrees a Notre-Dame de Bon Encontre en l'honneur du Bx P.-M,-L. Chanel, de la Societe de Marie, Agen, V. Lentheric, 1890, 14pp.

A solemn Triduum in Honour of the Blessed Peter-Louis-Marie Chanel, SM, protomartyr of Oceania, Friday, Saturday, Sunday, October 10, 11, 12, 1890, at the Church of Notre Dame des Victoires, San Francisco, San Francisco, McCormack Bros, 1890, 20pp. Despite its title, this is a biography of Chanel. A program leaflet was issued separately.

Le Bienheureuse P.-L.-M. Chanel. Triduum, a la Cathedrale de Saint-Brieuc, 14, 15 et 16 Novembre 1890, Saint-Brieuc, R. Prud'Homme, 1890, 107pp.

Le Bienheureux P.-L.-M. Chanel ... Triduum celebrees enl'Eglise de Saint-Aignon, a Chartres, les 15, 16 et 17 novembre 1890, Paris, D. Doumoulin, 1891, 65pp.

Grande Seminaire d'Agen, Triduum solennel en l'honneur du Bienheureux P.-L.-M. Chanel, [9, 10, 11 November 1890], Agen, V. Lamy, 1891, 70pp.

Oeuvre de la Propagation de la Foi. Le Triduum de Lyon et les Trois Discours prononces en l'honneur des martyrs J.-G. Perboyre et P.-L.-M.. Chanel, Lyon, Imprimerie de Pitrat aine, 80pp. Includes: Monseigneur d'Hulst, 'Chanel'; R.P. Tissot, 'Perboyre'; l'Abbe Lemann, 'L'avancement du royaume de Dieu par l'heroisme des bienheureuse Perboyre et Chanel'.

1890–1940

Panegyriques. Published copies of 35 of the sermons preached in this annual series have been located. For details, refer Rozier (1960), pp. 523–524.

1891

Nicolet, Claudius (trans. Carl Dilgskron), *Leben des seligen Peter Alois Maria Chanel, Preisters der Gesellschaft Maria und ersten Martyrers Oceaniens*, Mainz, Franz Kirchheim, 424pp.

———, *Quelques Guerisons et graces signalees obtenues par l'intervention du B. Pierre-Louis-Marie Chanel, pretre de la Societe de Marie et premier martyr de l'Oceanie*, Lyon, Vitte, 84pp.

Societe de Marie, *Compte rendu sommaire des solennites du triduum en l'honneur du Bienheureux Pierre-Louis-Marie Chanel, 1889–1890*, Lyon, Emmanuel Vitte, 39pp.

Tozer, Basil (ed.), *The Life of Blessed Peter Aloysius Mary Chanel, Marist, first martyr of Oceania and apostle of Futuna*, London, Art and Book Company, 89pp. 'From the French'.

1892

Morel, M., *Derniere Journee et Martyre du Bienheureux Pierre-Louis-Marie Chanel, mariste, premier missionaire de Futuna (Polynesie): drame en vers, trois actes*,

Lyon, Vitte, 64pp.

1894

[Burtin, Abbe], *Vie du B. Pierre Chanel, pretre du diocese de Belley, de la Societe de Marie, premier martyr de l'Oceanie, d'apres de nouveaux documents*, Grenoble, Imprimerie Centrale, 403pp.

Fabre, Monseigneur, *Un Miracle Recent du Bienheureux Chanel devant le tribunal du bon sens et de la raison*, Nice, C, Orengo, 61pp.

Rougier, Felix, *Le Martyre du Bienheureux Chanel: tragedie en cinq actes*, Barcelona, 113pp. 'Cette piece a ete representee pour la premier fois par le eleves de l'ecole apostolique de Barcelone, le 29 Avril 1894, et pour la seconde fois le 28 Juin de la meme annee, en presence du R.P. Jean Goyet, S.M., provincial de Lyon'. Handwritten polycopy, purple ink.

1895

Mangeret, Antoine, *Mgr Bataillon et les Missions de l'Oceanie*, Lyon, Vitte, 415pp.

1897

[Anon], *Devotion a Marie inspiree a la jeunesse, d'apres les examples et les maximes du bienheureux Pierre-louis-Marie Chanel, pretre mariste, premier martyr de l'Oceanie*, Tournai, H, and L. Casterman, 198pp.

1898

Giraudet, P.-A., *Le Bienheureux Pierre Chanel: tragedie en cinq actes*, Lille, Desclee-de Brouwer, 112pp.

1899

Planeix, R., *Le Bienheureux Chanel, premier martyr de l'Oceanie*, Paris, P. Lethielleux, 59pp.

[1900?]

[Anon], 'Le Bienheureux Pierre-Louis-Marie Chanel: premier martyr de l'Oceanie', in *Au dela des Mers: l'heroisme de la vertu dans les iles de l'Oceanie. Marins, missionaires, grands chefs Oceaniens, martyrs, adolescents. Recits varies offerts a la jeunesse chretienne*, Lille, Librairie Saint Charles, pp. 163–187. Others included: Marceau, Bataillon, Epalle, Collomb, Douarre, Goujon, Chevron, Breheret, Elloy, Delahaye, Vitoleo Faleone.

1901

P.S.M., *Petites Fleurs cueillies dans la vie et les ecrits du Bienheureux Pierre Chanel: conseils d'un sage directeur*, Tournai, H. and L. Casterman, 44pp.

1902

Falletti, L[uigi] M., *Vita del Beato Pietro Luigi Maria Chanel, protomartire dell'Oceania*, Asti, Opera, Pia Michelerio, 64pp.

1903

[Anon], 'Le Bienheureux Pierre-Louis-Marie Chanel, Mariste, premiere martyr de l'Oceanie (1803–1841),' *Les Contemporaines*, no. 535 (11 Janvier), pp. 1–16.

Nicolet, [Claude], *Vie du Bienheureux Pierre-Louis-Marie Chanel, pretre Mariste et premier martyr de l'Oceanie*, Lyon/Paris, Vitte, 385pp.

1907

Nicolet, [Claude], *Le Martyr de Futuna, vie du Bienheureux Pierre-Louis-Marie Chanel, pretre Mariste et premier martyr de l'Oceanie*, Boston, Catholic Foreign Mission Bureau, 385pp. Copy, re-set, of 1903 edition.

C.P.R. [Rinaldo Pavese], *Il Primo martire dell l'Oceania ossia il beato Pietro Luigi M. Chanel della Societa di Maria: brevi cenni della sua vita*, Torino, Ufficio delle Letture Cattoliche, 100pp.

1911

Sornay, F., *Meditations pour une neuvaine en l'honneur du Bienheureux Chanel*, Lyon, Paquet, 102pp.

1916

Wegener, Herm., *Blessed Peter Mary Aloysius Chanel: first marytr of Oceania*, Techny, Illinois, Society of the Divine Word, 25pp. No. 11 in series 'Heroes of the Mission Field, or Lives of Famous Missionaries and Martyrs'.

1917

Gilmore, Florence, *The Martyr of Futuna*, Maryknoll, NY, Catholic Foreign Mission Society of America, 199pp. 'Prepared from the French'.

1920–1927

Bulletin du Pelerinage du Bienheureux Chanel: organe du Pelerinage de Cuet, Janvier 1920 (1er annee, no. 1) – Janvier 1927 (8me annee, no. 84).

1920

Mijolla, R.P. de, *Sous l'Etendard de Marie: recits de Vocations et d'Apostolat*, Paris, J. de Gigord, pp. 7–36 (re. Chanel).

1922

Walsh, James A., 'Near Bourg: Blessed Peter Chanel', in his *In the Home of Martyrs*, Maryknoll, NY, Catholic Foreign Mission Society of America, pp. 67–104.

1923

Nicolet [Claude], *Vie du Bienheureux Pierre-Louis-Marie Chanel, pretre Mariste, et premier martyr de l'Oceanie*, Lyon/Paris, Libraire Catholic Emmanuel Vitte, 305pp.

1926

Kalin, Karl, *Der Gieger auf Futuna: Geschtliche Erzahlung aus Zentral-Ozeanien*, Freiburg, Herder and Co., 95pp.

1927

Courtais, E., i. *Blessed Peter Aloysius Mary Chanel, marist missionary and first martyr of Oceania*, Australian Catholic Truth Society (no. 517), Melbourne, 31pp.

———, ii. *Blessed Peter Chanel: the first martyr of Oceania*, Washington, DC, Marist Province, 29pp.

Later editions 1949, 1988.

1929

Falletti, P., *Il Beato Chanel (protomartire dell'Oceania)*, Casale Monferrato, Propaganda Mariana, 55pp. Contains a hymn by R. Pavese, 'Al Beato Pietro Chanel', pp. 52–55.

1935

Nicolet, [Claude], *Vie de Bienheureux Pierre-Louis-Marie Chanel, pretre Mariste et premier martyr de l'Oceanie*, Lyon/Paris, Vitte, 356pp.

1936

Boesch, Josef, *Der erste Blutzeuge der Sudsee: Petrus-Aloisius-Marie Chanel, Preister der Gesellschaft Mariens*, Meppen, Verlag 'Kreuz und Karitas', 235pp.

1937

Cloupeau, J., *Le Bienheureux Pierre-Louis-Marie Chanel, Mariste, premier martyr de l'Oceanie*, Chartres, Imprimerie Moderne de Chartres, 97pp. Revised edition 1954.

1941

Albillos, R.P., *El Beato Pedro Luis Maria Chanel, Marista, protomartir de Oceania*, Mexico, Imprenta Claret, 128pp.

[Boccassino, Paulo], 'Il Protomartire d'Oceania, Beato Pierluigi Chanel', *L'Araldo di Maria: rivista mensile del culto di Maria e delle missioni d'Oceania'*, Anno XVI, no. 4–5, (Aprile–Maggio), pp. 41–50.

R.-G.P. [Pavese], 'Ode al Beato Pierluigi Chanel', *L'Araldo*, as above, pp. 41–50.

1948

[Anon], *Pierre-Louis-Marie Chanel: missionaire mariste, premiere martyr d'Oceanie, 1803-1841*, Paris/Lyon, Chaplet des Enfants, 8pp. 'L'Oeuvre du Chaplet des Enfants a ete fondee en 1926, pour obtenir, par le priere des enfants a les Tres Sainte Vierge la regeneration chretienne de nos paroisses et le salut de la France'.

1949

Courtais, E., *Blessed Peter Aloysius Mary Chanel, Marist Missionary and first Martyr of Oceania*, Melbourne, Australian Catholic Truth Society (no. 436), 31pp. Other editions 1927 and 1988.

1950

Goyau, Georges, *Le Martyre du Pere Chanel et l'Apostolat Mariste*, Collection Don Bosco a l'Ecole des Saints, no. 26, Lederberg-Gand, 52pp. Marist edition published 1951.

1951

Goyau, Georges, *Le Martyre de Pere Chanel et l'Apostolat Mariste*, 'Avec une notice de Rd Willy Bilmeyer et un tableau general de la Societe de Marie 1949–1950', Mechlin, [Societe de Marie], 52pp.

1952

Jenner, Ernest, 'Short Oratorio in Honour of Blessed Peter Chanel SM, priest of the Society of Mary and first martyr of Oceania', Wellington, Catholic Supplies. Garin's composition (1889) adapted to English words. English translation by F. Durning SM.

1953

Barker, Anthony, *South Seas Martyr: Blessed Peter Chanel SM, 1803–1841*, Dublin, Catholic Truth Society of Ireland, 26pp.

Dardennes, Rose, 'Petelo chez les mangeurs d'hommes', *Peaux-rouges*, Paris, Coeurs Vaillants, pp. 43–53. Presented in comic form in a serial publication intended for children.

[1954]

Robitaillie, Henriette, *Le Grand Reve du petit berger*, [Paris], Editions Missions de Iles, album no. 1, 16pp. Illustrated, for children.

Soldati, Gabrielle, *Sangue sull'isola: Pierluigi Chanel*, Brescia, Padri Maristi, [7pp].

1954

Acta Societatis Mariae, no. 14 (15 August), 180pp. 'Celebrationes Romae habitae occasione canonizationis Sancti Petri Chanel'. Complete issue regarding Chanel.

[Boccassino, P.], i. *S. Pierluigi Chanel: protomartyr dell'Oceania*, Rome, Padri Maristi, 47pp.

———, ii. *Der Heilige Peter Chanel: erster martyrer von ozeanien*, Rome, Padri Maristi, 47pp.

———, iii. *Saint Pierre Chanel: premier martyr de l'Oceanie*, Rome, Padri Maristi, 47pp.

———, iv. *Saint Peter Chanel: first martyr of Oceania*, Rome, Padri Maristi, 47pp.

———, v. *San Pedro Chanel: primer martir de Oceania*, Rome, Padri Maristi, 47pp.

———, vi. *De Heilige Peter Chanel: de eerste martelaaar van Oceanie*, Rome, Padri Maristi, 47pp.

The original text of these works is the Italian one. They are all similar in format.

Cloupeau, J., *Au Pays des Tabous: Saint Pierre Chanel, religieux mariste, premier martyr d'Oceanie*, Sainte-Foy-les-Lyon, Procure des Missions d'Oceanie, 128pp. Original edition 1937. English translation: Darby (1954).

Corbie, Genevieve de, *Sous le Casse-tete des Cannibales: Saint Pierre Chanel, premier martyr d'Oceanie*, Paris, Bonne Presse, 36pp. 'Illustrations d'Hugues Ghiglia'.

Englebert, Omer, *Saint Pierre-Louis-Marie Chanel (1803–1841)*, Paris, Editions Albin Michel, 61pp. Spanish translation: Englebert (1984).

Giannini, Umberto, [with R. Pavese], *San Piero Luigi Chanel: protomartyr dell-Oceania*, Rome, Padri Maristi, 186pp. 'C'est celle que l'on peut appeler la "Biographie de la Canonisation", composee pour la Canonisation comme celle du P. Nicolet l"avait ete pour la Beatification'. (*Acta* 1954, p. 174).

Genet, M., *Soleil sur les Iles: vie de Saint Pierre Chanel S.M.*, Paris, Oeuvres Pontificales missionnaires, 14pp.

Joyce, James, *Hymn in Honour of St Peter Chanel SM*, Wellington, [Marist Fathers], 1p.

1. Pierre Chanel of Futuna (1803–1841): The making of a saint

La Secretaire d'Etat de Sa Saintete (ed.), *Les Ceremonies des Canonisation des 12–13 Juin 1954*, [Rome], Imprimerie Polyglotte Vaticane, 55pp. 'S. Pierre Louis Marie Chanel, S. Gaspard del Bufalo, S. Joseph Pignatelli, S. Dominique Savio, S. Maria Crocifissa di Rosa'.

Maher, P.K., *St Peter Chanel of the Society of Mary: proto-martyr of the Pacific*, Wellington, Marist Fathers, 43pp.

Marie-Andre, *Saint Pierre Chanel, premier martyr del'Oceanie*, Paris, Editions et Imprimeries du Sud-Est, 79pp.

Maria, Giugno (numero speciale), 16pp. 'S. Pierluigi Chanel: protomartire dell'oceania'.

Der Maristenbote: im Dienste der Weltmission, heft 7/8–62 – jahrgang (Juli/August), pp. 146–179. 'Seligen Petrus Aloysius Chanel'. Special issue.

Neufeld, Hubert, *Der Heilige und die Kopfjager: maristen-pater Chanel der erste Martyrer Ozeaniens*, Munchen, Vom Ludwig-Missions-Verein, 87pp. Revised edition 1966. English translation 1955.

Rouvray, Louis de, *Le Pere Chanel*, Toulouse, Editions du Clocher (Collection les Belles Histoires), 32pp.

'St Pierre Chanel, martyr: patron de l'Oceanie', *Missions des Iles*, no. 55 (May), pp. 1–32. Special issue.

Therol, Joseph, *Croisade en Polynesie: Saint Pierre Chanel*, Paris, Nouvelles Editions Latines, 153pp.

Verlingue, Charles, 'Il protomartire dell' Oceania', *Ecclesia: rivista mensile illustrata*, (Citta del Vaticano), anno XIII, no. 6 (Giugno), pp. 274–278.

Vezelay, Georges, *Futuna: ile sanglante*, Paris, Le Centurion, 127pp.

Voisine, R.P., *Pierre Chanel: premier martyr d'Oceanie*, Paris, Missions des Iles, 61pp.

1955

Fagan, Sean, *Life of Saint Peter Chanel, Marist:: first martyr of Oceania, apostle of Our Lady, mediatrix of all graces*, Dublin, Our Lady's Family, 72pp. 'Adapted from the German of Dr. Neufeld S.M.' (1954).

1957

Darby, James M., *In the Land of Taboos: life of St Peter Chanel, Marist, the first martyr of Oceania*, Paterson N.J., St Anthony Guild Press, 129pp. Translation of Cloupeau (1954).

1958

Neufeld, Hubert, *Abenteurier der Sudsee: grosse und kleine missionaire der Sudsee*, Munchen, Ludwig-Missions-Verein, 48pp.

1960

Rozier, Claude (ed.), i. *Ecrits de S. Pierre Chanel: etablis, presentes et annotes*, Rome, [Padri Maristi], 538pp.

—— (ed.), ii. *Ecrits du Pere Chanel, missionaire a Futuna: etablis, presentes et annotes*, Paris, Societe des Oceanistes, publication no. 9, 538pp.

1962

Alzin, Josse, *Saint Pierre Chanel, premier martyr d'Oceanie: sermons, lettres, testament, journal de mission*, Namur (Belgique), Les editions du Soleil Levant, 190pp.

1963

Symes, W[alter] J., *The Life of St Peter Chanel: the Marist missionary martyr*, Bolton, Catholic Printing Company of Farnsworth, 113pp.

1966

Neufeld, Hubert, Der Heilege und die Kopfjoger: Maristenpater Chanel der erste Martyrer Ozeaniens, Munchen (Grobenzell?), Manz Verlag (Hacker?), 128pp. Original edition. 1954.

1968

Laurand, Luce, *La Croix au bout du monde: Saint Pierre Chanel, mariste, premier martyr et patron de l'Oceanie*, Bruxelles, Editions Marie-Mediatrice, 165pp.

1975

Lynch, John W., *Saint Peter Chanel*, Rome, Society of Mary, [16pp].

1976

Laracy, Hugh, 'Roman Catholic "Martyrs" in the South Pacific, 1841–55', *Journal of Religious History*, vol. 9, no. 2 (December), pp. 189–202.

[1980?]

Finkler Pedro (Irmao Placido Xavier), *O Heroi de Futuna: Sao Pedro Chanel (1803–1841), primeiro martir da Oceania*, Porto Alegre, Brazil, Edicoes Paulinas, 253pp.

1984

Englebert, Omer (trans. Sergio Fernandez), *San Pedro Chanel (1803–1841)*, Claveria, Mexico, Libreria Parroquial de Claverio, 69pp.

1986

Mayere, Antoine, *Mission a Futuna: Pierre Chanel, le Saint patron de l'Oceanie*, Paris, Editions du Rameau, 48pp. Contains photographs, comic-strip and text.

1987

Walden, Russell, *Voices of Silence: New Zealand's Chapel of Futuna*, Wellington, Victoria University Press, 173pp.

1988

[Anon], *Patron of New Zealand, St Peter Chanel*, Auckland, Catholic Displays Bookshop, Onehunga, 20pp. 'The text of this book first published by the Marist Fathers in 1954'.

Burke, Roger and Michael Perry (eds), [E. Courtais], *St Peter Chanel, 1803–1841: Patron of Chanel College, Gladstone*, Gladstone, Australia, Chanel College, 63pp. Text mostly from Courtais (1927, 1949).

1989

Forde, Liam, *St Peter Chanel of Oceania: novena reflections*, [Sydney?], 24pp.

[1990?]

[Anon], *Pedro Chanel: Apostol de Futuna*, Mexico, Libreria Parroquial de Claveria, 56pp.

1990

Gioanetti, Franco, *S. Pier Luigi Chanel, proto martire dell' Oceania*, Brescia, Centro Vocazionale Marista, 26pp.

[1991]

[Anon.], *Avec Saint Pierre Chanel. Entrez dans la mission!*, Diocese de Belley-Ars, 125pp.

1991

Corbiere, A. de la, *St Pierre Chanel: 150e anniversaire du martyre*, Bourg, Diocese de Belley-Ars, 21pp.

Jannel, Louis, Monnier, Leon, Bruce, Agnes, Juilleron, Aime, Savey, Raoul, *Musee Oceanien et de Saint Pierre Chanel*, Cuet, Musee Oceanien et de St Pierre Chanel, 41pp.

The Marists: newsletter of the Third Order of Mary, [USA], vol. 2, no. 3, Framingham, Massachusetts. Special issue honouring 150th anniversary of Chanel's martyrdom.

Marquis, Jean-Claude, *St Pierre Chanel: de l'Ain au Pacifique*, Bourg-en-Bresse, Les Editions de la Taillanderie, 93pp.

[Morrissey, Paul F.], *Celebrating the Sesquicentennial of the Martyrdom of Saint Peter-Louis Marie Chanel, Marist priest and protomartyr of Oceania, 28 April 1841–1991: a Marist souvenir*, Saint Paul, Minnesota, The Church of Saint Louis, King of France, 22pp.

Rozier, Claude, *S. Pierre Chanel d'apres ceux qui l'ont connu*, Rome, [Padri Maristi], 254pp.

Stuart, William Joseph and Anthony Ward (trans and eds), *Ever Your Dear Brother, Peter Chanel: surviving letters and Futuna journal*, Rome, Padri Maristi, 466pp. Translation of Rozier (1960).

1994

Angleviel, Frederic, *Les Missions a Wallis et Futuna au XIXe Siecle*, Bordeaux-Talence, Centre de Recherche des Espaces Tropicaux, 243pp.

Graystone, Philip, *Saint Peter Chanel SM: first martyr of the South Pacific*, [Walsingham], England, Marist Fathers, 72pp. Draws on Rozier (1991).

Mayere, Antoine, *Pere Chanel, je vous ecris*, Paris, Les Editions du Cerf, 175pp.

Ronzon fms, Frere Joseph (ed.), 'Les Lettres de Frere Marie-Nizier', privately distributed, Rome, 148pp. Marie-Nizier (Jean-Marie Delorme) was on Futuna from 1837 to 1863. Some of his letters are also presented in Rozier (1961) and in Br Edward Clisby fms (trans. and ed.), 'Letters from Oceania: letters of the first Marist Brothers in Oceania, 1836–1850', privately distributed in four parts, Auckland, 1993, 1995, 1996, 1999, 266pp.

1995

Ronzon, Joseph, *Jean-Marie Delorme (Frere Marie-Nizier), 1817–1874: essai de biographie du compagnon missionaire du Pere Chanel*, Saint-Martin-en-Haut, Imprimerie des Monts du Lyonnais, 216pp.

1996

[Servant, Louis Catherin], *Ecrits de Louis Catherin Servant,* Paris, Editions Pierre Tequi, 375pp. Servant visited Futuna briefly in 1837. Subsequently, succeeding Chanel, he worked there from 1842 until his death in 1860.

1999

Girard, Charles (ed), *Lettres recues d'Oceanie par l'administration generale des peres maristes pendant le generalat de Jean-Claude Colin,* Centre d'etudes maristes, Rome, 4 vols. Contains much correspondence from Chanel.

2. The Sinclairs Of Pigeon Bay, or 'The Prehistory of the Robinsons of Ni'ihau': An essay in historiography, or 'tales their mother told them'

Of the *haole* (i.e. European) settler dynasties of Hawai'i there is none grander than that of the Robinsons of the island of Ni'ihau and of Makaweli estate on neighbouring Kauai, 24 kilometres away, across the Kaulakahu Channel. The family is pre-eminent in its long occupancy of its lands, in the lofty distance that it maintains from the outside community and in its inventive ennobling of its past. It has owned Ni'ihau since 1864 and, increasingly from the 1880s, when a new generation led by Aubrey Robinson assumed control of the family's ranching and planting operations, it has stringently discouraged visitors. Elsewhere in Hawai'i there is generally accepted public access to beaches below the high water or vegetation line, but—to the chagrin of some citizens—that is not so on Ni'ihau. There, according to the Robinsons, claiming the traditional rights of *konohiki*, or chiefly agents, private ownership extends at least as far as the low-water mark.[1] Not surprisingly, this intense isolation has attracted considerable curiosity and controversy, not least because the island contains the last community of native-speaking Hawai'ians, which numbered 190 in 1998.[2]

Philosophical and moral questions have arisen among commentators determined to find profound meanings in the way the Ni'ihauns' lives are strictly regulated (the use of liquor and tobacco, for instance, are forbidden) and their extra-insular contacts are restricted. That dyspeptic traveller and novelist Paul Theroux, for instance, argues not only that they are locked into a process of degeneration, but, conversely, that the opening up of Ni'ihau 'could eventually lead to revitalising the Hawai'ian language in the rest of the islands'. In the same vein, others have argued for the Ni'ihauans' right to have fuller access to 'civilisation', even though the Ni'ihauans have consistently shown themselves to be complaisant about the allegedly stultifying and exploitative regime under which they live. On the other hand, there are others who support what they see as preserving the Ni'ihauans' culture, as providing a chiefly substitute and as

---

1   Eric A. Knudsen, and Gurre P. Noble, *Kanuka of Kauai*, Honolulu, 1944, pp. 80–81; Wilmon Menard, 'The Widow Sinclair and Her Sea Search for Paradise', *Beaver*, Summer, 1981, p. 52; Paul Theroux, *The Happy Isles of Oceania*, London, 1992, p. 516; Edward R. Stepien, *Ni'ihau: a brief history*, Honolulu, 1988, pp. 115–117; Rerioterai Tava and Moses K. Keale, *Ni'ihau: the traditions of a Hawaiian island*, Honolulu, 1989, pp. 47–49; Gavan Daws, *Shoal of Time: a history of the Hawaiian Islands*, Honolulu, 1968, pp. 128; John E.K. Clark, *Beaches of Kaua'i and Ni'ihau*, Honolulu, 1990, pp. 88–92.
2   *Honolulu Advertiser*, 8 April 1998.

respecting their right to privacy.³ That suits the Robinsons. As Helen Robinson, the matriarch of the day, told a researcher in 1983, they cherish 'privacy and anonymity' and cannot see how 'maintaining the strict "seclusivity" of Ni'ihau can be of any great importance to Pacific studies', or to any other enquirers for that matter.⁴ And as recently as 1998, when the US navy was considering building a small rocket launch site on the island, guidelines for any military activity on Ni'ihau included the provision that 'any government employees or contractors must be escorted by a Ni'ihau Ranch representative at all times'.⁵

Even so, it is not as if the Robinsons have eschewed publicity. On the contrary, they have promulgated a widely circulated heroic myth of their dynastic origins.⁶ There is nothing unusual in that. Families and individuals are prone to glamourising their past. To that end, they will invent stories, or happily acquiesce in prevarication for a variety of reasons, perhaps to gain some presumed advantage. Or possibly because it seems to be an appropriate concomitant of the eminence, real or imagined, that they have attained, or to which they aspire. Examples abound, all of them versions of a phenomenon noted by Sigmund Freud and known as 'family romance'. In Gavin Daws's words, this 'involves a fantasy in which the child replaces his dull, ordinary parents by parents of more interest, elegance and power'. Thus, the *parvenu* politicians Shirley Baker of Tonga and Walter Murray Gibson of Hawai'i found it expedient to do so in order to reduce the social disadvantages with which they began life.⁷ And in 1911 W.J. Watriama, the canaque patriot from Lifu, styled himself 'king of the Loyalty Islands', in order to gain a hearing in Australia for his call for assistance to expel the French from New Caledonia.⁸ Later, the most distinguished of Polynesian scholars, Peter Buck, described the phenomenon elegantly with regard to his own people: 'many a family newly risen in the social scale has been known to deny the bar sinister that marks its origins'. In the same vein, Buck also quoted the Hawai'ian historian David Malo's observation that 'the expert genealogist is the washbowl of the high chief'.⁹

In the case of the Robinsons, the traditional version of their past smacks of the novelistic imaginings of a Barbara Cartland, and is without a hint of the

---

3   Menard, 'The Widow Sinclair', pp. 52–55; Theroux, *The Happy Isles*, pp. 515–520; Stepien, *Ni'ihau*, pp. 1–4, 184–194; Lawrence H. Fuchs, *Hawaii Pono: a social history* New York 1961, 76; 'Ni'ihau: the Hermit Isle', *Honolulu Advertiser*, 13 Dec. 1936.
4   Letter, Helen M. Robinson to Stepien, 18 April 1983, in Stepien, *Ni'ihau*, pp. 249–50.
5   *Honolulu Advertiser*, 8 April 1998.
6   See Appendix, 'Sinclair Bibliography'.
7   Gavan Daws, '"All the horrors of the half known life": some notes on the writing of biography in the Pacific', in Niel Gunson (ed.), *The Changing Pacific: essays in honour of H.E. Maude*, Melbourne 1978, pp. 297–307.
8   Hugh Laracy, 'William Jacob Watriama', in John Ritchie (ed.), *Australian Dictionary of Biography*, vol. 12, Melbourne 1990; and 'W.J. Watriama: pretendant et patriote (un homme noir defend l'Australie blanche)', *Mwa Vée: revue culturellekanak*, vol. 14, 1996, pp. 12–33.
9   Peter H. Buck, *Vikings of the Sunrise*, New York, 1938, p. 24.

subversive irony of a Jane Austen. It runs as follows. In 1824 Captain Francis Sinclair RN, aged 27, the son of Sir George Sinclair MP and a relative of the Earl of Caithness, 'over six feet two in height' and said to be the handsomest man in Scotland, married Elizabeth McHutcheson, the beautiful 19-year-old daughter of one of the leading citizens of Glasgow. So dainty was she that her husband could span her waist with the thumb and forefinger of his two hands. In 1815, after the battle of Waterloo, Sinclair had distinguished himself with some masterful seamanship when bringing the Duke of Wellington triumphantly back to England. Subsequently, Sinclair joined the Inland Revenue Service (true). In this position he is said (unreliably) to have spent a considerable amount of time travelling by coach between Edinburgh and London on government business. Then, and this is true, having joined a colonising scheme operated by the New Zealand Company, in 1840 he migrated to New Zealand aboard the barque *Blenheim*, accompanied by his wife and six children, plus Elizabeth's brother John.[10]

In some versions of his story Francis is linked not only to the Iron Duke but also to Lord Nelson. They cite him as having served in the battles of Copenhagen (1798), the Nile (1801) and Trafalgar (1805), and contend that he went to New Zealand to take up a land grant awarded by a grateful government to distinguished ex-naval officers. One account has him being 'given thousands of acres'.[11]

The flawed sources, the standard references, from which most of the foregoing is drawn do, however, also help direct the Sinclair chronicle across a few patches of somewhat thicker factual ice, especially from 1840, although they still lack precision. Fortunately, though, there are other less partisan sources, published and archival, available to provide material from which ancestral pretensions may be disproved and from which an account of events from about that date may be constructed that is more reliable, detailed and complete than one derived substantially from family tradition. The following narration draws extensively on these.

Francis Sinclair was the son of George Sinclair, a master mariner of Prestonpans. Given his father's occupation, his own later attested aptitude for sailing and an eventually thrice-demonstrated ability at boat-building (despite the loss of his craft the *Jessie Millar*), it is likely that Francis was familiar with the sea well before he left Scotland, although there are no details to prove it. One authority on maritime history surmises that

---

10   The most accessible source for this story is Ida Elizabeth Knudsen von Holt, *Stories of Long Ago: Niihau, Kauai, Oahu*, Honolulu, 1985. Von Holt consistently mispells McHutcheson as McHutchison.
11   von Holt, *Stories*, pp. 4–5; Knudsen and Noble, *Kanuka of Kauai*, pp. 70–71; Ruth M. Tabrah, *Ni'ihau: the last Hawaiian island*, Honolulu, 1987, pp. 92–93; Jack Teehan, 'Close-up on Place of Mystery: Niihau today, island without ulcers', *Sunday Advertiser*, 1 Nov. 1959.

at Stirling [between Edinburgh and Glasgow] as an excise officer he would have been familiar with the customs cutters on the Firth of Forth as well as vessels on the Clyde. The style of the *Richmond*, *Sisters* and *Jessie Millar* suggests he was building small ships resembling those whose design, tonnage and capabilities he knew and had probably sailed himself.[12]

In any case, it is as an excise officer that Francis enters the historical record, via the marriage register in 1824, aged about 26. Sixteen years later, now with a family, he enters it again, this time as a member of a party of Scottish emigrants, many of whom had been recruited by the laird Donald McDonald of Skye, who was also immigrating to New Zealand with his family.[13]

Departing from Greenoch near Glasgow on 25 August, the *Blenheim* reached Wellington, at the base of the North Island, on 27 December of 1840. From the beginning, Francis showed himself to be energetic and enterprising. As he told his brother William on 3 February 1841:

> I have bought a boat and I think that I shall be profitably employed with her till we get our place. The day after we landed I took a cargo of deals [sawn timber] from Petone to Wellington with her. G[eorge], J[ohn] and I started in the evening and landed them the next morning at six o'clock, and we had £2-5-0 for our job. It was the first and I was afraid to load heavier until I saw what she would do. I left J. and G. loading her to start on Monday morning at two o'clock and I shall (weather permitting) make three trips next week at £3 each, perhaps four. So we shall not starve in the interim. There is, however, a great deal of people here in consequence of the surveying stopt and the Gents not getting their land. We will, however, go ahead.[14]

True to his word, within a few months Sinclair shifted his family to the fledgling settlement of Wanganui, 200 kilometres north on the west coast, hoping to obtain a parcel of land to which he had bought an entitlement before leaving Scotland. Maori resistance to the New Zealand Company's operations, though, foiled that scheme. There, as elsewhere within much of the Company's putative domain of over 20,000,000 acres, opposition to land alienation and the obstruction of surveys by hostile Maoris impeded settler occupation of the land. Besides, individual blocks, even when shown on charts, were not always readily identifiable or in conformity with the topography. And there was still the

---

12 Letter, Amodeo to Laracy, 2 Mar. 2001.
13 Old Parochial Registers (Scotland), marriages 1820–1854, Latter Day Saints History Library, Christchurch, microfilm no. 102945; Nancy M. Taylor (ed.), *The Journal of Ensign Best, 1837–1843*, Wellington, 1966, p. 271; Louis E. Ward, *Early Wellington*, Wellington, 1928, pp. 78–79; Patricia Burns, *Fatal Success: a history of the New Zealand Company*, Auckland, 1989, pp. 190–191.
14 Sinclair to William, 3 Jan. 1841, Alexander Turnbull Library, Wellington, fMS Papers 460.

question of establishing legal title to a block. As a step to that end, in 1842 a land commissioner was appointed to investigate the New Zealand Company's claims. That was no easy task. As one commentator observes, '[William] Spain first had to establish the title of the sellers to the property which had been sold—a difficult task since the Maori often disputed amongst themselves as to their respective rights—and then find out whether the sale itself was legitimate'.[15] Thus one settler who had arrived on the *Blenheim* with the Sinclairs, James Brown, did not formally obtain his land in the upper Hutt valley, north of Petone, until 1853.[16]

But Francis was less patient than Brown, a former weaver from Paisley. After several months of cooling his heels within the confines of the embryonic settlement of Wanganui, he returned to Petone. There, with much ingenuity and with the aid of his sons and brother-in-law (our main informant on the matter), he set about building a boat. Later, family mythology would have it that at Petone the Sinclair's enjoyed the special protection of a Maori chief who stuck a spear in the ground outside their house as a sign of his favour, but that is sheer make-believe.[17] The story of the boat, though, a 30-ton schooner, is well attested. Named the *Richmond*, it was launched on 11 August 1842. The newspaper report of the event contains the earliest identified usage of the appellation 'Captain Sinclair'. The next month the *Richmond* went into service as a cargo vessel. In this guise it made five voyages plus an exploratory trip down the east coast of the South Island.

Then, between February and May 1843, Sinclair made three voyages to Banks Peninsula in the South Island to relocate three Scottish families—including his own—that had decided to take up land there instead of waiting for it to become available within the existing domains of the New Zealand Company. There were already a few Europeans in the area, including some French colonists who had settled at Akaroa in 1840, and claimed to have bought most of the peninsula from the Maoris. The first of the newcomers, the Deans, settled inland on the plains, but the less-monied Sinclairs and Hays, who followed them, settled (squatting at first) on the shore of an inlet that whalers had named Pigeon Bay.

---

15 Rosemarie Tonk, '"A difficult and complicated question": the New Zealand Company's Wellington, Port Nicholson, claim', in David Hamer and Roberta Nicholls, (eds), *The Making of Wellington, 1800–1914*, (quotation), Wellington, 1990, pp. 36, 39; Burns, *Fatal Success*, pp. 211–212; John Miller, *Early Victorian New Zealand: a study of racial tension and social attitudes, 1839–1852*, London, 1958, pp. 55–57; Edward Shortland, *The Southern Districts of New Zealand: a journal, with passing notices of the customs of the aborigines*, London, 1851, pp. 269–271.
16 J.A. Kelleher, *Upper Hutt, The History*, Upper Hutt, 1991, pp. 27–28, 31; Janette Williams, *Faith of Our Fathers: a history of St. Joseph's Catholic parish, Upper Hutt*, Upper Hutt, 2000. Brown was a forebear of my wife, Eugénie, who drew my attention to his experience.
17 von Holt, *Stories*, pp. 8–9.

In the larger history of settlement this Caledonian incursion was portentous. 'In this way', noted a contemporary, 'Lord Stanley's [that is, the Colonial Secretary's] project for discountenancing the further colonization of the Middle Island will be thwarted'.[18] Not that that worried the 'Pre-Adamites', as the early migrants to what would become the province of Canterbury were labelled after formal settlement began there with the arrival of the 'Pilgrims' in 1850. Their concern was to begin farming. Accordingly, the *Richmond* was soon sold to an Australian settler, W.B. Rhodes, for 18 cattle, of which Ebenezer Hay, who had bought a third share in the vessel before leaving Wellington, claimed six. Francis, who was to spend much of his time trading between Banks Peninsula and Wellington, thereupon built another schooner, the *Sisters*. He then sold this in 1845 to the French colonisation company, which claimed to have bought the whole of the peninsula from the Maoris, for 150 acres. Francis himself described the transaction:

> last voyage, when I was at home, the French Company was completing the purchase of the Peninsula, and arranged to pay away my schooner to the natives as part payment, selling me the little bay in which we are settled for her and a small balance more; so that the very thing that I had prepared for our removal has been the means, in the hands of a merciful and kind Providence, of fixing me down in perhaps the sweetest spot in this favoured country.[19]

Unfortunately, Francis and his son George, together with two other young men, were drowned in May 1846 when their newly built vessel, the *Jessie Millar*, foundered somewhere north of Kaikoura. They were en route to Wellington with a cargo of dairy produce for sale—the details of which are given by John Deans in a letter reporting the death of 'a Scotchman named Sinclair'—and not, as his grandson would later assure posterity, because Francis 'had received a letter from the Governor asking him to attend a conference'.[20] The poet Denis Glover has recorded the event in some sardonic verses:

> Captain Sinclair fashioned a schooner
> In a peninsula harbour
> That the dairy produce, the great cheeses,
> Might the sooner repay his labour;
> But he tempted too much the Pacific
> And was drowned with his lad,

---

18 *The New Zealand Gazette and Wellington Spectator*, 26 April 1843.
19 C.R. Straubel, *The Schooner 'Richmond' and Canterbury's First Farmers*, Wellington, 1948; James Hight and C.R. Straubel (eds), *A History of Canterbury, to 1854*, Christchurch, 1957, pp. 92–95, 239; L.G.D. Acland, *Pioneers of Canterbury: Deans letters, 1840–1854*, Dunedin, 1937, p. 110; A.H. Reed, *The Story of Canterbury: last Wakefield settlement*, Wellington, 1949, pp. 51–54; Francis Sinclair to William Sinclair, *New Zealand Journal*, London, vol. 5, 25 Oct. 1845.
20 Knudsen and Noble, *Kanuka of Kauai*, p. 73.

2. The Sinclairs Of Pigeon Bay, or 'The Prehistory of the Robinsons of Ni'ihau'

And the cheeses, the butter, the produce
Were nosed by the cod.[21]

Distressed by this loss, Elizabeth retreated with her remaining family to Wellington for a couple of years, but recovered to emerge as a matriarch. She returned to Sinclair Bay, as their particular site was known, in 1849, and soon began building a fine house that would be named 'Craigforth'.[22] Over the next 17 years the farm flourished and expanded (it eventually comprised 782 acres). And the family grew up. The daughter Jane married a widowed master mariner, Thomas Gay, captain at various times of the whalers *Offley* and *Corsair*, in 1849. And, in 1853, Helen married Charles Barrington Robinson, a dishonest and dissolute former magistrate. Rev. William Aylmer, the Anglican vicar of Akaroa, officiated.[23] Two years later, however, Helen parted from her husband and returned to 'Craigforth' with their son Aubrey. The family history notes the parting but, while commenting complaisantly on his profesional and social status, does not touch on Robinson's character, nor on the fact that he was violent towards his wife.[24] Nor does it mention a bold expansionary venture by Frank Sinclair and his uncle, John McHutcheson. In 1856 they took up a run of 10,000 acres in the newly opened-up inland plain of the Mackenzie Country. But the land, densely covered in heavy matagouri thorn bush proved too difficult to work, so they relinquished the run within two years.[25] Then, in 1863, probably because she could not obtain sufficient land to keep her family both properly occupied and cohesive where they were, and also possibly prompted by the personal discontent of Frank and Helen, Elizabeth decided that the time was right for the family to have a fresh start somewhere else.[26]

Accordingly, Craigforth was sold and, in March 1863, 12 members of the family set out with their furniture and livestock, under Gay's command in the *Bessie*, leaving the name Mount Sinclair as a mark of their sojourn in the area. Elizabeth, though, also left her two brothers, John and the recently arrived William, behind in New Zealand. Six months later the family came to Honolulu.[27] Then, in 1864,

---

21 Denis Glover, 'Captain Sinclair', in *Enter Without Knocking: selected poems*, Christchurch, 1964, p. 31; Gordon Ogilvie, *Denis Glover: his life*, Auckland, 1999, p. 125.
22 S.C. Farr, *Canterbury Old and New, 1850–1900: souvenir of the jubilee*, Christchurch, 1900, p. 32; H.L. Guthrie Hay, *Annandale, Past and Present, 1839–1900*, Christchurch, 1901, p. 123; H.C. Jacobson, *Tales of Banks Peninsula*, Akaroa, 1914, p. 301.
23 Aubrey (1853–1936), who in 1885 married his cousin Alice Gay, the daughter of Thomas Gay's second marriage, named one of his sons Aylmer (1888–1967). Another was named Selwyn (1892–1984).
24 von Holt, *Stories*, pp. 20–23; Gordon Ogilvie, 'Charles Robinson, Pioneer Magistrate—Also a Rake and Swindler', *Press*, Christchurch, 15 June 1984.
25 Johannes C. Andersen, *Jubilee History of South Canterbury*, Christchurch, 1916, pp. 82–83, 660; Oliver A. Gillespie, *South Canterbury: a record of settlement*, Christchurch 1971, pp. 94–97.
26 Isabella L. Bird, *The Hawaiian Archipelago: six months amongst the palm groves, coral reefs, and volcanoes of the Sandwich Islands*, London, 1905, p. 202.
27 The name Sinclair Bay was replaced by Holmes Bay. John McHutcheson eventually settled in Blenheim, where he became mayor in 1873. He died in 1899. William McHutcheson, born in 1810, came to New Zealand in 1862 and eventually settled in Oamaru, where he died in 1905.

in the aftermath of the Great Mahele of 1846 to 1855, by which traditional Hawai'ian communal land holding was replaced by individual freehold tenure, the Sinclairs bought Ni'ihau from King Kamehameha V for $10,000.[28]

The tale of the Sinclairs and of their peregrinations has been often told, but always partially and often with marked inaccuracies. The latter is especially the case with the extensive American literature on Ni'ihau. There, in contrast to the earlier and more matter-of-fact New Zealand tradition, which is grounded in memoirs recounting the European settlement of Canterbury, it is buoyed by the dashing figure of Francis, 'Captain Sinclair'. It has become part of the romantic myth of Hawai'i, and the 'human interest' dimension of the story—enhanced by roseate embellishments, flattering falsehoods and convenient silences—has tended to prevail. Whereas the New Zealand literature concerns a family that had still to make its mark, the Hawai'ian writings relate to a family that has become 'successful'. That is, until 1988. From that date, probably in response to the reservations (equivocal as they are) appended to the 1985 edition of Ida von Holt's family history, the Sinclairs have at last ceased to be romanticised, if not ignored, by commentators on Ni'ihau.

The conduit, if not the creative source, of the severely distorted view of the past, which entered the public domain when the oral account that presumably existed within the family was recorded in print, was Anne Knudsen. Her brother Francis, though, was not immune from grand delusions, either. He claimed to be heir to the Earl of Caithness.[29] The youngest of Francis and Elizabeth Sinclair's children, Anne was not yet two years of age when they reached Wellington in 1840, and was only seven when her father died. She was not well placed to be a first-hand authority on early family history. But she was also the most reluctant of the family to leave New Zealand. Perhaps that was conducive to nostalgia? After marrying Valdemar Knudsen, the Sinclair's neighbour from 'Waiawa' on Kauai, in 1867, she remained near the family centre for the next 30 years. She died in Hollywood in 1922, having outlived all her siblings. Like her sisters, she had married a financially well-off man who was appreciably older than herself.

Critically for the transmission of her version of events, two of Anne's children wrote works of family history drawing on stories derived from her. These have, in turn been plundered by other commentators, including a grand nephew.[30] Besides many uncritical newspaper stories, there have also been numerous

---

28 Ministry of Interior to J. McH. and F. Sinclair, 19 Jan. 1864; to Wahineaea, 25 Jan. 1864, State Archives of Hawai'i, Interior Department Letters, 1861–1866, Book 7B.
29 von Holt, *Stories*, pp. 3–4, 157.
30 Knudsen and Noble, *Kanuka of Kauai*, pp. 167, 172–173; von Holt, *Stories*, p. 1, passim; Lawrence Kainoahau Gay, *Tales of the Forbidden Island of Ni'ihau*, Honolulu, 1981, pp. 8–10.

treatments in magazines and books, a disconcerting number of them having links (and therefore an academic imprimatur?) to the staff or press of the University of Hawai'i.[31]

There was once a chance that the Hawai'ian tradition of Sinclairography might be launched by Somerset Maugham. According to his first biographer, Wilmon Menard, in 1969, Maugham heard the Sinclair story from Aubrey Robinson, Anne's nephew, in the Union Saloon in Honolulu in 1916, and intended turning it into a novel. Moving on to Tahiti, however, his attention was seduced by the story of Paul Gauguin, which he published as *The Moon and Sixpence* in 1919.[32] Following that false start, the Sinclair story did not come into print in its subsequently well-known and glamourised form until 1928. Then, appropriately, it was in an article on Anne herself in a celebratory volume called *Women of Hawaii*:

> Her father was Francis Sinclair, who as a young man entered the British navy and attained the command of a man-of-war at the end of the Napoleonic era.
>
> He distinguished himself immediately after the battle of Waterloo when he was conveying the Duke of Wellington home to England after his great victory over the Corsican. His ship, on which the Duke was a passenger, encountered a frightful gale in the English channel and was saved from being dashed to pieces on the cliffs of Dover by the superior seamanship of Captain Sinclair who personally took the wheel and guided the vessel safely to port. In recognition of this achievement, the Duke presented Sinclair with a handsome travelling desk which became a treasured heirloom in the Sinclair family.
>
> Captain Sinclair resigned his commission in the British navy about 1840. Then he, with his wife, who was Elizabeth McHutcheson, and their young family, including the infant daughter, Anne, went to New Zealand to direct large landed estates which he had acquired there.[33]

This story was repeated in the the second edition in 1938. Most of it also occurs in *Stories Of Long Ago* by Anne's daughter Ida, first issued privately in 1940, and again in 1953 and 1963, before being formally published in 1985. The story

---

31   See Appendix.
32   Wilmon Menard, *The Two Worlds of Somerset Maugham*, Los Angeles, 1965, p. 85; and 'Willie Maugham and the Wonderful Widow Sinclair', *Foreign Service Review*, Oct. 1969, pp. 40–43, 48–49.
33   George F. Nellist (ed.), *Women of Hawaii*, Honolulu [1928], pp. 157–159. This is a companion volume to the third volume (*Men of Hawaii*) of Nellist's *The Story of Hawaii and Its Builders* (Honolulu, 1925).

also appeared, substantially unchanged, in two 1984 volumes: *Notable Women of Hawaii*, in entries on Elizabeth and Anne; and, *History Makers of Hawaii*, in an entry on Anne.[34]

Given the apparent authority long conferred on this version by regular repetition, how could so many commentators not but accept it? One answer, at least, to that question is that they did not consult any archival records or the substantial—and independent—New Zealand literature bearing on the Sinclairs.

In the light of these other sources, as has already been indicated, a more mundane, if no less honourable, story emerges. Thus, Francis's father is not to be confused with the Sir George Sinclair MP who was prominently associated with the New Zealand Company, (and whose son Dudley, remorseful after declining a duel, shot himself in Auckland in 1844). Nor was Dr Andrew Sinclair, Colonial Secretary in New Zealand from 1844 to 1856, a relation.[35] As for his alleged naval career, Francis, born in 1797, was too young to have served with Nelson or to have commanded a vessel at the time of Waterloo (1815). Indeed, in an appendix to the 1985 edition of von Holt's book, Ruth Knudsen Hanner, Anne's grand-daughter, concedes that he was not in the navy at all. She thereby also gives the lie to a sentimental extension of the family myth, to wit that Anne's father and father-in-law were both present at the battle of Copenhagen, although on opposing sides. At the same time she is concerned to retrieve any lost ground. Thus, she compromises her concession by surmising that Francis was in charge of a merchant ship which was commandeered by the 'Iron Duke' to take him on a 'hurried' and 'secret'—and historically fictitious—journey to England. To this end she invokes the gift of the inscribed writing desk, for which no evidence exists and which is said to have been stolen from Francis during one of his business trips.[36] Still, it fuelled naive imaginations. 'As a child', wrote von Holt, 'I would dream of finding it in some old curiosity shop'.[37]

As for social status, the Sinclairs were undistinguished. While clearly 'respectable' and migrating as 'capitalists' (that is, prospective landholders) rather than as 'labourers', according to the rubrics of the New Zealand Company's colonisation scheme, they were, moreover, scarcely prosperous. They travelled steerage in the 374-ton *Blenheim*, not in the cabin like the McDonalds, and their

---

34   See Appendix.
35   von Holt, *Stories*, p. 2; Burns, *Fatal* Success, pp. 87, 104; 'Andrew Sinclair', in W.H. Oliver (ed.), *Dictionary of New Zealand Biography, 1769–1869*, vol. 1, Wellington, 1990, p. 397.
36   von Holt, *Stories*, pp. 157–158. None of Wellington's biographers report a 'secret' visit to England. The battle of Waterloo was on 18 June 1815, and his first visit after that was in July 1816. See, for example, Elizabeth Langford, *Wellington: the years of the sword* (New York, 1969) and Thomas Dwight Veve, *The Duke of Wellington and the British Army of Occupation in France, 1815–1818* (Westport, Conn., 1992).
37   von Holt, *Stories*, p. 6.

initial prospects were modest, if inflated by optimism and energy.[38] Far from having been assigned an estate, Francis had in 1839 purchased a £100 land order from the Company, entitling him to select 100 country acres and one town acre from its putative domains in New Zealand, when they became available for occupation.[39] The same payment, though, also covered the cost of passage for the family. To benefit further from that provision, and also to sidestep the Company's discouragement of unattached labouring men, Elizabeth's 24-year-old brother John was included among the Sinclair children. Four years were subtracted from his age to conceal the subterfuge.[40] John, who soon reverted to his own name, eventually became mayor of, for him, the appropriately named town of Blenheim.[41]

Characteristically ready to make the most of their chances, and adept at helping create opportunities for themselves, the Sinclairs had already made a promising start by the time Francis was drowned in 1846. And it was consistently their worthy qualities, rather than any suggestion of high rank, that, even in colonial society, caught the attention of commentators. For all that Francis's demise was lamented by the Governor, George Grey, and by the peripatetic Anglican bishop, George Selwyn, who had himself stayed a night with the Sinclairs in 1844, it was because he was regarded as a good type of settler rather than—as Anne's daughter, followed extravagantly by Menard, contends—because of any particular eminence.[42] Already, on the voyage to New Zealand, one diarist, the wife of a doctor, had noted 'Sunday 6 September 1840. Emigrants had prayers and a portion of the Bible read to them in Gaelic. We had the same in English by

---

38 The status terms were later replaced by 'colonists' and 'emigrants', respectively. Burns, *Fatal Success*, pp. 102, 147–148, 163–164; Nancy M. Taylor (ed.), *The Journal of Ensign Best, 1837–1843*, Wellington, 1966, p. 271; Louis E. Ward, *Early Wellington*, Wellington, 1928, pp. 78–79. For a discussion of steerage and cabin passage, see Tony Simpson, *The Immigrants: the great migration from Britain to New Zealand, 1830–1890* (pp. 78–79).
39 Francis's land order is in the National Archives of New Zealand, Christchurch, Canterbury Association papers L and S 40/2, no.35. For accounts of the company's land allocation system, see Burns, *Fatal Success*, pp. 100–102; Taylor, *Ensign Best*, pp. 45–46; Michael Turnbull, *The New Zealand Bubble*, Wellington, 1962, pp. 10–19.
40 This was brought to my attention by Mavis Donnelly-Crequer, who compared the passenger list of the *Blenheim* with relevant birth, marriage and death records.
41 For John, who died in 1899, see C.A. Macdonald, *Pages From the Past: some chapters in the history of Marlborough* (Blenheim, 1933, p. 260); William Vance, *High Endeavour: the story of the Mackenzie Country* (Wellington, 1980, pp. 6, 27–29, 166–167). For his and Elizabeth's brother William, who died in 1905, see *Press*, 28 Oct. 1905. See also, William McHutcheson, *The New Zealander Abroad*, 1888; *Camp-life in Fiordland, New Zealand*, 1892; 'The New Zealander at Home: fifty years of colonial life, or The Story of a Jubilee Colonist', *Otago Witness*, 14 August to 30 Ocrober 1890 (12 weeky episodes). The author was the son and namesake of Elizabeth Sinclair's brother William.
42 Wilmon Menard, 'The Cloistered Island: the lively widow and lonely Niihau', *Aloha*, April 1982, pp. 48–49; von Holt, *Stories*, 14; Shortland, *Southern Districts*, pp. 271–274; James Hay, *Reminiscences of Earliest Canterbury (pincipally Banks Peninsula)*, Christchurch, 1915, p. 147.

a very respectable steerage passenger of the name of Sinclair from Stirling'.[43] In 1844 a government official visiting Pigeon Bay spoke in similarly appreciative terms:

> I was invited by Mr Sinclair to rest at his house. His family is an example for settlers. Everything necessary for their comfort was produced by themselves—two young girls even making their own shoes. Mr. S. told me that he bought very few things; as his family—a wife, three sons, and two daughters—were able to do all the work required. They all appeared happy and contented; and as they resided on land which the natives had sold *bona fide*, they had never been annoyed in any manner by them.[44]

So, too, did Bishop Selwyn:

> I found some Scottish settlers of the right sort; living in great comfort by their own exertions, making everything for themselves, and above all, keeping up their religious principles and usages though far away from any ministerial assistance. The name of the family is Sinclair; I spent the evening [16 February] with them and conducted their family prayers.[45]

Later, in 1851, Charlotte Godley, the wife of the founder of the Canterbury settlement, would also write of their Swiss Family Robinson style of life:

> We went to stay the night at Mrs Sinclair's; I have told you about them and about the two daughters who came to stay here, at the time of our regatta. They are very nice simple people, excessively Scotch and old-fashioned, and live a regular colonial life, according to one's old ideas of it; plenty of cows, and milk and butter and cream, and doing everything for themselves; they have not a servant in the house. They have just built a pretty new house in a most lovely spot.[46]

These comments are similar in tone to those of the travel writer Isabella Bird, who visited the Sinclair's at Makaweli in 1874:

> The household here consists first and foremost of its head, Mrs [Sinclair], a lady of the old Scotch type, very talented, bright, humorous, charming, with a definite character which impresses its force upon everybody. [Wearing] a large, drawn silk bonnet, which she rarely lays aside, as light in her figure and step as a young girl [she looks] as if she had

---

43 Jessie Campbell, 'Diary', quoted in Macmillan to Stout, 15 Feb. 1951, Alexander Turnbull Library, fms Papers 460, Francis Sinclair, letter 1841.
44 Shortland, *Southern Districts*, pp. 269–270.
45 Quoted in James Hight and C.R. Straubel, *A History of Canterbury to 1854*, vol.1, p. 96.
46 John R. Godley (ed.), *Letters from Early New Zealand by Charlotte Godley, 1850–1853*, Christchurch, 1951, p. 262.

stepped out of an old picture, or one of Dean Ramsay's books. [And they all lived] much such a life as people live at Raasay, Applecross, or some other remote Highland place.[47]

None of these nineteenth century records—including an interview in 1893 with his grandson Francis Gay—glamourise Francis Sinclair, but they do acknowledge the authority within the family of his widow.[48] That was, however, probably severely tested by Anne's resistance to leaving Pigeon Bay. She was being courted by a young Scotsman named James Montgomery at the time.[49] The opportunity to shift, though, was not of the Sinclair's own making. Rather, it was presented to them with the scheme for building a tunnel through the Port Hills to link the inland town of Christchurch with the anchorage at Lyttelton. The Sinclair property lay to the east of Lyttelton, and was heavily wooded. In October 1862, therefore, George Holmes, the principle contractor, bought it in order to obtain timber for construction purposes. The price was £8707.[50]

Armed with money from this windfall, Thomas Gay went to Melbourne to buy what would be the family's 'Ark'. In 1863 he returned to Pigeon Bay with the *Bessie*, a three-masted barque of 262 tons.[51] Then, in mid-March, after refitting, and with its assorted Sinclairs, Gays and Robinsons aboard, plus furniture and farming equipment and some livestock, the *Bessie* cleared Lyttelton for Victoria in British Columbia, about which they had apparently heard promising reports. Travelling via Tahiti (3–11 April), they reached their destination in early June, but were were disappointed.[52] Victoria at that time was still little more that a fur-trading post, potential farm land in the region was covered in heavy forest and the indigenous people seemed less appealing than the Maoris. Consequently, after investigating settlement prospects, the group decided to look elsewhere. They even, it seems, contemplated returning to New Zealand. But, on the advice of one Henry Rhodes of the Hudson Bay Company, who had a brother in Honolulu, they decided first to consider Hawai'i, which may previously have been visited by Gay in the course of a voyage to the Bering Strait in 1851.[53] Thus it was that on 17 September 1863, after 28 days out, the *Bessie* dropped anchor in Honolulu. 'On going down to the wharf', Rev. Samuel Damon, the port chaplain, 'was surprised to find the trim barque with its large party on

---

47   Bird, *Six months*, pp. 202–204. Rev. Edward Bannerman Ramsay wrote nostalgic descriptions of Scottish folk culture. See, for example, his *Reminiscences of Scottish Life and Culture* (Edinburgh, 1857; 16th edition, 1912).
48   Mary H. Krout, *Hawaii and a Revolution: the personal experiences of a newspaper correspondent in the Sandwich Islands during the crisis of 1893 and subsequently*, London, 1898, pp. 132–134.
49   von Holt, *Stories*, p. 25.
50   *Lyttelton Times*, 29 Oct. 1862; Johannes C. Andersen, *Place-Names of Banks Peninsula: a topographical history*, Wellington, 1927, pp. 87, 126, 165; letter, Donnelly-Crequer to Laracy, 2 Mar. 2001.
51   *Lyttelton Times*, 7 Jan., 6 Feb. 1863.
52   *Messager de Taiti*, 11, 18 Avril 1863; *The Friend*, Oct. 1863; von Holt, *Stories*, p. 29.
53   von Holt, *Stories*, pp. 29–30, 98–99; Godley, *Letters by Charlotte Godley*, p. 269. The Hudson Bay Company had opened a branch office in Hawai'i in 1829.

board, with a beautiful old lady at its head, books, pictures, work, even a piano, and all that could add refinement to a floating home, with cattle and sheep of valuable breeds in pens on the deck'.[54]

Coming ashore, they rented a house in Honolulu as a base from which to search for a suitably large tract of land for farming, and eventually decided on Ni'ihau. In thus settling in Hawai'i they were, incidentally, following a path blazed by certain other ambitious Scottish migrants from New Zealand: notably, Harry and Eliza Macfarlane who settled at Waikiki in 1846, and Thomas Cleghorn who arrived in 1851 and who's son, Archibald Scott Cleghorn, later married Princess Likelike, the sister of King David Kalakaua. Archibald became the father of Princess Kaiulani.[55]

But the Sinclairs did not sever their links with New Zealand abruptly. Twelve days after arriving at Honolulu, Thomas Gay departed for Lyttelton with a cargo of sugar, molasses, rice and salt. He returned on 30 May 1864 with a cargo of coal from Newcastle in New South Wales, but left again for New Zealand in July with a cargo of 70 mules. That voyage was to be less successful. On reaching Auckland early in August, Thomas and his brother William were arrested, and charged with having assaulted an insubordinate seaman named Charles Boyle. After being held in custody for nearly two months they came to trial on 27 September and were found guilty. They were sentenced to six months imprisonment but, following a petition for clemency to Governor Grey, from certain 'southern gentlemen', including Anne's former beau, they were released in 1865. Thomas thereupon sailed the *Bessie* to Newcastle, apparently intending to sell her there. But, on 9 February, before that was accomplished, he died of pneumonia, probably contracted in prison.[56]

Even so, sporadic contact with New Zealand continued. In 1866 Francis, now aged 32, returned there to marry his cousin Isabella, daughter of William McHutcheson, and in 1902, following her death in 1896 or thereabouts, he married her widowed sister Williamina Shirriffs.[57] Meanwhile in 1881, Anne had brought her husband and five children to spend a year in New Zealand,

---

54 *Pacific Commercial Advertiser*, 24 Sept. 1863; *The Friend*, Oct. 1863, p 80; Bird, *Six months*, p. 202; von Holt, *Stories*, pp. 30–31. Isabella Bird, and the commentators who follow her on the matter, are mistaken in stating that the *Bessie* had previously called at Hawai'i after leaving Tahiti.
55 Don Hibbard and David Franzen, *The View From Diamond Head: royal residence to urban resort*, Honolulu, 1986, p. 66; obituaries of Archibald Scott Cleghorn: *PacificCommercialAdvertiser*, 2 Nov. 1910, *Paradise of the Pacific*, Nov. 1910, *Hawaiian Gazette*, Nov. 1910.
56 *Lyttelton Times*, 12 Nov. 1863, 1 Sept., 6 Oct. 1864, 28 Jan. 1865; *The Friend*, August 1864; von Holt, *Stories*, p. 33; R.G. Burkland to C.F. Amodeo, 15 Feb. 1985, private communication reporting movements of the *Bessie* from 17 Sept. 1863 to 6 June 1864, drawn from 'local [Honolulu] newspapers'; *Newcastle Chronicle*, 11 Feb. 1865.
57 *Lyttelton Times*, 29 August 1866; information provided by Mavis Donnelly.

mostly in Auckland.[58] That same year Francis bought a 12-acre property known as 'The Pines' in the Epsom district of Auckland. He held it until 1893, although for how long he lived there is unknown.[59] In 1883 he passed the management of the family's estates in Hawai'i over to his nephews Aubrey Robinson and Francis Gay; in 1885 he was in London with Isabella, overseeing the printing of her book *Indigenous Flowers of the Hawaiian Islands*; and, when his mother died in 1892, aged 92, he was living in California.[60] Later he settled in London, and devoted his time to writing about the Pacific, often under the name Philip Garth. He published five volumes of poems, essays and short stories. An amiable young itinerant, his character 'David Kinross of the *Lapwing*' is not unlike Louis Becke's 'Tom Denison'.[61] Francis Sinclair died on the island of Jersey on 22 July 1916, aged 83, and his sister Anne, 24 years a widow, six years later.[62] With that the emigrant adventure that began in Scotland in 1840 came to its close. But the Gorgon's teeth of imaginatively enhanced stories about her family's past that Anne had imparted to her children were just about to come into flower. Enemies of fact, they would continue to bloom vigorously for six decades.

Matters such as the subterfuge about John McHutcheson's age and name change, the scurrilous character of Charles Robinson and the criminal conviction of Thomas Gay have not hitherto figured in the various tellings of the Sinclair story. Indeed, they are inherently incompatible with the tone of the Hawai'i-generated literature. Even so, why draw attention to them, or to the Sinclair's relatively humble origins, or to any other flaws in the received narrative? The main reason is that, contrary to the 'repel all boarders' position stated by Helen Robinson 1983, the Robinson's do not 'own' their own history, or even that of Ni'ihau or of the Sinclair's. For these are all parts of other, larger and still evolving histories, not least that of the European colonisation of the Pacific, and so have something to contribute to an understanding of the events with which they are concerned. No history can be 'owned', but is the common property of all—even if it concerns Ni'ihau and the Robinsons.[63] That the Robinson's are

---

58 von Holt, *Stories*, p. 122. They departed Honolulu in the *Zealandia* on 26 Jan. 1881, and arrived back on 16 Feb. in the *City of New York*.
59 Private communication from John Stacpoole, 14 Nov. 1989; H.C. Jacobson, *Tales of Banks Peninsula*, Akaroa, 1914, p. 105.
60 Clark, John E.K., *Beaches of Kaua'I and Ni'ihau*, Honolulu, 1990 p. 89; Joesting, Edward, *Kauai*, Honolulu, 1984, pp. 195–196; Stepien, *Ni'ihau*, pp. 49–50; Tabrah, *Ni'ihau*, pp. 198–221; *Hawaiian Gazette*, 25 Oct. 1892; *The Friend*, Nov. 1892, p. 86.
61 Francis Sinclair's main publications are: *Ballads and Poems from the Pacific* (London, 1885); *Where the Sun Sets: memories from other years and lands* (London, 1905); *Under North Star and Southern Cross* (London, 1907); *From the Four Winds* (London, 1909); *Under Western Skies: life pictures from memory* (London, 1911). *Lapwing* was also the name of a trading vessel that operated out of Fiji. Dorothy Shineberg, *The People Trade: Pacific Island labourers and New Caledonia, 1865–1930*, Honolulu, 1999, p. 20.
62 *Honolulu Advertiser*, 22 July, 8 Sept. 1916; Peterson, Barbara Bennett (ed), *Notable Women of Hawaii*, Honolulu, 1984, pp. 223–224.
63 For a useful discussion of this matter, see Doug Munro, 'Who "owns" Pacific History? Reflections on the insider/outsider dichotomy', *Journal of Pacific History*, vol. 29, no. 2, 1994, pp. 232–237.

free, and quite properly so, not to cooperate with enquirers if they so choose is a different matter from what may or may not be of historical significance to any of those enquirers.

Besides, the infusion of Sinclair mythology, that amalgam of domestic phantasies, into the corpus of publicly available historical commentary obliges any serious enquirer to subject it to critical scrutiny. When private belief is transubstantiated into what purports to be objective fact, it thereby comes within the ambit of general curiosity, which is not subject to any inherent restraints.

A further, if somewhat extraneous, justification for attempting to clarify the history of the Sinclairs is that it offers a clear and salutary warning of the need for exercising particular care when dealing with what is too often euphemistically described as 'oral history', when what is really meant is 'the oral record'. 'I/you/he/she believe(s)/think(s)/say(s)' do not equate with 'it was', no matter how firmly a notion is held or how often a story is told. That *cogito ergo erat* is no less fallacious than *cogito ergo sum* is widely recognised. Thus, Jane Austen expressed misgivings about the reliability of oral transmission in *Persuasion* when she has Anne Elliot counter a would-be informant 'My dear Mrs Smith, your authority is deficient … we may not expect to get real information in such a [bendy] line. Facts or opinions which are to pass through the hands of so many … can hardly have much truth left'.[64] Oscar Wilde aired a similar view 1895 in *The Importace of Being Earnest*

> Miss Prism: Memory my dear Cecily, is the diary that we all carry about with us.
>
> Cecily: Yes, but it usually chronicles the things that have never happened.[65]

Certainly that was the case with Anne Sinclair Knudsen's story of her father. Nor was imaginative largesse restricted to her own family. Thus, her son Eric confidently writes that Knud Knudsen, Valdemar's father, 'was appointed President of Norway by the King of Denmark, and held that office until Norway seceded from Denmark in 1818', and the 1928 epiphany of family mythology describes him as being 'president of the Norwegian Legislature from 1814 to 1818'.[66] In fact, from 1810 to 1852 Knud was mayor and chairman of the town council of Kristiansand, a settlement on the south coast of Norway, (and not to be confused with Kristiania, the capital, which was to be renamed Oslo in 1925).[67] As for Norway itself: Sweden annexed it from Denmark in 1814, and

---

64 *Persuasion*, London, 1818, many subsequent editions, Chapter 21.
65 Act Two.
66 Nellist, *Women of Hawaii*, p. 271; Knudsen and Noble, *Kanuka of Kauai*, p. 93.
67 Sverre Steen, *Kristiansands historie*, Kristiansands, 1941, vol. 1, pp. 85–86; Karl Leewy, *Kristiansands bebyggelse og befolkning i eldre tider*, Kristiansand, 1980–1985, vol. 2, pp. 96–97; vol. 8, p. 10.

held it until it became independent in 1905. But such detail, such precision, found little place in a family history concerned to devise and foster a usable European past. *That* history was one that complemented the success of the migrant Sinclair–Robinson–Gay–Knudsen clan in the Pacific.

Appendix

Sinclair bibliography

A list of works which recount in some measure the history of the Sinclairs up to 1863. * denotes work with authorial or publication links to the University of Hawai'i.

1. The matter-of-fact tradition

a. New Zealand publications

1883

Jacobson, H.C., *Tales of Banks Peninsula*, Akaroa (3rd edn 1914).

1900

Farr, S.C., *Canterbury Old and New, 1850–1900: souvenir of the Jubilee*, Christchurch.

1901

Guthrie Hay, H.L., *Annandale, Past and Present, 1839–1900*, Christchurch.

1915

Hay, James, *Reminiscences of Earliest Canterbury (principally Banks Peninsula) and its Settlers*, Christchurch.

1937

Acland, F.G.D. (ed.), *Pioneers of Canterbury: Deans letters, 1840–1854*, Dunedin.

1938

Godley, John R. (ed.), *Letters from Early New Zealand by Charlotte Godley*, Christchurch.

1948

Straubel, C.R., *The Schooner 'Richmond' and Canterbury's First Settlers*, Wellington.

1949

Reed, A.H., *The Story of Canterbury: last Wakefield settlement*, Wellington.

1957

Hight, James, & Straubel C.R. (eds), *A History of Canterbury*, vol. 1: *To 1854*, Christchurch.

1981 Bromley Maling, Peter, *Early Sketches and Charts of Banks Peninsula, 1770–1850*, Wellington.

1990

Ogilvie, Gordon, *Banks Peninsula: cradle of Canterbury*, Christchurch.

'Elizabeth Sinclair', in W.H. Oliver (ed.), *Dictionary of New Zealand Biography: volume 1, 1769–1869*, Wellington.

1994

Amodeo, Colin, 'James Daymond and Pigeon Bay', 'What happened to the *Jessie Millar*'?, 'Thomas Gay to the rescue', *Akaroa Mail*, 4 November, 2, 16 December.

b. Hawai'ian publications

1988

Oyama, Kaikilani Eleanor, *The Kauai Guide on Niihau*, Lihue.

1989

Tave Rerioterio, & Keale, Moses K., *Niihau: the traditions of a Hawaiian Island*, Honolulu.

1990*

Clark, John R.K., *Beaches of Kaua'i and Ni'ihau*, Honolulu.

1998

Meyer, Philip A., (trans. Lei Pahulehua et al.), *Niihau*, Makaweli, (Hoomana Ia Iesu Church).

c. Published elsewhere

1992

Theroux, Paul, *The Happy Isles of Oceania*, London.

2. The romantic/inventive tradition

1928

Nellist, George F., *Women of Hawaii*, Honolulu.

1940

von Holt, Ida Elizabeth Knudsen, *Stories of Long Ago*, Honolulu.

1944

Knudsen Eric A. & Noble, George P., *Kanuka of Kauai*, Honolulu.

1953

von Holt, Ida Elizabeth Knudsen, *Stories of Long Ago*, Honolulu.

1963

* Daws, Gavan, & Head, Timothy, 'Niihau: a shoal of time', in *American Heritage*, vol. 14.

von Holt, Ida Elizabeth Knudsen, *Stories of Long Ago*, Honolulu. Privately printed.

1969

Menard, Wilmon, 'Willie Maugham and the Wonderful Widow Sinclair', *Foreign Service Review*, October.

1981

Gay, Laurence Kainoahou, *Tales of the Forbidden Island of Niihau*, Honolulu.

Menard, Wilmon, 'The Widow Sinclair and her Sea Search for Paradise', *The Beaver*, Summer.

1982

Beekman, Allan, *The Niihau Incident*, Honolulu.

Menard, Wilmon, 'The Cloistered Island—the Lively Widow and Lonely Niihau', *Aloha*, April.

———, 'To Find Niihau: "a bonny island of our very own"', *Oceans*, vol. 15, no. 5 (Sept.–Oct.).

1984

* Grove Day, A., *History Makers of Hawaii*, Honolulu.

* Joesting, Edward, *Kauai*, Honolulu.

* Peterson, Barbara Bennett (ed.), *Notable Women of Hawaii*, Honolulu.

* Stepien, Edward R., *Niihau: a brief history*, Honolulu.

1985

von Holt, Ida Elizabeth Knudsen, *Stories of Long Ago: Niihau-Kauai-Oahu*, Honolulu. First publication. With slight emendations.

1987

Tabrah, Ruth, *Niihau: the last Hawaiian Island*, Honolulu.

3. Insular Eminence: Cardinal Moran (1830–1911) and the Pacific islands

Patrick Francis Moran is a major figure in the story of the worldwide spread of Catholicism consequent upon the outpouring of Irish migrants in the nineteenth century. That is, he is prominently located within one of the two major, and occasionally converging, ethnic strands within the overall Church-building process of the period.[1] French Catholics, keen to compensate for the assault on the Church in their homeland by the votaries of the Revolution, may have led the Catholic missionary outreach to indigenous peoples in Africa, Asia and Oceania. But it was mostly from among the Irish, carrying their religion with them, that the Church was planted in the colonies that were built around settlers from the British Isles. Australia offers a case in point. There, Moran, Archbishop of Sydney from 1884 to 1911 and a cardinal from 1885, was concerned both to construct a strong ecclesiastical structure and, as a further triumph of Irish apostolic achievement, to identify the Church there in a particular way with the emerging nation. In Moran's view, a not uncommon one, Catholicism not only transcended, but might subsume, any other religious and intellectual tradition. At the same time, while being open to all peoples and cultures, in advancing its sway it was also deemed to have accorded an edge of pre-eminence to the Irish.[2]

Various manifestations of Moran's mythic beliefs are already well-known. For example, he was an enthusiastic Australian patriot and, in 1897, stood—albeit unsuccessfully, but not embarrassingly so—for election to a federal convention designed to draw the several colonies into a single country. He wished to take a lead in forming a 'union for the common good, [whereby] Australia, under the blessing of God, will work out its destiny, not as a group of colonies, but as a nation'. And he prophetically envisaged a national 'Parliament clothed with splendour and beauty like one of our cathedrals of old, the guarantee of freedom for Australia's sons, "strong as a fortress and sacred as a shrine"'.[3] Politically, Australia was to be an improved, alternative, liberated Ireland. Here, he rejoiced in 1885, 'we shape our own destinies and make our own laws'.[4] Within that nation he hoped to see the secure social and economic integration of Catholics. Consequently, he was a prominent supporter of the trade union movement and

---
1   See, for example, Hugh Laracy, 'Les Pères Maristes and New Zealand: the Irish connection', *Journal de la Société des Océanistes* (no. 105 (1997), pp. 187–198).
2   Patrick O'Farrell, *The Irish in Australia*, Sydney, 1987, p. 170; Patrick O'Farrell, *Vanished Kingdoms: Irish in Australia and New Zealand*, Sydney, 1990, pp. 110–111, 124–125, 221; Charles R. Morris, *American Catholic: the saints and sinners who built America's most powerful church*, New York, 1997, pp. 40–53, 115–117.
3   Quoted in James G. Murtagh, *Australia: the Catholic chapter*, New York, 1946, pp. 162, 165; Richard Ely, *Unto God and Caesar: religious issues in the emerging Commonwealth, 1891–1906*, Melbourne, 1976, pp. 13–20.
4   Quoted in Patrick O'Farrell, *The Catholic Church and Community in Australia: a history*, Melbourne, 1977, p. 195; O'Farrell, *Irish in Australia*, pp. 163–164.

of the emergent Labor party, both of which already tended to claim the loyalties of most of his co-religionists.[5] Furthermore, he believed it was the destiny of that nation to provide for 'this southern world a bulwark of civilisation and a home of freedom'; indeed, it was to 'be the centre of civilisation for all the nations of the East'. As a seminary student Moran had himself aspired to be a missionary in China and, from the time of his arrival in Australia, he harboured a plan to found a college to train missionaries. With reference to the heroic history created by the Irish missionaries of the sixth century, it was to be called St. Columba's and would, he hoped, become a new Iona, 'the spiritual lighthouse of the southern world'.[6]

That scheme was never realised, but something may be deemed to have been salvaged from it through his support of religious missionary congregations. Thus, he not only encouraged the Marist Fathers, whose province extended from the Solomons to Samoa and who had set up a 'Procure' house in Sydney in 1845; but in 1885 and 1900, respectively, he also assisted the Missionaries of the Sacred Heart and the Society of the Divine Word to establish similar bases in Sydney from which to service their newly founded missions in New Guinea, where they eventually established a strong indigenous church.[7] Indeed, there is a Pacific islands dimension that pervades various closely related facets of the cardinal's career. It occurs in his pastoral, political and polemical activities, but it is not just on this account that it warrants systematic study. It is also significant within the larger story of the complex and enduring engagement between Australia and its Oceanic neighbours.

Moran was born on 16 September 1830 at Leighlinbridge, Carlow, Ireland. He was the youngest of five children of Patrick Moran, a businessman, and his wife Alicia. His parents died while he was still young so, in 1842, he was placed in the care of his mother's half-brother Paul Cullen, a highly regarded Catholic priest who was rector of the Irish College in Rome. In 1849 Cullen, who became a cardinal in 1866, was reassigned to Ireland. His task, in which he succeeded firmly, was to reorganise the Catholic Church there after two centuries of English and Protestant oppression, and to resist a rising threat from secularism. By determining episcopal appointments he also extended his influence, with its emphasis on religious discipline and order, to Irish migrant communities worldwide. His nephew followed closely in his footsteps. Moran was ordained

---

5   O'Farrell, *Church and Community*, pp. 285–94; J.M. Mahon, 'Cardinal Moran's Candidature', *Manna*, no. 6, 1963, pp. 65–66; Patrick Ford, *Cardinal Moran and the A.L.P.: a study in the encounter between Moran and Socialism, 1890–1907: its effects upon the Australian Labor Party: the foundation of Catholic social thought and action in modern Australia*, Melbourne, 1966.

6   A.E. Cahill, 'Cardinal Moran and the Chinese', *Manna*, no. 6 (1963) pp. 97–106.

7   John Hosie, *Challenge: the Marists in colonial Australia*, Sydney, 1987, pp. 34, 249, 268–269; 'Couppé', in *Australian Dictionary of Biography (ADB)*, vol. 8 (1981), pp. 122–123; Cyril Hally, *Australia's Missionary Effort: opportunity? danger?*, Melbourne, 1973, pp. 15–16; Norman Ruffing (ed.), *The Word in the World, 1969: New Guinea*, Techny, 1969, pp. 9–24, 49–63.

to the priesthood in 1853, and himself taught at the Irish College. He was a capable scholar who, fluent in several European languages, both modern and classical, also wrote numerous substantial books on Irish church history that were based on archival research. In 1872 he was appointed Bishop of Ossory in Ireland and proved to be an energetic administrator and a formidable apologist. From there he went out to Australia where, on returning from Rome in 1885 not only as a cardinal but with the authority of Apostolic Delegate, or Papal envoy, he immediately set about strengthening, reordering and updating Church operations and discipline. To this end, orchestrating his own federal movement, he summoned three plenary councils of bishops in 1885, 1895 and 1905, and three national Catholic congresses in 1900, 1904 and 1909, each attended by upwards of 700 delegates.[8] And his sway extended beyond Australia. In 1901 a French Marist missionary in New Zealand, the symphoniously named Theophile Le Menant des Chesnais, extolled him as 'the highest representative of our Holy Father in the Southern Hemisphere'.[9]

Moran stepped rapidly onto his expanded stage. Early in 1886, assisted by a free pass on the railways obtained through his unrelated namesake the bishop of Dunedin, who was also a protégé of Cardinal Cullen, he made a triumphal monument-launching tour of New Zealand. In the course of two months he blessed St Joseph's Cathedral at Dunedin, St Patrick's College in Wellington and St Patrick's Cathedral in Auckland, laid the foundation for Mount Magdala convent in Christchurch and spoke of Ireland and the faith at numerous well-attended receptions.[10] Consequent on his position and public visibility, he was also enjoined to intercede on behalf of others. Thus, the Irish diocesan clergy, led by Bishop Moran, hoped through his influence to have Dunedin declared the Metropolitan See (archdiocese) while, in 1887, the Catholics of the Hokianga besought him to have their pastor, James McDonald, appointed Prefect Apostolic (bishop) for the Maoris.[11] In neither case were the petitioners' wishes gratified, but Moran's offshore role remained undiminished. For instance, he visited New Zealand again in 1905 and in 1908 and was only prevented from coming in 1900

---

8 'Moran', in *ADB*, vol. 10 (1986), pp. 577–581; also 'Cullen', in vol. 3 (1969), pp. 504; Murtagh, *Australia*, p. 175; Colin P. Barr, '"An ambiguous awe": Paul Cullen and the historians', in Dáire Keogh and Albert McDonnell (eds), *Cardinal Cullen and His World*, Dublin, 2011, pp. 415–417.
9   Quoted in Michael O'Meeghan, *Held Firm By Faith: a history of the Catholic Diocese of Christchurch, 1840–1987*, Christchurch, 1988, p. 225.
10 Redwood to Moran, 19 Dec. 1885, 5 Feb. 1886; Moran (Dunedin) to Moran, 26 Dec. 1885; Ginaty to Moran, 4 Feb. 1886, Moran Correspondence, 1885, 1886, Catholic Archdiocese Archives (Sydney); Pat Gallagher, *The Marist Brothers in New Zealand, Fiji and Samoa, 1876–1976*, Tuakau, 1976, p. 42; O'Meeghan, *Held Firm*, p. 153; E.R. Simmons, *In Cruce Salus: a history of the Diocese of Auckland, 1848–1980*, Auckland, 1982, p. 184; J.J. Wilson, *The Church in New Zealand*, vol. II, *In the path of the pioneers*, Dunedin, 1926, pp. 89–102.
11 Moran (Dunedin) to Moran (Sydney), 21 April, 26 May, 16 July 1887; Moran (Dunedin) to Moran (Sydney), 27 Oct. 1886, Remehio Te Tai Papahia to Moran, 28 Feb., 25 April 1887, Moran Correspondence, 1886, 1887; O'Meeghan, *Held Firm*, pp. 164–70; Simmons, *In Cruce Salus*, pp. 179–80, 185; Michael King, *God's Farthest Outpost: a history of Catholics in New Zealand*, Auckland, 1997, pp. 77, 122.

to lay the foundation stone of the Christchurch cathedral by the emergency that arose when his secretary, Monsignor Denis O'Haran, was named as co-respondent in the famous Coningham divorce case.[12]

Meanwhile, other islands also beckoned him. The first, through the connection with the Marists, was Samoa. Political turmoil, generated by shifting alliances within the two main indigenous groupings (Malietoa and Tupua) and erratic British, German and American interventions, had been intensifying there since the 1870s. Here Moran's sympathies were unambiguously directed towards the devoutly pious chief Mata'afa Iosefa. He was the nephew of Fagamanu who, at the request of chief Lavelua of the Catholic-aligned island of Wallis (Uvea), had welcomed the Marist missionaries to Samoa in 1845. Forsaking a loose attachment to the Protestantism of the London Missionary Society, which tended to have Malietoa sympathies, he had himself been baptised a Catholic in 1868, at the age of 46. He was also an adroit and forceful contender for power. A senior titleholder of the Tupua faction, but being also able to draw on substantial Malietoa links for support, Mata'afa had established a firm claim to be regarded as *Tupu* or 'king' of Samoa in December 1888. But he was deprived of the fruit of a military victory over his Tupua rival Tamasese—in a battle in which 16 German marines were killed—by resolute German opposition (and despite his having been supplied with arms by British and American settler factions).[13] Then, in March 1889, Samoa was devastated by a hurricane in which six German and American navy ships were sunk (with the loss of 155 lives) in Apia harbour. Moran responded to reports of starvation by sending food and other supplies to Samoa via the Marist procurator in Sydney, Henri Couloigner, for distribution among the needy. Mata'afa, signing himself *Tupu*, replied to this gesture with a letter of thanks in which he commented:

> I have been particularly gladdened by the fact that [the Marists, who distributed these gifts], have not made any distinction between people in need, but, on the contrary, have helped those who were neither of our party nor of our faith. What sorrows me is that I cannot reply to your kindness with similar generosity.[14]

Such even-handedness very likely strengthened Mata'afa's popular support among the Samoans, but it did not impress his foreign opponents. In June the Germans brought another of his rival claimants, Malietoa Laupepa, back from exile in the Marshall Islands and had him installed as *Tupu* instead. Following an outbreak of conflict between those two in 1893, it was Mata'afa's turn to

---

12 'Moran', in *ADB*; O'Meeghan, *Held Firm*, pp. 224–225.
13 J. Darnand, *Aux Iles Samoa: la forêt qui s'illumine*, Lyon, 1934, pp. 90–111; R.P. Gilson, *Samoa, 1830–1900: the politics of a multi-cultural community*, Melbourne, 1970, pp. 393–395.
14 Mata'afa to Moran, 19 July; Suatele to Moran, 20 July; Remy to Moran, 22 July 1889, Moran Correspondence, Marist Fathers, 1885–1930.

be exiled. He returned in September 1898, only to find his ambitions again being resisted, this time by supporters of Malietoa Tanumafili, the son of the recently deceased Laupepa. Predictably, fighting between the historic factions again broke out. And it continued spasmodically until May 1899 when, in the face of a coordinated initiative by the European powers, all parties agreed to find a diplomatic solution to the Samoan imbroglio.[15] To mark this achievement, Moran wrote to Mata'afa, sending him some personal gifts, congratulating him on the restoration of peace and identifying himself with

> the very many in Australia who deeply sympathised with you and your brother chiefs in the unjust warfare which was forced upon you, and which has been accurately described as one of the most grievous wrongs ever perpetrated in the name of civilisation. We rejoiced at the forebearance and humanity [notwithstanding the decapitation of German marines in December 1888?] which despite every provocation you constantly displayed. We now congratulate you on your prompt compliance with the Commissioners' decree, and we trust and pray that your self-denial and sacrifice for your country's good may be the harbinger of very many blessings to you.[16]

Apart from his personal regard for Mata'afa, Moran professed to explain his interest in Samoa on the grounds that the Samoans were, as he told his audience at the opening of the Christian Brothers' high school at Waverley, 'regarded as the noblest and most intelligent race in the South Pacific Islands'. The grand sweep of this utterance is characteristic of Moran's rhetorical style. So, too, is his expedient resort to authority—any authority—to affirm his belief. In this case it was Lloyd Osbourne, the stepson of another fervent admirer of Mata'afa, Robert Louis Stevenson: 'The Samoans are, without doubt, the finest race of half-civilised people in the world'.[17] But such sentiments were not the only reason for Moran's concern, as he explained at the opening of a fundraising bazaar at Erskineville in May 1899. 'It struck him how little weight the opinions of the people of New South Wales and the other colonies had in regard to the Samoan controversy, which was of vital interest to the Australians'. If only the colonies were federated, as occurred in 1901: 'They would [then] have voice and influence in all matters affecting their interests, and nothing would be done without consulting them'.[18] He feared that the United States, which seemed to regard the Samoans as the Turks did the Armenians, was 'bent upon making the

---

15 Paul M. Kennedy, *The Samoan Tangle: a study in Anglo-German-American relations, 1878–1900*, St Lucia, 1974, pp. 145–155; Malama Meleisea, *The Making of Modern Samoa: traditional authority and colonial administration in the modern history of Western Samoa*, Suva, 1987, pp. 40–42.
16 Moran to Mata'afa, 28 June; Mata'afa to Moran, 6 Aug. 1899, Moran Correspondence, 1899; Estienne to Aubry, 3 July 1899, Archivio Padri Maristi (Rome), OSS 208.
17 *Freeman's Journal*, 24 Jan. 1903.
18 *Sydney Morning Herald* (*SMH*), 8 May 1899.

Pacific Ocean a new American lake'. Consequently, he was disappointed when in November, in return for imperial concessions elsewhere, Britain, careless of any civilising mission, allowed Samoa to be divided between Germany and the United States.[19] As he lamented in 1903, 'thus the whole Samoan group, the gem of the Pacific, has been permanently withdrawn from the influence of the new Australian Commonwealth'.[20]

Meanwhile, in 1891, in a flurry of correspondence between ecclesiastical authorities in far-flung places—New Guinea, Issoudun in Belgium, Rome, Fiji and Sydney—Moran had been drawn into another matter of more explicitly pastoral concern. That is, the evangelisation of the Solomon Islands, which lay within the domain of the Missionaries of the Sacred Heart. Were they, he asked, 'going to be occupied by Catholic missionaries before Protestants got established there?'[21] Bishop Couppé of Rabaul in German New Guinea had announced that he did not have the resources to undertake the task, but suggested that the Marists might help, possibly by working within the British 'sphere of influence' that had been established over much of it by the Anglo-German Agreement of 1886. Subsequently, Julien Vidal who in 1887, after 14 years in Samoa, had been appointed the first vicar apostolic (bishop) of Fiji, declared that he was willing to take over the whole of the Solomons group, some of whose people he had already met as migrant plantation labourers, if the Marists were given sole jurisdiction over it. To this end he approached Moran for support—and received it.[22] The two men, who were already acquainted, were well matched. Builders and organisers, they were also energetic, enterprising and assertive. His Lordship of Suva, who annoyed the governor by hoisting the tricolour over his house and by flying the Marist banner above the British ensign, was of the same cloth as His Eminence of Sydney who, in 1903, denounced the allegation of a Wesleyan clergyman that he, Moran, had apologised to the Admiralty for saying that British ships had wilfully shelled Catholic property in Samoa in 1899 as a 'thumping Saxon lie'. Rather, he claimed, certain Protestant mission 'agents' had asked for this to be done, but the captains had declined. 'Sometimes', Moran explained to an appreciative audience, 'lies were stupid, sometimes lies were barefaced, but a thumping Saxon lie combined both a malicious and a barefaced lie'.[23] As for the Solomons, where pioneer Marists had been killed in the 1840s, the common cause of the two prelates bore fruit. In 1897 the group

---

19   Ibid., 1 May 1899.
20   *Freeman's Journal*, 21 Jan. 1903.
21   Vidal to Simeoni, 15 Dec. 1891, Archivio Padri Maristi, 410 Sancta Sedes.
22   Persico to Nicolet, 26 Aug.; Nicolet to Persico, 7, 30 Nov., 29 Dec.; Vidal to Simeoni, 15 Dec. 1891, Archivio Padri Maristi, 410 Sancta Sedes.
23   *SMH*, 26 June, 26 July 1899; *Freeman's Journal*, 3 Jan. 1903; Margaret Knox, *Voyage of Faith: the story of the first 100 years of Catholic missionary endeavour in Fiji and Rotuma*, Suva, 1997, pp. 53–73; Deryck Scarr, *The Majesty of Colour: a life of Sir John Bates Thurston*, vol. 2, *Viceroy of the Pacific*, Canberra, 1980, pp. 217–218.

was divided along the imperial 'spheres of influence' line and, over the next two years, Marist missionaries from Fiji and Samoa, respectively, occupied first the southern half (British) and then the northern half (German).[24]

In 1901 Moran was again prominently associated with the Solomon's mission. This came about when a Marist, Pierre Rouillac, arrived in Sydney on 23 April after a masterly 19-day voyage from Guadalcanal in his damaged 19-ton schooner *Eclipse*, accompanied by an inexperienced crew of four Fijian mission helpers, plus four young Solomon Islanders. The vessel had been driven onto a reef by the *koburu*, a strong north-west wind that blows in the Solomons from November to March, and needed extensive repairs. In May, at the laying of the foundation stone of the Christian Brothers school at Lewisham, Moran cited Rouillac as illustrating the 'intrepid … spirit which pervades the men in the mission'.[25] And, over the next three months, he was further involved in what became a well-publicised exploit. A four-page broad sheet reprinted admiring newspaper reports. For his part, Moran baptised the Solomon Islanders at Blessed Peter Chanel church in Woolwich; he gave a large donation to an appeal organised by the *Catholic Press*; he identified the remains of the martyred Bishop Epalle (recovered by Rouillac from the island of Ysabel, but which had first been drawn to Moran's attention by a local trader as early as 1891); and, in July, he presided at a Grand Concert. This latter was designed both to raise funds for Rouillac and, conveniently, to outclass a recent event arranged by the Orange Lodge. Unfortunately for the mission, the *Eclipse* was lost on a reef shortly after Rouillac's return to the Solomons, and could not quickly be replaced. When it was, though, in 1909, with the 30-ton *Jeanne d'Arc*, it was with a vessel financed from France but built in Sydney and ceremoniously blessed by Cardinal Moran.[26]

Moran also performed other noteworthy services for the Pacific missions. He interceded with colonial authorities on behalf of the Sacred Heart missionaries in the Gilbert Islands, where they had begun operations in 1888. He backed Marist lobbying for the beatification of Pierre Chanel, who was martyred on Futuna, near Tonga, in 1841; and he donated the altar for the chapel there built

---

24   Martin to President de la Propagation de la Foi, 17 Feb. 1897, Archivio Padri Maristi, 5SM 145; Hugh Laracy, *Marists and Melanesians: a history of Catholic missions in the Solomon Islands*, Canberra, 1976, pp. 11–22, 35–38. The British share of the Solomon Islands was increased in 1899, subsequent to any ecclesiastical arrangements.
25   *Freeman's Journal*, 11 May 1901.
26   Wolff to Moran, 19 Oct. 1891; Hollingdale et al. to Moran, 13 July 1901, Moran Correspondence, Sydney Archdiocesan Archives; Baptism Register, Villa Maria, 2 June 1901, Marist Archives, Hunter's Hill, Sydney; *Reports in Connection with the Rev Father Rouillac's Heroic trip from the Solomon Islands to Sydney in his 19 ton craft 'the Eclipse', also an appeal to all sympathisers for subscriptions towards then cost of repairing his beloved schooner*, Sydney, (incl. *Town and Country Journal*, 4 May 1901; *Freeman's Journal*, 11 May 1901; *Catholic Press*, 25 May 1901); *New Zealand Tablet*, 27 June 1901; Pierre Rouillac, 'Missionary Work in the Solomon Islands', *Australasian Catholic Record*, vol. X (1904), pp. 218–237; L.M. Raucax, *In the Savage South Solomons: the story of a mission*, New York, 1928, pp. 90–93; Hugh Laracy, 'Marists as Mariners: the Solomon Islands story', *International Journal of Maritime History*, vol. 111, no. 1 (June 1991), pp. 67–71.

in anticipation of that eventuality, which occurred in 1889.[27] Indeed, in 1903 he hoped to lead a pilgrimage cruise to the Pacific which would include a visit to Futuna and also to Suva for the opening of Vidal's cathedral, but it was not to be as he was called to Rome for a conclave following the untimely death of Pope Leo XIII. Another such tour, planned for 1909, also had to be abandoned, this time because of the aging cardinal's poor health.[28]

Extensive as they were, direct pastoral responsibilities were not the limit, nor the most conspicuous, of Moran's connections with the Pacific islands. With respect to the island of Santo in Vanuatu (formerly the New Hebrides), he also acquired a clear measure of prominence—and notoriety—as a would-be contributor to the general history of Australia. That is, by allowing his eagerness to establish a preemptive claim for Catholicism to override scholarly caution, he challenged the orthodox view that the land claimed by the Spanish explorer Pedro de Quiros on 14 May 1606 in the names of 'Jesus Christ, Saviour of all men … and of his Universal Vicar, the Roman Pontiff' was not connected to Santo but was, in fact, Australia. While drawing on newly published papers from Spanish archives, Moran did not deny that Quiros might have visited Vanuatu.[29] Rather, he simply contended that the bay Quiros had named after St Philip and St James, and in which he made his grand proclamation, was not 'Big Bay' on Santo but was Port Curtis on the Queensland coast, later the site of the town of Gladstone, nearly two centuries before the British landed at Sydney.

Following (but not citing) an assertion by the Spanish missionary Rosendo Salvado in 1853, Moran first presented this claim—and made it his own—in 1895 in his massive compilation *History of the Catholic Church in Australasia*.[30] Not surprisingly it was rejected by the recognised commentators on Australian history and geography such as Ernest Favenc and George Collingridge, who published authoritative refutations of it.[31] The parochial editor of the *Gladstone Advocate*, in contrast, was complaisant about accepting a putative accolade for his town. Visiting there in 1899, Moran was presented with an address which was

---

27 Moran to O'Brien, 9 Jan. 1899, Box B 16, MSC; Lamaze to Moran, 21 April 1888; Huault to Moran, 12 July 1907, Box B 16, SM, Archdiocesan Archives, Sydney; Moran to Vidal, 11 Feb. 1889, Catholic Archives, Suva, Pacific Manuscripts Bureau microfilm 444; Hugh Laracy, 'Saint-Making: the case of Pierre Chanel of Futuna', *New Zealand Journal of History*, vol. 34, no. 1 (April, 2000), pp. 154–156.
28 *Winter Excursion to the Islands of the Western Pacific*, 1903, Sydney, pp. 30; *Australasian Catholic Record*, vol. IX (1903), pp. 242–248; Knox, *Voyage of Faith*, p. 68.
29 Justo Zaragoza (ed.), *Historia del Descubrimiento de las Regiones Austriales hecho por el General Pedro Fernandez de Quiros*, Madrid, *1876–1882*; Clements Markham, *The Voyages of Pedro Fernandez de Quiros, 1595–1606*, London, 1904; O.H.K. Spate, *The Spanish Lake*, Canberra, 1979, p. 320.
30 Rosendo Salvado, *Memorias Historicas sobre La Australia*, Barcelona, 1853, p. 3; Moran, *History*, Sydney, [1895], pp. 13–14.
31 Ernest Favenc, review of address by Moran to Royal Society of Australia, *Australian Journal of Education*, Sept. 1904, p. 5; George Collingridge, *The First Discovery of Australia and New Guinea: being the narrative of Portuguese and Spanish discoveries in the Australasion regions, between the years 1492 and 1606, with descriptions of their old charts*, Sydney, 1906, pp. 84–122.

described as more than a testimonial of welcome but as 'a mark of appreciation of the Cardinal's work as an historian, his valuable work having established for Gladstone the foremost place in the annals of Australia'.[32] After all, in 1756, the distinguished French geographer Charles de Brosses—whom Moran cites—had placed Quiros's presumed continent Austrialia del Espiritu Santo on the then hypothetically drawn eastern boundary of New Holland.[33] But then, soon afterwards, the explorer James Cook had shown it to be otherwise. In 1774, after charting the east coast of Australia in 1769, he had located the bay of the two saints firmly offshore in the island of Santo.[34] Moran, though, simply believed Cook to be wrong on that point, and continued to say so, verbally and in print until at least 1908. For instance, he did so twice in the *Australasian Catholic Record*, a quarterly journal he founded in 1895, and in a 40-page pamphlet that he published in 1906.[35] In 1901, during Rouillac's visit, he was also pleased to link his claim to support for the mission in the Solomon Islands.

> It is a happy coincidence that the Marist Fathers who have charge of this group of islands in which Holy Mass was first celebrated in the South Pacific [in 1568] have during the past few weeks received the great pastoral charge of the Glasdstone district in Queensland, the site where Mass was first offered in Australasia on its discovery by Quiros.[36]

In urging his case, in this as in other matters, Moran was a resourceful apologist. Thus, in explaining away the significance of an eight degree difference in latitude between Santo and the more southerly Gladstone, he divined a subterfuge. That is, he claimed that by citing the position of the former, 15°S, but not that of the latter, Quiros was deliberately trying to conceal the location of his Australian discovery from Spain's rivals. As for discrepancies between Quiros's accounts of the Bay of St Philip and St James and actual descriptions of Big Bay, Moran made no allowances for literary exaggeration or for lack of technical precision or for any promotional intent in the documents. Instead, he postulated a literal coincidence between what they reported and the features of Port Curtis. For instance, Quiros said he had discovered a continent, but Santo was not a continent. Besides, the bay there was smaller than Quiros had said it was. As for the two great rivers that he had named the Jordon and the Salvador, there was only one river and several small streams running into Big Bay whereas Port Curtis could boast the Boyne and the Calliope. Then there was a matter of artefacts. Quiros said the people he saw had the bow and arrow. But

---

32 Quoted in *Freeman's Journal*, 28 Oct. 1899.
33 Collingridge, *First Discovery*, p. 113; Tom Ryan, '"Le Président des Terres Australes": Charles de Brosses and the French Enlightenment beginnings of Oceanic anthropology', *Journal of Pacific History*, vol. 37, no. 2 (Sept. 2002), pp. 162–163.
34 J.C. Beaglehole (ed.), *The Journals of Captain James Cook*, vol. 11, *The Voyage of the Resolution and Adventure*, Cambridge, 1969, pp. 516–520.
35 See Appendix for list of Moran's writings on the topic.
36 *New Zealand Tablet*, 27 July 1901.

the Aborigines did not have that weapon. Therefore, said the cardinal, on that point the Spaniard must have been mistaken.[37] Weak as such arguments are, even more effrontery was required to dismiss the evidence against Port Curtis implicit in the memorial of Quiros's second in command, Pedro de Torres.

After spending 41 days in the Bay of St Philip and St James, Quiros sailed away and did not return. Torres waited there for another 15 days before deciding to carry on with the voyage of discovery. To this end he left the bay and sailed sufficiently far down the west coast of Santo to decide that it was an island. Continuing, he then sailed several days south-west to a latitude of 21 degrees before turning to the north-east and then sailing due west, en route to Manila, through the strait that runs between Australia and New Guinea, and which bears his name. The ostensible problem for the cardinal with this voyage is that if Torres had sailed south-west from Port Curtis he would have been sailing inland, *across* Australia. But Moran was untroubled. Resourcefully, he dismissed the difficulty by interpreting the record to mean that Torres sailed along the coast south from Port Curtis to—and this figure is quite gratuitous—31 degrees latitude. By this contrivance the Spaniard was at length given a south-west bearing, if only just for two degrees south of Byron Bay, the easternmost point of Australia. It was from that point, near present day Kempsey in northern New South Wales, that Torres then made his turn to the north-east, and headed for home. At least, that is what the cardinal told an audience of distinguished guests at a ceremony held at St John's College at Sydney University on 14 November 1906 to celebrate the tricentenary of 'the discovery of our Australian Continent'.[38] The logic seems to have been *decet est, ergo erat* ('it is fitting, therefore it was'). This might be a theological principle of some limited application, but in history it is pernicious, despite finding favour among the structuralists, post-modern revisionists and 'tradition inventers' of later times.

Tendentious as they were, Moran's arguments about the discovery of Australia were politely, but consistently, refuted—and then largely disregarded. They generated a modest corpus of dissenting comment, but no heat.[39] It was different with the criticisms of Protestantism that became a staple of his oratory during the 1890s. They attracted vigorous public responses, only to be met with more

---

37 Moran, *Discovery of Australia by De Quiros in the Year 1606*, Sydney, 1906, pp. 20–34; Markham, vol. 1, pp. 248–275, vol. 2, pp. 379–382; Celsus Kelly, *La Australia del Espiritu Santo: the journal of Fray Martin de Munilla O.F.M.*, Cambridge, 1966, vol. 1, pp. 202–237; Robert Langdon, 'The Untold Story of "The Thing" in the Big Bay Bush', *Pacific Islands Monthly*, Aug. 1980, pp. 71–77.
38 Moran, *Discovery*, pp. 32–33; Collingridge, *First Discovery*, pp. 21–22; Kelly, *La Austrialia*, map 4, p. 75; Brett Hilder, *The Voyage of Torres: the discovery of the southern coastline of New Guinea and Torres Strait by Captain Luis Báez de Torres in 1606*, St Lucia, 1980, pp. 20–21; G. Arnold Wood, *The Discovery of Australia*, Melbourne, 1969, p. 132.
39 Henry N. Stevens, *New Light on the Discovery of Australia as Revealed by the Journal of Captain Don Diego de Prado y Tovar*, London, 1930, pp. 10–14; Celsus Kelly, 'The Narrative of Pedro Fernandez de Quiros', *Historical Studies Australia and New Zealand*, vol. 9 (May 1960), pp. 192–193, note 54.

of the same. For Moran there could be no surrender and no retreat, as shown by his rhetoric as he presided over a decade of extraordinary growth and expansion, one that was prodigally garnished with the laying of foundation stones and with the dedication of buildings and with celebratory assemblies. For these occasions he drew much of his verbal ammunition from the Pacific, mostly from Fiji. The first clear instalment of such intelligence was probably that received from his ally Vidal in 1892, reporting anti-Catholic utterances by a Methodist missionary named J.P. Chapman, a former horse dealer. To an audience at Nacula village, in the Yasawa group, Chapman had quoted the apostate No-Popery lecturer Charles Chiniquy to sustain allegations of immorality that he was making against priests and nuns. As a result he was subsequently tried for slander and libel, but, after a hearing that lasted for nearly three weeks, the charge was dismissed. In the case of *Nicouleau and Others v. Chapman* it was held, in a fine legal ruling, to be not proven that the offending words had been directed explicitly at the three Marist complainants. This evasion was abetted by the defence claim that Chapman had used the words Vanua Levu (literally, 'great land') not in reference to the Fiji island of that name but to America. Chapman, though, was scarcely vindicated by the decision. For the judge not only denied him costs in the matter but described him as a 'most dangerous and mischievous' man. His colleagues and the editor of the Australian *Methodist Review*, on the other hand, defended him without demur.[40]

Moran did not immediately react to this episode or to a controversy that erupted in Fiji in 1893 (and again in 1896) after the senior Methodist missionaries there, Frederick Langham and Henry Worrall, alleged that the Marists were obtaining converts through bribery.[41] (In particular, they cited an allegation, firmly rejected by his neighbours, of a man named Timoci Masira of Lokia village in Rewa province).[42] Such incidents were, though, steps on the way to sectarianism, and the shot that was to ignite a prolonged public conflict was fired by Moran on 17 June 1895. In a lecture on the 'Reunion of Christendom', moved by a recent letter of Pope Leo XIII on the subject, he discoursed on the weaknesses of Protestantism and the inadequacy of its achievements—and advised its adherents to turn to Rome. Predictably, there was an outcry. The most notable protest came from George Brown, the best known Methodist missionary in the Pacific, who regaled a public meeting with severe criticisms of his Catholic competitors. A week later, on 2 July, the cardinal returned to the attack. To 'repel the envenomed charges' of failure that Brown and Langham had recently made against Catholic missions,

---

40 Vidal to Moran, 22 Dec. 1892, 26 Feb. 1903, Moran Correspondence, 1892, 1903, Archdiocesan Archives, Sydney; *Australian Methodist Missionary Review*, 4 Nov. 1892; *Fiji Times*, 18, 23 Nov. 1893; Basil Thomson, *The Diversions of a Prime Minister*, London, 1894, pp. 209–210; 'Chiniquy', in *Dictionary of Canadian Biography*, vol. XII, Toronto, 1900, pp. 189–193.
41 *Fiji Times*, 8, 18 Mar., 12, 24, 29 July 1893, 15, 29 April 1896; *Australian Methodist Missionary Review*, 5 June 1893; *Advocate*, 25 April, 2, 9 May 1896.
42 *Fiji Times*, 18 Mar. 1893, 15, 18, 22 April 1896.

he addressed a large public meeting on the subject of 'The Mission Field in the Nineteenth Century'. There, attended on the platform by various consular and clerical representatives, including (surprisingly) Langham, newly retired to Australia after 38 years in Fiji, he told a stirring story of worldwide Catholic progress through heroic self-denial and charity. Then, with scant regard for empirical evidence, he concluded by asserting that in the Protestant-dominated islands of the Pacific the native populations were dying out, whereas in those where the Catholics prevailed they were thriving. Brown, in turn, took issue with these claims with an audience of his own, which he also advised that 'the priests of the Roman Catholic Church have never given the people one chapter of the sacred Scriptures in the native tongue'. Vidal, in contrast, responded gratefully to his eminent patron. 'The Catholic Mission of Fiji', he wrote a few months later, in a letter advising Moran of affairs there, could 'rejoice at having found an able advocate'. He then went on to blame Wesleyanism for an alleged decline of morals in Fiji.[43] An endorsement of that claim, along with allegations of superficial Christianity prevalent among its indigenous devotees and of Eucharistic blasphemy among its ministers—artfully illustrated by anecdotes from a kindly observer such as Constance Gordon-Cumming—was again offered by the cardinal in a long letter to the *Sydney Morning Herald* in July 1899, during another flare-up in the campaign.[44]

Moran, meanwhile, in a long-remembered jibe, had also touched deep sensibilities about the cult of temperance, which had prevailed among Nonconformist Protestants, and especially the Methodists, since the 1880s. As an aside during his 'Missions' address in 1895 he had charged their close allies, the Congregationalists of the London Missionary Society, with carrying liquor aboard their ship. He referred to 'the *John Williams*'s "spiritual cargo", in the sense of whisky, wine and rum, much more than in the number of Bibles', and was 'cheered to the echo' for it. The authority for this insolent statement was a mistaken report in the *Sydney Morning Herald* of 27 March 1880 that had included some of the cargo of another vessel, the *Au Revoir*, with that of the *John Williams*. The paper had subsequently corrected the error, but Moran, although aware of that correction, had still drawn on the original report. When the error was pointed out to him he was, though, (encouraged by notes in his files reporting liquor in the general cargo of various mission ships, including the *John Williams*, during the 1860s and 1870s) far from contrite. Indeed, he again got a laugh from the same joke (and thereby provoked a Methodist protest meeting at the Town Hall) in 1899, and was equally insouciant. As he told a

---

43 *SMH*, 3, 31 July 1895; Vidal to Moran 5 Sept. 1895, Marist Fathers, Archdiocesan Archives, Sydney.
44 *SMH*, 26, 27 July 1899.

reporter, 'the Parthian arrow which I fired seems to have remained fixed, and I have no intention of withdrawing it'.[45] In 1903, at the annual meeting of the Hibernian Society, the joke was aired a third time.[46]

Clearly, the tensions that surfaced as acrimonious conflict in 1895 did not soon abate. Undeterred by a denial from Vidal during a visit to Australia, Langham introduced the Fiji 'conversion by bribery' issue to Sydney in April 1896. Again the newspapers feasted off sectarian conflict, even though Langham's informant of 1893 had already been discredited and the putative briber, Emile Rougier of Nailalili, was exonerated.[47] Again the matter brought Moran's name into the news in what for Langham, at least, was an exhilarating contest. As he reported to Worrall:

5 June 'went for the Cardinal a while ago'.

1 July 'gave an address on "Romanism in the Pacific", and another to the Balmain Orange Lodge. I went into them very lively … made the priests squirm'.

12 August 'You will be delighted to read the scorching Cardinal Moran has been getting in the *Telegraph*'.[48]

Nor did Moran tire easily. The Samoan imbroglio became the focus of acute sectarian animadversions, as well as of political concern, in 1899, especially after Moran claimed that Protestant missionaries had attempted to persuade Captain Leslie Stuart of HMS *Tauranga* to shell Catholic establishments in Apia. Indignant public denials of any such overtures or intentions, though, brought no retraction of the charge.[49]

Even stronger passions were aroused in 1903 after it was reported from Fiji that, in February, Rougier had publicly burned 238 Methodist-distributed Bibles in his lime kiln at Naililili. One story had it that a 'brass band had played selections' during the auto-da-fe, and there was even talk of sending a British gunboat to Fiji to quell feared disorder. The Methodists cried blasphemy, and at their annual conference in Sydney they denounced Moran as a traducer and cheered a missionary from Fiji who vowed to have 'no peace with Rome'. For his

---

45 *Freeman's Journal*, 22 June 1895; *SMH*, 20, 27 Mar. 1880, 28 July 1899; notes, M76, Moran Correspondence, Archdiocesan Archives, Sydney; Ford, *Moran and A.L.P.*, p. 208; Niel Gunson, 'On the Incidence of Alcoholism and Intemperance in Early Pacific Missions', *Journal of Pacific History*, vol. 1 (1966), pp. 60–61.
46 *SMH*; *Freeman's Journal*; *Daily Telegraph*. Late Feb./Mar. 1903. CHECK.
47 *SMH*, 1, 9 April 1896; *Fiji Times*, 15, 18, 22 May 1896.
48 Langham to Worrall, 12 Aug. 1895, 5 June, 1 July 1896, Methodist Overseas Mission, Item 90/OM295, Mitchell Library; *Daily Telegraph*, 15 June 1896.
49 Stuart to Cousins, 17 Oct. 1899, London Missionary Society, South Seas Letters (microfilm); *Daily Telegraph*, 26 June 1899, 8 Jan. 1903; *Freeman's Journal*, 24 Jan. 1903.

part Moran, advised by Vidal, dismissed the story—the first versions of which were based on hearsay—as a hoax. Certainly, the reality was more prosaic. In 1902 the inland people of Namosi, led by their chief Matanitobua, had rejected Methodism for Catholicism. The reasons were political rather than religious. Unlike most other chiefs, Matanitobua was sympathetic to a proposal for Fiji to federate with New Zealand and, on that score, had been denounced by a Methodist minister as being disloyal to Britain. Consequently, he sought an alternative denomination, and the Marists were not reluctant to oblige. Rougier and his confrère Jean de Marzin visited Namosi to collect their windfall. Whilst so doing they gathered up various religious books surrendered by the former Methodists and took them back to Naililili, where most of them still were in June. (The figure of 238 was a fabrication). What Rougier had done on 12 February, as more careful enquiry revealed, was to dispose of two small boxes of worn and tattered volumes from among them in an appropriate and respectful way, at least according to Catholic ritual, by burning them. In so doing he inadvertently provoked an outcry in Austalia, and elsewhere.[50] Perhaps sadly for the press, for these disputes had been a journalist's delight, this proved to be the last episode in an eight-year long boilover of sectarian animadversion.

Moran was a tall, spare, aloof figure who tended to attract respect rather than affection, even within his own Catholic tribe. When he died on 16 August 1911 at the age of 81 he left behind a Church that was institutionally solid, but pragmatic in its style of operation and still at odds with the society of which he had once hoped it would be the leaven. It was shaped by the historic conflict with Protestantism and by distaste for the secularist legacy of the French Revolution (and why not, *contra* O'Farrell, since these were still potent and contrary forces?), but at least it was Antipodean.[51] Moran might have been building on Irish foundations, but his vision, like his rhetoric, was emphatically not inwards and backwards to Ireland; rather it was forward and outwards, to a Church which realised its being within a strong and independent Australia—and in the Pacific islands. Despite his disappointment over Samoa, he accepted the growing importance of the United States in Pacific affairs and, while supporting the creation of an Australian navy, he also welcomed the US fleet when it visited Sydney in 1908. Like the trading firm of Burns, Philp and the Presbyterian mission to the New Hebrides and the Methodist mission to

---

50   Vidal to Moran, 26 Feb. 1903, Moran Correspondence, Archdiocesan Archives, Sydney; Vidal, 'A Few Conclusions Drawn from the Bible-burning Affair', 18 April 1903, Catholic Archives, Suva (PMB microfilm 463); *SMH*, 27 Feb. 1903; *Australasian Methodist Missionary Review*, 4, 18 April 1903; files CSO 1196 and 3980 of 1903, Fiji National Archives; *Manchester Guardian*, 18 June 1903; A.W. Thornley, '"Heretics" and "Papists": Wesleyan-Roman Catholic rivalry in Fiji, 1844–12903', *Journal of Religious History*, vol. 10, no. 3 (1979), pp. 294–312.

51   O'Farrell, *Church and Community*, p. 296.

New Guinea, Moran did much to lay the foundations of an awareness of the Pacific islands within Australia. One commentator estimates that 'he was ahead of his time in visualising Australia as a new Pacific nation'.[52]

Within his own denomination, this disposition bore particular fruit, which was followed by a strong continuing interest, in 1930. That occurred when an American Marist named Thomas Wade of the North Solomons (principally the island of Bougainville) became the first English-speaking Catholic bishop appointed to any of the islands missions. Wade chose to be consecrated not in his home town of Providence, Rhode Island, as might have been expected, but at the Marist church of St Patrick in the archdiocese once presided over by Cardinal Moran.[53] *Decet erat*.

Appendix

Moran's writings on the Quiros 'discovery'

1895

History of the Catholic Church in Australasia, Sydney.

1900

'The Discovery of Australia by the Spanish navigator de Quiros in the Year 1606', *Australasian Catholic Record*, vol. 5 (June), pp. 153–172.

1901

Was Australia Discovered by de Quiros in the Year 1606?, Sydney. 'A paper presented to the Royal Geographical Society of Australia by Cardinal Moran, Archbishop of Sydney, 1 May 1901'.

1906

Discovery of Australia by de Quiros in the Year 1606, Sydney.

1907

'Discovery of Australia by de Quiros in the Year 1606', *Australasian Catholic Record*, vol. 13, pp. 1–41.

---

52 Murtagh, *Australia*, p. 183.
53 *Freeman's Journal*, 16, 30 Oct. 1930; Hugh Laracy, 'Imperium in Imperio: the Catholic Church in Bougainville', in Anthony J. Regan and Helga Griffin (eds), *Bougainville Before the Conflict*, Canberra, 2005, p. 134.

1908

Discovery of Australia by de Quiros in the Year 1606, Melbourne. Australian Catholic Truth Society, pamphlet, no. 5.

Note: for an extended bibliography covering the debate on this matter, see Celsus Kelly, 'The Narrative of Pedro Fernandez de Quiros', *Historical Studies Australia and New Zealand*, vol. 9 (May 1960), pp. 192–193, note 54.

4. Constance Frederica Gordon-Cumming (1837–1924): Traveller, author, painter

'Eka', as Constance Frederica Gordon-Cumming was generally known to those acquainted with her, was an assertive and self-assured woman of independent means.[1] She came from a large and socially well-connected family and was unconstrained by domestic obligations. Genteelly but not delicately brought up, she achieved distinction in the 1880s as a productive author and as a skilled and prolific painter of watercolour landscapes. Her accomplishments in these areas during that epiphanic decade derived mainly from a sustained bout of travelling that she undertook in various parts of the world, not least in the Pacific, between 1868 and 1880. She was a tourist on a grand scale. Indeed, among much else, she is a notable example of a social type formally identified and labelled by Dorothy Middleton in *Victorian Lady Travellers* (1965), and one which has since attracted a good deal more attention.[2] As a result, the ranks of historically identified specimens—typically middle-aged and socially advantaged—have increased markedly. Among the best known are Isabella Bird and Marianne North, both of them friends of Gordon-Cumming, and both of whom followed some of the same paths as she did.

Independently of their particularities, these people—like any other category of being—may have significance conferred on them from various perspectives. From the point of view of feminist notions, for instance, they might be seen as archetypes of untrammelled, resourceful womanhood. Maybe, but anachronism is insidious. A balanced understanding of them would need to take into account the fact that, while relishing freedom in the form of physical and occupational mobility, they tended also to be conservative in their standards of morality and in their notions of what constituted proper behaviour. Or, and no less pertinently, in venturing to and returning from distant parts, and by recording in print and picture what they saw there, they may be regarded as an important adjunct of Empire. They were engaged in packaging and ordering, and thus seemingly tamed and rendered in some way familiar, places, peoples and habits that would otherwise have remained alien, or beyond the pale of

---

1 Frederica, *not* the occasionally seen Frederika, is the correct spelling of her second name. C.F. Gordon-Cumming, *Memories*, Edinburgh, 1904, p. 34. While not consistently so elsewhere, the surname is hyphenated in *Burke*.
2 Middleton, London; Leo Hamalian (ed.), *Ladies on the Loose: women travellers in the 18th and 19th centuries*, New York, 1981; Jane Robinson, *Wayward Women: a guide to women travellers*, Oxford, 1990; Mary Russell, *The Blessings of a Good Thick Skirt: women travellers and their world*, London; Shirley Fenton Huie, *Tiger Lilies: women adventurers in the South Pacific*, Sydney, 1990.

their audience's comprehension. That the meanings thus conveyed might be in some ways distorted and could create misleading impressions, imposed as they were from without by transient observers, is something of which a later age might be critical. But that does not of itself vitiate the authenticity of the first-hand experience that begot them. The records of that experience are inherently valuable, even when they are coloured by the ideas of the recorder. Despite the layers of interpretation and explanation and generalisation that may be applied to them and their works, the lady travellers were at base individuals with personal interests, abilities, idiosyncrasies and—commonly—the tellingly advantageous support of class and family. As for any eyewitnesses, they are valuable suppliers of detail.

Gordon-Cumming inherited considerable advantages. Her family was listed in *Burke's Peerage and Baronetage*, claimed descent from Charlemagne through the Counts de Comyn (the name Cumming derives from Comyn), and had a place in Scottish national history. One of her ancestors, a contender for the kingship, was killed by Robert Bruce. Fittingly, given the family mottoes of 'Courage' (Cumming) and '*Sans Crainte*' (Gordon), there was also an inspirational tradition of adventuring. 'There are', she wrote, 'perhaps few families in the Mother Country to whom the farthest corners of Greater Britain have (from the colonising or sporting instincts of its members) become more really familiar than that into which I was welcomed'. Besides, in preference to 'trade', the British colonies were 'the natural destination of the younger sons of great houses'.[3]

Gordon-Cumming's grandfather, Sir Alexander Cumming, the first baronet, inherited through his wife the name and arms of Gordon of Gordonstoun in 1804. On that account he adopted the double surname, the components of which are hyphenated in Burke. The same usage is followed here, although it was not consistently employed by members of the family. Her father Sir William Gordon Gordon-Cumming, 'as splendid a Highlander as ever trod the heather', and also heir general of the ancient (but diminished) Penrose family of Cornwall, was the second baronet. He married Eliza Campbell, the granddaughter of the Duke of Argyll in 1815. They had six sons, four of whom became army officers, and five daughters, of whom Gordon-Cumming was the youngest.[4] She was born at the family seat of Altyre in Morayshire, Scotland, on 26 May 1837. There was also a large extended family containing 'numerous centres of cheery and hospitable welcome' within which she would live much of her life.

---

3   *Two Happy Years in Ceylon*, Edinburgh, 1892; *Memories*, pp. 14, 80.
4   Gordon-Cumming, *Memories*, p. 5; *Burke*, pp. 440–441. In at least two places Eka claims to have been the 12th–born in the family, but *Burke* lists only 11 *in toto*, so it is likely that she is counting one who died in infancy. Moreover, since she had a younger brother there must have been another infant death, making a total of 13 births. Indeed, she states that her mother left 13 living children and that, of her father's 16 children, 14 'lived to man's estate'. If there is an error, it is likely to be one of omission in *Burke*. See *Two Happy Years*, p. 1; *Memories*, pp. 43, 52.

4. Constance Frederica Gordon-Cumming (1837–1924): Traveller, author, painter

> I started life with fifty first cousins, about twice as many second and third cousins and collaterals without number, for the family tree had roots and branches ramifying in every direction; and as each group centred around some more or less notable home, it followed that England and Scotland were dotted over with points of family interest, in those good old days when … kinship, however much diluted, was fully recognised.[5]

Gordon-Cumming's mother died in 1842, a month after giving birth to her youngest brother, Francis. He later soldiered in India, and his son William settled in New Zealand. In 1846 her father married again, and sired two more daughters and a son. The latter was killed in action in Burma in 1890.[6] Meanwhile, the grandson of one of her father's employees, the Australian-born traveller and journalist George Ernest Morrison, who would find fame in China, was becoming well-known through his early writings on the New Hebrides and New Guinea.[7]

Frustratingly for the would-be biographer, for someone who wrote so much, Gordon-Cumming left few private papers and is less than prodigal in providing personal details in her published writings. Thus, even in her autobiography, *Memories*, published in 1904, her early years are skimmed over, as are the last 47, following her return from China, yet the assiduous gleaner does not go unrewarded. Gordon-Cumming probably had some early instruction from resident tutors. In any case, the household in which she grew up appears to have been an intellectually lively one. Her mother was interested in geology and was acquainted with noted authorities in that field such as Robert Murchison, who identified the Devonian and Silurian periods, and Louis Agassiz, the glaciologist, who proved the existence of Ice Ages. Other noted visitors to Altyre included painters, such as Edwin Landseer and Charles Saunders, who painted elaborate portraits of Eliza and William in about 1830. Another broadening influence was the Swiss maid, Cherie, a family retainer, who instructed her young charges in French. Following the death of her mother, Gordon-Cumming went to live with her eldest sister in Northumberland, but in 1848, at her step-mother's benign insistence, she was sent to 'a first-rate school near London', Hermitage Lodge at Fulham, where she was enrolled until 1853. An annual highlight of this period for her was the sea voyage home from London to Inverness for the summer holidays, even though it was often uncomfortable.[8] A year after leaving school she attended her first London 'season' and her first 'Northern Meeting' at Inverness, thus beginning a round of visiting and of social activity that endured throughout her life.[9]

---

5   *Memories*, pp. 5–6.
6   *Memories*, pp. 43, 107–108, 194.
7   Cyril Pearl, *Morrison of Peking*, Ringwood, 1970, p. 1.
8   *Memories*, pp. 36, 38, 43, 48, 102–112.
9   Ibid., pp. 124–129, 131, 151, 169.

Together with any refinements of taste and behaviour that they may have acquired, the Gordon-Cumming children grew up with a sturdy appreciation of the outdoors that extended to an admiration for rural culture and to a fondness for wandering in wild, isolated places. Some remote reinforcement of such avocations may have come via the marriage of their uncle, Charles Cumming-Bruce MP, in 1822, to the granddaughter of the explorer James Bruce of Kinnaird, who in 1769, had visited Abyssinia, seeking the source of the Nile. 'The Abyssinian', as he became known, he reached the headwaters of the Blue Nile.[10] For Gordon-Cumming, there were also more personal and immediate sources of inspiration for adventurous exploits. About the time that she was reading *Robinson Crusoe*, her eldest brother, Alexander, returned from Canada and the next eldest, Roualeyn, returned—as a celebrity—from Africa. After leaving Eton and having a spell of soldiering in the Madras Cavalry and in the Cape Mounted Rifles, Roualeyn had acquired fame as a pioneer big game hunter. His book, *Five Years of a Hunter's Life in the Interior of South Africa. With notices of the native tribes and anecdotes of the chase of the lion, elephant, hippopotamus, giraffe, rhinoceros etc*, first published in 1850, and for which his sisters served as amanuenses, enjoyed a wide and admiring readership, while his trophies were displayed at the great Crystal Palace exhibition of 1851.[11] Then there were Gordon-Cumming's fourth and fifth brothers, who each set forth in December 1845. John became a coconut planter—and hunter—at Batticoloa in Ceylon, where he died in 1866. And William, who later married the daughter of a baron, attained the rank of lieutenant-colonel before returning from Bombay that same year. In 1871 he published a book about his soldiering and hunting exploits there titled *Wild Men and Wild Beasts*: the former he tamed, the latter he slew. The work is dedicated to a kinsman, Col. Walter Campbell who, writing as 'The Old Forest Ranger', had first turned William's youthful 'thoughts to the hunting grounds of India'. Regular letters from these two over 20 years, wrote Gordon-Cumming, ensured that 'life in the forests of Ceylon and Bombay became as familiar to our thoughts as grouse shooting or salmon fishing in Morayshire'.

> One mail brought me a letter from India, telling me of thirty tigers as the chief item of a two month's bag; while my Ceylon letter of the same date told of the rejoicing of the villagers over the slaughter, by their white friend, of twenty-five leopards—a highly satisfactory riddance of dangerous foes!

Yet she did not condone the wholesale assault on wildlife, especially against elephants:

---

10   Ibid., p. 12. James Bruce, *Travels to Discover the Source of the Nile, In the Years 1768 ... 1773*, London, 1790; Alfred E. Lomax, *Sir Samuel Baker: his life and adventures*, London, [1894], pp. 27–28.
11   *Memories*, pp. 116–120; *Two Happy Years*, p. 1.

4. Constance Frederica Gordon-Cumming (1837–1924): Traveller, author, painter

such is the havoc by ivory hunters, that the country south of the Zambesi is already well-nigh cleared, and no wonder, when we consider that the twenty-five tons of ivory annually required by one English firm (Messrs Rodgers and Sons of Sheffield) involves the deaths of eight hundred tusk elephants! How rarely people investing in nice ivory-handled knives think of such antecedents.[12]

Gordon-Cumming's own travels began modestly enough. She was at Fort Augustus, overlooking Loch Ness, with one of her sisters, nursing Roualeyn when he died there on 24 March 1866. Another brother, Alexander, died five months later. Then, in April 1868, initially with her half-brother Frederick, she set off on a painting tour of the Western Islands. Departing from Greenoch, the port of Glasgow, they travelled by sea and by coach around the Firth of Clyde and through the Inner Hebrides to Skye. As she 'willingly yielded to most hospitable invitations to linger amid such delightful sketching ground … month after month slipped by' until, by October, as she told one of her sisters, she was back where Roualeyn had died.[13] The subjectivity, intimate but not mawkish, that marks her writing, even in passages of description and of historical reflection, is well shown in her account of the last part of that journey.

> A beautiful drive down Glen Garry brought us to old Inverary Castle and so to Fort Augustus, still called by the Highlanders Cill Chumein, in memory of that Cuming the Fair who twelve hundred years ago held the bishopric of the Isles as seventh Bishop of Iona, but known to the Sassenach only by the name of the old grey fort whose rough walls still bear the names the Duke of Cumberland's soldiers carved in their idle leisure in those grim quarters.
>
> To you and to me those grey walls bring forth other memories—such memories as consecrate some few spots on earth …
>
> Many a time during the intervals of anxious watching, you and I have looked down from those windows on to the wild wintry storms which, sweeping over the cold grey hills, turned the blue waters of Loch Ness to inky darkness.[14]

Her writing also displays a taste for topographically enlivening anecdotes. Characteristically, her representations were of a peopled universe and even her paintings of New Zealand's volcanic 'wonderland' would be domesticated by the inclusion of small human figures. Thus, in approaching the Isle of Skye and

---

12 *Memories*, pp. 42, 173; *Two Happy Years*, pp. 1–2; Lt. Col. Gordon-Cumming, *Wild Men and Wild Beasts: scenes in camp and jungle*, Edinburgh, 1871.
13 *Memories*, pp. 194–195.
14 Gordon-Cumming, Constance F., *From the Hebrides to the Himalayas: A sketch of eighteenmonths wanderings in Western Isles and Eastern Highlands*, London, 1876, vol.1, p. 374.

being pleased to catch a glimpse of the home of the Macdonalds, the Lords of the Isles, she recalled a story of one on them named Donald Gorm. Once, when visiting Ireland, he was invited to dine with the lord lieutenant. He arrived late, and took a vacant seat near the door of the banqueting hall. But his host noticed, and sent a servant to bid him come up to the head of the table. To this request, says Gordon-Cumming, mingling patriotic fondness with only faint disapproval, 'the chieftain's reply, more proud than courteous, was to "tell the earle [sic] that wherever Macdonald sits, that is the head of the table"'.[15]

Meanwhile, there were beckonings from afar. Gordon-Cumming was still at Loch Ness in October when she received an invitation from her half-sister, Emilia Sergison, suggesting that 'having seen the finest hills' she should visit India and spend a summer in the Himalayas. Emilia, who later contributed to literature by translating into English a book on Russian explorers in Asia and another on the French writer Germaine de Stael, was married to an army officer who, before returning to England to take over his family estates, wished to spend a year touring in India.[16] Gordon-Cumming's first impulse was to decline the proposal to join the party. As she explained in 1904, 'in those days such travel was still very expensive', though, thanks to the development of steam power, less so and more comfortable than when her brothers set out in the 1840s. Besides, 'no one dreamt of going to India unless they were obliged to do so', especially women, and then 'as wife or sister of some official [or missionary], more or less under compulsion', and certainly not for pleasure. That is the only reason she later gave for the her own travels, but she needed little persuading. There was not much to hold her at home. After her father's death in 1854 she had left Altyre and found a home—'headquarters' was the term she came to use for her places of abode—with her eldest sister, Anne, at Harehope in Northumbria. On Anne's death, four years later, she shifted in with another sister, Eleanora, and her husband, George Grant, who had a fine residence beside the Spey river in Scotland. That is, until 1867, when George lost much of his capital in a stock exchange speculation. So the household, with Gordon-Cumming loosely in train, needed to shift to a smaller and cheaper house. They found one nearer to Edinburgh, first at Comrie and in 1869 at Crieff. Travelling, which she had begun in Scotland in 1866, offered Gordon-Cumming an escape from some of the strains of these domestic disruptions. More broadly, accepting Emilia's invitation also gave her—in 1904—the retrospective satisfaction of being, in her own view, and without intolerable hyperbole, 'the pioneer of the multitude of women who now run to and fro throughout the earth! I am glad I had first

---

15 *From the Hebrides*, p. 99; Leonard Bell, 'Travel Art and its Complications: Constance Frederika Gordon Cumming's 1877 visit to New Zealand, and the Colonial and Indian Exhibition of 1886', *Bulletin of New Zealand Art History*, vol. 16 (1995), pp. 36–37.
16 J. Gordon-Cumming (trans., from Russian), Pavel Yakovlevich Pyasetsky, *Russian Travellers in Mongolia and China*, 2 vols, London, 1884; J.E.G. Cumming (trans., from German), Charlotte Julia Blennerhassett, *Madame de Stael: her friends and her influence in politics and literature*, 3 vols, London, 1889.

innings'! Had she not accepted, 'the twelve years of enchanting travel which followed would never have been dreamt of, for link by link that pleasant chain wove itself'.[17]

So, on 14 November 1868, equipped with painting materials and, presumably, her 'excellent English side-saddle', Gordon-Cumming left Southhampton on the P&O liner *Pera* for Alexandria.[18] As the Suez Canal linking the Mediterranean to the Red Sea did not open till the following year, she travelled from there by train across the desert to Suez, to join the *Candia* bound for Calcutta. Then followed 'a year of unmitigated enjoyment'. She spent 'seven months seeing the glories of the great mountains [and] five months exploring some of the principal cities of the plains'. Her impressions and observations of the people, places and customs that she encountered during that time were recorded in long letters to family members, which provided the basis of a book. Her first published work, an article titled 'Camp Life in the Himalayas' appeared in 1869 in *Good Words*, a popular, religious-toned periodical founded by a kinsman. Thereafter she wrote extensively for a wide range of journals. Her first book, covering her Scottish and Indian travels, was published in 1876, but had to be seen through the press by Isabella Bird, because Gordon-Cumming had left hurriedly for Fiji.[19]

Features of this book, as of those that followed, are Gordon-Cumming's intense and sympathetic interest in what she saw; her approval of the work of Christian missions, which was rooted in her own deep attachment to the Episcopal Church of Scotland but coexisted with a tolerant regard for indigenous people and their ways; and a concern for reducing the discomforts and constraints to which women might be subject. Thus, in her account of Benares, where her host was Rajah Sir Deo Nareien Singh, 'one of the kindest and most courteous gentlemen, she had ever met', she extolled the work of the Zenana missionaries, who aimed to befriend their 'Hindu sisters and impart to them some of the commoner branches of civilised education', such as literacy. Consistent with such views, she was critical of those of her fellows

> in whose eyes a touch of the tar brush is the worst form of evil ... . Too often the owner of a white skin seems to consider himself at liberty to address his darker brethren, no matter how highly educated, in an imperious tone of superiority [that is] painful and amazing to a newcomer ...

---

17 *Memories*, pp. 137, 156, 159, 191–195; *From the Hebrides*, p. 1; C.F. Gordon-Cumming, *Granite Crags*, Edinburgh, 1884, p. 211; *Strathearn Herald*, 1 June, 1912.
18 *At Home in Fiji*, p. 276; C.F. Gordon-Cumming, *A Lady's Cruise in a French Man-of-War*, Edinburgh, 1882, p. 215; *Granite Crags*, p. 113.
19 *Memories*, pp. 107–108, 196–197, 477–480; *From the Hebrides*, pp. i, 1; *Two Happy Years*, p. 16.

> [Furthermore], I have often marvelled to see English ladies returning from church, where they had been paying devout homage to the memories of saintly Syrian Jews (the tradesmen of 1,900 years ago), yet shrinking with contemptuous aversion from contact with their own servants—men differing in colour by but a few shades.[20]

By the same token, she was moved by the plight of the slave-like Egyptian *fellaheen*: 'they are said to be an utterly degraded race, but who can wonder if they are? Poor wretches ... no sunshine of happiness ever seems to gild their sad days'. And she was saddened by the extermination of the Madoc Indians of California: 'One would imagine that some sense of fair play might have induced a certain amount of sympathy with the wild tribes'.[21] If indignation is restrained in such utterances, that does not frustrate the humane outlook that infuses them. While being indifferent to race, Gordon-Cumming was sensitive to class as a distinct and socially relevant category. This is reflected in a comment on food: 'the rice and dahl [of the Indians] is not much worse than the potatoes mashed with mustard and milk which form the ordinary dinner of a vast number of our own sturdy Scots'. Similarly balanced is her response to a comment of one pro-consular predator, Sir Samuel Baker, that 'three first-rate shots' in three days bagged 104 elephants in Ceylon: 'the really disturbing part of such slaughter is the waste of so much good meat'. She was also disquieted by the crass impudence of imperial naming practices:

> I do think it is a pity that wherever the Anglo-Saxon race settles, it uproots the picturesque and generally descriptive native names of mountains and streams, and in their stead bestows some new name, which at best is commonplace, and too often vulgar.[22]

Having been gratifyingly diverted, and with her portfolios replete with paintings, Gordon-Cumming left India from Bombay in December 1869. En route to England, she stayed in Malta for a month as a guest of the governor, and eventually landed at Portsmouth from HMS *Simoon* on 14 February 1870.[23] Immediately, armed with her paintings, she dutifully set about paying 'a multitude of visits to kinsfolk and friends' all over the country. Among them, she notes with some satisfaction, were Lord and Lady Middleton of Birdsall, near York, whose eldest son had married her niece Eisa whilst she was in India. Probably, she made her 'headquarters' with her brother William at Auchintoul, but it was not to be for long. In the autumn of 1872 she was invited by the

---

20 *From the Hebrides*, vol. 11, pp. 65, 334; Gordon-Cumming, Constance F., *In the Himalayas and on the Indian Plains*, London, 1884, pp. 553, 583 [note: this is a revised edition of vol.2 of the 1876 *Hebrides/Himalayas* book].
21 Gordon-Cumming, Constance F., *Via Cornwall to Egypt*, London, 1890, p. 301; *Granite Crags*, pp. 146–152.
22 *In the Himalayas*, p. 33; *Granite Crags*, p. 201; *Two Happy Years*, p. 222. Alfred E. Lomax, *Samuel Baker*.
23 *Memories*, pp. 202–203.

widowed Rev. Hugh Jermyn, formerly the parson at Altyre and latterly Bishop of Colombo (and Primus of Scotland from 1886 to 1901), to visit him and his daughter in Ceylon. This time there was no hesitation.[24]

On 23 November 1872 she boarded the *Hindoo* on its maiden voyage from London bound for Calcutta. It was an inauspicious start, at least for the ship. Scarcely had the *Hindoo* put to sea than it was damaged in a storm and had to put into Portsmouth. Gordon-Cumming thus had a month on her hands before her journey was resumed in the *Othello*. She took advantage of the time to explore Cornwall and Devon. An account of that sojourn, together with her impressions of Egypt, which she visited coming and going on three later voyages beyond Europe was published in 1885 as *Via Cornwall to Egypt*. She eventually reached Colombo on 5 February 1873. Then began, to cite the title of her book on the subject, *Two Happy Years in Ceylon* (1892). For Gordon-Cumming the highlight of this period was an excursion, begun in August 1873, accompanying the bishop and his daughter 'on one of his extensive rounds of visitation, riding and driving circuitously across Ceylon'. In particular it brought her to Batticoloa, on the east cost of the island, opposite Colombo, where she visited the grave of her brother John and reflected on some of the personal costs of the imperial enterprise:

> We returned to Batticoloa at sunset, and in the peaceful moonlight I stood on the grassy grave in the little 'God's Acre' with an intensified sympathy for many of 'our boys' leaving the happy home-nest to carve their fortunes in distant lands.[25]

More fortunate than her brother, Gordon-Cumming arrived back in England at the end of July 1874. Immediately, and without even establishing any 'headquarters', she launched herself with undiminished energy into a strenuous campaign of visiting, as well as doing 'much writing, sketching and other work'. Wherever she went within her circle, her peregrinations attracted approval. 'Everyone seemed to consider it a matter of course that I should continue the travels which had hitherto proved so pleasant'. Indeed, it was through one such admiring acquaintance that her next chance for foreign travel arose. The circumstances are reported in a retrospective introduction to her 1875 diary, which also offers a minute account of her incessant social round. Returning from Ceylon, she

> landed first at Lady Jane G.-G. [her step-mother]. Thence with Janie [her unmarried half-sister] to Settringham, where I spent August. Thence with Eisa to Cresswell. Next to Harehope with Conty. A week with Lady

---

24 *Memories*, pp. 171, 205–207; 'Jermyn, Hugh Willoughby', in *Who Was Who, 1897–1915*, London, 1920/1988, p. 276.
25 *Memories*, pp. 207–210; *Via Cornwall to Egypt*, p. 10; *Two Happy Years*, vol. 11, pp. 172.

> Emma McNeill. Thence to Raigmore for consecration of the cathedral. To the Otters at Oban. Week at Inverary. Via Loch Lomond to the Lees at Gartmore. The Murrays at Gartur. Thence with little Nelly Jenkinson to Crieff, where I spent Christmas and New Year, only going once to Edinburgh, for the Incurable Bazaar, where I had a special exhibition of Ceylon pictures. Returning to Crieff, found a letter from Mrs Rate, suggesting an expedition to Fiji with the Hamilton-Gordons. A very busy fortnight finishing exhibition pictures and my book 'From the Hebrides to the Himalayas', which Sampson, Marston and Low accepted. A few very busy days in Edinburgh with the Lees. Three days at Settringham. Thence to London to stay with Ellinor Hughes (Feb.24th?). Next evening with Jane, Lady G.-C., I dined at the Rates, to meet Sir Arthur and Lady Gordon. A cosy pleasant evening. Mr Ferguson (rude stone monuments) came to look at my Buddhist temples, and we did [the] portfolio extensively.[26]

As anticipated, at the Rates' dinner Lady Gordon formally invited Gordon-Cumming to accompany her to Fiji, where her husband had been appointed governor. 'Needless to say', wrote Gordon-Cumming, 'I accepted with delight'. Despite the shared name, Gordon-Cumming was not—as is commonly thought—related to the governor. Maudslay has left it on record that Lady Gordon did not know 'much of her until they met on board ship', and Gordon-Cumming never claimed any relationship to Sir Arthur.[27]

On 23 March 1875 the Fiji party assembled at Charing Cross railway station. It then crossed to France and boarded the *Anadyr* at Marseilles for Singapore, before transferring to the *Brisbane* for the trip to Sydney. There Gordon-Cumming was billeted with the ill-fated Commodore James Goodenough who she would later, with sententious piety, describe as 'a saint, and martyr'; for, in August, he was killed, partly through his own negligence, while trying to establish friendly contacts with the Santa Cruz islanders. Meanwhile, the Gordons had stayed at Government House with Sir Hercules Robinson who had effected Britain's annexation of Fiji on 10 October 1874. But Gordon was anxious to reach his post without delay so, less than two weeks after reaching Sydney, he departed with most of his party in Goodenough's vessel HMS *Pearl* for Levuka in Fiji, leaving his family to follow when he had arranged suitable accommodation for them. By so doing he also offered Gordon-Cumming another lengthy—and avidly seized—opportunity to explore and paint in yet another country before the remnant, too, departed Sydney, on 9 September. Here she made two notable expeditions, one to the Blue Mountains and, the other, 300 kilometres into the

---

26 *Memories*, pp. 214–216; C.F. Gordon-Cumming, 'Log for 1875. Fiji', National Library of Australia, M1167.
27 *Memories*, pp. 216–217; *At Home in Fiji*, pp. 9–10; Alfred P. Maudslay, *Life in the Pacific Fifty Years Ago*, London, 1930, p. 86.

bush to Duntroon, a sheep station on the site of modern Canberra.[28] On both journeys she was escorted by Alfred Maudslay, a young man newly appointed to Gordon's staff. Maudslay has also left a useful, firsthand description of her:

> a tall plain woman … no tact, no tact, very pushing when she wants anything done, and yet one of the best natured creatures in the world … . She is sufficiently clothed in suits of brown holland or blue serge [which by her own account, also, was her standard garb] and wears an enormous pith helmet. Her *tavi*, as we say here [Fiji], is to wander about the world and 'see things and paint them'.[29]

Another, but somewhat snide and conceited, young man who also described her was the ethnologist Baron Anatole von Hugel. She met him soon after arriving in Fiji, where they both shared the Gordons' hospitality at Government House, 'Nasova'. He was more critical of her, especially at first:

> 16 October [1875] She certainly is a character—very tall, lanky, and pronounced ugly, though clever features; of exhorbitant dress … . She talks much and pleasantly.
>
> 24 October The 'lion killer' nearly kills me with her loud jabber, for it is incessant and intended to be clever.
>
> 7 April [1876] … very gushy … . I wish the 'lion killeress' joy.
>
> 16 May … rather distinguished herself by bumptiousness.
>
> 20 May Sat some time with her while she was sketching. She is so different alone, all her corners and prickles disappearing and the goodliness of her sweet woman's soul coming out to perfection.
>
> 26 September … in excellent spirits and capital company.
>
> 30 September … she ran along the sand waving her hands frantically and vociferating loudly … but it was only the exuberance of her spirits which was causing these antics.[30]

As for her hosts, Arthur Gordon seems to have found her trying at times. In July 1876, for instance, she complained that he refused to take her with him on a trip to Kadavu, Fiji's southernmost island, even though 'there was room' in his boat.

---

28   *Memories*, pp. 218–219; *At Home in Fiji*, pp. 11–26. For Goodenough, see Jane Samson, *Imperial Benevolence: making British authority in the Pacific Islands* (Honolulu, 1998, pp. 171–174).
29   Maudslay, *Life in the Pacific*, p. 84; *Memories*, p. 217.
30   Jane Roth and Steven Hooper (eds), *The Fiji Journals of Baron Anatole Von Hugel*, Suva, 1990, pp. 178, 182, 299, 322, 324, 430, 436.

His wife, in contrast, was quite complaisant, even though Gordon-Cumming took little interest in their children and showed scant inclination to stay put. Shortly after reaching Levuka, she had written sympathetically:

> Eka seems very happy and is looking forward with intense delight to what she thinks will be a life of incessant picnics and sightseeing in Fiji. But I cannot make her believe what a very quiet and monotonous life it will be, and that seeing anything out of [the island of] Ovalau for many months will, at any rate, for her and me, be out of the question.[31]

She need not have worried. On the voyage from Sydney, Gordon-Cumming had become acquainted with Rev. Frederick Langham and his wife. They had been Methodist missionaries in Fiji since 1858, and regularly invited Gordon-Cumming to join them on their pastoral visitations. Thus, in December 1875, she ascended to the upper reaches of the Rewa River; in April and May 1876 she cruised around the islands of the Koro Sea; and, in August, she circumnavigated Vanua Levu. Then, on 22 December, *en route* to a holiday in New Zealand, she set out with Lady Gordon and the children for Kadavu. That was where, until 1882, when the capital of Fiji was shifted to Suva, the trans-Pacific steamers used to meet to exchange or pick up mail and passengers for Sydney, Auckland and San Francisco. From Auckland the New Zealand prime minister, Frederick Whitaker, despatched the Fiji party northwards in the government steamer *Hinemoa*, to spend several months with Sir George Grey at Kawau. Gordon-Cumming, though, in characteristic fashion, 'determined to see something of the country', particularly the Rotorua thermal area. Accordingly, she broke away from the group early in March and rejoined it in mid-April, in time for the return to Fiji. Two months after that, still unsated, she embarked on a six-week visit to a coconut plantation at Lomaloma in the Lau group, then returned to Levuka to find that fate had yet again intervened in her favour.[32] As she put it:

> a counter-charm was brought to bear upon the spell which for [two years had] held me entranced [with Fiji]. The chief magician appeared in the guise of a high ecclesiastic of the Roman Church, clothed in purple and wearing the mystic ring and cross of amethyst; while his coadjutor, a French gentleman of the noble old school, was the commander of a large French man-of-war, which had been placed at the service of the Bishop of Samoa, to enable him to visit all the most remote portions of his diocese.

---

31 'Log for 1876', 6 July; [Arthur Gordon], *Fiji: records of private and public life, 1875–1889*, Edinburgh, 1897, vol. 1, pp. 119, 265.
32 *Memories*, pp. 219–223; *At Home in Fiji*, pp. 70, 158, 183, 189, 219, 259–263, 272–287, 306, 319, 324; [Gordon], *Fiji*, vol. 1, pp. 348, 399–400, 415–416, 424; vol. 11, pp. 375–378, 403–405, 586, 590; Maudslay, *Life in the Pacific*, p. 175; Tilly, Captain, *Brett's New Zealand and South Pacific Pilot with Nautical Almanac for the Years 1887–88*, Auckland, 1886, p. 299; *New Zealand Herald*, 9, 10, 13 April 1877; C. Hartley Grattan, *The United States and the Southwest Pacific*, Melbourne, 1961, pp. 110–111.

In other, plainer words, Captain Aube of the *Seignelay*, recognising her 'keen appreciation of scenery and inveterate love of sketching', invited her to join the voyage which was taking Bishop Elloy on a *tour de mission*, 'and so fill fresh portfolios with reminders of the beautiful scenes which the vessel was about to visit'. Predictably, she accepted.[33]

Leaving Levuka on 5 September, the *Seignelay* spent eight days in Tonga and two weeks Samoa. There Gordon-Cumming had planned to disembark, and then take ship for Sydney, where she was due to spend Christmas with Lady Gordon. But, given the political instability in Samoa consequent upon the power struggle between the Tupua and Malietoa factions, of which she offers a clear account, probably supplied by Rev. George Turner of the London Missionary Society (LMS), she prudently decided that Samoa 'would not be an inviting place in which to lie stranded'. So, buoyed by an axiomatically romantic expectation, she joyfully carried on to Tahiti.

> Every creature on board is rejoicing at the prospect of returning to the Tahitian Elysium. To me this has been a dream ever since my nursery days, when the big illustrated volumes of old voyages that lay in my father's dressing room were the joy of many an hour.

Even when the *Seignelay* reached Papeete on 7 October, she was still hopeful of reaching Sydney via Honolulu or Auckland—or even via San Francisco, which had become a major hub of the Pacific transport system with the completion of the transcontinental railway in 1869. But that scheme was soon abandoned, as was a return to Fiji. The visit to Tahiti became a sojourn of six months, leaving the hard-pressed Lady Gordon, who herself left Fiji in June 1878, with the task of repatriating her itinerant guest's pictures and other possessions in 'four immense cases'.[34]

At first, on the strength of an introduction from George Turner, Gordon-Cumming stayed with the Rev. James Green, also of the LMS. Later, she moved in with the newly widowed Titaua Brander, a wealthy aristocrat of mixed blood whose Scots-born husband ('one of the Branders of Pitgaveny') had built up the largest trading company in the Society group. It was an interesting time for an inquisitive, gregarious visitor such as Gordon-Cumming to be in Tahiti. Three weeks before her arrival the monarch, Queen Pomare IV, had died. Two days after the burial, to forestall a looming succession dispute and to smooth the way for the full annexation of what had been a French protectorate since 1843, the acting administrator, Rear Admiral Serre, astutely had her compliant son, Ari'iaue, installed as Pomare V. To consolidate this arrangement, Serre then escorted

---

33   *A Lady's Cruise*, pp. v–vi.
34   *A Lady's Cruise*, vol. 1, pp. 5, 9, 41, 79, 94–95, 125, 248, 253; *Memories*, pp. 227–228; [Gordon], *Fiji*, vol. 111, p. 69.

the new king on an elaborately arranged tour, like a Samoan *malaga*, around Tahiti and the neighbouring island of Moorea, where Mrs Brander, who was also Pomare's sister-in-law, held high rank, to receive the acclaim of his subjects. At the admiral's invitation, Gordon-Cumming joined the official party for these expeditions. Clearly, it would seem, people found pleasure in her company. In early November 1877 she even turned down another invitation to board the *Seignelay*, this time for a voyage to the Tuamotus and Marquesas. But she was not dabbling in self-denial. Rather, she declined because she was expecting to depart on the *Marama*, a vessel the Maison Brander was despatching to Hawai'i to collect a cargo of cattle. At the last moment, however, by which time the *Seignelay* had sailed, she was persuaded—probably easily—to stay on until the next voyage of the *Marama*. As it happened, that vessel was long overdue on its return. Consequently, it was not until March 1878 that Gordon-Cumming left Tahiti, and then in another Brander vessel, the 230-ton *Paloma*, carrying a cargo of oranges and mail for San Francisco. *En route*, the *Paloma* coasted Kauai and Ni'ihau where, much to Gordon-Cumming's disappointment, she could not be put ashore to visit the Sinclairs. As she put it:

> In the course of many wanderings, I had already experienced enough of the hospitality of the Colonies to know that had I landed, the name I bear would have ensured a hearty welcome from my countrymen and their mother ... . But, alas! so rigid are the regulations of the French government concerning its postal service that our good Danish captain dared not even send a boat ashore, as he would thereby have broken his mail contract.[35]

Then followed six months in California, which she mostly spent painting in the Yosemite valley, and generating another book, *Granite Crags*, before departing in August for Japan. Here her host was Henry Dyer, another Scot, and founder of the Imperial College of Engineering, which contributed much to Japan's industrial modernisation. Three months later Gordon-Cumming was in China where she ranged northwards along the coast from Hong Kong and Canton to Tsientsin, and inland to Peking. She then returned to Japan for another two months, during which time she ascended Mount Fujiyama, before departing once again for San Francisco. A highlight of that crossing was dining at the captain's table with the former US president Ulysses S. Grant and his wife, who were completing a round-the-world trip, and whom she 'had met repeatedly in China'. Next, a week after reaching San Francisco, she embarked at length for Hawai'i—and its volcanoes. This visit, which Gordon-Cumming describes in

---

35 *A Lady's Cruise*, vol. 1, pp. 256, 265, 296, 303, vol. 11, pp. 1, 42, 73–75, 86–92, 151, 215, 237–245, 287–288, 300, 304–307; *Granite Crags*, pp. 1–2; C.F. Gordon-Cumming, *Fire Fountains: the kingdom of Hawaii, its volcanoes, and the history of its missions*, Edinburgh, 1883, vol. 1, p. 3; C.F. Gordon-Cumming, 'The Last King of Tahiti', *Contemporary Review*, vol. 41 (1882), pp. 819–836; Colin Newbury, *Tahiti Nui: change and survival in French Polynesia, 1767–1945*, Honolulu, 1980, pp. 194–195.

Fire Fountains, lasted two months. In that time, assisted with introductions from John Dominis, the king's brother-in-law, she toured the islands of Oahu, Hawai'i and Maui (with Isabella Bird), and met King Kalakaua and Queen Likelike. She then returned to San Francisco from where she travelled by train across the continent and visited Maryland, the Niagara Falls and Boston, before boarding the *Montana* at New York for the homeward leg in March 1880. Ironically, after two near misses, one off the Eddystone rocks in 1872 and another near the Goto Islands of Japan in July 1879, this also proved to be her most dangerous trip. Approaching journey's end, the *Montana* ran on the rocks at Holyhead and the passengers had to be taken off by lifeboat. Gordon-Cumming declined to join them, for fear of having her paintings damaged by salt water, and she persuaded the captain to allow her to stay on board at her own risk, until she was rescued several hours later by another vessel which delivered her to Liverpool on 13 March 1880.[36]

With that, Gordon-Cumming's career as a far-ranging traveller was over. She established her headquarters at Crieff, in the house of her by-then-widowed sister Eleanor (where she continued to live after Eleanor's death in 1889) and entered upon a decade of literary and artistic industry that took her name well beyond the circle of family and friends to which it had hitherto been confined. Between 1881 and 1886 she published six more large books on the places that she had visited—Fiji, Polynesia, Hawai'i, California, Egypt and China—followed in 1892 by one on Ceylon. The only country not so dignified was Japan, for which her publisher said there would be no market as the subject was currently overwritten. Accordingly, she bided her time, and included a substantial account of Japan in *Memories* in 1904.

In tone and style, Gordon-Cumming's writings are consistent. They are descriptive and personal, immediate and amiable. They record her experiences and observations of places, people and customs and, while often light on detail, avoid excesses of effusiveness and exoticism. Nor are they padded out with pretentions to ethnological analysis or by lengthy excursions into history. On the other hand, even while extolling the 'civilising' influence of missionaries, for instance, in Fiji and Hawai'i, they do reveal an assimilative, relativistic sympathy for native ways, especially—in accord with artistic convention—those of Polynesia. Thus, after watching Melanesian plantation labourers in Fiji, she commented:

---

36 *Granite Crags*, pp. 6, 37, 55, 348; C.F. Gordon-Cumming, *Wanderings in China*, Edinburgh, 1888, pp. 1, 25, 75, 83–88, 351, 355, 372–373, 507–519; *Fire Fountains*, vol. 1, pp. 10, 64–66, 253, vol. 11, pp. 10–13; *Memories*, pp. 230–243, 308, 334–343, 356–357; *Via Cornwall to Egypt*, p. 1. Lydia Wevers, 'Visiting the Volcano: Isabella Bird and Constance Gordon Cumming in Hawaii', *Turnbull Library Record*, vol. 34 (2001), pp. 59–72.

their dances are strange and uncouth—utterly devoid of grace. Certainly, from an aesthetic point of view, these races are as inferior to those of Fiji, Tonga and Samoa, as the Australian blacks are to the noble Maoris of New Zealand [who had an exceptional ability to 'assume the broadcloth of civilisation'].

Not least to the Samoans' credit, were their funeral customs:

> No Highlander is more careful to have his bones or those of his kindred, laid beside the dust of his forefathers than is the Samoan. To him the idea of a common cemetery is repulsive. His desire is to be laid in the tomb in the garden, on land belonging to his family.[37]

For her own part, she was not dogmatic. In 1904 she declared that she hoped to be buried 'in the sweet God's-acre at Ochtertyre [Auchtertyre]', near Crieff, but later expressed a preference for further north, near her ancestral ground:

> I desire that I may be buried without a coffin on the banks of the Findhorn [river], near the Soldier's Hole, and that a cairn of stones be erected over me … . personally I have no feeling about consecrated ground for we know that the earth is the Lord's and guards his people where their dust lies.[38]

The same adaptable outlook made her a pioneer advocate of cremation, a practice she had noted and approved of as 'cleanly' in India, Japan and China. She published a well-regarded article on the subject and, in 1884, she was gratified by a legal decision which declared that 'cremation was not contrary to the law', and which paved the way for the opening in 1885 of Britain's first public crematorium.[39] Less gratifying would have been another legal decision, in 1891, in which her nephew William, the fourth baronet and a Lt. Colonel in the Scots Guards, was found guilty—though on dubious evidence—of having cheated while playing cards with the Prince of Wales, afterwards King Edward VII. Known as the Baccarat or Tranby Croft case, after the country house in which the incident occurred, the trial was one of the most sensational of Queen Victoria's reign and led to Sir William's disgrace.[40] Another nephew, Walter, distinguished himself more conventionally as an army officer in Africa.[41]

While achieving prominence as a writer, Gordon-Cumming also found a vast— and unanticipated—audience as a painter. Similarly to many women of her

---

37 *At Home in Fiji*, pp. 154, 336; *A Lady's Cruise*, p. 113.
38 Unidentified newspaper clipping.
39 *Memories*, pp. 244–252.
40 *Daily Graphic*, 1 June 1891; W. Teignmouth Shore (ed.), William Gordon Gordon-Cumming, *The Baccarat Case: Gordon-Cumming v Wilson and others*, London, 1932; Giles St. Aubyn, *Edward VII, Prince and King*, London, 1979, pp. 163–172.
41 Harry H. Johnston, *The Story Of My Life*, New York, 1923, pp. 300–301.

time and class, she had learned how to use watercolours and, as early as 1866, had publicly exhibited her work in Edinburgh and, from 1867, in Glasgow. Her subjects were typically expansive landscapes. They were representational, numerous and painted quickly on site, but often finished later. Her own assessment of their intrinsic quality was modest—perhaps overly so—and eschewed claims to 'fine art':

> Undoubtedly their real value was collective, in presenting successively a number of realistic pictures of each district in each country, where I sojourned and worked so diligently.[42]

Her aim was to depict remote parts of the world for the benefit of people who were never likely to see such places for themselves. In this, she offered reassurance as well as instruction and diversion. Propaganda attends the picturesque (a word she often employs). For instance, the peacefulness of 'White Terraces, Roromahana' belies the hostility and cupidity she encountered from the Maoris of the Rotorua area. The picture has the terraces flowing into the space where the viewer is located and the 'wonderland' is humanised by showing Maoris bathing and cooking in the hot pools, while Europeans sit nearby, relaxed and admiring the scenery. Such harmony, though, is not sustained by her written account of her experiences, which led her to smuggle her pictures out, or risk having them destroyed.[43]

By her own account, Gordon-Cumming worked on the principle 'never a day without at least one careful-coloured sketch' and, in India at least, she always began work before 'gun-fire' (five am). Others, too, testify to her assiduity. Thus, in Ceylon in 1875, Lady Gordon noted

> [Eka] had a carriage lent her by someone … . She asked me to take a drive with her, 'you won't mind waiting for about an hour while I a make a sketch?' But I found I should have about half a mile of walking up a hill to the place of the same sketch so I declined, and she went alone. She has already painted nearly everything in Ceylon, so she is not very keen about it, as she never cares to do a thing twice.

And in Fiji in 1876:

> Eka generally goes off by herself either morning or afternoon and climbs up to some spot where she can get air and a nice view, and where she sits for hours.

---

42   *Memories*, p. 351.
43   *At Home in Fiji*, vol. 11. pp. 199, 223–227; Bell, pp. 38–39.

Gordon-Cumming, she further adds, delighted in 'roughing it', never walked if she could help it 'except to sketch' and 'usually sits on the ground by choice'. Maudslay also commented

> No subject is too big for her, the larger and the more imposing it is the better she likes it. She sketches in her outline with wonderful rapidity and accuracy, and when her pictures are about three parts done they are often most admirable, but then she insists on taking them home to finish them.

That, he thought, led to inaccuracies.[44] Illustration of the 'finish later' comment is found in four of the Rotorua paintings: they are all dated 4 April 1877, but could not have been completed then. In any case, she did not always work in easy conditions, as a catalogue of her Fiji pictures noted in 1886:

> In submitting to the public this series of travel-sketches [as well as those of other places], Miss Gordon Cumming would venture to ask that criticism from an Art point of view, may be tempered by the consideration of the manifold difficulties under which the majority were produced.
>
> Many were obtained during exposure to scorching heat, others in the intervals between tropical rain storms, during which the artist's ingenuity was often sorely taxed to keep herself and her paper from being washed away! Not least among the sketcher's troubles are the swarms of musquitoes and sandflies, and the inquisitive crowding of human beings.
>
> Worst of all is the impossibility of preserving paper from mildew, which in a few days converts the best drawing-paper into most thirsty blotting-paper, which at its best absorbs wash after wash of colour in the most trying manner. More frequently, however, the mildew reveals itself by absorbing the colour in stars and blotches all over the picture, making the drawing which has cost hours of careful work look as if it were afflicted with small-pox. Under these circumstances, the sole possible expedient is to coat the paper thickly with Chinese white paint, which of course is fatal to all clear water-colour painting, and to all brilliancy of effect.

---

44   *Memories*, pp. 199–200; *Two Happy Years*, p. 5; [Gordon], *Fiji*, vol. 1, pp. 5, 407, 421, vol. 11, p. 397; Maudslay, *Life in the Pacific*, p. 85. The *Memories* reference offers a good description of her working methods.

Moreover, in very beautiful remote places, the traveller is apt to find that the supply of even mildewed drawing-paper has run short, and many of the sketches here shown are painted on pieces of waste paper, such as old estate maps kindly contributed by planters and other friends.[45]

Perhaps? She did have to contend with practical problems, but there is also an element of false modesty in these comments. In the words of an academic authority familiar with her extant oeuvre, 'The watercolours are quite wonderful'.[46]

By the time she returned to Britain in 1880 Gordon-Cumming 'had accumulated about five hundred large landscapes in water colour, and about as many small ones'. Marianne North coped with a similarly large quantity of botanical paintings by presenting them to the nation in a gallery she built at Kew Gardens in 1882. Gordon-Cumming, lacking the means to establish a similar permanent exhibition of her work, acted as a 'private show-woman' until her 'portfolios became a weariness' to her. There was, though, respite to be had in having her pictures displayed in temporary exhibitions, most notably at the great Indian and Colonial Exhibition of 1886. In that triumphal assertion of imperial achievement she, too, found a moment of glory: 27 of her paintings, more than of any other artist, were hung in the New Zealand section; 66 paintings and 112 pages of artefact studies in the Fiji one; plus further paintings depicting India, Ceylon and Australia. By her count, she had over 300 paintings of 'Greater Britain ... exhibited ... at South Kensington and at the subsequent Colonial Exhibitions in Liverpool and Glasgow'. They were probably seen by more people than the work of any other female artist of the period. But she found a disadvantage in such otherwise gratifying exposure. When the pictures came back they were clad 'in large frames, with heavy glass, whereby they became to me a sort of white elephant, requiring stables'.[47]

In the late 1880s, therefore, she records, 'I made over about two hundred and fifty of my most important pictures in India, Ceylon, New Zealand and the Fijian Isles to my eldest nephew [William, the fourth baronet] to be added to the family travel-accumulations at Altyre and Gordonstoun'. Many more were 'scattered in the homes of other relations', leaving what she considered to be 'a more manageable series of portfolios in my own hands'. Unfortunately this mode of dispersal, for she never sold her paintings, which, in their formal qualities and despite their historical and ethnographic value, were 'popular art' has had serious consequences. Most of her paintings were lost (perhaps they were

---

45   Colonial and Indian Exhibition, *Colony of Fiji*, London, 1886, p. 52.
46   Personal letter, Peter Gathercole to Hugh Laracy, 12 May 1986.
47   *Memories*, pp. 349–351; Colonial and Indian Exhibition, *Catalogue of New Zealand Exhibits*, pp. 7–9, and *Fiji*, pp. 52–55; Graham Bateman (ed.), *A Vision of Eden: the life and work of Marianne North*, London, 1980, pp. 9–13; Bell, 'Travel Art', p. 32.

seen as 'Aunt Eka's foibles', and were disposed of when Gordonstoun, which later became famous as a school, passed out of family hands?). Even Gordon-Cumming's name became virtually unknown to art historians.[48] Some of the lost items survive as illustrations in her books; a very few are in art galleries.[49] The largest known collection of her work, consisting of 29 paintings, mostly of Fiji, and her folios of Fijian artefacts, are in the Cambridge University Museum of Archaeology and Anthropology. This was set up in 1883 by her old acquaintance Anatole von Hugel, with the support of his friends Alfred Maudslay and Arthur Gordon, both of whom were Cambridge graduates. Through the benefactions of these early residents of 'Nasese', the Fiji collection is central to the museum's holdings.[50]

As for Gordon-Cumming, of all the places that she had visited, it was not any of the territories of 'Greater Britain' that held her abiding interest, but China. Consequently, among the few paintings she kept were 60 illustrating scenes 'where our missionaries are at work' there. During the 1880s, thanks to the efforts of the American Methodist advocate of missions J.R. Mott with his slogan 'The Evangelisation of the World in this Generation', and which culminated in the World Missionary Conference in Edinburgh in 1910, Protestants—Gordon-Cumming among them—had become intensely concerned about China. By 1904 her paintings had 'occupied a definite place in twenty-five great Missionary Exhibitions … in many large cities'. Her motives, though, were not narrowly religious. There was another issue involved besides the eternal salvation of the Chinese and that was the temporal salvation of Greater Britain, and beyond. Noting the 'colonising spread' of the Chinese, she believed that 'they will continue more and more to overrun the earth', taking the curse of opium smoking with them. Accordingly, but conveniently overlooking the Opium Wars (1839–1842, 1856–1860) that Britain and its allies had earlier forced on China, she declared that 'from self-interest it behoves all nations of the earth to help in this mission work'.[51]

---

48 She is not mentioned in Una Platts, *Nineteenth Century New Zealand Artists: a guide and handbook* (Christchurch, 1980), or in Deborah Cherry, *Painting Women: Victorian women artists* (London 1993). John Parker, *Prince Philip: his secret life*, New York, 1991, pp. 56–57 (re Gordounstoun School).
49 Those known to the writer are: 'Moorea. Baie de Pao Pao en 1877' and 'Papeete, Tahiti, from Mrs Brander's Verandah, Feb. 1st 1877' (Musee de Tahiti, Papeete); 'Sir George Grey's home on the Kawau', 1877 (Auckland City Art Gallery); 'The Gininderra Creek looking forward to Murrumbidgee Hills, County Murray, N.S. Wales', 30 Aug. 1875 (National Library of Australia). Another painting, 'Temporary Chimney's and Fire Fountains, Kilauea, 1879', was shown in an exhibition entitled 'Hilo 1825–1925' at the Lyman House Memorial Museum, Hilo, Hawai'i in 1983–1984, but it was on loan from a private collection in Honolulu.
50 *Memories*, pp. 251–252; Bell, 'Travel Art' pp. 29, 42–43; Roth and Hooper, 'Von Hugel', p. xvii.
51 *Memories*, p. 252; *Wanderings in China*, p. 436. For this Protestant missionary impulse, see Stephen Neill, *A History of Christian Missions*, Harmondsworth, 1964, pp. 393–396; and for the Catholic reaction, which had significant implications for the Pacific Islands, see Hugh Laracy, 'Maine, Massachusetts and the Marists: American Catholic missionaries in the South Pacific', *Catholic Historical Review*, vol. LXXV (1999), pp. 566–590.

She also had a more personal interest. When visiting Peking in 1879 she was intrigued to meet William Hill Murray, a Scots missionary who was attempting to devise a method whereby blind and illiterate Chinese could be taught to read by means of a Braille-based system in which sounds were represented by numbers. She did not think about him again until 1885 when, writing *Wanderings in China*, it occurred to her 'to wonder how the teaching of the blind was progressing'. Thereupon she entered into correspondence with Murray, and became so impressed with what she learned of the pedagogic effectiveness of his method and of his scheme for producing a Bible in numeral type, that assisting his work became her principal occupation. In 1894 she was instrumental in setting up a Glasgow-based operation, the Mission to the Chinese Blind, to raise funds for him and, in 1898, she published a biography, *The Inventor of the Numeral-Type for China*, to extend public recognition of what he was doing.[52]

Constance Frederica Gordon-Cumming died at Crieff on 4 September 1924, aged 82, and was buried locally. That may have been some distance from the banks of the Findhorn, but, like so much of northern Scotland, it was still hallowed by family associations. A Samoan would not have asked for more. Nor need such overlaps with the cultures of the Pacific islands end there. If her missing pictures of the islands, such as any of the *meke* (celebration) at Bau in Fiji in May 1877, are ever found, they will offer glimpses of a world that was never just a pro-consular playground, and of a past that increasingly, since the 1960s, has come to belong to the citizens of independent nations, no less than it does to the heirs of those who left graphic records of it.

Appendix I

The travels of C. F. G-C.

1. India

a. Depart from Southampton (*Pera*) 14 November 1868; Gibraltar (19 Nov), Malta (23 Nov), Alexandria. By rail to Suez, to join *Candia*. Aden, Galle. Arrive at Calcutta (23 December).

b. Allahabad, Cawnpore, Lucknow, Delhi, Agra, Futteyporesickri (joined Emilia and Warden Sergison), Meerut, Umballa, Simla (April–May 1869), Massourie (Oct), Dehra Doon, Hardwar, Benares, Allahabad, Jubbulpore, Calcutta.

---

52 *Memories*, pp. 252–270; *Wanderings in China*, pp. 414–438; C.F. Gordon-Cumming, *The Inventor*, London, 1898, pp. 24–26.

c. Depart from Calcutta. From Suez to Cairo to Alexandria by rail. Depart from Alexandria 1 January 1870. Stay for a month in Malta. Depart from Malta in HMS *Simoon*. Gibraltar. Arrive at Portsmouth 17 February 1870.

2. Ceylon

Depart from London (*Hindoo*) 23 November 1872. Interlude in Cornwall and Devon. Depart from Plymouth (*Othello*) 30 December 1872. Suez Canal. Arrive at Colombo 5 February 1873. Return to Britain 'end of July' 1874.

3. Pacific

a. Depart from London (rail-ferry for Paris) 23 March 1875. Depart from Marseilles (SS *Anadyr*) 28 March 1875. Port Said, Aden, Galle (stay three days), Singapore (stay one week). Depart from Singapore (*Brisbane*) 3 May 1875. Brisbane 21–23 May. Arrive at Sydney 25 May. Visits to Duntroon and Blue Mountains. Depart from Sydney (*Egmont*) 9 September.

b. Arrive at Levuka 19 September 1875. Suva to Kadavu 22–25 December. Depart from Kadavu (SS *City of Sydney*) 26 December 1876. Arrive at Auckland 30 December. Kawau (8 January – c. 9 March 1877), Thames (23 March), Kati Kati (29 March), Tauranga, Ohinemotu (1 April), Rotomahana (3 April), Te Wairoa (5 April), Ohinemotu, Tauranga. Depart from Tauranga (*Rowena*) 6 April. Arrive at Auckland 7 April. Depart from Auckland (*Zealandia*) 12 April. Arrive at Kadavu 16 April 1877. Kadavu to Suva (*Barb*) 16–17 April. Arrive at Levuka 27 April.

c. Depart from Levuka (*Seignelay*) 5 September 1877. Tonga (7–15 Sept), Samoa (18 Sept – 2 Oct). Arrive at Papeete 7 October. Depart from Papeete (*Paloma*) 9 March 1878. Arrive at San Francisco 21 April.

d. Depart from San Francisco (*Gaelic*) 16 August 1878. Arrive at Yokohama 6 September. Depart from Nagasaki mid December. Arrive at Shanghai (stay for three days). Hong Kong (25 December – ?), Canton 9–24 January 1879), Amoy (23 Feb), Foo Chow, Nantai, Ningpo, Shanghai (26 April – 28 May), Tien Tsin, Peking (5–16 June), Tien Tsin. Depart from Chefoo (*Thorkild*) 21 June.

e. Arrive at Nagasaki 5 July 1879. Depart from Yokohama (*City of Tokio*) September. Arrive at San Francisco 21 September. Depart from San Francisco (*City of Sydney*) on 1 October.

f. Arrive at Honolulu 7 October 1879, stay till 13 October. Hawai'i (16 Oct – ?Nov), Maui (mid November – ?), Honolulu (23 Nov). Depart from Honolulu (*Australia*) 24 November 1879.

g. Arrive at San Francisco 2 December 1879. Across continent by train. Baltimore (Christmas). Depart from New York (*Montana*) 2 March 1880. Shipwrecked at Holyhead 13 March. Arrive at Liverpool (*Sea King*) 13 March 1880.

Note: the dates in brackets indicate with varying degrees of completeness when Gordon-Cumming was at the places referred to.

Appendix II

Books by C. F. G-C.

1876

From the Hebrides to the Himalayas: a sketch of eighteen months' wanderings in western isles and eastern highlands, London, 2 vol.

Subsequently revised and re-published as two separate and enlarged works: *In the Hebrides* (London, 1883) and *In the Himalayas and on the Indian Plains* (London, 1884).

1881

At Home in Fiji, Edinburgh and London, 2 vol.

1882

A Lady's Cruise in a French Man-of-War, Edinburgh and London, 2 vol.

1883

Fire Fountains: the kingdom of Hawaii, its volcanoes, and the history of its missions, Edinburgh and London, 2 vol.

1884

Granite Crags of California, Edinburgh and London.

1885

Via Cornwall to Egypt, London.

1886

Wanderings in China, Edinburgh and London, 2 vol.

1892

Two Happy Years in Ceylon, Edinburgh and London, 2 vol.

1898

The Inventor of the Numeral-Type for China, London.

1904

Memories, Edinburgh and London.

Note: This list indicates dates of first publication only, and not of reprints or new editions.

5. Niels Peter Sorensen (1848–1935): The story of a criminal adventurer

'From villains like "Bully" Hayes, James Toutant Proctor, the murderous Rorique brothers, the cowardly *Rainbow Warrior* terrorists—and numerous others of their ilk—may we be protected'.[1] No such litany of the miscreants whose crimes have brought them more than a passing mention in the historical records of the Pacific would be complete without the name of Niels Peter Sorensen. Indeed, it would seem to be not unfitting that most of what is known of him relates to his misdeeds and that much of what he made known about himself was demonstrably untrue. The violence, robbery and deceit, though, that mark his career are well documented. If he touched the lives of others in more benign ways, and it may be assumed that he did, there is scant evidence of it. In mitigation it may be suggested that on one occasion at least he was used by men more socially advantaged than himself, but there is nothing to indicate that he was to any extent an unwilling tool. Often enough in the course of a long life, he demonstrated ample ability to arrange his nefarious affairs without any such prompting. The information to be gleaned from the files of government agencies concerning the way he conducted himself during several commercial expeditions to the Solomon Islands is consistent, and provides no grounds for disputing the view of those of his contemporaries who judged him to be a singularly and deservedly disreputable fellow. He was one of the 'white savages' whose activities supplied a moral reason for Britain's imperial presence in the Pacific.[2]

According to court records, Sorensen was Lutheran in religion and was aged 42 at the time of his trial in Brisbane in 1886 for robbery and assault under arms. According to his birth certificate, presented in the course of a fraudulent—and unsuccessful—claim for a pension, which he maintained from 1899 to 1930, he was born at Rudkobing in Denmark on 4 January 1848. Parish records confirm that date and place, but spell his name in the Danish style, Niels Peder Sorensen, and cite his parents as Soren Christensen, a day labourer, and Ane

---

[1] 'Hayes', in W.H. Oliver (ed.), *Dictionary of New Zealand Biography, 1769–1869*, vol. 1, Wellington, 1990; Christopher Legge and Jennifer Terrell, 'James Toutant Proctor', *Journal of Pacific History*, vol. 5 (1970), pp. 65–84; Henri Jacquier, *Piratie dans le Pacifique: de Tahiti a l'Ile du Diable*, Paris, 1973 (trans. *Piracy in the Pacific: the story of the notorious Rorique brothers*, New York, 1976); John Dyson, *Sink the Rainbow: an enquiry into the 'Greenpeace Affair'*, London, 1986.
[2] Jane Samson, *Imperial Benevolence: making British authority in the Pacific*, Honolulu, 1998, pp. 24–42.

Marie Andersen. At the age of 11, so Sorensen told a court in 1911, he found his own way to New York from le Havre in 1860 and lived in a boarding house in Market St for two years until joining the navy.³

He told an extended version of his story to the US Bureau of Pensions in 1915: he was in New York in 1863, aged nearly 14, illiterate, not speaking English, when he was shanghied, and taken to the Brooklyn Navy Yard, where he was forced to enlist as Peter Peterson, under which name he served first on the *Miantonomah* and then on the *Susquehanna* until being discharged in 1865.⁴ If there was any truth in this story, several investigations by the bureau failed to uncover it. No Peter Peterson served aboard either vessel during the Civil War; indeed, the *Miantonamah* was not commissioned until October 1865. As for the *Susquehanna*, he claimed to have witnessed the famous clash between the ironclads *Monitor* and *Merrimack* at Hampton Roads, from its decks in 1863; but that battle occurred on 9 March 1862 and, in any case, the *Susquehanna* was in the Gulf of Mexico at the time. Nor was he aboard it, as claimed, at the capture of Fort Fisher, North Carolina, in January 1865. Also false was a claim to have worked as a diver in helping raise 'Old Ironsides' (the USS *Constitution*), for it was never sunk; no divers are shown among the 100–120 workers listed monthly while it was being rebuilt at the Philadelphia Navy Yard between 1871 and 1878. Likewise unsubstantiated, and thus not earning him an invalid pension, were claims made in 1900 to have suffered various injuries during a genuine period of service in the Navy after the Civil War. So, too, was a claim to have been awarded a land grant of 160 acres near Chicago at the time of his discharge in 1870, for the practice of giving bounty land grants was dropped in 1855. Documents which Sorensen declared would support his various claims were, he said, stolen from his hotel in Antwerp in November 1872. Official records, though, amply attest the mendacity of his self-serving assertions.⁵

At the same time they do provide a good deal of accurate information about him. On 12 September 1867, aged 19, he enlisted in the navy at New York. He signed

---

3   Chief Secretary to Governor, 10 Sept. 1915, enclosed in Foreign Office to US Ambassador (London), 19 Nov. 1915, Inwards Correspondence General (later changed to series 4), 32/16, Western Pacific High Commission, Public Record Office, Kew; Neils (sic) P. Sorensen, pension file, NAVY SO 45548, can no. 135, bundle no. 58, National Archives US, Washington DC; *Sun* (New York), 29 Mar. 1911. Information from parish records was supplied by Professor Rolf Kuschel of the University of Copenhagen in a personal communication.
4   Sorensen, deposition, 5 Oct. 1915, pension file.
5   Records relating to enlisted men in the US navy are extremely difficult to trace; personal files containing details of service are kept only for officers. Were it not for the kindness and expertise of Becky Livingstone in locating material relating to Sorensen in the following files this paragraph could not have been written, and much personal data would also have remained unaccessible. The paragraph is based on data gleaned from various documents in: Sorensen, pension file; RG 24, Records of Bureau of Naval Personel, *i*. Bureau of Navigation Records re Enlisted Men Who Served in the Navy 1842–1885, Box no. 249, 260 (note: Sorensen correspondence is filed under Serensen), and *ii*. Enlistment Returns, Changes and Reports, 1846–1942. Weekly returns of Enlistments at Naval Rendevous, Jan. 6 1855 – Aug. 8 1891, vol. 049 of 110, P1 123, E.219; Navy Muster Rolls: *Idaho* (1867–1868), *Piscataqua* (1868–1869), *Iroquois* (1869–1870); Bureau of Yards and Docks, Philadelphia 1871–1875 Payrolls (civilian). *Sun*, 29 Mar. 1911.

the shipping articles with a mark, and answered 'none' when questioned about previous naval service. He was a seaman aboard three vessels *Idaho*, *Piscataqua*, and *Iriquois*, and served in east Asia before being discharged at Philadelphia on 23 April 1870. He was twice treated for venereal disease. Physically he was a thickset man with fair hair and blue eyes and, at the age of 52, was 168 centimetres in height (slightly taller than he was in the navy) and weighed 74 kilos. His later alias of Peter Peterson may have derived from a man of that name who had served with him aboard the *Piscataqua*.[6]

Following his discharge, according to his own account, Sorensen worked on 'Old Ironsides' until having to dive through a hole in the ice made him ill, and so—and here his word may be accepted—he turned to shipping on merchant vessels. In 1873 he went as boatswain on an emigrant ship from England to New Zealand. On board he met 21-year-old Annie Smith, and married her in Christchurch on 20 October 1874. At the time of the marriage he was working in a sawmill.[7] A year or two after the marriage and the birth of two children,[8] the family shifted to Auckland, where Sorensen was employed mainly as a diver. Hence the name by which he was sometimes known, 'Peter the diver' although, in 1898, the *San Francisco Chronicle* would offer the variant, 'Pirate Pete'.[9]

It was as a diver that Sorensen made his first trip to the Pacific islands, aboard the schooner *Mary Anderson*, chartered by the trading firm of McArthur and Co., which left Auckland on 15 March 1877, bound for Noumea.[10] From there it went to the Loyalty Islands to recruit labourers for work on plantations in the New Hebrides, before going on to the Solomons to collect pearl shell and copra. The diving station there was located at Cockatoo Island in Thousand Ships Bay, at the southern end of the island of Ysabel, a district under the sway of the powerful chief Bera. Sorensen was left to run the station while the *Mary Anderson* went in search of trade. Soon afterwards, on 27 May, the Anglican mission vessel *Southern Cross* anchored nearby. The Rev. Alfred Penny noted in his diary a visit from Sorensen:

> A man who is here to dive for pearl oysters came on board. He came alongside in his boat. A rough Bulldog looking fellow. He stayed to

---

6 Sorensen, Nelson (sic) P., Enlistment Returns; Muster Rolls; Report of Medical Examination, Nov. 14, 1900, Sorensen, Nelson (sic) P., pension file. For fuller identification and location of these files, refer note 5.
7 Sorensen, Notice of Intention to Marry, Christchurch, 1874, BDM 20/19, p. 595/3414, National Archives New Zealand; Marriage Certificate, Christchurch, 1874, no. 1962; Sorensen, deposition, 5 Oct. 1915, pension file; *Sun*, 29 Mar. 1911.
8 In 1915 Sorensen deposed 'I have not lived with her for thirty years, she having left me, and the last I knew of her was about six months ago when she was living in Sydney, Australia. I was never divorced from her. I have two children, a boy, Washington Sayres Sorensen, now in Seattle, Wash., and a girl, Anna Dennybrook, in Sydney, Australia. That is the only marriage I ever contracted.'
9 Sorensen, deposition, 5 Oct. 1915; *San Francisco Chronicle*, 1 Sept. 1898; *Sun*, 29 Mar. 1911.
10 *New Zealand Herald*, 12 Mar., 26 Oct. 1877; *Evening Star*, 15 Mar., 25 Oct. 1877.

service, the Bishop remarking that he supposed it was the first time a man had attended service in the *Southern Cross* with a revolver in his belt.[11]

If Hamilton Wright, the supercargo of the *Mary Anderson*, is to be believed, Sorensen needed to carry the weapon for his own protection. When Captain Caffin of HMS *Beagle* anchored in Havannah Harbour on Efate in the New Hebrides on 5 October he met the *Mary Anderson* on its way back to New Zealand. Sorensen came aboard and complained of being ill-treated by the captain, H. Shipman, and the supercargo of the *Mary Anderson*, and claimed that they had threatened to abandon him there. Wright and Shipman, however, had a different story. Wright said that the diving station at Cockatoo Island had been closed prematurely because of a series of incidents that had occurred between 19 May and 15 July. He had learned of them from Captain W. Schwartz of the *Zephyr* while trading at Uki. As that was after having met HMS *Conflict*, which was on a patrol through the Solomons, Wright said that he had been unable to report the matter to the naval authorities any earlier, but that he did return immediately to Cockatoo Island to investigate. Sorensen, he found, had terrorised the islanders by 'generally maltreating all the men under his control': in one case to the extent of killing a man named Biu and in another by flogging one named Bima. So, 'finding things wrong I removed the cause and closed the station'; although the *Mary Anderson* did remain trading in the Solomons until 17 September.

Subsequently, at Havannah Harbour in the New Hebrides, on the homeward run, Shipman had put Sorensen ashore for being 'drunk and riotous'. Exactly how much fire accompanied all this smoke cannot now be known, although there was probably a good deal. Yet neither of Sorensen's accusers were themselves models of gentility or reliability. An officer of the *Beagle* who went aboard the *Mary Anderson* found Shipman the worse for alcohol and noticed that the log had not been kept for six weeks; and Wright, who was to be killed on Uki in 1896, appeared to one contemporary 'to have been a foolish quarrelsome fellow'. Despite their objections, Caffin ordered them to take Sorensen back to Auckland. While considering that Shipman was unfit for his position, Caffin also recommended that an enquiry be made into the charges against Sorensen, who claimed in defence that Wright had 'ordered him to ill-treat natives'. This investigation was duly conducted by the collector of customs at Auckland, which the *Mary Anderson* reached on 25 October with 'a valuable cargo', but in the absence of reliable witnesses he could not establish the facts and so no

---

11 Alfred Penny, Diary, 27 May 1877, MS B 808, Mitchell Library, Sydney; David Hilliard, *God's Gentlemen: a history of the Melanesian Mission, 1849–1942*, St. Lucia, 1978, p. 87.

prosecution was possible. The available evidence was all hearsay. The only European acknowledged to have observed Sorensen's alleged brutalities was a trader named Lars Nielson, who was still in the Solomons.[12]

In the latter half of the nineteenth century, as European activity in the area intensified, British authorities were considerably exercised by the problem of regulating the conduct of British subjects and British shipping in those islands of the south-west Pacific not claimed by any colonial power. In 1817 the Supreme Courts of New South Wales and Van Diemen's Land had been empowered to try 'Piracies, Felonies, Robberies, Murders ... and other Offences' committed in such places, but more precise regulations, and administrative machinery to enforce them, were needed before judicial processes could be effective. From 1859, with the setting up of the Australia Station of the Royal Navy by the Admiralty, British naval vessels made more regular and frequent cruises through the islands; and, from 1868, with the *Polynesian Labourers Act*, the recruiting of islanders for work in Queensland began to be supervised more closely. Various other measures followed. For instance, in 1877 the governor of Fiji, which had been annexed by Britain in 1874, was given extra jurisdiction applicable within those islands of the region not subject to 'any civilised power'. To enforce this authority he was heavily reliant on naval commanders to assist in investigating complaints, in apprehending malefactors, in collecting evidence and in securing witnesses. A cumbersome set of arrangements evolved, but its deterrent value was reduced by the reluctance of colonial juries to convict white men for offences committed in the Pacific islands, at least against Islanders. In fact, steady policing was only to be achieved after colonial regimes had been erected in the island groups. Nevertheless, by the mid-1880s, the measures already taken to impose law and order, or at least to punish offenders, were beginning to be felt especially, as Sorensen was to learn to his cost, in Melanesia.[13]

Sorensen appears to have been based in Auckland for the next five or six years following the *Mary Anderson*'s return there. In 1883 he was employed as a diver in Sydney and, early the following year, he was at Cooktown in northern Queensland. At this point he again steps vigorously into the historical record.[14] In April 1884, he sailed from Cooktown aboard the two-masted schooner *Albert*. Newly purchased by T.G. Leslie, a Melbourne businessman, the *Albert* was bound for the Solomon Islands to procure copra and pearl shell. Again, Sorensen was the expedition's diver. By the time the vessel completed its trip at Sydney

---

12 Wright to Caffin, 6 Oct. 1877, Caffin to Hoskins, 6 Oct. 1877, Hill to Secretary of Customs, 3 Nov. 1877, Royal Navy Australia Station 14, National Library of Australia (microfilm G 1811); *Evening Star*, 25 Oct. 1877; Judith Bennett, *Wealth of the Solomons: a history of a Pacific archipelago, 1800–1978*, Honolulu, 1987, pp. 55, 58, 126, 382, 391.
13 John Bach, *The Australia Station: a history of the Royal Navy in the south west Pacific, 1821–1913*, Sydney, 1986, pp. 131–150; Deryck Scarr, *Fragments of Empire: a history of the Western Pacific High Commission, 1877–1914*, Canberra, 1967, pp. 6–35.
14 Sorensen, deposition, 5 Oct. 1915.

with a satisfactory cargo on 26 January 1885, having left Uki in the Solomons three weeks before, he was once again the subject of serious accusations. At Rua Sura near Guadalcanal, in late December, a lieutenant from HMS *Diamond* had come aboard to enquire if there had been 'any murders or disturbances anywhere [the *Albert*] had been'. He was assured by the captain, E. Ancell, 'that everything was quiet' and that, moreover, the *Albert* was not licensed to carry Pacific Islanders. Four days later, though, Ancell, went aboard the *Diamond* to report something that, he said, had earlier 'slipped his memory'. That is, that three men taken aboard at the island of Ranongga in June 1884 to work the diving pump had, 'for no visible cause', absconded ten days later in the Lambatana Passage at Santa Ysabel, and were rumoured to have been killed by local people. Apparently trying to down play the discord that had attended the expedition, and to discourage further enquiry, Ancell offered no more details. And none appear to have been sought.[15] His crew, however, probably fearful of being implicated in any wrongdoing that had occurred, were less complacent and, on reaching Sydney, reported other incidents to the police. Besides the Ranongga men, a man recruited at Makira and three islanders brought from Cooktown had also deserted at Santa Ysabel. 'The causes of these natives deserting', was given as

> the cruelty of the diver Sorrenson [sic] to them by beating them, overworking them and feeding them badly. On one occasion one of the natives had his hands lashed behind his back, his feet tied and lashed to his hands, and kept in that position all day by order of the diver Sorrenson [sic].
>
> There were five other natives taken on board at the island of Gaieta and remained on board for about two weeks when they expressed a wish to go home but were forcibly detained for two weeks longer and made to work hard by the diver Sorrenson, but were eventually returned to their home.
>
> On another occasion a Guadalcanal man was forcibly put in irons aboard the vessel and secured to a ring bolt on deck, his canoe taken from him, also his ornaments, and sold to the natives for trade.[16]

Once again, fortune favoured the felon, again with a near miss. Since Sorensen was not the master of the ship (though he appears to have been the owner's agent), since none of the injured parties were available to give evidence, and

---

15   Tryon to Loftus, 5 Feb. 1885, enclosing notes of E. Ancell and Francis T. Barr, ADM 122/21, Public Record Office (photocopies C2f, GBA, Division of Pacific and Asian History, Australian National University).
16   Statement of Walter Hollingsworth, 30 Jan. 1885, enclosed in Douglas to Inspector General of Police, 16 Feb. 1885, ADM 122/21.

since it would be necessary for witnesses from the crew to be detained in Sydney for a month before a trial could be held, the attorney-general decided not to prosecute him.[17]

The vessel's owner, in contrast, was less disapproving. When it left Sydney on its next voyage on 13 April 1885, laden with trade goods, Sorensen had been promoted to master. Moreover, with the collusion of Thomas Cooper, the Portuguese consul in Melbourne, and Carlos Strauss, an impecunious Portuguese subject who was persuaded for a small fee to let himself be listed as the nominal owner, the ship's registration had been changed from British to Portuguese and its name changed from *Albert* to *Douro*. The reason that Leslie gave for these changes was that they might save it from being seized by the Russians in the event that, as was widely feared at the time, Russia should decide to attack British possessions in Asia and the Pacific.[18] A more pertinent reason, but one that would prove to be legally inadequate, was the presumption that Portuguese registration would exempt the vessel from British authority while on the high seas. After the formalities had been completed, Sorensen is said to have remarked 'I'm now out of all English law; I'm my own master; I can trade now with what I like—with rifle, cartridge, powder and dynamite'.[19] In fact, as he had already shown, he preferred to trade without giving anything in exchange if that could be managed. Nor would his presumed licence do anything to sweeten his temper. The knavery that marked the *Mary Anderson* and *Albert* voyages was magnified on that of the *Douro*.

Ten days out from Sydney the vessel reached Makira Bay in the Solomons. No labourers could be recruited there on account of the non-return of some previously taken by the *Albert*, but a few were collected at Marau on Guadalcanal with the lying promise of a four or five months voyage seeking pearl shell and bêche-de-mer. (In fact, Sorensen intended to stay away for at least 15 months). A few days later, on 23 May, he severely beat the ship's cook, Charles Leslie, no relation of the owner, over a trivial dispute, and knocked five of his teeth out. 'At the least provocation', recalled the mate, 'he addressed everyone with the coarsest epithets'. At Cockatoo Island, off southern Ysabel, he coerced seven recruits aboard; and, at Wagina, in the Manning Straits, south of Choiseul, he abducted the chief, 'King John', and demanded a ransom from his supporters under the guise of compensation for the escapees from the *Albert* whom the chief had harboured the year before. The price was high, and was paid in produce, much of which was already pledged by the islanders as payment for goods received from a Sydney trader named Niel Brodie. Only after 4,000 bêche-de-mer, 24

---

17 Crown Solicitor to Inspector General of Police, 13 Feb. 1885, ADM 122/21.
18 Police Dept., inquiry report, 7 Nov. 1885; extract from Police report, 13 Nov. 1885; statement of Carlos Strauss, 16 Nov. 1885, ADM 122/21; Leslie to Hunt, 26 July 1912, A1, 1912/21196, Australian Archives; Glynn Barratt, *Russophobia in New Zealand, 1838–1908*, Palmerston North, 1981.
19 *Brisbane Courier*, 3 April 1886.

turtle shells, three recruits and one pig had been handed over was the chief released. Moving northwards to the Carteret Islands to collect bêche-de-mer, Sorensen, with the assistance as always of a well-armed entourage, continued his Viking-like raid. He commandeered canoes, coerced four girls to come aboard for the entertainment of his crew, plundered the people's huts and, in an attempt to put it off limits to other traders, presumed to 'purchase' the group from the islanders. To the consternation, if not to the conscientious objection, of the mate, Otto Ashe, further depredations were planned. 'We were', Ashe said later, 'convinced that should we assist him he would thus commit another piracy and perhaps implicate us', and so, when the opportunity arose, he and several companions, 'determined to seek protection by reporting Sorensen to a man-of-war.'[20]

Accordingly, on 23 June, the shore party, consisting of Ashe, two seaman named Anders Apitz and Anders Olsen and seven Solomon Islands labourers, set out in an open longboat, with meagre provisions and no ballast, for Mono in the Treasury group. The British navy had had a coaling station there since 1884, and so they were hopeful of finding a naval vessel there. They arrived on 1 July and fell in with Sam Craig, the master of the Sydney trader *Princess Louise*, but there was no man-of-war to assist them. They then decided to follow the trader to the closest European trading station in the area, namely, Mioko in the Duke of York Islands in German New Guinea. From there, Craig took the three white men and four of the islanders to Ralum in New Britain, where the former took ship for Australia They reached Cooktown aboard Thomas Farrell's vessel *Golden Gate* (which flew an American flag) on 29 August.[21]

Their story quickly attracted attention. On 2 September the *Sydney Morning Herald* published a long report under the heading 'Outrages in the South Seas', a style more usually employed for accounts of Islanders attacking Europeans. Official indignation was also strong, especially in the case of Admiral George Tryon, the commander of the Australia station, and a notably high-minded officer. As early as 6 September, he had initiated an enquiry into the *Douro* for 'improperly flying the Portuguese flag; and alleged piratical proceedings' in which Sorensen 'it is averred has behaved shamefully to the natives'. Two months later, fearing that Sorensen might attempt to sell the vessel in some distant port, but fortified by a legal opinion that the sale to Strauss and the subsequent Portuguese registration of the ship were invalid, Tryon appealed to all the colonial authorities in the region to help apprehend the '*Douro* late *Albert*' and ordered his captains to arrest her if met.[22]

---

20   *Sydney Morning Herald*, 2 Sept. 1885; Bennett, p. 55.
21   *Daily Telegraph*, 2 Sept. 1885; *Sydney Morning Herald*, 1, 2 Sept. 1885; statements of Otto Ashe, 29 Aug., 29 Sept. 1885, ADM 122/21.
22   Tryon to Loftus, 6 Sept. 1885; Tryon to Admiralty, 12 Nov. 1885; Attorney General to Governor, 12 Nov. 1885; Tryon to Lock, 18, 20 Nov. 1885; Tryon to Thurston (WPHC), 19 Nov. 1885; Tryon, General Memo. No.

5. Niels Peter Sorensen (1848–1935): The story of a criminal adventurer

Meanwhile, oblivious to the events in Australia, Sorensen had been conducting business with his customary directness. From the Carterets he, too, had sailed to Mioko, and then to Carpenter Island in the Admiralty group, north of New Guinea. There, on 19 October, about a dozen canoes containing close to 30 people came out to the *Douro* to trade, just over two kilometres out from shore. As they drew near Sorensen opened fire on them with a 15-shot Winchester rifle, forcing the occupants to jump overboard. Next, having taken the cargo of bêche-de-mer, pearl shell and betel nut from the abandoned canoes, he ordered that the craft be broken up—and then sailed on. After calling at the Hermit group (26 October) and at Mono (17 November), he eventually put into Cooktown on 24 December. There the *Douro* was promptly seized, and Sorensen was arrested.[23]

Four months later he came to trial. Despite his Danish citizenship, he was held liable for offences committed on what was deemed to be still a British ship. On this occasion enough of his former crew, particularly a Swede named Sven Laland, a former Hernsheim employee who had joined the *Douro* in New Britain on 5 August, were available to testify against him. He was found guilty on charges of assault and robbery and was sentenced to ten-years imprisonment. In a related decision, the *Douro* was 'condemned as forfeited to Her Majesty for violation of the Merchant Shipping Act of 1854'. It was subsequently sold for £280.[24]

These decisions gratified Tryon. Concerned to demonstrate the navy's effectiveness in promoting law and order in the south Pacific, and fearful that harsh treatment of islanders could lead them to retaliate violently and indiscriminately, he had been disappointed by Sorensen's previous escape from justice and was pleased to see an example being made of him at last.

> It will not escape observers that the original charges were for evil conduct towards natives, but it is practically too often impossible to establish such charges in the eyes of the law, while such conduct leads too often to the death, at the hands of natives, of well disposed white men who subsequently visit the scene.[25]

46, 4 Dec. 1885, ADM 122/21. Tryon was destined to go down with his ship in the Mediterranean in 1893. J.K. Ware, *An Outline of Australian Naval History*, Canberra, 1976, p. 11.
23   *Brisbane Courier*, 3 April 1886; *Sydney Morning Herald*, 28 Dec. 1885; *Central Queensland Herald*, 16 Mar. 1933 (included in 'Australia's Maritime Heritage', a collection of newspaper articles by 'Junius', F. Rhodes, in Mitchell Library). The events are also referred to in German sources: Oertzen to Bismarck, 30 July, 10 Nov. 1885; Consul to Bismarck, 3 Sept. 1886, Reichskolonialamt records, Vol. 2335, Zentrales Staatsarchiv, Potsdam.
24   Musgrove to Lock, 1 Mar. 1886, ADM. 122/21; *Brisbane Courier*, 2, 3, 7, 8, 10 April 1886. For the judge's report on the case, see Mein to Colonial Secretary (Brisbane), 30 April 1887, enclosed in Foreign Office to US Ambassador (London), 19 Nov. 1915, Inwards Correspondence General 32/1916, Western Pacific High Commission.
25   Tryon to Admiralty, 21 May 1886, ADM 122/21.

Even so, he had a few misgivings, derived from an affronted sense of *noblesse oblige*, that businessmen of some standing such as Leslie, secretary of the Brighton Gas Company, and Cooper, consul for Portugal since 1868, should be involved in such an affair and yet escape prosecution. Leslie escaped that embarrassment by giving Queen's evidence against Sorensen, and Cooper did so because of the difficulty of obtaining sufficient evidence to convict him of conspiracy. 'For Cooper and Leslie' wrote Tryon, 'to escape scot free is a disgrace to civilisation in my opinion'.[26]

> I cannot but feel that if there were no Leslies and no Coopers there would be no Sorensens. Leslie and Cooper's cool deliberate actions in pursuit of gain appear to me to be such as to preclude the possibility of their being treated with any consideration and no pains in my opinion should be spared to repress such conduct.
>
> Sorensen has been punished for assault and robbery and I think that taking all circumstances into consideration ... Leslie and Cooper are greater criminals than even Sorensen and I trust that they will be made to feel the full power of the law.
>
> Conspiritors to remove the vessel beyond the range of the Pacific Island Acts, the selectors of the tools employed, men of education, holding some social position, are surely more culpable than the uneducated disgrace to humanity, their tool, Sorensen.[27]

Even so, Sorensen's conviction was scarcely an injustice, although the penalty was uncommonly severe for that time. For instance, he was in prison for two years longer than McNeil and Williams of the *Hopeful* who, in 1884, had been found guilty of murder whilst kidnapping off New Guinea.[28] Imprisonment also marked his final parting from his wife, although she may occasionally have visited him during his term behind bars.[29] Predictably, though, incarceration did little to reform him. He was released from Queensland's St. Helena prison in March 1894 and, over the next four decades, repeatedly yielded to the temptation to make a dishonest fortune, only exchanging violence for chicanery as a means of doing so.

During his imprisonment Sorensen had read a reference in Findlay's navigation directory to the existence of abundant copper deposits on the Rennell Islands in the Solomons. This was, in fact, an impossibility since the islands were composed

---

26 Tryon to Lock, 15 Oct. 1886; Tryon to Admiralty, 15 Oct. 1886; Crown Solicitor, memorandum, 29 Sept. 1886; Attorney General, 4 Oct. 1886, ADM 122/21. *Votes and Proceedings of the Legislative Assembly of Victoria* mentions both Cooper (1872, 2, blue book), and Leslie (1892–1893, 4, 382).
27 Tryon to Lock, 12 Aug. 1886, ADM 122/21.
28 Scarr, p. 157.
29 Ann Sorensen to Secretary of Navy, 4 Sept. 1886, Box 260, RG. 24, Records of Bureau of Naval Personnel.

of pure coral.[30] Nevertheless, on the strength of that belief, and rumours of gold elsewhere in the group—and possibly spurred by the knowledge that other entrepreneurs were also interested in Rennell—late in 1896 he attempted to interest certain Sydney speculators in a mining venture.[31] He failed there, as he also did at Victoria in British Columbia in mid-1897, but was soon to fare better in San Francisco.

He turned up there in July, reportedly wearing a ring with a pearl as large as a hazelnut and promoting an enterprise called The South Sea Commercial Company, which was designed to exploit the putative gold and copper resources of the Solomons. Pearling was also talked of. Even if Sorensen believed that minerals could be found, his scheme was fraudulent in its fulsome promise, in the assurances of success that drew authority from his acquaintance with the country and in the mineral samples—supposedly assaying as high as $US5,000 to the ton—that he presented to support his claims.[32] Nevertheless, the prospect he offered induced a group of businessmen, including E.B. Pond, an ex-mayor of San Francisco, to invest $US16,000 in the scheme. This was more than sufficient to enable him to purchase a 156-ton three-masted schooner named the *Sophia Sutherland*, to hire a skipper and to equip an expedition.[33] There could scarcely have been a better time for such a speculation. The Klondike gold rush had begun on 15 July, when a group of prospectors staggered off the steamer *Excelsior* at San Francisco 'carrying bulging suit cases, carpet valises, leather saddle bags, even cartons of jelly jars—all full of gold'. Ten days later, the steamer *Umatilla*, licensed to carry 290 passengers, sailed from San Francisco with 471 aboard, including the young Jack London, bound for Alaska.[34]

Even so, the lure of wealth allied to the romance of the South Seas, offered an attractively warm alternative to the Klondike. It led a number of young men both to support Sorensen's scheme financially and to sail with him. Already, on 25 February, a 101-strong colonising expedition of Utopians-on-the-make called The United Brotherhood of the South Sea Islands had sailed from San Francisco in the brigantine *Percy Edwards* bound for the Solomons via Fiji. If the failure of that venture, which was reported in San Francisco the following August, cost

---

30   Woodford to Escott (WPHC), 2 Sept. 1912, enclosed in Escott to Colonial Office, 22 Nov. 1912, CO 225/106 (2). Alexander G. Findlay, *A Directory for the Navigation of the Pacific Ocean*, London. The reference was not in the first edition, 1851; but was in the subsequent ones—1863, 1875, 1877, 1884.
31   Docker to WPHC, 23 Dec. 1896, Inwards Correspondence General 12/1897; Constable to WPHC, 3 Mar. 1897, 87/1897; Docker to WPHC, 12 Mar. 1897; Grien to WPHC, 11 Mar. 1897, 91/1897, Western Pacific High Commission (microfilm no. 593); Foreign Office to Colonial Office, 12 Feb. 1897, CO 225/53(2) (microfilm no. 2332).
32   Deposition of Alexander McLean, 11 Mar. 1911, p. 8, Sorensen v Sun New York Supreme Court, index reference 5917. Note: the records of this case are indexed under Sorensen (sic); *New York Sun*, 29 Mar. 1911.
33   *San Francisco Chronicle*, 28 July 1898.
34   Joyce Milton, *The Yellow Kids: foreign correspondents in the heyday of yellow journalism*, New York, 1989, p. 173; Franklin Walker, *Jack London and the Klondike: the genesis of an American writer*, San Marino, 1966, p. 49.

Sorensen any support it was not sufficient to scare off his backers or to deter a few 'clerks and mechanics' from leaving their jobs, handing over their savings and joining him.[35]

In all, the party numbered 15, and included a mining engineer. The captain was the formidable Alexander McLean. He was a man renowned along the Pacific coast for his skill as a mariner and seal hunter and was notorious for his readiness to engage in commerce beyond the fringe of the law, such as seal poaching in Russian waters and smuggling. He has been accorded a place in literary history as the model for Wolf Larsen, the masterful, well-read, brutal, unscrupulous Nietzschean superman in Jack London's novel *Sea Wolf*, which was published in 1904. William Randolph Hearst's *San Francisco Advertiser*, the exemplar of 'yellow press' journalism began—and promoted—that identification in 1905, when reporting an illegal voyage that McLean had made to the Bering Sea in the *Carmencita*. For his part, while admitting superficial similarities, such as their both being sailors and hunters, McLean subsequently denied having committed any of the murderous deeds attributed to Larsen, whose character was as much a product of London's own egoistic phantasy as of McLean's exploits. Incidentally, London had himself sailed in the *Sophia Sutherland* on a seal hunting trip in 1893, although Larsen's vessel *Ghost* is based not on her but on another of Mclean's commands, the *James Hamilton Lewis*.[36] As for Sorensen and McLean, they were two of a kind, in recklessness and self-assured opportunism, with Sorensen having an edge in duplicity and guile. He was to be fortunate, when that part of his character was revealed, that McLean was not really a Larsen.

The party sailed from San Francisco in the *Sophia Sutherland* on 3 September, ignoring the advice of the British Consul who, following recent instructions from the Foreign Office after the *Percy Edwards* fiasco, tried to dissuade them from going.[37] The *San Francisco Chronicle*, a more sedate journal than the *Advertiser*, observed that:

> Among the stores were large number of muskets, rifles, and pistols, besides a quantity of mining machinery ... . The crew and passengers

---

35 The *Percy Edwards* expedition is described in my paper '"Quixotic and Utopian": American adventurers in the South Pacific, 1897–1898', *Pacific Studies*, vol. 24, no. 1–2 (2001), pp. 39–62.
36 *San Francisco Examiner*, 15 June, 6, 7, 11 Sept. 1905; Earle Labor et al., *The Letters of Jack London*, Stanford, 1989, vol. 11, p. 492. For more subtle accounts of Larsen, see Carolyn Johnston, *Jack London—an American radical?* (Westport, Conn., 1984, pp. 83–84); Peter Murray, *The Vagabond Fleet: a chronicle of the North Pacific sealing schooner trade* (Victoria, B.C., 1988, pp. 142–143); Andrew Sinclair, *Jack: a biography of Jack London* (New York, 1977, p. 95); Franklin Walker, 'Afterword', in Jack London, *The Sea Wolf and Selected Stories* (New York, 1964, pp. 344–345); Dan McGillivray, personal communication. Despite errors of *Sea Wolf* identification, the following offer useful accounts of McLean and his ships: E.W. Wright (ed.), *Lewis and Dryden's Marine History of the Pacific Northwest* (New York, 1961 (first published), pp. 369, 425–428); Gordon Newell (ed.), *The H.W. McCurdy Marine History of the Pacific Northwest* (Seattle, 1966, pp. 63, 212, 232, 248).
37 Warburton to Salisbury, 14 Sept. 1897, CO 225/54(1).

> on the *Sophia Sutherland* are made of stern stuff, and a few Solomon islanders more or less will not be allowed to stand in the way of the daring spirits engaged in the venture.
>
> The *Sophia Sutherland* is provisioned for eighteen months … . The members of the expedition expect to remain on the islands for three years, and come back with more gold than the luckiest miners of the Klondike region … . While some explore Island mountains, others will devote their attention to fishing for pearl oysters. Two expert pearl divers accompanied the expedition, they will engage native talent to assist them. Others will devote their time to visiting the various islands of the group and trade with the natives.[38]

They reached Apia in Samoa a month later, and there they might have—should have—turned back, if McLean had heeded the forebodings of two men more familiar with Sorensen's nefarious history and character than anyone else he had met hitheto. One was William Churchill, the US consul to Samoa who, between 1883 and 1888, had travelled extensively in the south Pacific; the other was John Strasburg, a trading captain who, in 1886, as mate of the *Princess Louise*, had met the refugees from the *Albert* at Mono and Sorensen himself at Mioko. They both warned McLean that Sorensen was a dangerous person to be involved with, and was not to be trusted. Accordingly, he continued the voyage resolved to 'keep a sharp look out on Mr Sorensen' in order to avoid any repetition of the *Douro* roguery, but apparently unaware that he had already been severely hoaxed.[39]

After calling briefly at Suva in Fiji (25–29 October) to allow McLean to consult British officials about conditions in the Solomons, and to reassure them that his party was not intending to found a colony there, the *Sophia Sutherland* reached Tulagi in the Solomons on 8 November. There, another veteran of the Pacific, the resident commissioner, Charles Woodford, issued mining licences and again advised McLean to be wary of Sorensen. The vessel then left for Rennell. Naturally, no copper was found. Woodford recorded the story in 1912:

> Having visited the North West end of Rennell Island where he said a solid cliff of pure copper too hard to be blasted out by dynamite existed and failing to find it, he told his dupes that he must have mistaken the end of the island and that it was at the South East end. The S.E. end was visited with the same result and he then accounted for its absence by saying that it must have disappeared in an earthquake.

---

38   *San Francisco Chronicle*, 5 Sept. 1897.
39   McLean, deposition, pp. 14–19; Captain Strasburg, 'Trading in the South Seas', *The Lone Hand*, 1 Jan. 1914, p. 147; Joseph Theroux, 'William Churchill: a fractured life', *Hawaiian Journal of History*, vol. 29 (1995), pp. 97–123.

Sorensen's credibility was further weakened after attempts to find gold, which included sinking a shaft near a river on Makira, also proved abortive. It was altogether obliterated when after two months in the Solomons, during which time McLean prudently refused to allow Sorensen to take the steam launch to go pearling or trading, the *Sophia Sutherland* returned to Tulagi. It carried rock samples from 16 different localities, but the expedition's assayer found, after two days work, only the faintest traces of precious metal in them:

> the result of the assays showed only the presence of silver ranging from 0.15oz to 0.3oz per ton with a minute trace of gold in all. One other, the richest found, gave 0.44oz of silver per ton and 0.03oz of gold: the value of this sample was stated to be about 4/– per ton.

Chastened and bitter, the miners then turned angrily against Sorensen. He replied by producing a power of attorney fom the owners in San Francisco 'empowering him to take possession of the vessel and cargo and to start trading in the Solomons', but one of the party then countered by presenting a document of a later date rescinding Sorensen's one.[40]

At that point, Woodford and McLean, fearing that Sorensen was in danger of being lynched, agreed that he should leave the party and take the next steamer to Sydney. Accordingly, McLean took him to the adjacent islet of Gavutu, leaving £5 with Woodford to pay for his fare on the *Titus* which was due shortly (and which reached Sydney on 5 February). It is likely that the two men who took the deceiver ashore gave him a beating before leaving him to seek shelter in a coal hut.[41]

For two more months the *Sophia Sutherland* explored rock formations on Nggela and Guadalcanal, until 19 May. Then, with nearly everyone suffering severely from malaria, McLean turned for the Golden Gate, via Samoa, but leaving behind four of the party, who had decided to find their own ways home. Perhaps they were wise to do so. After battling headwinds and an outbreak of scurvy, which killed four men and incapacitated all the others except McLean, the *Sophia Sutherland* put into Apia on 11 May. There McLean told his story to L.W. Osborn, Churchill's successor, and L.W. Chambers, the chief justice. The first news of the debacle reached San Francisco on 2 June.

---

40 Woodford, 'Report on Solomon Islands, Jan. 1897 – Mar. 1898', enclosed in WPHC to CO, 28 Sept. 1898, CO 225/55(1); Woodford to Hunt, 2 Sept. 1912, A1/1, 12/21196, Australian Archives; Woodford to Escott, 2 Sept. 1912, enclosed in Escott to CO, 22 Nov. 1912, CO 225/106(2); Woodford to WPHC, 14 July 1913, CO 225/119(2) (microfilm no. 2938, p. 666); *San Francisco Chronicle*, 2 June 1898.
41 McLean, deposition, pp. 41, 45, 115, 130; Woodford to Hunt (also to WPHC), 2 Sept. 1912; Woodford to WPHC, 30 Dec. 1913, Inwards Correspondence General, 494/14, WPHC; *New York Sun*, 16 July 1908, 29 Mar. 1911.

After two months in Apia and with a crew that now contained only one other member from the original complement, McLean put to sea once more, on 9 July. He reached San Francisco on 31 August. Among the crew, reported the *Chronicle*, were 'two members of the *Percy Edwards* expedition. They were in full sympathy with the folks of the *Sophia Sutherland* as they, too, had left home to follow a phantom.'[42]

Sorensen, meanwhile, having sailed from Newcastle, New South Wales, as boatswain aboard the coal carrier *Bedford*, had arrived in San Francisco on 19 June. He was still talking—but now to more sceptical hearers—of the mineral wealth of the Solomons, and also of how he had first been cruelly mistreated and then abandoned by McLean, and of how, from the deck of the *Titus*, he had last seen the *Sophia Sutherland* lying wrecked near Oscar Svensen's trading station at Marau Sound on Guadalcanal. In fact, the vessel had been heaved over for careening and a slight mishap had put it over too far and it had taken on water—but that was easily remedied. Prudently, Sorensen left town a few days before McLean's return.[43]

For the next decade Sorensen disappears from historical view. That period is like an interval in the drama of his life. In Act II he would revisit his past, and his past would revisit him. Between acts, when he may even have been making an honest living, he was also bombarding the US navy with his fraudulent pension claims.[44] And he remained an incorrigible commercial adventurer. That is the guise in which he next came to public notice. In July 1908, taking his place in an enduring succession of fabulists, he arrived in New York and announced his intention of organising a company to recover gold from the *General Grant*, a Britain-bound vessel from Australia that had sunk in the Auckland Islands, south of New Zealand, in 1866. The 24th-place holder in the ignoble line of descent of *General Grant* schemers was, incidentally, convicted of fraud by a New Zealand court in February 1998 (although the conviction was later quashed on appeal). For his part, Sorensen had a map purporting to show the whereabouts of the wreck (which has never been precisely located) and claimed that it held $20 million worth of gold bars and minted guineas.[45]

Unfortunately for Sorensen, a nemesis was at hand in the form of William Churchill, the former consul. For the past six years he had been on the staff of the *New York Sun* newspaper. Unwilling to see people risk lives or money

---

42 Osborn to Department of State, US Consular Despatches, Apia, T 27, microfilm roll 24, National Archives; *Examiner*, 2 Sept. 1898; *San Francisco Call*, 2 June 1898; *San Francisco Chronicle*, 2 June, 28 July, 2 Sept. 1898; *New York Sun*, 29 Mar. 1911.
43 McLean, Deposition, pp. 107–110; *San Francisco Call*, 21 June 1898; *San Francisco Chronicle*, 1 Sept. 1898.
44 Neils (sic) P. Sorensen, pension file, NAVY SO 45548, National Archives US.
45 Keith Eunson, *The Wreck of the General Grant*, Wellington, 1974; *Sunday Star-Times*, 29 Jan. 1995, 22 Feb. 1998; R v Baxter, *New Zealand Law Reports: Court of Appeal*, 1998, pp. 144–158.

in the scheme, Churchill promptly provided information for a story that was published in that journal denouncing Sorensen and recounting the history of the *Douro* and *Sophia Sutherland* expeditions.[46] Sorensen replied with a hundred thousand dollar libel claim.

The case came to court in March 1911. Sorensen's past was raked over in detail and reported on at length and, in the proceedings, McLean at last had his chance of revenge. Then living in Canada, and reluctant to enter the United States lest he be arrested for having taken the *Carmencita* out of San Francisco in 1904 without clearance and under a Mexican flag, he gave evidence by deposition on behalf of the *Sun*, affirming Sorensen's record of chicanery. In the course of this he also rebutted strenuous efforts to discredit his testimony by identifying him with the vicious Wolf Larsen. His evidence was supported by that of Churchill and of William Chambers, who was now practicing law in Washington. The jury, though, while not impressed by Sorensen's disclaimers of sharp practice, was not indifferent to the niceties of the rules of evidence. Churchill had left Samoa before the *Sophia Sutherland* called there the second time; most of what he knew of the events in the Solomons had been acquired from Chambers, who had learned of them from the 'beachcombing' residents of Apia. Besides, the article contained slight inaccuracies regarding the *Douro* voyage. Consequently, much of the *Sun* report was deemed to be based on hearsay. After a hearing that lasted a week, the jury divided on the matter. Six jurors considered that the published statements were justified while the other six held out for a verdict in favour of Sorensen, though only wishing to award him nominal damages of six cents, on the grounds that the *Sun* had failed to furnish technically acceptable proof for all its assertions of Sorensen's misconduct. A new hearing was, accordingly, scheduled for as soon as Sorensen, the plaintiff, elected. The *Sun*, which reported the proceedings under the heading 'Sorensen of the South Seas Loses', intended to offer additional testimony. In the event, it was not obliged to for, in September, the parties agreed to discontinue the action. For Sorensen, New York had proved to be no more obliging than the Solomons. He was likewise unsuccessful with another *General Grant* scheme which he tried to promote in New Zealand in 1912.[47]

If not treasure, then real estate, and again the Solomons, were the elements of Sorensen's next formula for financial gain. In 1911 and 1912, from an address in Dunedin, New Zealand, Sorensen resumed contact with his old business partner T.G. Leslie of Melbourne. He proposed to buy Leslie out of any claim he might have to the ownership of Mono or Treasury Island, near south-west Bougainville. Sorensen had entered into a form of purchase of the island with the

---

46   *New York Sun*, 16 July 1908; Robert W. Ritchie, Deposition, Sorensen v Sun.
47   McLean 'Deposition'; *New York Sun*, 29 Mar. 1911; Eunson, pp. 141–143; Fergus B. McLaren, *The Auckland Islands: their eventful history*, Wellington, 1948, p. 100.

chief Mulekupa when he called there *en route* to Cooktown in the *Douro* on 17 November 1885. He did so on his own account, and not as the shipowner's agent, as Leslie maintained. Subsequently, probably about the time of Sorensen's trial, Leslie apparently obtained possession of the log of the *Douro* and other papers from Sorensen's wife. About 1905 he apparently handed them over to a colonial official named Oliphant, through whom he hoped to obtain a title of ownership, but no such document had been issued when Sorensen resurfaced. So Leslie tried again to have his tenuous interest in Treasury formally recognised. Again it was to no avail; no trace or even record of the papers he said he had given to Oliphant was to be found in colonial files in Fiji or in the Solomons; no such purchase had ever been registered. In any case, as Woodford noted, Mulekupa had no authority to dispose of the ownership of Treasury, while at the same time 'British subjects were not permitted to acquire land in the unsettled portions of the Western Pacific'. Other germane points cited by Woodford, who knew Treasury well, were that not only had the Royal Navy had a coaling station there since 1884, but that, in 1886, a German trading company had bought some land there: consequently, the whole island could not all have been for sale, or have been sold, in 1885.[48]

Still, Sorensen did not despair of establishing an independent claim to Treasury. If an extract copied from the log is to be believed, a paper existed 'signed and understood by [Mulekupa] and three other natives that the whole Group belong[s] to Capt. N.P. Sorensen and no other man'.[49] As early as 1890, while in prison, he had asserted his ownership, and had attempted to profit from it, by appealing to the US Government to annex Treasury. It could, he said, provide 'safe anchorage for ships of the heaviest armament'.[50] That request was ignored, but, in 1913, Sorensen revived the issue, thereby generating a round of correspondence that endured until 1930, and which established that the arguments marshalled against Leslie's claim applied also to his own. But, being more persistent, in June 1913, Sorensen visited the Solomons again. This time he was aboard the regular steamer *Mindini* from Sydney, but was no more welcome there than in the past. Woodford, who was still Resident Commissioner, met him on arrival and told him that, unless he returned forthwith, a deportation order would be issued against him.

Sorensen continued with the *Mindini* to the port of Faisi in the Shortland Islands. There he went ashore, apparently intending to go across to Treasury to refresh

---

48   Woodford to External Affairs, 2 Sept. 1912, enclosed with Leslie to Hunt, 26 July, 5 Aug., 14 Aug. 1912, and Sorensen to Leslie, 12 July 1912, and Hunt to WPHC, 30 July 1912, and WPHC to External Affairs, 25 Sept. 1912, A1/1, 12/21196 Australian Archives (much of this correspondence is also in CO 225/106(2), microfilm reel 2929, pp. 801 et seq.); Woodford to WPHC, 14 July 1913, Inwards Correspondence General, 1479/13, WPHC.
49   Law to WPHC, 2 Oct. 1913, 1972/13, WPHC.
50   Baggs to Wharton, 28 July 1890, enclosing Sorensen to Harris, 10 April 1890, RG 24 Records of Bureau of Naval Personnel, Box 249, National Archives US.

his ideas on its development prospects, but the district officer ordered him to re-board the ship. Reluctantly, he complied. Even so, Woodford wished to prevent any further visits and, considering Sorensen's presence in the Solomons 'dangerous to peace and good order', issued a prohibition order against him. Despite representations on Sorensen's behalf by the US ambassador in London, that action was not only upheld by the Foreign Office but the order was renewed in 1916.[51]

A further approach in 1925 to the British prime minister, Stanley Baldwin, complaining about the order and also outlining a grandiose development plan for Treasury brought no more satisfaction. Nor did a similar proposal, which was put foward in 1929 on behalf of a company called United States Treasury Islands Incorporated, of which Sorensen was president—a duplicitous designation, even if it was not untrue. Sorensen at that time was described as 'a widower, about eighty years old, and a retired sea captain, living in Brooklyn, N.Y.' An enquiry by J.P. Morgan and Company, on behalf of the British consul, showed that his 'company has no bank account, its present capital is nominal and the account is not found active in a credit sense'.[52]

Niels Peter Sorensen, also known as Peter Saunders, of 991 Flushing Ave, Brooklyn, New York, was admitted to King's County Hospital on 3 February 1935 suffering from 'senile psychosis arterio sclerotic type' and died there five days later.[53] He was buried in the City Cemetery. His had scarcely been a noble life, though it had undoubtedly been useful in providing employment for the clerks who recorded his escapades, and helps justify the efforts of colonial authorities to bring 'law and order' to the south-west Pacific. He was hardly, as Peter Corris describes him, a 'psychopath'; yet, he truly earned the 'notorious character' and 'evil reputation' proclaimed by Woodford and his successor.[54] Of the *Sophia Sutherland* episode, Woodford commented 'the most charitable explanation of his proceedings is to suppose that he was mad'.[55] Certainly, it would seem prudent to say 'Amen' to the prayer 'from Niels Peter Sorensen and his like may we be protected'.

---

51 Woodford to WPHC, 14 July 1913, and 'Affidavit to ground Prohibition Order', 14 July 1913, 1475/13; Law to WPHC, 2 Oct. 1913, 1972/13; Woodford to WPHC, 30 Dec. 1913, 494/14; FO to US Ambassador, Aug. 1914, 2596/14, WPHC.
52 Schachne to Baldwin, 24 Mar. 1925, 1837/25; Ashley to WPHC, 15 Feb. 1930, and enclosures, 202/30. WPHC.
53 Death register, Brooklyn, 1935, no. 4002, Peter Sorensen(sic), Feb. 8, age 90.
54 Woodford to WPHC, 14 July 1913, 1479/13; Barnett, affidavit, 14 Jan. 1916, 421/16, WPHC.
55 Woodford to Escott, 2 Sept. 1912, enclosed in Escott to CO 22 Nov. 1912, CO 225/106(2); Peter Corris, *Passage, Port and Plantation: a history of Solomon Islands labour migration, 1870–1914*, Melbourne, 1973, p. 102.

6. John Strasburg (1856–1924): A plain sailor

John Strasburg's is not a conspicuous name in the maritime history of the Pacific. Hitherto it has rated barely more than a footnote in the literature. Yet, he is still a significant figure. This is not on account of any magnitude of achievement, for any dramatic acts of villainy or, indeed, for establishing a notable claim on the attention of his contemporaries by any other means. Rather, it is mainly because—unusual among his kind—he generated sufficient written records to reveal his participation in the busy and burgeoning commercial life of the Pacific islands between the 1880s and World War I. With a career that ranged from Tonga to New Guinea, and that lasted for over 30 years, he thus emerges as an accessible—and clearly identifiable—representative of an important, but relatively reticent and historically under-studied, class of people. That is, the seafarers who maintained the shipping networks that sustained European interests and activities in the islands during the colonial heyday; and, conversely, who were drawing island peoples into ever closer contact with Europeans, and so into increasing dependence on the goods and services that they could provide. While the lives of missionaries, merchants, adventurers and administrators in the islands remained strongly linked to the worlds beyond the horizon whence they had come, those of their indigenous clients, the capsule of their traditional self-sufficiency cracked if not yet broken, were also tending in the same direction.

By the middle of the nineteenth century, traders of diverse kinds—whalers and other predators of natural resources being prominent among them—had located virtually every serviceable anchorage in the Pacific. Regular mercantile operations were developing rapidly. 'Beach communities' of displaced Europeans had formed at commonly frequented ports.[1] By the 1880s, from Sydney to San Francisco, from Auckland to Honolulu, from Valparaiso to Guam, and at various places in between, the Pacific shipping news had become a vital item in the local newspapers and in harbourside gossip. Most of the people who operated the vessels involved in this maritime efflorescence have, though, slipped into irreversible obscurity. That John Strasburg stands out from the crowd and becomes available for an extended discussion, one which also throws a rare light on the enterprises in which he was involved, is fortuitous.

It is largely due to two instances of self assertion on his part. In the first case, he published two retrospective magazine articles about trading voyages to the

---

1   Caroline Ralston, *Grass Huts and Warehouses: Pacific beach communities of the nineteenth century*, Canberra, 1977.

Solomon Islands in the early 1880s.² In the second, he entered into a dispute concerning his service during the Australian military occupation of German New Guinea in 1914. This affair not only produced a voluminous correspondence but culminated in a parliamentary committee of enquiry.³ From these records, supplemented by meagre fragments of information from other sources, essential biographical details may be extracted. A picture of the man himself also emerges: energetic and enterprising at first, but eventually frustrated, broke and disappointed. Sadly, his was—and is—a not uncommon life trajectory. Nor is it one reserved to mariners, although it is difficult to avoid the impression that it was disproportionately so. Their's has traditionally been a precarious occupation, despite the success of some, such as Robert Towns, who prospered in the south-west Pacific sandalwood trade of the mid-nineteenth century.⁴

John Strasburg (originally Axel Johan Leonard Stridsburg) was born at Soderkoping, near Stockholm, in Sweden, in 1856, but grew up in the north of England. He was the son of a builder, whose name he also gives as John, and his wife Elizabeth. Little more is known of his early years, but he seems to have set out on a seafaring life at a young age, having served an apprenticeship on a north of England collier. In 1871 he became a naturalised British citizen. That procedure was repeated in Sydney, Australia, on 28 October 1892. Possibly it was required because the original papers of citizenship had been lost and he needed such evidence to obtain the pilot's certificate for Sydney and Newcastle, which was issued two weeks later.⁵

Meanwhile, Strasburg had resurfaced in the historical record in Fiji in 1883. This time it was as mate of the 69-ton fore and aft schooner *Sea Breeze*, which had been engaged in recruiting Melanesian plantation labourers since March 1882.⁶ According to the local newspapers, the vessel made three such voyages in 1883, although Strasburg says that he sailed on only one of them. With a crew of 33, and with 87 time-expired labourers to be returned to their homes, the *Sea Breeze* left Suva for the Solomons on the first of these trips on 1 April, at the end of the three-month-long hurricane season. Its other departure dates that year, in which the fleet of 16 vessels brought a total of 2,221 labourers to Fiji, were 5 August and 24 November.⁷

---

2   Captain [John] Strasburg, 'Trading in the South Seas', *Lone Hand*, Jan. 1914, pp. 117, 147–148; 'A Labor Recruiting Voyage in the Solomon Islands', *Lone Hand*, November 1918, pp. 508–510.
3   'Report on the Claims of Captain J. Strasburg for a War Gratuity', in *Journals of the Senate, Parliament of Australia* (*Senate Report*), 1922, No. S.1., pp. vii, 14.
4   Dorothy Shineberg, *They Came for Sandalwood: a study of the sandalwood trade in the south-west Pacific, 1830–1865*, Melbourne, 1967.
5   *Senate Report*, pp. 3, 12; *Sydney Morning Herald* (*SMH*), 6 May 1919; Strasburg to Naval Secretary, 1 Mar. 1915, National Archives of Australia (NAA), A518, G822/1/3; Strasburg, death certificate.
6   *Fiji Times*, 18, 29 Mar., 10 May, 5 July, 9 Sept. 1882.
7   *Fiji Times*, 2 April, 2, 20 June, 25 July, 1, 15 Aug. 1883, 9 Jan. 1884; *Suva Times*, 28 July, 1 Aug., 8, 14 Sept., 14, 28 Nov. 1883; Strasburg, 'Labor Recruiting', p. 508.

6. John Strasburg (1856–1924): A plain sailor

By his own account, contained in an imaginatively embellished memoir, Strasburg arrived in Fiji from Europe early in 1883, and quickly launched himself into the shipping industry servicing the burgeoning commerce of the south-west Pacific.[8] The pace of development had picked up with the advent of the big German firm of Godeffroy, which had begun operations in Samoa in 1857 and, in the mid-1860s began purchasing land for plantations, and importing island labour to work them. At about the same time, other would-be estate holders were becoming interested in Fiji. By 1874 the number of foreign settlers there exceeded 2,000. Such were the problems of law and order attendant on this growth that the British Government—reluctantly—found itself impelled to take responsibility for governing the group. As had happened in New Zealand 30 years before, annexation stimulated further immigration. That, in turn, brought an expansion of planting and further demand for auxiliary services. In 1879, when European settler numbers had reached 2,671, people from India began to be introduced to Fiji. This was done in order to meet a surging demand for plantation labourers that could not be satisfied from generous but limited Pacific island sources.[9] At the same time—in accordance with government policy—the Indians helped cushion the disruptive impact of settler activity on the traditional way of life of the native Fijians (*taukei*) by excusing them from plantation labour. In a further major response to the increasing scale and complexity of the European (*kai vulagi*) presence, in 1882 the capital of the colony was transferred from the confines of Levuka on the island of Ovalau to the more spacious and accessible location of Suva on the south coast of Viti Levu.

It was probably there that Strasburg landed in Fiji a year later. He promptly joined the *Sea Breeze*, captained by an experienced master, James Taylor, and set out to try his hand at recruiting. This was a precarious business. To the inherent, and frequently realised, perils of the sea was to be added the possibility of clashes with islanders when landing returned labourers or collecting new ones. Caution was always necessary, but, in the event, it was often insufficient. Strasburg spells this out in his *Sea Breeze* narrative, although with regard less to any experience of his own than to the massacre of the crew of the Fiji-based *Borealis* which had been attacked at Malaita in 1880.[10]

Contrary to his statement that he embarked 'in the beginning of 1883', it is more likely that Strasburg sailed not on the first of the *Sea Breeze*'s three-month long voyages for that year, but on the second one. The itinerary he gives for

---

8   Strasburg, 'Labor Recruiting', p. 508.
9   *Fiji Times*, 9 Jan. 1884.
10 Strasburg, 'Labor Recruiting', p. 509. For the *Borealis*, see Peter Corris, *Passage, Port and Plantation: a history of Solomon Islands labour migration, 1870–1914*, Melbourne, 1973, pp. 33, 57. Strasburg claims to have witnessed the reprisal that quickly followed the *Borealis* attack but the dates make that impossible. He also invents a story of a punitive raid by a naval vessel.

the vessel's movements in the Solomons does not accord at all closely with that given for the first voyage by Taylor. Thus, Strasburg offers Santa Ana, Malaita (where in Uru harbour he mused on the *Borealis* attack), Mono (where he met the flamboyant chief Mulekupa), Buka, and then back to Santa Ana for three weeks for repairs before returning to Fiji. Taylor, in contrast, reports visiting Efate in the New Hebrides before going to the Solomons, where he called at Nggela, Guadalcanal, Isabel, New Georgia, Choiseul, Mono, Bougainville and Buka, before returning—without incident—to Fiji.[11] Besides, if Strasburg was on the second voyage (the exact track of which cannot, unfortunately, be ascertained) that would give credibility to his claim to have been in the Solomons when the survivors of the labour ship *Stanley* were rescued from Indispensible Reef, where they had been marooned for two months, by the trading schooner *Venture*. The timing fits better, for that dramatic set of events occurred during July and August.[12] Alternatively, it is not inconceivable that Strasburg was on the third voyage of the *Sea Breeze* rather than the second, and not 'early' but *late* in 1883 (and that he merely 'borrowed' the story he tells of that vessel's being forestalled in going to the rescue of the *Stanley* by learning of the *Venture*'s intervention, in order to add colour to his own narrative). Favouring this hypothesis is the fact that the master's report of the third cruise gives a route not too unlike that given by Strasburg: Santa Ana, Malaita, Buka, Malaita, Santa Ana.[13] Why such uncertainty about which voyage? Perhaps Strasburg's memory was fading 35 years after the event? Even so, there is no reason to doubt that he did sail on a recruiting voyage in the *Sea Breeze*, or to question his statement that afterwards he never saw the ship or its captain again.

After two more long trips, the second of which extended to the islands at the eastern end of New Guinea, the *Sea Breeze*, bound for Sydney, sailed from Levuka in ballast on 28 March 1885—and vanished. No sign of it was ever found.[14]

Likewise in 1885, Strasburg, rather more fortunate than his erstwhile shipmates, entered the colony of New South Wales, where he would eventually settle. On this occasion he arrived on the *Ly-ee-moon*, probably from Melbourne. This vessel, built for the China opium trade and used as a blockade runner during the American civil war, had been employed by the Australian Steam Navigation Company on the Melbourne–Sydney–Brisbane run since 1876. Occasionally, it

---

11   Strasburg, 'Labor Recruiting', p. 508; *Suva Times*, 28 July 1883.
12   Strasburg, 'Labor Recruiting', pp. 508–509; correspondence re R v McMurdo and Davies, *Fiji Royal Gazette*, 1884, pp. 203–226; *Suva Times*, 10, 20 Sept. 1884; William Wawn, *The South Sea Islanders and the Queensland Labour Trade*, (1893), Peter Corris (ed.), Canberra, 1973, pp. 330–331; Hector Holthouse, *Cannibal Cargoes: the story of the Australian blackbirders*, Sydney, 1986, pp. 165–169.
13   *Suva Times*, 27 Feb. 1884.
14   *Suva Times*, 26 Mar., 17 Sept., 8 Oct. 1884; *Fiji Times*, 7 Jan., 4 Feb., 1 April, 27 June, 27 July 1885.

also relieved the *Gungha* on the regular Sydney–Fiji run, but there is no record of it having done so in 1885. It was lost off the south coast of New South Wales on 30 May 1886.[15]

Soon after reaching Sydney, Strasburg states that he signed on as mate aboard the 100-ton *Princess Louise*, under Captain Sam Craig, bound for a trading voyage to the Solomon Islands. In 1891 Craig, then mate of the *Sandfly*, was killed at Makira by a returned labourer in revenge for some of his fellows who had died in New Caledonia.[16] According to an article Strasburg published in the *Lone Hand* in 1914, he sailed on the *Princess Louise* voyage in 1884. This would have meant a trip that lasted from 25 June 1884 to 7 January 1885.[17] But, in addition to the contradictory statement that he did not reach New South Wales until 1885, internal evidence suggests otherwise. Strasburg mentions that during the voyage the *Princess Louise* rescued the crew of the German-crewed, Samoa-based labour ship *Haapai*, which had run aground near Fauro in the Bougainville Strait, and took them to Mioko, the Deutsche-Handels und Plantagen-Gessellschaft trading post at the Duke of York Islands—and that while there he met the piratical Niels Peter Sorensen. These claims, though, relate to events that occurred in 1885. Consequently, to have participated in any of them Strasburg must have been on the next voyage of the *Princess Louise*, which lasted from 21 March to 14 December 1885.[18] Again, faulty recall presumably explains his factual error about the order of events.

In the Solomons the *Princess Louise* traded principally for coconuts and the oil derived therefrom, plus some bêche-de-mer and pearl shell, which it obtained in return for 'trade goods'. These Strasburg describes as being

> about the most weird assortment of goods ever brought together in one ship—colored beads of every variety; porpoise teeth (which pass for currency among the island natives); Jews' harps; prints of various gaudy patterns, but mostly of the variety known as 'Turkey Red'; hoop iron; knives of all sorts; tomahawks and axes; "='Tower' muskets (worth about 3s. 6d.), powder and shot; tobacco (of a particularly vile kind); clay pipes; calico; fish-hooks and lines; medicines; arm rings of porcelain; zinc mirrors; and, last of all, live dogs.

The last, he explains, were to be used for hunting wild pigs. But the method of collecting them 'was more ingenious than creditable':

---

15 Certificate of Naturalization, *Senate Report*, p. 12; Jack Loney, *Australian Shipwrecks*, vol. 3 (1871–1900), Geelong, pp. 163–164; *Fiji Times*, 21 May 1880, 5, 19 April, 13 May 1882.
16 *SMH*, 23 Jan. 1891; Dorothy Shineberg, *The People Trade: Pacific Island laborers and New Caledonia, 1865–1930*, Honolulu, 1999, pp. 89; Judith Bennett, *Wealth of the Solomons: a history of a Pacific archipelago, 1800–1978*, Honolulu, 1987, p. 394; Corris, *Passage*, p. 68.
17 Strasburg, 'Trading', p. 117; *SMH*, 25 June 1884, 8 Jan. 1885.
18 Strasburg, 'Trading', p. 117; *SMH*, 21 Mar., 14 Dec. 1885; 'Sorensen'.

On the return voyage to Sydney all the spare corners of the ship were filled with cocoanuts, and when the trader moored in Wooloomooloo Bay, the usual place, hundreds of small boys came on board and inquired for cocoanuts. They were told that if they brought a dog on board they would get three cocoanuts. Where the boys got the dogs the traders never inquired, but they got them; and it was quite a common thing for a trading schooner to leave Sydney with 150 dogs barking farewells.

It made for a lucrative exchange, even allowing for literary exaggeration:

[For each dog] the natives paid ten cockatoos, those usually sold as South American birds, at any price up to £5 a-piece: but the traders had a set price of 10s each at the Sydney market. So a stolen live dog brought a trader £5 cash on his return to Australia. And £5 for three cocoanuts is profitable trade.

In words that should strike a sympathetic chord with anyone perplexed by the latter day widespread—and commonly illegal—trade in exotic and endangered species, he comments 'the thing I never could understand was the unfailing demand for these green cockatoos'.[19]

With that voyage completed, the record of Strasburg's career becomes meagre for most of the next 20 years. It can be glimpsed only in fragments of information that resemble reported sightings of rare animals or of wanted criminals 'on the run'. A consistent feature of them, though, is that he is now in full command of a trading vessel. He was issued with an ocean-going master's ticket (OM 14) in Fiji on 13 August 1887 and in November he was reported there in charge of the 66-ton schooner *John Hunt*.[20] Formerly owned by the Methodist mission, this vessel, which had been employed—among much else—to make an annual three-month visit from Fiji to the Methodist mission in New Britain, was sold as a wreck in 1884. It was subsequently salvaged, and then operated by Henry Cave and Company of Levuka in the recruiting trade (in which they also controlled several other ships, including the *Sea Breeze*). In 1884 the company procured labourers at a cost of £17 2s 6d per head, exclusive of government charges and commission, which would be included in the price eventually paid for them by employers.[21] But Strasburg did not remain long in the company's employ.

Two years later, in 1889, when he next appears, it is as master of the 588-ton barque *Coulnakyle* out of Newcastle, New South Wales, carrying coal and general cargo for the Colonial Sugar Refining Company. 'After discharging which',

---

19 Strasburg, 'Trading', pp. 117, 147.
20 Strasburg, 'Log of the *Federal*: Sydney–New Britain–Sydney, 11 April – 14 Sept. 1912', Mitchell Library, MS, A1475; Strasburg to Naval Secretary, 1 Mar. 1915; Strasburg to Collector of Customs, 2 Nov. 1887, National Archives of Fiji (NAF), Colonial Secretary's Office (CSO), Vol. 14, 1887/2859.
21 *Fiji Times*, 1 Feb. 1882, 12 Mar., 10, 28 May 1884, 7, 31 Jan. 1885; *Suva Times*, 27 Feb., 12 Mar. 1884.

reports the *Fiji Times*, 'she proceeds to Tonga and the Eastward Islands [that is, Wallis and Samoa], where she takes a full cargo of copra for Europe'.[22] Then, in 1897, he is mentioned in a news report from Tonga. 'We have yet one more buyer in our copra market. Captain Strasburg, late of the *Meg Merrilies*, now acting in that capacity for Lever Bros., Ltd., of Sunlight Soap fame'.[23] Once commanded by the lightly scrupled Finlay McLiver on behalf of Charles Hennings and Co of Fiji, the *Meg Merrilies* had long been a stalwart of the labour trade, since at least 1882, but about 1895 it was transferred to the then flourishing Tongan copra trade.[24] Strasburg's association with the *Coulnakyle*—if not that with the *Meg Merrilies*, for Levers did not open their Sydney factory until 1900—suggests that by the late 1880s, he had made Australia his home, even if he did not spend a lot of time there. In June 1893, when he married Mary Dolling at St John's Church of England at Darlinghurst in Sydney, he gave his address as Darlinghurst. The couple had two children: a daughter, Florence Mary, born in August 1894 and a son, John Leonard, born in August 1897. The latter's birth certificate notes that his father was 'away in Samoa' at the time.[25] There, two months later, Strasburg encountered the by now notorious Sorensen for a second time.

With that, Strasburg again largely disappears from historical view for several years, except for numerous tantalising will-o'-the-wisp sightings of him. He was again in Samoa in 1899; after which he reportedly worked for the Australasian New Hebrides Company; and then served as master of the government yacht *Lahloo* in the British Solomon Islands.[26] But research has yielded no details on these matters.

When Strasburg next appears at all clearly, the principle focus of his maritime orientation has shifted markedly from that of his earlier years. It is no longer eastwards to Fiji but northwards to German New Guinea. There, early in 1904, he became master of the schooner *Monantha*, recruiting labour for Octave Mouton of Kinigunan plantation near Rabaul. It was a position he held for 18 months, until the *Monantha* was wrecked off Buka and his employment terminated. The mishap, though, did not deter him from practising his trade (in 1909 he was master of *La Carbine*, when it was used by the government for a punitive expedition to the Admiralty group), or from risking his own capital in business ventures in what he believed to be 'the most valuable [islands] in the Pacific'. One writer has identified him as a founder 'of the New Britain Corporation, established in Sydney in 1907', but by his own account Strasburg's investing centred more certainly on the island of Bougainville.[27] Geographically the most

---

22 *Fiji Times*, 20, 23 Nov., 11 Dec. 1889, 29 Mar. 1890.
23 *Fiji Times*, 24 April 1897.
24 *Fiji Times*, 23 Dec. 1882, 6 Nov. 1895.
25 Information summary, by courtesy of Australian Dictionary of Biography.
26 Strasburg to Naval Secretary, 1 Mar. 1915.
27 Peter Biskup (ed.), *The New Guinea Memoirs of Jean Baptiste Octave Mouton*, Canberra, 1974, p. 130.

northerly of the Solomon group, Bougainville (with Buka) had been frequented by labour traders since the 1880s but was late in attracting more intensive forms of commerce. The first European settlers, Catholic missionaries, arrived only in 1901. Then, planting interests, British ones prominent among them, began acquiring land there along the fertile north-east coast in 1912.[28]

In March of that year Strasburg bought into such a syndicate and, the following month, together with his partners (C.G. Piggott, H. Howard, A.E. Kendall, and C.G. Banko) he left Sydney as commander of the auxiliary brigantine *Federal*, the company's vessel, to begin the new venture. They travelled via Rabaul, Kavieng and Buka before, on 25 May, apparently on Strasburg's recommendation, coming to Numanuma, north of the small administrative centre at Kieta, founded in 1905. (The trading ship *Ripple* had been attacked and its captain, Alexander Ferguson, and three of his complement were killed at Numanuma in August 1880, thereby attracting a severe reprisal raid by the chief Gorai from the Shortland Islands). After Piggott and his fellow passengers had been ashore to look at the land in which they were interested, Strasburg took the *Federal* to Aropa, south of Kieta, where a Dane named Peter Hansen was clearing land. There he picked up 38 labourers for return to Hernsheim's station at Rabaul. Turning for the north, he stopped again at Numanuma. Piggott, Banco and Howard then left the vessel and began work. With the aid of 56 local labourers, they too set about clearing land while two Chinese carpenters erected a prefabricated house for them. These tasks were under way when, on 1 June, August Döllinger, the district officer, arrived in the steam launch *Buka* from Kieta to inspect and approve the project. The following day, with the boundaries marked, he supervised the formal purchase of 300 hectares of land from the indigenous owners for 250 marks, plus one mark for each of the 137 mature coconut trees growing on it.

Trading on behalf of the company and bringing supplies for Numanuma, Strasburg made two more trips in the *Federal* to Rabaul over the next couple of months before being despatched to Sydney to sell the vessel. The company, it seems, was foundering, both financially and because of personal divisions. Besides, Piggott, the managing director, deemed the *Federal* to be too big for the company's needs. Unfortunately for Strasburg, this also meant that his services as master were no longer required. After an arduous 30-day passage from Kieta, one made more difficult by a mutinous engineer who allegedly tried to wreck the ship for the sake of the insurance money, he was shorebound. At least, that is, until the outbreak of World War I meant that his familiarity with the waters of German New Guinea came once again to be valued by an

---

28   Hugh Laracy, '"Imperium in Imperio"? The Catholic Church in Bougainville', in Anthony J. Regan and Helga M. Griffin (eds), *Bougainville Before the Conflict*, Canberra, 2005, p. 126; Laracy, '1914: changing the guard at Kieta', Ibid., p. 140.

employer. In this instance it would be the Australian navy although, as with the Numanuma venture, Strasburg would again find that his expertise earned him scant reward.[29]

Responding to Germany's invasion of Belgium, Britain—and with it the Empire—declared war on the aggressor on 4 August 1914. In Australia, where the prime minister, Joseph Cook, declared that 'our duty [to stand alongside Britain] is quite clear', his patriotic sentiments were fervently endorsed by the public at large. Recruiting for an Australian 'Expeditionary Force' began on 11 August and by 20 August over 10,000 men had enlisted in Sydney alone.[30] Nor was Strasburg slow to answer the call. Friends, including a Major Lark whom he had met at the Sydney Club, who knew of his 'experience in the South Seas … for 35 years' advised him 'to offer to help the Navy by piloting in the islands'. Accordingly, on 12 August he presented himself at the Navy Office at Garden Island. There he was welcomed by a Lieutenant-Commander H.P. Cayley who, three days later, on the advice of the Naval Board in Melbourne, informed him that he was commissioned as Acting Lieutenant R.N.R. and was to proceed on board HMAS *Berrima*, a chartered P&O liner, where he would serve as pilot and navigator.[31]

Carrying troops for the occupation of German New Guinea and escorted by Australian, British and French warships, the *Berrima* left Sydney on 19 August. It travelled via Moreton Bay and Port Moresby, and reached Rabaul at 7 am on Friday 11 September. There the troops were quickly landed, but, despite being of overwhelming strength, they soon encountered considerable resistance from an enemy force of three dozen Europeans and 210 native policemen, who were not averse to night-fighting. It was not until Saturday at 1 am that, with four Australians dead and several wounded, the radio station at the administrative centre of Herbertshohe (later Kokopo) was captured. Later that day, preparing for the ritual completetion of the exercise, Strasburg went ashore at Rabaul with Major Francis Heritage to obtain a flag pole (they commandeered a mast from the Nord Deutsche shipping line office) and to find a suitable spot on which to erect it in preparation for the formal reading of a statement proclaiming the Australian military occupation of 'the whole Island of New Britain and its dependencies'.

That event, performed by the commanding officer, Colonel William Holmes, took place the following afternoon outside the administration offices, in what became known as Proclamation Square.[32] It was followed by the reading of a

---

29 Strasburg, 'Log of the *Federal*' and other papers, Mitchell Library, MS A1475.
30 Phillip Knightley, *Australia: a biography of a nation*, London, 2001, p. 62; Bill Gammage, *The Broken Years: Australian soldiers in the Great War*, Canberra, 1974, p. 6.
31 *Senate Report*, p. 1.
32 For the text, see B. Jinks et al. (eds), *Readings in New Guinea History*, Sydney, 1973, pp. 202–203.

second proclamation in pidgin English (*tok pisin*) which was directed to a native audience. This document had been drafted by Strasburg but was delivered from the verandah of the chief of police's quarters by a Warrant-Officer Wilkinson. Predictably, as the occasion required, the listeners were promised better treatment than what they had received under the previous regime. Conversely, but no less predictably, they were addressed as a labour force. Fittingly, given the severity that was to become a mark of the Australian administration, a clear hint of punishment for any insubordination was also contained in the address.

> Supposing you work good with this new feller Master, he look out good along with you. He look out you get plenty good feller kaikai [food]. He no fighting black feller boy along nothing. You look him new feller flag; you savvy him, belong British, English. He more better than other feller. Supposing you been making paper [signing a labour contract] before this new feller Master come, you finish time belongina him first. Finish time belongina him, you make him new feller paper long man belong new feller master. He look out good along with you. He give you more money and more good feller kaikai. Supposing you no look out good along him, he cross [get angry] too much. British, English, new feller Master he like black man too much. He like you all the same you picanin [children] along him.

To conclude, the audience of about 500, which had been marched from Proclamation Square to the space outside the police headquarters for the second reading, was enjoined to 'give three feller cheers belongina new feller Master'. This they duly did. They were deemed, thereby, so Strasburg later commented, articulating the ingenuous detachment of the invaders, to have shown 'that we were welcome visitors'.[33]

Composing this speech was not the last of Strasburg's contributions to the occupation of German New Guinea, an event that proceeded without further Australian losses on land but which was marred by the mysterious disappearance of submarine *AE1* with all hands south of Rabaul on 15 September.[34] For the next four months he was busily engaged in facilitating and extending the process. At first this was mainly by recruiting labour. Then, after 4 October, when the *Berrima* left for Sydney and he was transferred to the staff of the military administrator, it was by commandeering and commanding numerous smaller vessels formerly operated by Germans. He was an assiduous factotum.

---

33 Strasburg, 'Log and Diary, 19 Aug. – 7 Oct. 1914: a voyage aboard HMAT *Berrima*', Mitchell Library, MS A1476; 'Abstract of my Logs and Diaries', NAA, A518, G822/1/3; *Senate Report*, p. 10; *Sun*, 7 Oct. 1914; S.S. MacKenzie, *The Australians at Rabaul*, Sydney, 1937. Strasburg's proclamation was first published in the *Sydney Mail*, 14 Oct. 1914 and later elsewhere, including *Government Gazette: British Administration – German New Guinea*, vol. 1, no. 2 (1 Nov. 1914), and in MacKenzie, *Australians*, p. 76.
34 *SMH*, 14 Oct. 1914.

On 17 September he recruited 84 Chinese labourers to coal the *Berrima* and, when they went strike after two days for more pay and easier conditions, he supplemented them with 135 indigenous labourers, who were willing to accept far less generous terms. In his diary for 22 September Strasburg noted 'We finished coaling the *Berrima* at 6 am—970 tons. The coal bill: Chinese labour £87-10s; native labour £23-7s-6d. The natives did the most of the coaling and all the night work, and the Chinese day work only'.[35]

Once the main objectives of the expedition were secured (and these extended to the towns of Lae and Madang as well as to Rabaul), the new administration's writ had also to be made to run through the scattered islands of the Bismarck archipelago. To this end, on 7 October Strasburg took the *Lorengau* to the Duke of York Islands. Ten days later he took the government yacht *Nusa* to Kavieng in New Ireland where a party of troops led by Major Heritage rescued the British consul, F.R. Jolley, who was being held prisoner by diehard German settlers. In the course of that voyage Strasburg's navigation also led to the capture of three other German craft—the 490-ton steamer *Siar*, and the auxiliary schooners *Matupi* and *Senta*—which had been hidden in a small uncharted cove on Gardner Island called Tekarake. On 24 October he was despatched in the *Madang* to capture the *Samoa*, hidden in Kalili Bay on New Ireland. And, on 26 October, he returned to New Ireland in the steamer *Meklong*. It carried troops to establish a garrison at Kavieng, and then landed a shore party at Namatanai to apprehend some Germans who had sought to assuage their damaged pride by flogging an Australian Methodist missionary named W.H. Cox. The same week the *Meklong* captured the cutter *Hilalon* in open sea.

In their geographical extent, the shipping services for New Britain and New Ireland that occupied Strasburg's attention during October and November seem also to have accorded with a calculated lack of official urgency to complete the occupation once the bulk of the task had been accomplished. Thus, the German regime on Bougainville was not replaced until December, bringing closure without relief to the expectant officials there. Two ships that had put out from Bougainville shortly before the occupation bound for Rabaul were early apprehended by Australian vessels (the *Sumatra* on 11 September and the *Madang* on 13 September); and, in late November, in a gesture of resigned defiance, the district commissioner had scuttled his two-year old, 60-ton steam launch, *Buka*. But the German flag still flew at Kieta. Indeed, it was not lowered until 90 days after the Australians had reached Rabaul. The countdown to that formal sign of defeat began on 7 December when the *Meklong*, a 438-ton former Norddeutscher Lloyd vessel, sailed from Rabaul. Captained by Strasburg and

---

35 Printed versions of Strasburg's diary for the period 12 Aug. – 12 Dec. 1914 are contained in *Senate Report*, pp. 9–12, and NAA, A518, G822/1/3; the manuscript in the Mitchell Library only covers the period 19 Aug. – 7 Nov. 1914.

carrying 230 troops commanded by Lt. Col. W.R. Watson, it reached Kieta two days later, after a brief stop at the village of Rorovana to enquire about German strength on the island. The transfer of power was swift and undramatic. A shore party changed the flags; Dollinger with his staff of four, together with their families, and several other Germans, were taken aboard; and a 54-strong party of soldiers was left behind. By 6 pm, after a stay of barely five hours at Kieta, the *Meklong* was again at sea. Before quitting Bougainville, it stopped briefly at Tinputz and at Soroken and so became, said Strasburg, the largest ship to have hitherto passed through the then unsurveyed Buka Passage. The *Meklong* regained Rabaul on 12 December. The commander of the expedition was generous in his praise: 'The services of Lieut. Strasburg, the master of the *Meklong* were invaluable, and his navigation of the difficult waters of these islands relieved me of all anxiety as to the safety of our ship.'[36]

With that, though, Strasburg's service to the military administration came virtually to an end, not because he could no longer be useful but because—it seems—of the resentment towards him of a more senior naval officer, Commander R.L. Lambton, the harbour master at Rabaul. It was through Lambton's influence, Strasburg alleges, that he was not asked to pilot the transport *Eastern* which ran on a reef at Kavieng in January 1915 and cost £4,000 to repair. The advice of the Japanese merchant Isokihi Komine was preferred, even though Strasburg had twice entered that port in darkness and without any external navigation aids. Again, whereas under the first administrator, Col. William Holmes, Strasburg had hopes of being appointed government pilot for the whole of the ex-German New Guinea territory, he believed that when Holmes was replaced by Col. Pethebridge it was Lambton who induced the new administrator to terminate his employment, as occurred on 18 January.[37]

Nor was that the only misfortune to blight Strasburg's naval career. On 4 January 1915 he had written to the Naval Board in Melbourne 'intimating that I had not received any official notification of my commission having been gazetted'. He also enclosed a bill for £285 for outstanding pilotage fees in respect of the captured vessels. The reply, which he received on 22 February, a week after returning to Sydney, was singularly disconcerting. Despite the undertakings of August 1914, he was told that he had not—and could not have—been given a commission because of his alien birth. Therefore, notwithstanding official recognition of his subsequent meritorious service (and, indeed, the award of

---

36 Strasburg, 'Diary' and related papers, NAA, A518, G822/1/3; Lt. Col. W. Russell-Watson, 'Military Occupation of Bougainville, German New Guinea', *Government Gazette, British Administration – German New Guinea*, no. 5 (15 Dec.), p. 4; Holmes to Minister of Defence, 15 Dec. 1914, Australian War Memorial, series 33, control 39.
37 Strasburg to Senator Needham, 4 Aug. 1915, and to W.M. Hughes (Prime Minister), 12 Sept. 1919, NAA, A518, G822/1/3. For Komine, see C.D. Rowley, *The Australians in German New Guinea, 1914–1921*, Melbourne, 1958, pp. 84–85.

medals to mark his participation) he had not actually been a member of the Naval and Military Expeditionary Force to German New Guinea, with which he had been prominently associated. To make matters worse, concerning the pilotage bill, the Naval Board was willing to pay only £125 of the total amount charged. In an attempt to persuade it otherwise by approaching officials and politicians directly, Strasburg took himself to Melbourne for two months (March to May 1915), but to no avail. The authorities were unmoved by his insistent and well-documented entreaties.[38]

A year later, with his fortunes declining but with his spirit of enterprise (if not his good judgement) still intact, Strasburg again comes into view, but briefly, and from another angle. On 13 May 1916 he left Sydney aboard the SS *Van oon Stratten* for the six-day voyage to Port Moresby, apparently intending to set up in business on his own account as a trader. Accordingly, on arrival he bought the small auxiliary-engined schooner *Niue* and, on 8 June, with a crew of three, set out for Faisi in the Shortland Islands, south of Bougainville. The vendor of the *Niue*, a Captain Dean, had told him that 'the vessel was tight, the copper good and she had not been on shore anywhere'. Too late, the crew told him she had, in fact, been on the reef three times. Evidence was soon to hand. The *Niue* reached Faisi on 3 July, leaking so badly that the crew refused to go further in it and insisted on being sent home on the regular Burns Philp steamer *Matunga* from Sydney bound for Port Moresby. Strasburg thereupon engaged another crew and headed for Roviana in the central Solomons. There, at Lambetti, on 19 July he was forced to abandon the *Niue*. Two days later he joined the *Matunga* on its return voyage to the south.[39]

That ignominious episode, though, was not to be the last of its kind in what was proving to be a dismal end to Strasburg's career. In February 1918 he returned once more to New Guinea, at the invitation of Jean Baptiste Octave Mouton. He was to be master of the motor schooner *Takubar* that Mouton used to recruit labour for his fine plantation at Kinigunan near Rabaul, but the one voyage he made in it was unsuccessful. On 14 April after an absence of 49 days, during which period it anchored at no less than 22 places along the south coast of New Britain and Rooke Island, the *Takubar* returned to Kinigunan with only seven recruits. Strasburg attributed this poor result to the rough treatment meted out to villagers by two other recruiting expeditions that had recently preceded him along that route. One of these had been conducted by two women, Ettie Kaumann and Lulu Hoepfels, part-Samoan relatives of the redoubtable pioneer planter 'Queen' Emma Coe. While not unsympathetic to the complaint that

---

38 Correspondence enclosed in Strasburg to [Needham?], 5 June 1915, and Strasburg to Needham, 4 Aug. 1915, NAA, A518, G822/1/3.
39 Strasburg, 'Log of the *Niue*', bound with volume two of 'Log of the *Federal*', Mitchell Library, MS, A1475.

Strasburg duly registered, the administration was unable to offer any remedy. Mouton, on the other hand, was moved by the meagre catch to reassess the case for maintaining his own recruiting vessel at a cost of £1,500 per year, and decided not to continue. Accordingly, Strasburg was given a month's notice and a contract for supplying labour to Kinigunan was let to the Hamburgische Suedsee-Aktiengesellschaft, managed by a German named Mirow.[40]

With that, Strasburg went ashore for the last time. He was 62 years old, unemployed, disappointed and hard-up. He was battered; but he was not yet beaten. Over the next two years he wrote numerous letters, berating the Australian government on two counts. One was for allowing recruiting abuses, especially, he alleged, by Germans; German civilians having been allowed to stay when officials were deported.[41] Given his *Takubar* fiasco, such irregularities could, he claimed damage the commercial economy of New Guinea by alienating potential labourers. Interestingly, in the light of his own difficulties, and in contrast to his views of a few years before, economic considerations were now alloyed with a measure of sympathy for the island peoples. In 1914 he had publicly expressed the view, not uncommon among those whose interest in the islands did not extend beyond making a living from them, that the natives were more a bane than a blessing.

> Inhabited by a white race [the islands] might be a real terrestrial paradise. But the brown savage is a brand across the beauty, and while he remains the white man will never be more than a trader and an exploiter there. Had the South Sea Isles been uninhabited, a wonderful chapter of history might have commenced. They would probably have been flooded with white farmers, and become a great nation or confederation of small nations, beside which the Isles of Greece would have faded into ordinary and commonplace.

By 1919 this rhetoric of fanciful aspiration had given way to sentiments that, regardless of the frustrated self-interest that begot them, were still philanthropic. Strasburg became apologetic about his proclamation.

> I am sorry to say that none of the promises in that address made to the natives has been carried out and that the natives of these Islands instead of being protected under our rule have been very cruelly treated, kidnapped, taken by force. Men and women [have been] compelled to work against their will for the German planters; flogged and kicked, some to death, because they were starving and could not do sufficient work for the German plantation overseers.

---

40 Strasburg, 'Report of a Recruiting Voyage in the M.S. *Takubar*, 27 Feb. – 14 April 1918', enclosed in Strasburg to [Johnston], 12 Sept. 1918; Johnston to Secretary of Defence, 16 Oct. 1918, NAA, 457, 710/3.
41 C.D. Rowley, *The Australians in German New Guinea*, pp. 47–60.

Strasburg's other grievance concerned the discounting of his war service. This, he also wrote in September 1919, had cost him dearly:

> I tried very hard for a settlement, went again to Melbourne for another 60 days, my case was brought before parliament, again turned down. I became bankrupt, penniless, lost my good home. Worst of all, lost a good and true wife.[42]

There is no evidence to suggest that his situation had improved when, three years later, he was at length awarded a token measure of relief. In August 1922, after exhaustive deliberation, a committee of the Australian Senate recommended that he be awarded a gratuity in terms of the *War Gratuity Acts* 1920. Even then it was not a unanimous decision and might not have been arrived at without the aid of some benignly inventive legal logic from the Solicitor-General, Sir Robert Garran. In the absence of any statutory definition of the 'Naval and Military Expeditionary Force' to New Guinea, argued Garran, Strasburg might be deemed to be 'a member of the Forces, even though he was not a member of the Military or Naval Forces'. How one could belong to the whole but to neither of the constituent parts, he did not explain. Senator T.W. Glasgow was, therefore, moved to dissent from the majority view of Strasburg's claim, but did concede that he was 'morally entitled to receive an amount equal to the War Gratuity'. That is, £133-4s.[43] Not that he would have much time to enjoy his vindication. John Strasburg died at Rookwood Asylum, Sydney, on 21 July 1924, survived by his estranged wife and two children. Cause of death was given as senility. He was aged 68.[44]

Writing of the pioneer trader Peter Dillon, who in 1826 solved the mystery of the disappearance of the La Perouse expedition that had vanished in 1788 whilst looking for the Solomon Islands, J.W. Davidson commented that Dillon, whom he admired, 'was not a "great man" in the conventional sense'. Notwithstanding 'the one brief flush of glory' after a fortuitous find at Vanikoro, 'his life as a whole was a failure, not only in conventional terms but as it must have seemed to himself'. Dillon had been an adventurous, enterprising captain, ranging the Pacific from Tahiti to Sydney in search of cargoes and charters when he came across wreckage from the expedition. But the bubble reputation so earned did not bring prosperity to him. Dillon spent much of the rest of his life in relative poverty. With anxious assiduity, he tried to improve his situation by petitioning government agencies, private capitalists and missionary organisations interested in the South Seas to employ his services, but to no avail.[45] His was career and a

---

42 Strasburg to Hughes (Prime Minister), 12 Sept. 1919, NAA, A518, G822/1/3.
43 *Senate Report*; Minister for Repatriation to Sen. A Gardiner, 6 Oct 1922, NAA A2487, 1922/14485; *Melbourne Age*, 19 Aug. 1922; *SMH*, 21 Aug. 1922;
44 Death certificate.
45 J.W. Davidson, *Peter Dillon of Vanikoro: Chevalier of the South Seas*, Melbourne, 1975, p. 308

fate, which, in its essential outlines, would later be paralleled by that of John Strasburg. The practical sailor had a moment of notability (in Strasburg's case it was because of the proclamation of 1914 that historians have acknowledged his existence) but that was followed by a terminal decline of fortune and of official appreciation. On the other hand, the names of Dillon and Strasburg have at least survived and the salient facts of their lives have been retrievable. The names of most of their ilk, deckhands on the barque of commerce, remain 'writ in water'.

7. Ernest Frederick Hughes Allen (1867–1924): South Seas trader

Salt water ran strongly in the veins of Ernest Allen. In the seventeenth and eighteenth centuries there were admirals in the family and, in the nineteenth century, there was a post-captain. About 1850 the latter's son, Frederick Kenneth Allen, was invalided out of the Royal Navy and migrated to New Zealand. There, at Wellington, in 1851 he married Frances Stratford Elizabeth Houghton, the 19-year-old daughter of another ex-navy man, Robert Houghton. Said to be an illegitimate son of one of the Cochrane family, to which Admiral Thomas Cochrane, 10th Earl of Dundonald (1775–1860), and the model for Frederick Marryat's heroic Hornblower-like Captain Savage, had belonged, Houghton arrived in Wellington with his family in the New Zealand Company vessel *Aurora* in January 1840. There he established a successful lightering business and acted as harbour master. The family name is preserved in Houghton Bay. Frederick and Frances, in contrast, took up sheep farming on Forsyth Island in the Marlborough Sounds at the top of the South Island. It was there that their only son, Ernest Frederick Hughes Allen, the youngest of their four children, was born in 1867.[1]

Information about Ernest Allan's childhood and education is scarce, but it seems that about 1870, after his father, who died in 1871, was struck with paralysis, the family shifted to Wellington. There, about 1880 he was articled as a clerk in the law firm of Cutten and Edwards, but—as with 'Banjo' Paterson's Clancy—that sort of work was not to his taste. 'I doubt he'd suit the office, Clancy of the Overflow'. A more active life at sea beckoned. Thus it was that in 1882, according to a report in 1920 in the *Samoa Times*, Ernest Allen launched himself on what would be a four decade career as a South Sea trader, planter, mariner and ship owner.[2]

In embarking on this course, there is nothing to suggest that Allen was running away from anything, or yielding to a romantic, literature-fired indulgence. Nor was he escaping into a balmy nirvana, like many of the shore-based 'resident traders' who managed small trading stations, either independently or on behalf

---

[1] Ernest Tanumafili Allen, 'Memoir'. This is an unpublished and undated [c. 1980] TS of ten pages. Copy in my possession by courtesy of the author. Allen family tree, by courtesy of Eric Allen. Nell Hartley, *Colonial Outcasts: a search for the remittance man*, Morrinsville, 1993, pp. 162–166. Frederick Marryat, *Peter Simple*, London, 1834.
[2] *Samoa Times*, 20 Mar. 1920; *Fiji Times*, 22 Sept. 1924. The *Samoa Times* states, 'Captain Allen, was a resident in Suva from 1882 to 1885', but it is more likely that 1882 was the year he left Wellington in the *Albatross*.

of larger ship-based operators, and who gradually 'went native', and whom he eventually helped displace from their place in the commercial spectrum. Such men have been well described by Doug Munro:

> Despite their diversity of social backgrounds, the overwhelming impression is that [they] were a group of men, dissatisfied and often unsuccessful in other walks of life, who found a refuge on the margins of the Island trade. They were social casualties by and large. Most went into trading in the first place as a last resort after drifting in and out of various occupations—and sometimes in and out of trouble as well—in various parts of the world.[3]

Nor was Allen as restless a soul as his near contemporary Louis Becke. From 1869 to 1892 Becke wandered from Sydney to San Francisco and back and spent at least ten years in a desultory trading career in various islands of the Pacific before becoming a writer at the age of 37. He then found fame but not fortune with unvarnished tales of his adventures.[4] In contrast, despite his evident relish for the less constrained style of life that the islands had to offer him, Allen showed himself to be consistently entrepreneurial and broadly conventional in the way he managed his affairs. And there were numerous others such as he. Many of them had been drawn to the Pacific by the big German firm of Godeffroy und Sohn (forerunner of the Deutsche Handels- und Plantagen-Gesellschaft or DHPG) which opened in Samoa in 1857, and by the 'rush' of would-be cotton planters to Fiji in the early 1870s. By 1905 there were 400 *palagi* (Europeans) in Samoa, 250 in Tonga and 2,675 in Fiji—and overall almost 2,500 half-castes, of whom 700 were in Samoa. Collectively, within each island group, these people constituted a distinct and self-sustaining, but by no means exclusive, demographic and social category, with half-castes tending to be identified as 'European' rather than 'native'. What the leaders among them were doing and had accomplished is described and lauded, though not egregiously so, in the biographical entries in two *Cyclopedia* volumes published in 1907 to chronicle 'the history, traditions and commercial development of the islands'.[5]

In joining the ranks of these *arrivistes* of the pelagic littorals, Allen sought to make a comfortable living, if not his fortune. And he succeeded moderately well. He thus played—within the region in which he operated—a significant

---

3   Doug Munro, 'The Lives and Times of Resident Traders in Tuvalu: an exercise in history from below', *Pacific Studies*, vol. 10, no. 2 (1987), pp. 79, 97.
4   A. Grove Day, *Mad About Islands: novelists of a vanished Pacific*, Honolulu, 1987, pp. 124–143.
5   *Cyclopedia of Samoa, Tonga, Tahiti and the Cook Islands*, Sydney, 1907, p. 27; *Cyclopedia of Fiji*, Sydney, 1907, pp. 24–26. For useful discussions of the 'mixed-race' community in Samoa, see J.W. Davidson, *Samoa mo Samoa: the emergence of the Independent State of Western Samoa* (Melbourne, 1967), pp. 197–201); Malama Meleisea, *The Making of Modern Samoa: traditional authority and colonial administration in the modern history of Western Samoa* (Suva, 1987), pp. 155–182; Damon Salesa, '"Troublesome Half-castes": tales of a Samoan borderland' (MA thesis (History), University of Auckland, 1997).

part in an important and pervasive double-sided process. It was one in which, on the one hand, the European settler presence in its various manifestations was supported and serviced while, on the other, the local peoples acquired new appetites and expectations as they were drawn ever more closely into the European-controlled economic system. Allen himself, though, was never absorbed into indigenous life. In 1924 the *Fiji Times* would recall him as 'a fine type of Britisher'.[6] But he did become well integrated on the advancing *palagi*-defined margins of island society through long and familiar acquaintance with places and people, not least by marriage, and by his fluency in the language of Samoa. From such a position the established and enterprising trader such as he, like the veteran missionary and the energetic colonial official, might exert an appreciable influence on the multiple rhythms of islands affairs.

Allen left Wellington as an apprentice on the trading schooner *Albatrosss*, under Captain McLever, and stayed with her for several trips until coming ashore in Fiji, probably in 1884. There he worked as a boatbuilder in the yards of J. Darrach in Suva before moving to Samoa in 1885, where he found employment with the Auckland-based trading firm of William McArthur and Co.[7] At that time McArthurs, which had come to Samoa about 1876 and was the largest British company in the group, was locked in a bitter and protracted legal contest with an ex-missionary turned planter, Frank Cornwall, over the ownership of 300,000 acres of land. McArthurs claimed the land, with some limited early success, on account of money owed them by Cornwell. It seems that Allen was first employed managing the cotton plantation at Magia, 24 kilometres west of Apia, which a court had awarded to McArthurs in 1882. The dispute, however, dragged on until 1890, when the Privy Council in London ruled in favour of Cornwall. McArthurs left Samoa in 1892.[8] Apparently more than just an impartial observer of the drama, Allen is reported to have come around to supporting Cornwall in his claim and in return to have received from him, although in his wife's name, 1,200 acres of land at Iva on eastern Savai'i. In any event, Allen had settled there by 1892. There he built himself a small schooner, the *Manu Tagi* ('Bird that Cries'), and also started a trading business of his own, which he at

---

6 22 Sept. 1924.
7 *Samoa Times*, 20 Mar. 1920; *Fiji Times*, 22 Sept. 1924; Allen, 'Memoir', states 'After about four years on sailing ships around the Pacific, he left the sea and worked in a boat building yard in Suva for a few months. He then settled in Samoa'. Thomas M'Cullagh, *Sir William M'Arthur: a biography*, London, 1981, pp. 60–61, 219, 223.
8 Cornwall to Derby, Mar. 1883, enclosed in Jervois to Derby, 22 April 1883, *Appendices to the Journals of the House of Representatives* [NZ], 1884, A4, pp. 214–218; Deryck Scarr, *Fragments of Empire: a history of the Western Pacific High Commission*, Canberra, 1967, pp. 78–81; R.P. Gilson, *Samoa 1830–1900: the politics of a multi-cultural community*, Melbourne, 1970, pp. 341, 376–379, 413–414; Doug Munro, 'Planter versus Protector: Frank Cornwall's employment of plantation workers in Samoa, 1878–1881', *New Zealand Journal of History*, vol. 23, no. 2 (1989), pp. 174–177; Thomas Trood mistakenly has 1902 instead of 1892 for McArthur's withdrawal; *Island Reminiscences*, Sydney, 1912, p. 71.

first conducted from a vessel named the *Kawau*.⁹ Unfortunately, for the sake of a good story, there is no evidence that during these years Allen ever met, let alone 'knew intimately', Robert Louis Stevenson; or other celebrated literary figures such as Becke and Jack London. These were specious claims to fame, but ones with which he later apparently impressed Donald Kennedy, an administrative officer in the Ellice Islands, who passed them on to other sympathetic listeners.¹⁰

Politically, the 1890s were an uncertain decade for the European community in Samoa, with rival chiefly lineages, backed by rival foreign powers, contending for the kingship of the group. It was a problem that had become acute in the 1870s and which continued to beget sporadic outbursts of warfare until 1899 when, in a spurt of imperial expansion, America annexed the small island of Tutuila with its port of Pago Pago and Germany took the larger, agriculturally valuable islands to the west. The last phase of the conflict had been precipitated by the death of the incumbent, Laupepa of Sa Malietoa, in August 1898. The contenders for succession were Laupepa's 18-year-old son Tanumafili, who was backed by the British and Americans, and the venerable Mata'afa Iosefa of Sā Tupua, who was backed by the Germans. Following the installation of Tanumafili as king on 31 December, heavy fighting, most of it centred around Apia, occurred between January and April 1899.¹¹

On several occasions during that period civilians sought refuge aboard naval vessels. Allen, however, joined in the conflict. He was present at the opening of hostilities on 1 January and, from 12 March to 23 May, he was carried on the books of HMS *Porpoise*, under Captain (later Admiral) A.C.D. Sturdee, at the rate of £1 per day to serve as interpreter, pilot and intelligence adviser aboard any of the four British craft deployed in Samoa. In that capacity, in mid-April, he went in the *Royalist* to Salelologa in Savai'i to bring in 215 men who were defecting from the Mata'afa cause. A few days later he was hurt in a fall from his horse during a skirmish at Vailima. Yet it had all been to little purpose. In June all parties agreed to abolish the institution of kingship in Samoa. After all, it had never been a more than notional office, despite the turmoil caused by those seeking it. They had engaged in what was essentially a contest for titular supremacy rather than for supreme power. Allen, though, clearly showed where his sympathies lay by naming his fifth son, born on 14 May 1899, Ernest

---

9   Allen, 'Memoir'; tape of interview with Eric Allen, Brisbane, 7 Sept. 1987, courtesy of Doug Munro. In 1926 the 1,200 acres were still in the family. Power of attorney of Frederick Kenneth Allen, 13 April 1926, copy courtesy of Eric Allen.
10 Colin Amodeo (ed.), *The Waterlily Diary of Jack Atkinson*, Christchurch, 2001, p. 68.
11 Gilson, *Samoa*, pp. 426–431; Paul M. Kennedy, *The Samoan Tangle: a study in Anglo-German-American relations, 1878–1900*, St. Lucia, 1974, pp. 150–155.

7. Ernest Frederick Hughes Allen (1867–1924): South Seas trader

Tanumafili, but later generally known as 'Joe', apparently in honour of another chief. Contrary to Joe's own belief, he was not born aboard the *Royalist*, for it had left Apia for Suva en route for Sydney on 2 May.[12]

With the coming of German rule the economic development of what would in 1962 emerge as the Independent State of Western Samoa accelerated markedly. New planting companies were formed, Chinese workers were imported (from 1903) to expand the available labour force, extensive public works were undertaken—and shipping requirements increased. From about 1900 Allen had in some measure been operating in conjunction with William Blacklock, a merchant who had come to Samoa in 1883. Whatever their arrangement, it became closer in 1903, when Blacklock sold his business and he and Allen jointly purchased a ship, the *Maori*.[13] Subsequently, in 1908, they set up the Samoa Shipping and Trading Company and, in September 1910, registered its head office in Sydney with Blacklock as manager.[14] In line with the post-annexation economic growth, the *Kawau*, in addition to its other inter-island work, had been kept busy making a weekly run from Apia to Pago Pago to connect with the San Francisco mail steamers of the Oceanic Line.[15] The importance of this service to the residents of Apia—and evidence of some deep anxiety about even being there? – is revealed in a dramatic newspaper report of 1901:

> There seemed to be mystery around the sudden departure of the S.S. *Kawau* for Tutuila on last Friday. Some of the foremost businessmen were disconcerted, thus forestalling the shipment of goods by that boat. However Captain Allen knew best. On mail-day the *Kawau* had not arrived. Great suspense hung over entire Apia. All looked seaward during the day. At last, at half past six, the gun of the *Kawau* was heard. Intense excitement prevailed. By nine o'clock the post office was thronged with eager citizens. So packed were the verandah and the streets that men nudged the ladies; the girls were not afraid of the boys—and many forgot their customary decorum in the excitement. Only by ten o'clock the window was opened, and the mail distributed. Then it was made known that the *Kawau*'s delay was principally due to the fact Mr Allen

---

12 New Zealand National Archives, Royal Navy Australia Station 40, Stuart to Pearson, 14, 18, 26 April 1899; Thomas Trood, *Island Reminiscences*, Sydney, 1912, pp. 108–111, 129; interview Joe Allen.
13 Allen, 'Memoir'. *Samoanisch Zeitung*, 19 July 1902, stated 'From this date no passengers will be carried [by S.S. *Kawau* to Tutuila] unless thay have tickets from the office of W. Blacklock'. On 17 June 1905, quoting from the *New Zealand Herald* of 18 May, it referred to 'The steamer *Maori*, belonging to Messrs W. Blacklock and E.F Allen'. *Cyclopedia of Samoa*, p. 99.
14 Trood, *Reminiscences*, p. 129. *Samoanische Zeitung*, 20 June 1908, contains the earliest discovered reference to the company. An unidentified newspaper clipping, probably from *Sydney Morning Herald*, Feb.–Mar. 1925, gives the date of incorporation in New South Wales. Courtesy of Eric Allen.
15 Refer *Samoanische Zeitung* for shipping movements. Trood suggests that Blacklock may have had more to do with the *Kawau* than selling tickets: 'Allen initiated with Mr. Blacklock that steam service between Apia and Pago Pago'. *Reminiscences*, p. 129; C. Hartley Grattan, *The United States and the Southwest Pacific*, Melbourne, 1961, pp. 110–111.

had the boiler repaired, had the pipe newly painted—all in Pago Pago—
and, as it rained heavily there he had to wait patiently until the pink
paint had dried. This satisfactory explanation was sufficient to reconcile
the Apians with their day's suspense, and to acknowledge that Captain
Allen knew perfectly well what he was about.[16]

Such was the increasing demand for shipping that the *Kawau* was replaced in
February 1903 by the larger *Maori*, which also made regular runs to Niue and
to Tokelau. Niue was a source of labourers for, among others, the Upolu Cacao
Company which began planting at Tanumapua in 1901.[17]

Of 174 tons gross tonnage, with room for 163 tons of cargo, built in Glasgow in
1868 and carrying a crew of 25, the *Maori* had been the first vessel acquired
by the newly incorporated Union Steam Ship Company of New Zealand in
1875.[18] The shipping news from the *Samoanische Zeitung* regarding it conveys
an impression of constant activity. For instance, on Thursday 26 May 1904 the
Maori arrived at Niue, where it landed passengers and recruited plantation
labourers; five days later it left for Pago Pago, arriving there on Thursday 2
June, and leaving that night for Apia; the next day it left Apia for Safata on
the south coast of Upolu to land labourers and cargo and to load copra, and
returned to Apia on 5 June; next day, Monday, it left with passengers and the
'colonial mails' for Pago Pago, via Leone; arriving on Tuesday, it received mails
and cargo from the SS *Sonoma* during the night; and, at noon the following day,
after taking on passengers, it departed for Apia, which it reached 11 hours later.
Similarly, in June 1905, the *Maori* took '100 tons of copra from Savai'i to Pago
Pago for shipment to San Francisco'. And in September it was employed to take
the members of the Sports Club, founded in 1903, and of which Allen was vice-
chairman, on an excursion to Savai'i. There followed a succession of excursions
during the first part of 1906, following volcanic eruptions that began on Savai'i
in August 1905. The *Maori* regularly carried sightseers to view the volcanic lava
flowing into the sea at Sale'aula on the north coast of the island.[19]

In June of that year Allen extended his operations to Tokelau, thereby
establishing a profitable but harshly applied paramountcy within that group,
which would last until 1923. As the historians of Tokelau observe:

> Allen [enjoyed] a monopoly not only in trade but also in communication
> between Tokelau and the world outside, specifically between the local

---

16 *Samoanische Zeitung*, 26 Oct. 1901.
17 Ibid., 28 May 1904. *Cyclopedia of Samoa*, pp. 91–93.
18 *Samoanische Zeitung*, 30 Dec. 1903, 17 June 1905; J.E. Hobbs and D.F. Gardner, *The Union Steam Ship Company Steam Ships*, Wellington, 1982, p. 13.
19 *Samoanische Zeitung*, 28 May, 11 June 1904, 17 June, 2 Sept. 1905, 7 Jan., 2 Feb. 1906. *Cyclopedia of Samoa*, pp. 8–9, 67. J.E. Newell, 'The Most Active Volcano in the World', *The Lone Hand*, vol. 7 (Aug. 1910), pp. 274–278.

polities and their colonial administrators. He alone tendered for Tokelau tax copra; he bought all other copra and supplied all imports. He transported all travellers in and out, ignoring port of entry regulations if it suited him … . He had a captive labour force to recruit either for Olohega or the Phoenix Islands. People sentenced to serve time in the Funafuti gaol, often at the instigation of Allen, were conveyed to gaol on the *Dawn* and, after serving their sentences, returned on the *Dawn*.

The first voyage, to Tokelau had also been something of a social occasion. As the *Samoanische Zeitung* noted, 'Messrs Partsch, Meredith, Forsell, Hall and Hallbauer' went with Allen 'to enjoy a well-earned week's respite from the cares and worry of business'.[20] About the same time the Lever Brothers vessel *Upolu* was busy carrying seed coconuts from Samoa for planting in the Solomon Islands. Allen was similarly optimistic about the prospects for his own business. In 1908 the *Maori* was replaced by the 522-ton *Dawn*, which (to the irritation of established operators) he would occasionally take to Tonga and New Caledonia.[21] And in 1910 he also acquired the wooden-hulled *Rob Roy* of 80 tons. The company later operated, in addition, the *Laura*, *Jeanette* and *Samoa*.[22]

Then, in 1911, there was another portentous move. In September Allen sailed the *Dawn* to the Ellice Islands (since 1976, Tuvalu). He made several more such voyages over the next three years. After obtaining access to land in May 1913, he built a substantial establishment there on the atoll of Funafuti, and formally made it his operational base in June 1914. A wharf for ocean-going ships was not practicable, but there was a jetty for launches and barges and large coal, cargo and copra sheds, as well as a well-equipped shipyard and a slipway that could take vessels of up to 100 tons. Electricity was installed and the machine shop was complete with power-driven lathes, drills and machine saws. There was also a blacksmith shop. Fresh water was assured by a system of ducts from the buildings into a huge concrete cistern, and the main residence of about 280 square metres was of concrete, with high ceilings, French windows and wide verandahs. The precise reasons for Allen's move from Apia (where he left an agency) are not recorded. One suggestion, made in 1920, well after the event, is that he had 'become tired of German rule', but is seems more likely that in the face of increasing competition in the Samoas Funafuti was deemed to offer better business opportunities. It is also possible that politics on the other side of the border was impeding the flow of commerce, as the *Samoanische Zeitung* hints in 1913:

---

20 *Samoanische Zeitung*, 23 June 1906. Judith Huntsman and Antony Hooper, *Tokelau: a historical ethnology*, Auckland, 1996, pp. 261–264.
21 *Samoanische Zeitung*, 8, 22 May, 12 June 1909, 27 Aug. 1910, 4 May 1912; Allen, 'Memoir'; 'The Diary of Captain William Ross' (1927), TS copy in University of Auckland Library, p. 223.
22 *Samoanische Zeitung*, 20 June 1908, 16 April 1910. The *Maori* was scuttled at Saluafata in 1908. *Samoa Bulletin*, 28 Sept. 1962. Hugh Laracy (ed.), *Tuvalu: a history*, Suva, 1983, pp. 62–64.

It is not certain when the Government at Tutuila will grant pratique [entry] for ships arriving from Apia. For this reason the mail may not go by the Samoa Shipping and Trading Company's steamer on 2nd July, as advertised. If it is possible the Imperial Post Office will forward the mail via Pago Pago but it is advisable to post via Fiji, Vancouver.[23]

Besides, whatever other reasons there may have been, coming from the British-ruled Ellice offered easier access to Tokelau, which had been attached to the Gilbert and Ellice Islands Protectorate in 1910, and for which Apia would become an official port of entry only in 1923.[24]

Meanwhile, Ernest Allen also had a personal and domestic life. On 4 June 1888, in the British consulate in Apia, he married Maria Miller Meredith. She was the daughter of Thomas Meredith, an English-born merchant who had come to Samoa with his brother James in the 1870s, and his wife Maria, a woman of notable parentage. Maria's father, Jonas Coe, was one of the earliest European settlers in Samoa, and her mother, Le'utu, belonged to the chiefly family of Sa Malietoa. Ernest and Mary had six sons, but, to ensure that they were brought up *palagi* style, Ernest entrusted them during their formative years to the care of his sister Frances, known in the family as 'Auntie'. In 1896 she joined the family in Samoa, but, in 1899, the four eldest boys were sent to Auckland to live with her in the waterfront suburb of Devonport. They were followed by the next two in 1901 and 1905, respectively. About the latter date Ernest and Mary were divorced. Then both remarried: Mary to a German named Bayerlein, and Ernest to Mary Eliza Coe, a product of Jonas Coe's fifth—and final—marriage to Litia, the daughter of a Tongan missionary. This second union yielded one daughter and two sons.[25] They, too, were brought up by Frances, but—together with their youngest half-brother, William—mostly in Sydney, where their father bought a house in Lane Cove. They remained there from 1914 to 1921, before returning to Samoa. There Frances continued to devote herself to the family until shortly before her death in 1936.[26] Another child, not brought up in the family, was Lucy Pereira, Ernest's daughter by a Tokelau woman.[27]

As the older boys of the first family completed their schooling they also acquired skills that could be useful in their father's business. Fred served his time as an apprentice aboard the *Louisa Craig* which ran between Sydney and

---

23 *Samoanische Zeitung*, 21 June 1913; *Samoa Times*, 20 Mar. 1920; Allen, 'Memoir'; Sarah Jolliffe, 'Funafuti Diaries', 1 May 1913, LMS Records, South Sea Personal, National Library of Australia, microfilm M646.
24 *Samoanische Zeitung*, 30 Sept. 1911, 8 Feb. 1913, 30 May, 13, 20 June 1914; *Samoa Times*, 20 Mar. 1920; Allen, 'Memoir'; Huntsman and Hooper, p. 264.
25 Western Pacific High Commission 4, 64/1897, Cusack-Smith to WPHC, 4 June 1888; R.W. Robson, *Queen Emma: the Samoan-American girl who founded an empire in 19th century New Guinea*, Sydney, pp. 32–33; Allen, 'Memoir'; interviews with Eric Allen and Pat Steer. Thomas Meredith died in 1902.
26 Obituary, Frances Annie Amelia Allen, unidentified newspaper cutting.
27 Allen, 'Memoir'; letter, Briar Wilson to Laracy, 27 Aug. 2001.

Auckland; Reg worked in a warehouse; Tom in a engineering firm; Bert (Robert) in a shipping office; and, Joe had studied commercial subjects at Auckland Technical College. Thus, when on 28 February 1914 Joe joined the *Dawn* in Apia as an assistant supercargo, or floating shopkeeper, he was one of five brothers working for the Samoa Shipping and Trading Company. That first voyage took him north to Olohega (Swain's Island), which was owned by a planter named Eli Jennings, then up through the Tokelau group—Fakaofo, Nukunono, Atafu— before turning north-west for Funafuti, where Reg had married a local girl, Katerina. Soon afterwards the barquentine *Laura* arrived from Sydney carrying coal and general cargo, with Fred as first mate and Tom as able seaman. After loading copra, the *Laura* returned to Sydney. Then, as Joe later recalled in a memoir offering an unusually detailed and immediate description of trading operations, he began work in earnest.

> We traded mainly in the Tuvalu and Tokelau groups, with occasional trips to Samoa and islands north of the Cook group and Fiji. Our ship would arrive at an island at daybreak and I would go ashore with a supply of empty copra sacks. These I would distribute around the village in accordance with the amount of copra in each house … . The platform scale would be set up on the beach and the natives would bring their copra down in the sacks provided. On weighing I would give a ticket to the seller showing weight and cash value. The natives would then take their tickets on board where Bert would then cash them, and then sell them back goods. Meanwhile, I would supervise the carrying of the sacks of copra to waiting surf boats for transport over the reef to the ship … . Once over the coral reef, the depth went down suddenly to about 500 feet. Therefore, the ship had to steam in close and parallel with the reef, haul up the sacks of copra from the surf boats, and then steam or drift out again. I would go on board with the last boat load of copra and help Bert in the trade room. We usually got back in sales about 95% of the amount paid out for the copra. When trading was complete we would head away for the next island, usually an overnight trip. It would be 7pm by the time we had straightened up the trade room, replenished shelves, balanced the cash, and collected any passage monies from inter-island passengers. A popular custom was for groups of young men to go on holiday to another island in the group. This was also an exercise in practical eugenics, as it reduced inbreeding on each island.[28]

While strongly established in the Ellice group, the Allens did not have everything their own way there. The large firm of Burns, Philp sometimes competed for trade. So, too, did Sarah Jolliffe of the London Missionary Society, who ran a

---

28 Allen, 'Memoir'.

school at Papaelise on Funafuti. Her enterprise led Ernest Allen to complain to her Samoa-based superior, in a revealing letter on one of the classic tensions of Pacific islands life in the decades before World War II.

> I am sorry to say that Miss Jolliffe is rather seriously cutting into our business throughout the group. Miss Jolliffe imports goods for sale to the girls of the school. She no doubt believes that they are for the use of the girls only, but after careful enquiries I find that the girls buy for numerous other people, who bring the goods to us and tell us how much cheaper they can get them through Miss Jolliffe than through the ordinary course of trade.
>
> We keep a full and well assorted stock of goods which we sell at fair prices. Consequently I consider that it is very unfair that anyone engaged in mission work should import goods for trade at all.
>
> One instance I might point out. We sell a number of chemises at 2/–. These we used to get made at Sydney, the factory price for sewing being 2/6 per dozen. I thought it would be good practice for the girls if they made them, also allowing them to earn a few shillings, so through Miss Jolliffe got as many made as they could do. I now learn that Miss Jolliffe has a lot made up from her own material for sale.
>
> I would call your attention to the fact that we are under rather severe trading regulations in the Protectorate, all buildings etc having to be erected according to ordinance, which conditions we have faithfully carried out; also the licences: £100 for a ship, £12 per store and also a capitation tax of £5 per head per annum on all other than natives of the Protectorate in our employ that remain in the group for a longer term than two months.[29]

Besides its shipping and trading activities, the company also owned and operated island coconut plantations. These were Niulakita (Sophia) in the Ellice Islands, bought from H.J. Moors of Samoa in 1914; Nassau in the northern Cooks, also previously owned by Moors; and leaseholds, purchased from Levers, of five of the seven islands of the Phoenix group. Servicing these islands was a welcome diversion from the trading routine.[30]

World War I, though, would soon disrupt familiar routines in less congenial ways. Fred and Tom came ashore from the *Laura* in Sydney shortly after the outbreak of hostilities and enlisted forthwith in the Australian Imperial Force. They were both wounded at Gallipoli. Later Tom transferred to the Australian

---

29 Allen to Hills, 13 May 1915. Courtesy of Eric Allen.
30 *Samoanische Zeitung*, 27 Sept. 1902, 20 June 1908, 9 Aug. 1913. Laracy (ed.), *Tuvalu*, p. 62. Allen, 'Memoir'.

Flying Corps, and was killed in a training accident. In due course three other brothers, Bert, Joe and Bill likewise enlisted. That left only Reg of the immediate family to work with their father, who continued to captain the *Dawn*, and to endure the abuse and moodiness deriving from his habitual heavy drinking.[31]

By 1919 the surviving brothers were back with the firm, and business prospects looked good. In the immediate postwar years the price of copra was high, as was the demand for building materials and trade goods. Allen was also receiving a retainer from a family in Ireland for bringing to Funafuti and taking care of its Trinity College-educated son, J.G. Whibley, who had slipped into dereliction as a beachcomber on the island of Niutao.[32] Then, in 1920, there was a windfall contract to repatriate 73 'time expired' Melanesian labourers, recruited during the German regime, from Samoa to Rabaul. For Fred, who captained the *Rob Roy* on this expedition, and for Bill, who was 2nd engineer, it was also welcomed as an opportunity to meet some of their maternal relations, including their great-aunt Phoebe Parkinson and various descendants of her sister, the pioneering New Guinea planter 'Queen Emma' Coe.[33]

As an index of his continued optimism, Allen bought Blacklock out of his share in the company in 1918. And, in 1920, according to his son Joe, he even refused an offer from Burns, Philp 'of $1,000,000 for a half share in the company'. That statement, though, can at best be no more than half true. Even if there was an offer the amount cited is certainly not to be credited.[34]

But if a serious offer ever was made, Allen was unwise not to have accepted it. As early as 1915 Frederick Wallin of Burns, Philp, in a critical appraisal of the company, considered that it might not be as sound as it appeared.

> [They] will rue the day they locked up so much capital in Funafuti [he estimated £3,500] as, in addition thereto, they have the small steamer *Rob Roy* laid up in the lagoon for the last five months, it is said, owing to her machinery being done. The steamer *Dawn* and the barque *Laura* are also reported to be ancient and ripe. Withall, [though] I should say the Samoa Shipping and Trading Company's running expences will be cheap, Captain Allen having [his sons] working with him.[35]

---

31 Allan, 'Memoir'.
32 Ibid.; Hartley, *Colonial Outcasts*, pp. 164–165; Lucille Iremonger, *It's a Bigger Life*, London, 1948, p. 25; interview Joe Allen.
33 Allen, 'Memoir'; *Samoa Times*, 14 Feb. 1920.
34 Allen, 'Memoir'; notes by R.C. and M.E.A. Allen, courtesy of Eric Allen. Whatever the sum that was offered, Briar Wilson is surely correct in saying that it was in pounds, not dollars; letter to Laracy, 27 Aug. 2001.
35 K. Buckley and K. Klugman, *South Pacific Focus: a record in words and pictures of Burns Philp at work*, Sydney, 1986, p. 31.

As experience would show, these were perceptive comments. The *Rob Roy* broke down on the return voyage from Rabaul and drifted for 65 days before coming to Ocean Island, where the crankshafts could be repaired. About the same time the *Dawn* was long overdue on a voyage to Noumea for repairs. Instead of three weeks, it was there for three months. These problems were compounded in 1921 when Allen bought a wooden steamship, the *Samoa*, of about 400 tons from the American administration in Pago Pago for the seeming bargain price of $10,000. It was a disastrous purchase. The then new German-built vessel had been interned in Pago Pago on the outbreak of war in 1914. But it had lain there idle until 1921. Moreover, unseasoned oak had been used in its construction, so leading the company to undertake 'an abortive and financially crippling effort … to build a new hull around the engines'.

In the midst of these concerns Allen also lost an invaluable asset, his sons, through his excessive drinking and abusiveness, followed by fits of remorse. By 1922 not one of them was working for him, but had sought employment elsewhere. Robert and Joe, for instance, joined the colonial administration in Apia, in the native affairs and customs departments, respectively.[36] There, in a department rather too glibly maligned, as revisionist research has shown—and as his own presence suggests—as being careless of Samoan interests and out of touch with Samoan opinion, Robert worked closely with the administrator (1923–1928), Sir George Richardson. Like Richardson, Robert saw O.F. Nelson, a wealthy *afakasi* (half-caste) businessman and leader of the antigovernment Mau movement, as something of a carpetbagger tending to mislead and exploit the Samoans for his own advantage, rather than as an unalloyed nationalist.[37]

The last Robert and Joe saw of their father was in 1924 when he passed through Apia with his wife en route to Sydney. In an apparent salvage attempt, he asked Joe if the brothers would go back and take over the business as he would like to retire and live out his days on Stanley Point in Auckland, near Devonport. While being unable to speak for the others, Joe declared himself to be willing—but time had run out. Returning from Sydney the Allens reached Suva in August 1924, intending to join the brigantine *Jeanette* for the trip to Funafuti. Instead, Ernest was admitted to hospital, and died there from cirrhosis of the liver on 20 September. He was aged 57.[38] His company, of which his widow was now the sole director, was liquidated in 1925, on the petition of a San Francisco-based

---

36 Allen, 'Memoir'.
37 Richardson to Robert Allen, 27 July 1928, courtesy of Eric Allen; I.C. Campbell, 'New Zealand and the Mau in Samoa: re-assessing the causes of a colonial protest movement', *New Zealand Journal of History*, vol. 33, no. 1 (1999), pp. 92–110.
38 *Fiji Times*, 22 Sept. 1924; Allen, 'Memoir'.

firm to which it owed money. By Allen's own estimation shortly before his death there was an excess of assets over liabilities of £59,000. These were duly offered for sale by tender and were bought by Burns, Philp for £20,000.[39]

With the death of Ernest Allen—'the last of the overseas owner-captains', as one commentator has called him—and the demise of the Samoa Shipping and Trading Company, the day of the island trader as an independent operator was finally over.[40] Conversely, the long foreshadowed ascendancy of 'the big firm', a public company run from a corporate boardroom outside the islands in which it operated was complete. Both events, though, were but phases of the larger process of economic change that had begun for the islands before the middle of the nineteenth century with the visits of whalers and the growth of 'beach communities' around serviceable anchorages, such as Apia, and which has continued into the age of international aid and development programs. Allen played a discernable, and not inconsiderable, role in that process. He also finds significance in another, but related, area of enquiry through his family. Although they defined themselves as Europeans, and although by the 1930s his children had nearly all left Samoa for administrative, professional and commercial employment in New Zealand, Australian and England, they did not forget their ancestry. They thereby remained witnesses to the permeability and imprecision that may be attendant on convenient ethno/racial classifications such as European and 'native', Samoan and *palagi*, indigenous and alien. Accordingly, when Polynesians began flooding into New Zealand (and America and, later, Australia) in the 1960s many of them were entering a society in which they already had some well-established *afakasi* relations and acquaintances. The descendents of Ernest Allen are a case in point. So, too, are the Kronfelds, a German–Samoan family with Tongan connections, who settled in Auckland about 1890, and who cared for the future Queen Salote of Tonga during her school years there.[41] Such people as these point to a history not just of contact and encounter between Oceaneans and Europeans but also to one of integration and, indeed, of symbiosis.

---

39   *Evening News*, 15 Jan. 1925; unidentified newspaper clipping [*Sydney Morning Herald*, 30/31 Jan. 1925?]; Allen, 'Memoir'.
40   A.D. Couper, 'The Island Trade: an analysis of the environment and operation of seaborne trade among three island groups in the Pacific', PhD thesis, ANU, 1967, p. 87.
41   Elizabeth Wood-Ellem, *Queen Salote of Tonga: the story of an era, 1900–1965*, Auckland, 1999, pp. 13, 311; Margaret Hixon, *Salote, Queen of Paradise*, Dunedin, 2000, pp. 43–53.

8. Beatrice Grimshaw (1870–1953): Pride and prejudice in Papua

Of all the writers connected with the Pacific islands, probably the most prolific has been Beatrice Ethel Grimshaw, who lived from 1870 to 1953. Initially a journalist, she began her Pacific career as a propagandist for commercial and settler interests, but later, after becoming a settler herself, she concentrated on fiction writing. She was the author of nearly four-dozen books. Most of them were escapist outdoor romances with an exotic, titillatingly dangerous, Pacific setting. As a supplier of the popular market for easily digested entertainment, as an author whose characters tend to be stereotyped 'goodies' and 'baddies' and whose mechanically contrived plots invariably move to a 'happy ending', she is, admittedly, not a great literary figure. Yet, neither is she to be dismissed with a damning phrase, as James A. Michener presumed to do in describing her as the 'Queen of gush'.[1] For she does succeed in entertaining. The denouements are never entirely predictable, the variations on the basic elements of her stories are often ingenious and the prose is periodically enlivened by a tongue-in-cheek wryness of observation, often at the expense of her compatriots (for instance, 'when an Irishman is vulgar, be sure he's an Ulsterman').[2] *The Times* obituarist gave her no more than justice when he remarked that her 'long sequence of novels and short stories ... achieved high competence'.[3]

The more enduring significance of Grimshaw's writing, however, is in its being an historical source. For it reflects with unequalled volume and consistency some of the basic values, assumptions, aspirations and fantasies of the European settler community in Papua, to which she belonged from 1907 to 1934. She was their Rudyard Kipling (a writer to whose work she regularly alludes). She was the laureate of what has been described as:

> a dusty, lower middle class, Australian version of the British Raj. It lacked the grace and magnificence of the Empire at its zenith. Its security derived less from a sense of pride in its technological superiority and splendour than from a mean and pedantic insistence on the importance of innate racial differences.[4]

Approaching imaginative writing as a historical source can be a precarious activity. But the dangers are minimised in the case of Grimshaw by the clarity with which she shows the characters she approves of, by the supplementing

---

1 James A. Michener, *Return to Paradise*, London, 1952, p. 5.
2 Beatrice Grimshaw, *When the Red Gods Call*, London, 1911, p. 5.
3 *The Times*, 1 Aug. 1953.
4 Edward P. Wolfers, *Race Relations and Colonial Rule in Papua New Guinea*, Sydney, 1975, p. 45.

of her fiction with a considerable body of non-fiction, by the well-established place she enjoyed in settler society, and by the recorded views of many of her followers.[5] These factors all attest to a profound assurance of European racial superiority. This is a characteristic theme throughout her work. (After all, she was writing for a British readership at the heyday of Empire). It has been explored at length by Susan Gardner, and with a subtlety that identifies contradictions and tensions within the characters who populate her pages and, indeed, in her attitude to her own representations. Thus Grimshaw glamourised female individuality while affirming women's dependence on their menfolk, and their special responsibility for maintaining European standards of propriety in an alien setting. As for Pacific Islanders, she articulated a general disdain for them in the present but pragmatically foresaw a future in which they would be less easily dismissed.[6]

Paradoxically for one who wrote so extensively, Grimshaw was a private person. Her own writings, even those concerning herself, contain little personal information. An autobiography, reported in 1935 as having been written, was never published and few of her personal papers appear to have survived.[7] Yet, there are documentary gleanings enough from which to construct a basic chronology. She was born on 3 February 1870 at Cloona House, near Dunmurry, County Antrim, in the north of Ireland. Her father, Nicholas, was a linen merchant turned wine and spirit trader (in 1868) Her great-great-grand-father had, about 1760, moved from Lancashire to Belfast. There he set up the first cotton mill in Ireland and founded the Ulster Spinning Company. Her mother was the daughter of Ramsay Newson of Cork. Beatrice was the fifth child in a family of eight, four boys and four girls. The family were members of the Church of Ireland.[8]

Her early life Grimshaw reports as happy, being spent with a loving family in a pleasant home in the country where horse riding was the chief amusement. Later, as her father's business failed—a fact she does reveal—the family relinquished its country seat and moved into Belfast city, to 19 College Gardens.[9] She had left there long before her mother (1905) and father (1907) died, but, given the

---

5 See e.g., the views discussed in Hank Nelson, 'Papua—with the right sort of woman', *New Guinea*, vol. III (1969), pp. 39–56, also published as 'European attitudes in Papua, 1906–1914', in *The History of Melanesia* (Canberra, 1969), pp. 593–623; and Don Dickson, 'Murray's Education Policy', *New Guinea*, vol. IV (1970), pp. 15–40.
6 Susan Gardner, 'For Love and Money: early writings of Beatrice Grimshaw, colonial Papua's woman of letters', *New Literature Review*, no. 1 (1977), pp. 10–20; and 'A '"vert to Australianism": Beatrice Grimshaw and the Bicentenary', *Hecate*, vol. 13, no. 1 (1987–1988), pp. 51, 56–57.
7 *Pacific Islands Monthly* (*PIM*), July 1935, p. 4.
8 Birth certificate by courtesy of Mr P. Grimshaw, and copy of family tree by courtesy of Dr H. Nelson, Canberra, Australian National University; Ian Budge and Cornelius O'Leary, *Belfast: approach to crisis. A study of Belfast politics 1613–1970*, London, 1973, p. 17; Susan Jane Gardner, 'For Love and Money: Beatrice Grimshaw's passage to Papua', PhD thesis, Rhodes University, 1985, p. 202.
9 Matthew Hoehn (ed.), *Catholic Authors*, St Mary's Abbey, 1948, p. 294.

decline in fortune associated with it, it is likely that she had Cloonagh rather than its successor, opposite Queen's University, affectionately in mind when she wrote to an Australian correspondent in 1912:

> I was very glad to hear that you are well and that your home affairs are happy. You don't know how different life looks when the home breaks up and you warm yourself henceforth by other folk's fires. Of course yours never may; there may always be some of your people left in the old place. I hope there will be.[10]

Houses were a recurrent, and wishful, symbol of comfort and reassurance in Grimshaw's writings. In 1919 she was pleased to have her house at Samarai in Papua featured in an Australian magazine.[11]

Never 'a girl to sew a fine seam', Grimshaw appears to have been allowed to grow up without too much parental constraint. Her formal education was broad and expensive, though desultory. She was first taught by private tutors and governesses. Later, in 1877, during a lengthy interlude abroad, at Caen in Normandy, she attended a school kept by Mlle Retaillaud (whose name she afterwards used in a novel). A decade on, during 1887, she attended Bedford College, University of London, where her main subjects were Latin, Greek, Mathematics Physics and Chemistry. During the 1890–1891 academic year she attended Queen's College, Belfast. She never took a degree. At some time she appears to have tried nursing.[12]

Grimshaw's parents' hope, so she says, was that she would become a lecturer in classics at a women's college, though they might even have been content for her simply to take her place in society. For her part, the evidence suggests that she was attracted by the possibility of—and, as the family money ran out, presumably felt the need for—a professional career of some sort. Whatever the particular reasons, Grimshaw emerges as the very model of the liberated 'New Woman' of the 1890s. Indeed, she applied the term to herself. She had enjoyed something of the new opportunities for female higher education; she also rode the newly fashionable bicycle, which became an important sign and symbol of liberation by enabling respectable young ladies to assert their individuality, and escape from the traditional restraints represented by chaperones; she found paid professional employment; and, ultimately, she travelled.[13] Dorothy

---

10 Beatrice Grimshaw to Margaret Windeyer, 20 July 1912, Sydney, Mitchell Library, Ag 66.
11 Gardner, 'A '"vert" to Australianism', p. 31; Thos J. McMahon, 'The House of Miss Beatrice Grimshaw, Papua's novelist', *Lone Hand*, Jan 1919, 34.
12 Hoehn, p. 294; B. Grimshaw, *From Fiji to the Cannibal Islands*, London, 1907, p. 219; pers. comms from Sir Arthur Vick, Queen's University, Belfast, 30 Oct. 1974, L.P. Turnbull, Bedford College, London, 7 Nov. 1974, and Gildas Bernard, Archives Departmentales du Calvodos, 15 Oct. 1975.
13 Hoehn, p. 294; Beatrice Grimshaw, *Isles Of Adventure*, London, 1930, pp. 14–16.

Middleton's generalisations in *Victorian Lady Travellers* (all of them middle class women, and not eccentric aristocrats such as Lady Hester Stanhope) apply in their essentials to Grimshaw:

> Travel was an individual gesture of the housebound, man-dominated Victorian woman. Trained from birth to an almost impossible idea of womanly submission and self-discipline, of obligation to class and devotion to religion, she had need of an emotional as well as of an intellectual outlet. This she found often late in life, in travel, and though her dignity never wavered and she seems to have imposed her severe moral standards on the very rough company in which she often found herself, she was able to enjoy a freedom of action unthinkable at home.[14]

This individual liberation, relished by Grimshaw, was not allied to a concern for the condition of women in general. The 'New Woman' was not necessarily a suffragette, nor, in any explicit way, a precursor of the modern feminist. Grimshaw not only held rigidly to conventional moral standards but also readily conceded that 'women are not as clever as man—let the equality brigade shriek if they like—but neither are we as stupid'.[15]

In *Isles of Adventure*, a semi-autobiographical travelogue on New Guinea published in 1930, Grimshaw writes that she left 'a perfectly good home, where the manners and the food are better than she found anywhere else, but where life was infested by the giving and taking of loathsome parties. And nobody was really serious'.[16] The evidence of later straightened circumstances (her father left an estate of only £30), suggests that this picture of delightful domestic decadence was unduly roseate (and based on Cloonagh?). In any case, when she was 21, and with the reluctant blessing of her parents, she went to Dublin to take up journalism. There, with a vagueness of detail characteristic of her style, she relates that she edited a 'Social Journal' and subedited a sporting journal. In fact, she worked on *The Irish Cyclist* (1891–1895) and *The Social Review* (1895–1899), two of a stable of magazines controlled by a notable sportsman and publisher, Richard James ('Arjay') Mecredy. Her decade in Dublin was also marked by several other notable assertions of self. In 1894 she became a Catholic. About the same time she set, so she claims, a new women's 24-hour road cycling record, but this was at best a gross transmogrification of a more modest feat.[17] Under the pseudonym 'Graphus', in her 'Lady Cyclist' column in *The Irish Cyclist*, 29 June 1898, Grimshaw reported that

---

14   D. Middleton, *Victorian Lady Travellers*, London, 1965, p. 4.
15   B. Grimshaw, *In the Strange South Seas*, London, 1907, p. 152.
16   Grimshaw, *Isles*, p. 11; Gardner, thesis, p. 194.
17   Grimshaw, *Isles*, pp. 11–36; Hoehn, p. 293; Harold J. Hood (ed.), *The Catholic Who's Who, 1952* (London n.d.); *Freeman's Journal* (Sydney), 21 Oct. 1905. Gardner, thesis, p. 5. *The Times* obituary, among other reports, accepts Beatrice's record claim, but offers no details and is probably relying on her own statement in *Isles of Adventure*.

> I hear that a lady cyclist—name unknown—shortly contemplates going for a 12 hours road record ... once in my 'salad days', when machines were rather different, and riders very much less knowing, I thought of trying for a 100 miles ride in private, and without any pace-makers, though checks, of course, were to be obtained ... the result, on a three-figure ride, did not come within 4 miles an hour of the 100 record as it stood then! After which, as Kipling would say, I quit! Unless a woman cyclist is prepared to ride under the best possible conditions, in exactly the same way as a man, her ride cannot amount to anything worth noticing.[18]

Another achievement was the publication in 1897 of her first novel, a romance about an assertive young woman like herself, and titled *Broken Away*. Then, in 1901, she turned from 'pure' to 'applied' journalism, to writing advertising material for tourist and travel firms and promoting emigration. In 1902, following a move to London, she became responsible for the organisation and control of the Cunard shipping company's literary department, but resigned the following year to travel further afield herself, on assignment for the *Daily Graphic*.[19]

Equipped with travel passes, writing commissions and personal introductions, she crossed America, touched at Tahiti, and went on to New Zealand. There the Union Steam Ship Company commissioned her to write attractive descriptions for tourists of the places visited by its vessels in the eastern Pacific. Before the end of 1904 she had visited and enthused over the Cook Islands, Tonga, Samoa and Niue. Two articles on this voyage, which allowed her several lengthy sojourns ashore, were serialised in 1906 and 1907 in the *Red Funnel*, a literary magazine published by the Union company.

Also in 1904 she was commissioned to tour and report on New Zealand, particularly on the geothermal 'wonderland' of the central North Island, for the Government Tourist Department. Next, in 1905, she was commissioned by the Fiji Government to undertake a horseback journey through the two main islands of Fiji 'to see just what the native and his life were like, and what value the country might be for possible settlers'. The governor, Sir Everard im Thurn, later declared himself pleased with the resulting publicity.[20] Sir Basil Thomson, a former colonial official familiar with Fiji and Tonga, though, was more sceptical:

---

18   Quoted in Gardner to Laracy, 7 June 1979, personal communication.
19   Grimshaw to Deakin, 1 Oct. 1908, Canberra, Australian Archives, CRS A1 1919/3935; *PIM* Feb. 1947, p. 36; J.E. Nixon Westwood 'Notes', Canberra, National Library of Australia (NLA), Nixon Westwood papers.
20   Grimshaw to Deakin, 1 Oct. 1908, Canberra, Australian Archives, CRS A1 1919/3935; Beatrice Grimshaw, 'A Lady in Far Fiji', *The Wide World Magazine*, vol. XVIII (1906–1907), p. 218. Beatrice had a cousin, Edward Grimshaw, who lived in Fiji from 1883 to 1941, but there is no evidence that she was ever aware of him. *Fiji Times and Herald*, 20 Jan. 1941.

> Nor must her invitation to Englishmen with small capital to emigrate to the South Pacific be taken seriously. First impressions of these beautiful islands are apt to breed enthusiasm, but the stern reality is that, while many traders, by dint of hard living and careful management, contrive to save money, the planter landing in the islands without experience generally stays only long enough to part with his capital.[21]

Maybe, but Grimshaw was scarcely intemperate or even uncautious in her advocacy:

> the young Englishman wishing to seek his fortune as a planter should have at least £500 to start on, exclusive of passage-money. He can do excellently with a few hundreds more, but it is as well to put things as low as possible. Copra—the dried kernal of the cocoanut—is the usual, and the safest, investment. It is always saleable, and the demand increases year by year—so much so, that the large soap-making firms, who are the chief users of the product, are of late planting out islands for themselves. The cost of clearing and planting the land is about £5 an acre. ... In about seven years, the returns begin to come in, and in ten years time the land should be bringing in £5 net profit for every acre of trees. This is, of course, a long time to wait, but bananas can grow on the same land meantime, and will generally yield a quick return. ... [On the other hand] banana growing may be managed with less capital, but the profits are not so sure, since fruit is perishable, and cannot wait for the steamer as copra can.[22]

From Fiji, Grimshaw travelled to Sydney and thence to the then New Hebrides. Early in 1906 she returned to Europe.[23] Her main achievement over the next 18 months was the completion of three books, all published in 1907. Two, *In the Strange South Seas* (reviewed by Thomson), and *From Fiji to the Cannibal Islands*, were expansions of her *Red Funnel* articles, and one, *Vaiti of the Islands*, was a novel.

In 1907 she again set forth: this time for Australia and from there, in November, to Papua. She intended to stay two or three months. Instead, it became her home for the next 27 years. One reason for this was the encouragement she received from Hubert Murray (at that time the acting administrator and soon to be lieutenant-governor), who accommodated her for the first few weeks at Government House. Irish, Catholic, well educated, travelled, a 'loner', a noted sportswoman, and an advocate of commercial development for tropical colonies, Grimshaw was in many ways a female analogue of Murray, who found her an

---

21 *Times Literary Supplement*, 14 Nov. 1907, p. 346.
22 Grimshaw, *Strange South Seas*, pp. 57–58.
23 Grimshaw, *Fiji to the Cannibal Islands*, pp. 124, 169, 224; Grimshaw, *Isles*, p. 298.

agreeable guest. He described her to his brother, Gilbert, the famous Greek scholar, as 'an extremely nice woman, and not a bit superior; also she is an Irish Catholic and Fenian and if she was also Australian there would be nothing more to be desired'.[24] While the designation 'Fenian' is tongue-in-cheek (there is no evidence that her unabashed Irishness extended to political partisanship), Grimshaw was, likewise, attracted to Murray. Unfortunately for the prurient romantics, though, there is no evidence that their relationship was ever closer than that of friendship; the details of their mutual history must remain professional rather than personal. Impressed with Murray's work she was to find in Papua ample scope for her ability as a publicist. She was concerned to help him attract settlers, and to defend him against criticisms of rivals who, at the time of her arrival, were hoping to prevent his appointment as lieutenant-governor.

On 31 January 1908 *The Times* published her report 'that new liberal land laws have been promulgated and the natives are contented. For this state of things credit must be given to Mr Murray's administration'. During 1908 she also took it upon herself to write a series of letters to Alfred Deakin, then Prime Minister of Australia, praising Murray and urging upon Deakin his responsibility towards British settlers in Australia's neighbourhood. In January she wrote to advocate a stronger British presence in the New Hebrides; to assure Deakin of the Papuans' great personal respect for Murray; and, to inform him that she had a 'very satisfactory system for spreading information through the press of the world, not necessarily under my own signature'. In March she wrote in praise of Murray: 'he is of the type that I know well at home—the kind that can handle an Indian Presidency, or an African colony with ease'.

On 2 June she urged that Australia take over the Solomon Islands and the New Hebrides from Britain, and also made some revealing comments about missions and her view of their place in the colonial polity. While describing herself as a rough believer in and supporter of missions, she deplored their tendency to usurp the functions of government. She also charged that they did not want countries developed by white settlers. Rather they wished 'to keep out capital, to retain supreme power themselves, to prevent the natives engaging in plantation work, and above all (as a rule) from learning English'. Three weeks later she wrote again, defending Murray.[25]

When she visited Melbourne later in the year she twice called on Deakin.

---

24 Beatrice Grimshaw, *The New New Guinea*, London, 1910, pp. 3–5; 'Into Unknown Papua', *Wide World Magazine*, vol. XXIV (1909–1910), p. 387; "Australia's Island Asset', *Life* (Sydney), 1909, p. 360; Francis West (ed.), *Selected Letters of Hubert Murray*, Melbourne, 1970, p. 34.
25 Grimshaw to Deakin, 25 Jan, 21 Mar., 2, 26 June, 2 July, 1 (two letters), 3, 14 Oct. 1908, NLA, Deakin Papers, Box 40 MS 1540/40/499. This correspondence is also discussed in J.A. La Nauze, *Alfred Deakin, a biography* (Melbourne 1964), vol. II, p. 468.

One result of thus making herself known was that, for £85 and free transport to and within Papua, she was commissioned by Deakin to publicise Papua's need for settlers and capital.[26] On 14 November 1908 Murray wrote to his brother: 'Miss Grimshaw returned today after a short visit to Australia. She is to write pamphlets advertising Papua. I owe much to her'.[27] She lost no time on this task. On 5 December she reported to Atlee Hunt, secretary of the Home and Territories Department, that she had completed three leaflets for distribution among the county families of England and that she would do 'about half a dozen more before concluding the work'. She was as good as her word. She then ensured that copies were sent to the main London clubs, shipping companies and magazines as well as to 800 people listed in *Whittaker's Peerage, Baronetage, Knightage and Championage* (*Burke's Landed Gentry* was unobtainable in both Melbourne and Sydney at the time). She hoped to assure 'families ... who have "younger sons" with capital that there is not a place in the British Empire where a fortune, can be made more surely and safely with a small capital' (recommended minimum £2,000).[28] Meanwhile she continued to 'puff' Papua in newspaper articles, and later in books. In 1910 there appeared *The New New Guinea*, an account of her travels in Papua similar in style to her travel books of 1907. Murray paid her £100 from government funds for *The New New Guinea* and probably corrected the proofs himself while on leave in England. Considering, so she wrote in 1909 (and as the academic community was to decide in the 1960s), that 'the market is ripe for New Guinea literature', she also applied herself to fiction.[29]

Following her initial stay at Government House, Grimshaw had several addresses in Port Moresby. First, the 'Top Pub', one of Port Moresby's two. Then a double canoe anchored offshore, against the hull of which, it has been said, crocodiles used to scratch their backs at night; and, later, a house, which she bought on Paga Hill.[30] She was generally acknowledged as a celebrity and took prominent part in the social life of the town. She attended functions at Government House, helped organise 'at homes' in the schoolhouse, attended the Catholic church regularly and was one of a group of ladies who made vigorous use of the public swimming pool. To gather material for her writing she persistently sought the conversation of schooner men, planters and goldminers, in addition to visiting the Lake Kamu goldfield herself and taking advantage of almost any opportunity to travel. For a while, it seems, she may even have been engaged to a well-known

---

26   Hunt to Grimshaw, 8 Oct 1908, Canberra, Australian Archives, CRS A1, 1910/3935.
27   West, p. 52
28   Grimshaw to Hunt, 5 Dec. 1908, NLA, Atlee Hunt papers, 52/2179; Hunt to Grimshaw, 10 Oct. 1908; Grimshaw to Campbell, 16 June 1909; memoranda re 'Circulars', CRS A1 1910/3935, Australian Archives, *Daily Mail Overseas Edition*, 4 Sept. 1909.
29   West, p. 40; Grimshaw to Murray, 23 Dec. 1909, Sydney, Mitchell Library, Murray papers, A3138.
30   Nixon Westwood 'Notes', 4, NLA, Nixon Westwood Papers; *Argus* (Melbourne), 28 Sept. 1912; Grimshaw, *Isles*, pp. 183–186, 217–218; Ian Stuart, *Port Moresby: yesterday and today*, Sydney, 1970, pp. 175, 225, 254.

miner, William Little, who died in 1920. At least she wore his ring.[31] In 1913 she was invited to visit Dutch Timor to advise on development and, in 1915, she left Port Moresby to live on the island of Sariba, near Samarai. From 1917 to 1922—turning to pioneering on her own account—she tried her hand at developing a plantation on the mainland opposite Sariba. Then, in 1922, she sold out and visited Britain, staying several weeks in the Moluccas on the way. On her return, Port Moresby again became her home, though she spent considerable time at a cottage, which she built, overlooking the Rouna Falls, 32 kilometres inland.[32]

During the 1920s Grimshaw made several notable excursions. In 1923, visiting the Mandated Territory of New Guinea, she accompanied a Divine Word Mission party over 300 kilometres up the Sepik River. And, in 1926, Murray took her on an expedition nearly 500 kilometres up the Fly River to Lake Murray where, she records, the people stole from him a history of Ireland written in Gaelic. On both trips Grimshaw rejoiced to have been the first European woman to have ventured so far inland.[33] Late in 1930 she departed, travelling via the Cook Islands and Tahiti, for the United States and Europe, returning in 1932. Then, in 1933, she took over five acres of land that had been previously leased by the film actor Errol Flynn, on the Laloki River, 24 kilometres from Port Moresby. Here, with her brother Ramsay, an ex-marine engineer, she hoped to establish a tobacco farm. But in 1934 the farm was sold and, with Ramsay and another brother, Osbourne, who was retiring after 20 years in the Papua Government Service, she left Papua. As for her previous departures from Port Moresby, Murray stated his deep regret at losing a good friend and commented further that 'we had come to look on her as part of the territory'.[34] She again visited Fiji, Samoa and Tonga before finally retiring in 1936 to a cottage at Kelso, near Bathurst in New South Wales, where Ramsay was farming.[35] Her last novel, *The Missing Blondes*, was published in 1945. Grimshaw died at Bathurst on 30 June 1953.[36]

In her nonfiction writing Grimshaw had two, clear-cut objectives. The first was to entertain and divert armchair travellers. The second was to promote European enterprise: tourism in Polynesia and settlement in Melanesia, immediately, at least, in Fiji and in Papua. For the New Hebrides, she saw the absence of a clear

---

31 Grimshaw to Windeyer, 20 July 1912, Sydney, Mitchell Library, Ag 66; Nixon Westwood 'Notes', 4, NLA, Nixon Westwood Papers; *Papuan Times*, 1 Mar., 8 Nov. 1911; *PIM*, Feb. 1947, p. 36; Grimshaw, *Isles*, pp. 182–183; B. Malinowski, *A Diary in the Strict Sense of the Term*, New York, 1967, pp. 17, 58, 75; *PIM*, July 1932, p. 39.
32 West, pp. 73, 88–89; *The Times*, 1 July 1953; *PIM*, Feb. 1947, p. 36; Grimshaw, *Isles*, pp. 208–218.
33 Grimshaw, *Isles*, pp. 37–82, 109–145. This book is largely a reprint of articles published in *Wide World Magazine* and *Windsor Magazine* in the 1920s. For details see bibliography.
34 West, pp. 73, 89, 170. *PIM*, June 1931, p. 4; May 1932, p. 33; Feb. 1933, p. 31; May 1933, p. 45; Oct. 1933, p. 33; Aug. 1934, p. 13. John Hammond Moore, *The Young Errol: Flynn before Hollywood*, Sydney, 1975, pp. 77–79.
35 *PIM*, Apr. 1935, p. 9; July 1935, p. 4; Oct 1935, p. 26; Nov 1936, p. 54.
36 *Western Times*, 1, 2 July 1953; *The Times*, 1 Aug. 1953.

colonial authority as inhibiting commercial development, and urged Australian intervention.[37] Underlying these notions is another significant theme, a racialist one, of the distance which, according to an evolutionary theory of human development, allegedly exists and must be maintained between Europeans and Pacific Islanders. Her attitude toward the islanders, ranging from patronising to disgusted, was one that the present age would damn, but which a school of thought fashionable earlier in the century rationalises in terms of what has since become known as 'social Darwinism.'[38]

Following the convention established by the eighteenth century explorer Bougainville, whose romantic description of the Tahitians led to their being widely regarded as 'noble savages', she is indulgent towards the Polynesians.[39] They are amiable children of nature—'jolly, laughing, brown-skinned, handsome men and women', 'straight haired, light brown in colour, gentle and generous in disposition, ready to welcome strangers and feast them hospitably … aristocratic to the backbone'.[40] The Tongans she describes as 'a Christianised and partially civilised if a coloured race … they are handsome, with intelligent faces, and a dignity of pose and movement that is sometimes unkindly called the Tongan "swagger"'. And the Samoans are delineated as 'a singularly beautiful race and most amiable in character'.[41] Fijians, on the boundary line between Polynesia and Melanesia, are, however, placed on the border between good and evil. Seeing a Fijian making fire by rubbing two sticks together led Grimshaw to comment:

> It was my first example of the truth that the Fijian civilization is only varnish deep.
>
> Cannibalism has been abandoned, cruelty and torture given up, an ample amount of clothing universally adopted, yet the Fijian of 1905, freed from the white control and example that have moulded all his life would spring back like an unstrung bow to the thoughts and ways of his fathers. This is a truth doubted by no one who knew the inner life of Fiji.[42]

Westward of Fiji, the undiluted Melanesians are worst of all. Darker skinned than the Polynesians, living on much larger islands but in smaller non-chiefly

---

37 Gardner, 'A "'vert to Australianism"', pp. 43–48.
38 For a discussion of ideas regarding race, see Michael Banton, *Race Relations* (London, 1967), pp. 36–54.
39 For a discussion of the origins of Polynesian noble savages see W.H. Pearson, 'European Intimidation and the Myth of Tahiti', *The Journal of Pacific History*, vol. IV (1969), pp. 199–217, and Bernard Smith, *European Vision and the South Pacific, 1768–1850*, Oxford, 1969, pp. 24–31.
40 Grimshaw, *Strange South Seas*, pp. 91, 190.
41 Ibid., pp. 257, 282.
42 Grimshaw, *Fiji to the Cannibal Islands*, p. 39.

communities, divided from their neighbours by fear of sorcery and by language differences and being, admittedly, less acculturated, Grimshaw had little good to say of them although she was to live among them for 27 years. She speaks of

> The dark, wicked cannibal groups of the Solomons, Banks [New Guinea] and New Hebrides, where life is more like a nightmare than a dream, murder stalks openly in broad daylight, the people are nearer to monkeys than to human beings in aspect, and music and dancing are little practised, and in the rudest state possible.[43]

She developed her views of the New Hebrideans at some length. They were 'ugly creatures with flat, savage features; creatures of appalling ugliness and evil, as for the Malekulans, worst fiends in hell or out of it … the wildest imagination of mad-houses could [not] picture'.[44] But they were not entirely unimproveable:

> In some cases the New Hebridean is found capable of receiving education, filling the post of plantation overseer or learning to be a good house servant: though such instances are rare. The people of Aneityum and Erromanga, being Christianised and civilised as far as possible to the race, have reached a general level about equal to that of an intelligent English child of seven or eight.[45]

Such improvement was, however, to their disadvantage rather than advantage: 'to the traveller original savages are a good deal more interesting folk such as the clean, tidy, school attending, prosaically peaceful people of Aneityum'.[46] The mental process of all new Hebrideans were, she thought, different in kind from those of Europeans:

> The New Hebridean mind is what Lewis Carroll would call 'scroobious and wily' and no white man can follow its turnings. It is quite capable of planning to kill you, for no conceivable reason, and abandoning the plan, also without the reason, and in a minute. All one can be certain of about a New Hebridean is that there is no certainty in him.[47]

Yet, despite the New Hebrideans' lowly status in the scheme of human development, European planters were not entitled to ill-treat their labourers.

---

43   Ibid., p. 14
44   Ibid., pp. 138, 162, 165.
45   Ibid., p. 139.
46   Ibid., p. 237.
47   Ibid., p. 213.

> Let it be allowed that the New Hebridean is a devil at heart—it does not improve even a devil to underfeed him, abuse him and flog him for the smallest cause, and count his life worth nothing more than the few pounds you have paid the schooner captain for recruiting him.[48]

Nevertheless, such was the disorder that prevailed among the islanders that Grimshaw wished

> most earnestly, that I could see the strong hand of Great Britain or her colonies grasp the bridle of this wretched country, as unfit to be left on its own guidance as any runaway horse, and pull it firmly and determinedly into the road of civilization and law-abiding peace.[49]

The cries of certain men from Tana, who had worked on plantations in Queensland—'Tana for the Tanese', 'if the white man won't have us in his country we won't have him in ours'—she dismissed as 'unpleasantly significant'.[50] What was needed to bring real fulfilment and nobility to the Pacific islands, as Beatrice saw things, was settlers: 'The South Seas hold out hands of peace and plenty, begging for a respectable white population'. For,

> The brown races are dying out with fearful rapidity; at their best they never touched the limitless capacities of the golden pacific soil. Its richness has always seemed to the original inhabitants an excellent reason for abstaining from cultivation. When the earth produced of itself everything that was necessary for comfort why trouble to work for it .... In the promise of the future, grey or golden, they have no shame. Today is theirs but they have no tomorrow.

But for the 'more progressive' white man in the Pacific islands 'honesty, sobriety and industry repay their possessor as almost nowhere else in the world'.[51] An example of a desirable settler was

> Mr X ... a young Oxonian, not twenty four years of age, who had been through most of the Boer War, and found himself unable to settle down to an office job at home afterwards. Accordingly he bought a plantation on Efate ... this adventurous young Englishman remains alone among his men, managing the plantation without help ... these are things that mere school boys of the British race can do when you take them from their Grandmothers and Aunts at home, and turn them loose in the wilderness to shift for themselves.[52]

---

48   Ibid., p. 139.
49   Ibid., p. 220.
50   Ibid., p. 229.
51   Grimshaw, *Strange South Seas*, pp. 56–57.
52   Grimshaw, *Fiji to the Cannibal Islands*, p. 149.

Another admirable example was that of a family on a well-established plantation who lead a life in full accord with metropolitan standards of gentility.[53] Indeed, to Grimshaw, they owed it to their race to do so. She makes her own conviction of racial superiority clear in describing her reaction to the volcanic activity of Mt Yasur on Tana. She had been looking into the crater:

> [and then] I found myself running down the side of the cone, hand-in-hand with two extremely frightened niggers .... It was not courage, for I had none left, that stopped me half a dozen yards below the crater lip. White people must not be frightened before the blacks. So I went back and sat on the edge again ... and looked down once more.[54]

Given the corollary of such notions of racial superiority, the importance of maintaining white racial purity, it is logical that Beatrice should have deplored interracial marriage (even between European and Polynesians), unlike one Englishwoman she writes of who 'sinned against her race'—and was punished with misery and an early death for her folly. In the idyllic island of Rarotonga, so she wrote, 'there are no social distinctions, save that between white and brown'.[55] Such was the proper state of things, in contrast to the situation of the Dutch East Indies, where, she was later to observe, miscegenation was bringing 'nearer to Holland the fate that befell Portugal and Spain when they forgot the Pride of race'.[56]

The same attitudes, together with more urgent promotional purpose, are also found in Grimshaw's work on New Guinea. In *The New New Guinea*, she wrote of 'the Port Moresby native' and the locality he inhabited as being of scant interest and that '[it is] the new plantation life that is the real attraction in Papua today'. Indeed, between '1907 and 1909 it changed from being a useless tract of land, where the natives were more than half out of hand ... to a peaceful, habitable and flourishing colony'. The reality of this transformation she presumed to demonstrate by citing statistics: in 1906, 28,999 acres of land were in European hands; by March 1909 this had risen to 319,853.[57] Such was progress, and if the Papuans were to have any share in the glorious future to which it pointed, it would be through working as plantation labourers or 'house-boys': 'All Pacific history seems to show that the conquered, tamed, civilised, and idle Oceanian inevitably dies out. All Malaysia seems to prove that the working savage lives'.[58] But work was not totally reforming. By the 1920s increased contracts between Papuans and Europeans had given rise to what Grimshaw calls the 'Black

---

53   Ibid., p. 145.
54   Ibid., p. 233.
55   Grimshaw, *Strange South Seas*, pp. 91, 244.
56   Beatrice Grimshaw, 'East Beyond the East', *Wide World magazine*, vol. LII (1923–1924), p. 30.
57   Grimshaw, *New New Guinea*, pp. 33, 53.
58   Beatrice Grimshaw, 'The Progress of Papua', *Australia Today*, 1 Nov. 1911, p. 141.

Peril'—the alleged sexual desire of dark men for white woman. She admits that sexual assault was rare; after all very few white women would 'insult' their race in 'the deepest possible manner' by directly encouraging the advances of their servants. But since 'brown men [were] violent and unrestrained of feeling, like all savages' their lusts could easily be aroused through carelessness in dress and demeanour. The answer was simply for European women to be more careful, and to keep a revolver in the bedroom.[59]

Opinions such as these were firmly entrenched among the settler caste in Papua. This is shown by the pressure that in 1926, following several assaults (not all of them unambiguously sexual) on European females, led Murray to issue the White Women's Protection Ordinance. This blatantly discriminatory regulation allowed the death penalty to be imposed on anyone convicted of rape or attempted rape of 'any European woman or girl'.[60]

Sustaining Grimshaw's distrust of the New Guineans' sexuality was a firm belief in their diabolically supported capacity for evil. In her view the devil, working through sorcerers, had assisted the people of the then German New Guinea in 1904 to organise a plot, covering the whole of the territory, for getting rid of the Europeans. This opinion is a construction based on two separate and unrelated incidents—one an unsuccessful plot by dispossessed villagers to attack the European settlers at Madang, and the other the massacre of Catholic missionaries in the Baining district of New Britain. For Grimshaw, as for the Australian settlers of Rabaul after their employees struck for higher wages in 1929, the instinctive response to any form of Melanesian aggression or self-assertion was one of hysterical opposition.[61]

The themes and values that characterise Grimshaw's nonfiction writing also occur in her fiction, which is particularly concerned with glamorising the settler class to which she belonged. Consistently, she builds her stories around the same basic plot structure—hero meets heroine, they survive dangers from cannibals or some other species of miscreant, they discover some impediment to marriage, as well as great riches, but in the final chapter the impediment is disposed of and they settle down to a blissful and prosperous future. Virtue always triumphs, and marriage provides the happy ending. Autobiographical echoes, and wishfulness, abound.

---

59   Grimshaw, *Isles*, pp. 28–29.
60   Amirah Inglis, *'Not a White Woman Safe': sexual anxiety and politics in Port Moresby, 1920–1934*, Canberra, 1974.
61   Grimshaw, *Isles*, pp. 80–81. For the Madang plot, see Peter Lawrence, *Road Belong Cargo. A study of the cargo movement in the Southern Madang District, New Guinea* (Bari, 1968). For the Rabaul strike, see Ian Willis, 'Rabaul's 1929 Strike', *New Guinea*, vol. V (1970), pp. 6–24; and, Bill Gammage, 'The Rabaul Strike, 1929', *Journal of Pacific History*, vol. X, nos 3–4 (1975), pp. 3–29.

Beatrice's second novel, *Vaiti of the Islands*, covers the same geographical range as her first two travel books, also published in 1907. In it, Polynesia provides a more gentle setting than Melanesia, where most of her novels are set. The conflict of colour is pronounced and, indeed, the heroine, Vaiti, is a mixed-blood. Like any Grimshaw heroine she is beautiful, wellborn, resourceful and brave, in addition to being an accomplished sailor and a good shot with a gun. Her mother was a Cook Islands princess, her father a disgraced English nobleman. As a result she was 'doubly dowered … with the instinct of rule', as well as with the half-caste's taste for extravagant clothes (she buys one very expensive and quite unsuitable gown from 'Madam Retaillaud's Emporium in San Francisco'). After several adventures escaping from a villainous and ultimately degraded Irishman named Donahue ('a white man cannot live native without going downhill fast'), an affair with an English naval officer named Tempest, and after terrorising a party of foolish, over-genteel, thrill-seeking tourists in the New Hebrides, she ends up in the 'Liali Group' (Tonga). There she marries the king, Napolean Timothy Te Paea III.[62]

In 1920 Grimshaw published a sequel, *Queen Vaiti*. It begins with Vaiti, her husband having died, fleeing from the Lialians who think she has killed him. She again meets Tempest, who had resigned from the navy after an incident in which he had neglected his duty for the sake of some amorous escapade, and marries him. For Tempest the marriage is both a conquest and a defeat. He unashamedly tells his new wife 'I've ruined my life, as far as anything decent goes', while the author explains that 'his marriage with a half-caste … was the final cutting of the last link that bound him to all he had known, desired or cared'.[63] Still, they both remained worthy characters in their own way—he brave and she an aristocratic Polynesian—so Grimshaw contrived a honourable demise for them. In the finale, the sudden eruption of an underwater volcano destroys their schooner. But the lovers go down with it, embracing on the poop deck as it sinks.

No such countenancing of a breach of the code of white supremacy occurs in Grimshaw's Melanesian novels in which the heroes are less ambiguous and the author's identification with her heroines is complete. These are all white, nearly all of mature years, and tend to be New Women. They represent her ideals. Eve Landon in *The Coral Queen* is, we are told, the prettiest girl in Papua, but is also a competent businesswoman. She 'represented the twentieth century and the future'. Aged 26, 'she was the incarnation of the youth in the twentieth century'. She demonstrates this, among other ways, by disrupting a strange cult, the Altiora Settlement, in an imaginary island group called the New Cumberlands. The Altiora Settlement is a community of Europeans who believe that human

---

62 Beatrice Grimshaw, *Vaiti of the Islands*, London, 1907, pp. 14, 212, 278, 284.
63 Beatrice Grimshaw, *Queen Vaiti*, Sydney, 1920, pp. 73, 121.

development had reached its highest point in polite society in England in the 1870s, and who dedicate themselves to maintaining the manners and fashions of that decade. In the last chapter Eve marries Ronald who, in Chapter One, had been forced by economic necessity and family duty to marry someone else. After the death of his first wife he is able to return—with a title and a fortune—to his first love.[64]

Another typical heroine is the beautiful Isola in *Red Bob of the Bismarks*. An able sailor and a skilled pump operator for pearl divers, she is a worthy companion for 'Red Bob' Gore, MA, LLD, FRGS, FRS, an internationally famed traveller and adventurer. A more roundly drawn heroine is Stephanie, the daughter of the governor of Papua in *When the Red Gods Call*. She is like 'a blade of steel in a silken scabbard'. Dismayed shortly after her marriage to the planter Hugh Lynch to learn of her husband's earlier marriage to a Papuan girl (who had since died) she returns indignantly to England. After some years, recognising the marriage bond as indissoluble, she goes back to Papua to rejoin the man whom she 'had loved and married—whom God had given to me', and who has long since repented of his folly.[65] Like, Isola, and like Deirdre Rose in *Conn of the Coral Seas*, she rejoices that in Melanesia there is no Mrs Grundy to object to white women travelling about unchaperoned. 'Besides', comments the author, 'there are many things that a women of thirty can do without a remark that would be impossible for a young girl'.[66] Thus, were it not that she had been shipwrecked, it is unlikely that the Honourable Alexandria Meredith, aged 19, maid of honour to the Queen of England, would have entered the pages of *The Terrible Island*. The sophisticated Martha Lyle, however, aged about 30, of *My Lady Far-Away*—she 'the last flower of civilisation', 'fragile but with nerves of whip cord and steel', 'a thousand ages had gone into the making of her' (a phrase which echoes a line of Kipling)—was in Papua with as much right as Grimshaw herself.[67] Similarly Deirdre Rose, born in the north of Ireland, educated at a university in Dublin, and arriving in the Pacific at the age of 28. In order to obtain her inheritance she had, while in Dublin, entered into a marriage of convenience with a man who shortly afterwards was committed as a mental asylum. Since neither divorce nor adultery were solutions for a Grimshaw heroine, Deirdre is condemned to living alone. Thus she wanders the world, until, learning that her husband had been released, had 'gone native' among the cannibals of the 'New Cumberlands' and had died there, she was free to marry Stephen Conn. Death is also required in *The Wreck of the Redwing*, to free the beautiful Susan Pascoe from her brutal husband, Herod, and there enable her to marry the brave, considerate Albert

---

64 Beatrice Grimshaw, *The Coral Queen*, Sydney, 1919, pp. 14, 136, 140, 149, 219.
65 Grimshaw, *Red Gods Call*, pp. 182, 331.
66 Ibid., pp. 311, 321; Beatrice Grimshaw, *Red Bob of the Bismarks*, London, 1915, 223; *Conn of the Coral Seas*, London and New York, 1922, p. 108.
67 Beatrice Grimshaw, *My Lady Far-Away*, London, 1929, pp. 55, 184, 270. In 'Et Dona Ferentes', 1896, Rudyard Kipling described the polite and well-bred British as 'the heir of all the ages'.

Polson, MA It is almost the same for Stacy Holliday in *The Sands of Oro*. While she possesses 'delicate shell-white skin' and 'the prettiest foot in Oceania' she, 'like the average decent woman [she] knew only of one way out of her marriage' to the despicable Charlie: he must die. It is eventually revealed, however, that Charlie Holliday had previously gone through a form of marriage with a native woman. This conveniently invalidates the marriage to Stacy, thereby leaving her free to marry Mark Plummer, who has recently struck gold.[68]

Like her heroines, Grimshaw's heroes also are conspicuously high-minded. To steal a kiss would be to besmirch a lady's honour, and that they would not do. Physically and in their ability to master the difficulties of the frontier they are, likewise, paragons of manhood: strong, taciturn, of better than average social and educational background and usually well into their 30s. One such is Mark Plummer in *The Sands of Oro*, 'like most Australians an entirely masculine man'. He is known as the surest gold prospector and bravest man in Papua. When Stacy asks him what he did when cannibals ate some of his mates on the Yodda goldfield he did not answer but his eyes 'suddenly narrowed and turned hard as flint. Out of them looked, in that instant the tameless spirit of the wilderness; the lightning flash of stark masculinity that dazzles a woman's soul and makes it cower away'.[69]

The Wreck of the Redwing has two heroes: an elder one, Albert Polson, who eventually wins the villain's widow, and younger one, Paul Bowen, a master mariner at 25, who wins her stepdaughter, an heiress. In one of the high points of the story Bowen, fearless and unarmed, bluffs his way through a horde of cannibals to rescue Polson. It is a brilliant manoeuvre emulated, Grimshaw tells us, with scant regard to historical fact, years later by 'Papua's famous Governor Murray' near the village of Goaribari when he was investigating the killing of the missionary James Chalmers.[70]

Also to be admired is Percival Flower of *The Terrible Island*. A big man aged 37, he completed a medical course before becoming a surveyor. Then, on the death of his wife, he comes to Papua where he discovers an island of phosphate rock, and wins the Honourable Alexandrina. Another typical hero is Stephen Conn. Descended from Irish royalty, university educated, and the discoverer of a cache of pearls, he is eventually appointed administrator of the 'New Cumberlands'—to which he proposes to bring the kind of development that Grimshaw had in 1908 urged Deakin to provide for the New Hebrides.

---

68   Grimshaw, *Sands of Oro*, London and New York, 1924, pp. 81, 111, 149, 225.
69   Ibid., pp. 82, 149, 284.
70   Beatrice Grimshaw, *The Wreck of the Redwing*, London, 1937, pp. 154–5. For a description of Murray's visit to Goaribari, on which Beatrice accompanied him, see Grimshaw, *New New Guinea*, pp. 222–238.

A less consistent hero, and as such a typical one, is George Scott, the Irish gold miner in *Guinea Gold*. Having deserted his wife Janie, he bigamously marries an Australian divorcee in Papua. Soon afterwards she dies in childbirth; women in Grimshaw's novels rarely make mistakes but when they do there is no second chance. But George struck gold. He then returns to his true wife with his newborn son, his respectability attested by his repentance and his great wealth, and guaranteed by his wife's unwavering sense of propriety, as described at the close of the book:

> The Scott's have a beautiful country house, not very far from Balmoral on the Lismore road. There are leather chairs in the dining room, and velvet chairs in the drawing room, and there are conservatories, and a motor garage, and a stable, with one or two good saddle horses. Scott has a small yacht with a motor and uses it in the summer time. Janie has carriages and furs, and more than one solid silver tea set. They agree excellently well. Scott is growing a little stout, and thinks of standing for Parliament one of these days.
>
> Janie is a just and kindly stepmother. The toys of the little girls are never better than Rupert's, and she always remembers to kiss him every night and to call him dear. Sometimes, when she sees his father holding him nursed in his arms of an evening, looking at the honey brown eyes and scarlet lips of the child as a man may look at the picture of something loved and lost, she goes away to her own room and sorts linen determinedly, with a hard set lip. She does not believe in crying. Sometimes, too, when Scott takes one of his rare fits of restlessness and disappears for a week at a time, flying down the channel in his yacht—southward, always towards the sun—she feels a strange fear creep about her heart. But she does not believe in worrying: there are the children, and there is duty.[71]

The most complex of Grimshaw's heroes is Hugh Lynch of *When the Red Gods Call*, a title derived from Kipling's poem 'The Feet of the Young Men',[72] Lynch was educated at Harrow and Sandhurst and is said to be the strongest man in the Western Pacific, but he is not beyond indiscretion. Having taken up land in Papua and believing that it would be wrong to ask 'any white woman to share' the rugged life of breaking in a plantation, he commits 'the unforgivable sin of folly' by marrying a native woman. He is, however, after much suffering and remorse to find redemption, as a result of Stephanie's recognition of her wifely duty, but he is not undeserving of her. His first marriage was an error

---

71 Beatrice Grimshaw, *Guinea Gold*, London and New York, 1912, pp. 341–342.
72 'For the Red Gods call me out and I must go!' That is, the deities that inhabit strange and distant places are summoning adventurous young men to come and prove themselves.

of judgement rather than a repudiation of basic values. He entered into it with high, if misguided, motives and, moreover, refused to go native in any way other than that, for he knows that it is not true that a 'white man cannot lose his race'.[73] The same salutary truth was also known to Paul Corbet, 'Red Bob's' companion. In Malaysia, on their way to New Guinea, the scent of nutmeg had suggested to him 'the clinging poisonous peace that wraps itself about the white man in the East beyond the East … [that had made] eyes of English grey … empty happy, as no white man's eyes should ever be', though, for his own part, he knows that, whatever his faults, he 'was not one of the kind that "goes black"'.[74]

Grimshaw's villains, on the other hand, characteristically, show no such regard for their heritage. Indeed their villainy be it greed, or murder, lying or infidelity—tends to lead them to the degradation of accepting native standards of behaviour, from which there is no escape. Thus it is in *Sands of Oro*, with Charlie Holliday, a scion of an old but inbred family. So it is with Herod Pascoe who brought a licensed native minister from Thursday Island in the Torres Strait to officiate at his intended marriage to the heiress Laurie. 'Nobody', comments Grimshaw, 'had ever heard of one of them marrying a white couple, no doubt because racial feeling ran strong in the North, and such an outrage had never been contemplated'.[75]

Behind such sentiments is the belief that Europeans represent several thousand years of progressive evolution from the Stone Age. This is seen as a disgusting stage of existence, one at which the Melanesians still find themselves, and to which Europeans could easily fall if they are not careful. In *The Wreck of the Redwing*, Polson, the hero–narrator—Grimshaw commonly writes in the first person—discusses the Papuans:

> It's the gap between these Stone Age creatures and us—the certainty that we are dealing with something almost as pre-historic as the mastodon, as little comprehensible as a crocodile—that makes the horror. No Parisian Apache committing deeds of violence, no shipwrecked sailor driven to loathsome crimes against his fellow by the goad of hunger, horrifies us like the cannibal savages of New Guinea. We understand those other; bad as they are, they belong to our own age; they are moulded of the same stuff as you and I.[76]

When the natives attack in *My Lady Far-Away*, the author comments: 'It was as if past centuries far back in the world's history, had suddenly arisen and

---

73 Grimshaw, *Red Gods Call*, pp. 8–11, 24, 31.
74 Grimshaw, *Red Bob*, p. 45.
75 Grimshaw, *Wreck of the Redwing*, p. 99.
76 Ibid., pp. 140–141.

spewed forth the slime and scum of their darkest eras—creatures who lived in caves, saw the great mastodon, and fought with sabre tooth tigers, hardly more fierce than they'.[77] An ambiguous mingling of fear, hostility and contempt is contained in these comments, and in the attitudes that follow from them. For example, when they are not feared, Melanesians count for nothing, as the following comments suggest: 'A 60 ton schooner is a small place for two lovers to exchange confidences unless they have it to themselves—save for "coloured boys" who do not count as human beings';[78] and again: 'To be alone with the woman you love (for surely a couple of Papuan cook boys count as nothing) on an exquisite, remote coral island … should be Paradise'.[79]

Nevertheless, it always remains important for whites to maintain their individual and collective self-esteem. Thus, Hugh Royden, in *My Lady Far-Away*, distressed at learning of Martha's marriage to his rival, soon composes himself: 'It was not meant that the inferior races should witness the humiliation of their superior'.[80] Deirdre Rose feels the same way when Stephen Conn's house is broken into: 'the solidarity of the race felt by all Europeans who live among dark people, forbade her to go away and leave the natives destroying a white man's property'.[81] So, too, does Hugh Lynch when his Melanesian escort wishes to attack the villainous Sanderson: 'I had no intention in the world of letting loose this pack of black hounds on a man who was at least outwardly white like myself'.[82] To break ranks is to betray the race, especially with regard to sex, as is implied in the description of Stacy Holliday's response to learning of her husband's affair:

> [Shocked she did not answer]. She was not looking at him, as he stood there, but he figures in her memory of the group of native girls who a few minutes before she had seen walking past the house … brown creatures, with great puffball heads, bare bodies hung over with grass skirts, prehensile monkey toes which clasped the ground.[83]

The reasons for Stacy's disgust are, appropriately, spelled out most clearly by Simon, 'the white savage', the hero who, of all Grimshaw's characters, lives closest to the Papuans. Raised by Papuans until he was 16, then educated in Sydney and at Oxford before fighting in World War I, he eventually returns to the simple island life of his youth. Even so, he refuses to take a native wife:

---

77 Grimshaw, *Lady Far-Away*, p. 307.
78 Grimshaw, *Wreck of the Redwing*, p. 174.
79 Grimshaw, *Sands of Oro*, p. 148.
80 Grimshaw, *Lady Far-Away*, p. 248.
81 Grimshaw, *Conn of the Coral Seas*, p. 112.
82 Grimshaw, *Red Gods Call*, p. 99.
83 Grimshaw, *Sands of Oro*, pp. 50–51.

> I respect my race … . I will have no son or daughter thousand years behind myself … . White Australian to the roots of my soul, I would not give my name nor the mothering and care of my children to a woman with one dark drop in her veins. [84]

Besides, children who were born of such a union could be relied on to be cowardly, like the half-castes in *My Lady Far-Away*, or dissolute. Hence it is that Susan Pascoe should for a while be concerned about the swarthiness of her mysterious stepdaughter. The girl is eventually discovered to be a Brazilian, which explained it satisfactorily, but in any case by the time she was 16.

> It did not need the clear almond of white at the base of each finger nail, the high silver coloured voice, the delicate laughter of Laurie to tell us all that she was as white as we were. Her character told us. Laurie was not especially interested in boys. That is where the dark drop talks.[85]

White was not only the best, but was intrinsically virtuous.

The racial views expressed in Grimshaw's writing have interesting implications. Racial pride was needed to ensure purity of race, which should in turn ensure continued racial progress. Even conceding ability to improve to the Papuans it was, therefore, scarcely possible that they should ever catch up with the Europeans. They could never win. For, presumably, the Europeans themselves would keep on improving. But, even allowing that continued European progress was not in the nature of things, Grimshaw's assumptions were in tune with the belief that in her time the Europeans had reached the highest stage of their development. Whatever conclusion one cared to draw it was, for the race-proud settlers of Papua, a consoling one. Indeed it may be regarded as one of their main consolations. For none of them made much money. Despite Grimshaw's propaganda, the natural resources of the country proved to be limited, while the aftermath of World War I led to a diversion of Australian settlers and capital to the richer territory of former German New Guinea, captured by the Australians in 1914.[86] In Papua there was an audience that not only could enjoy her books, but also had a need for them. With the passing of that audience and of the much larger one elsewhere that thrilled to tales of the colonial frontier, she has slipped into obscurity. Papua New Guineans now write novels themselves. Yet Grimshaw's voice is not entirely still. It may be heard, by all races, in the bell inscribed with her name which she gave to the Catholic church in Port Moresby in 1924, and which now hangs in the cathedral there.[87]

---

84 Beatrice Grimshaw, *White Savage Simon*, Sydney, 1919.
85 Grimshaw, *Wreck of the Redwing*, p. 50.
86 P. Biskup et al., *A Short History of New Guinea*, Sydney, 1970, pp. 77–78.
87 Frank Flynn, *St Mary's War Memorial Cathedral, Port Moresby*, Port Moresby, 1969, p. 2.

Appendix

A bibliography of the writings of Beatrice Grimshaw

Much of Beatrice Grimshaw's writing was first published in serial form in magazines. This bibliography, especially in regard to her fiction, attempts to record its first publication in book form. Much of her work appeared in several editions, but, so far as it has been possible to ascertain them, only the first editions are listed here.

Fiction

1897

Broken Away, London and New York.

1904

'Miss Silver's Attic', *Temple Bar*, vol. CIII, pp. 184–193.

1907

Vaiti of the Island, London.

1908

'The Tale of the Scarlet Butterflies', *Sunset Magazine* (San Francisco), pp. 680–688.

'The Tale of the Missing Passengers', ibid, pp. 721–729.

1911

When the Red Gods Call, London and New York.

1912

Guinea Gold, London and New York.

1914

Sorcerer's Stone (stories), London.

1915

Red Bob of the Bismarks, London (published in Chicago in 1916 as *My Lady of the Islands*).

1917

Kris Girl, London.

Nobody's Island, London.

A Coral Queen, New York.

1919

The Terrible Island, New York and London.

The Coral Queen, Sydney.

White Savage Simon, Sydney.

1920

The Coral Palace 'Twixt Capricorn and Cancer (stories), London.

Queen Vaiti, Sydney.

1921

My South Sea Sweetheart, London and New York.

The Little Red Speck and other South Sea Stories, London.

1923

Nobody's Island, New York.

1924

Sands of Oro, London and New York.

Helen of Man-O-War Island: a story of the South Seas, London.

1925

The Candles of Katara, London.

1926

The Wreck of the Redwing, London and New York.

1927

Eyes in the Corner, and other stories, London.

Black Sheep's Gold, London and New York.

1928

Paradise Poachers, London.

1929

My Lady Far-Away, London.

1930

The Star in the Dust, London and New York.

1931

Beach of Terror, and other Stories, London.

1932

The Mystery of the Tumbling Reef, London and New York.

1933

The Long Beaches, and other South Sea Stories, London.

1934

Victorian Family Robinson, London.

1935

Pieces of Gold, and other South Sea Stories, London.

1937

The Wreck of the Redwing, London.

1939

Rita Regina, London.

1940

South Sea Sarah (and) Murder in Paradise: two complex novels, Sydney.

Lost Child, London.

Wild Mint of Moresby [London].

1945

The Missing Blondes, Sydney.

Nonfiction

1905

'Life on a South Sea Schooner', *Pall Mall Magazine*, vol. XXXVI: pp. 47–58, 147.

'A Princesses Love Story', *Wide World Magazine*, vol. XIV, pp. 241–244.

'The Dancing Island of Manihiki', ibid., pp. 278–283.

'A Comic Opera Kingdom', ibid., pp. 494–497.

1906

'Sheep and Cattle Farming in New Zealand', *World's Work and Play*, vol. VII, pp. 374–381.

'An Imperial Wonderland: the hot water country of New Zealand', *World's Work and Play*, vol. VIII, 33–39.

'The Samoans at Close Range', *Metropolitan Magazine* (New York), pp. 615–624.

'Three Wonderful Nations: a tour through Tonga Samoa and Fiji', *Red Funnel*, vol. II, pp. 173–182, 170–174.

'New Zealand: in the Geyser land', *Canadian Magazine*, vol. XXVII, pp. 232–238.

1907

'Islands of the Blest', *Red Funnel*, vol. III, pp. 250–257; vol. IV, pp. 82–88, 149–157, 261–268.

In the Strange South Seas, London.

From Fiji to the Cannibal Islands, London (Published in New York *as Fiji and its Possibilities*).

'A Lady in Far Fiji', *Wide World Magazine*, vol. XVIII, pp. 217–225, 354–363, 425–436.

1908

'In the Savage South Seas', *National Geographic Magazine*, vol. XIX, pp. 1–19.

'Under the Southern Cross', in the *P.&O. Pocket Book*, London, pp. 125–156.

1909

'Australia's Island Asset', *Life* (Sydney), pp. 357–362, 483–488, 602–606.

'Australia's First Colony', *The Times*, 21 Sept. 1909.

1910

'Into Unknown Papua', *Wide World Magazine*, vol. XXIV, pp. 387–380.

The New New Guinea, London.

The Islands of the Blest: something about Raratonga, Mangaia, Atiu, Mauke, Aitutake, Tahiti, Raiatea, Huahine, Dunedin.

Three Wonderful Nations, Dunedin.

1911

'The Progress of Papua', *Australia Today*, pp. 141–145.

1913

Adventure in Papua with the Catholic Mission, Melbourne.

1922

'Sorcery and Spiritualism in Papua', *Wide World Magazine*, vol. L, pp. 208–215.

1923

'East Beyond the East', ibid., vol. LII, pp. 25–32.

1924

'The Head-hunters of the Sepik', ibid., pp. 240–246, 283–288, 381–387, 501–504.

1925

'The Sea Villagers of Humboldt's Bay', ibid., vol. LIV, 325–331.

1927

'Adventures in Papua with the Catholic Mission', *Annals of our Lady of the Sacred Heart*, pp. 301–305, 338–341, 490–494; 1928, pp. 17–19, 115–116, 172–175.

1928

'Head-hunters of Lake Murray', *Windsor Magazine*, pp. 543–555.

1930

Isles of Adventure, London.

1934

'The World's Worst Cannibal Island', *Asia*, vol. XXXIV, pp. 348–351.

1946

'Island of my Own', in the *'Man' Gift Book: a presentation of the best Australian writers of today*, Sydney, pp. 150–158.

9. W.J. Watriama (c. 1880–1925): Pretender and patriot, (or 'a blackman's defence of White Australia')

According to W.M. Hughes, Australia's prime minister during World War I, Australia entered that conflict to ensure its national security and 'to maintain those ideals which we have nailed to the very topmost of our flag-poles—White Australia, and those other aspirations of this young democracy'.[1] Given the one aspiration which Hughes chose to specify in that comment, and although the White Australia policy was mainly concerned with the exclusion of Asians, there is some irony in the fact that when White Australians went to war in 1914, black Australians went too. Admittedly, their number was small and their contribution to the fighting nowhere decisive, although several were decorated. Still, their presence on the battlefields, and the price they paid for it was sufficient to ensure that, in so far as an abiding sense of Australian nationhood was created in 1914–1918, this was not the exclusive achievement of white Australians. Although the army was at first reluctant to recruit Indigenous Australians, about 300 of them eventually served in the First Australian Imperial Force, and about one-third of them were killed or wounded. Not all the dark-skinned members of the First AIF, however, were Indigenous. American-born Jack Dunne, of New South Wales, was black.[2] Another, William Jacob Watriama, was a Melanesian from the Loyalty Islands of French-ruled New Caledonia.

Little seems to be recorded about the reasons why Indigenous Australians enlisted, although there is no reason to assume that their motives were greatly different from those of most other Australian recruits. Hughes and White Australia notwithstanding, and allowing for personal motives, it is likely that they responded to the then generally accepted belief that, in time of war, Australian patriotic duty implied support for Britain. Certainly, by all accounts, this was so in Watriama's case. By 1914 he had lived in Sydney for almost 25 years. He had already proved himself as a patriot by serving in the Boer War and, since 1911, had gained considerable publicity through agitating for the extension of British imperial responsibilities in the Pacific. Indeed, through a well-reported claim to being the exiled 'king' of the Loyalty Islands, a group for which he sought British protection, he had also acquired a reputation as a 'character', one of those people whose idiosyncrasy brought a leavening touch of theatricality

---
1 Quoted in Manning Clark, *Sources of Australian History*, Melbourne, 1977, p. 567.
2 C.D. Clark, 'Aborigines in the First AIF', *Australian Army Journal*, no. 286 (1973), pp. 21–26. See also, Humphrey McQueen, *Social Sketches of Australia, 1888–1975* (Harmondsworth, 1978), p. 88; *Canberra Times*, 27 Mar. 1987; *Sydney Morning Herald (SMH)*, 24 April 1987.

to the life of the city. Even so, he was well respected. His death in 1925 was extensively reported in the newspapers, which paid unstinting tribute to his patriotism while remaining affectionately and sympathetically noncommittal about his claim to the throne of the Loyalty Islands. The National Association of New South Wales, an organisation that favoured a socially conservative type of Australianism, similar to that espoused by D.H. Lawrence's 'Kangaroo', described Watriama in its monthly journal as an 'earnest and active Nationalist, and a popular member of the Association'. It applauded him for being 'in every way a good citizen' and respectfully noted his claim to have been kept out of his kingdom 'because of his loyalty to Britain and his hostility to French rule'.[3] Hughes, who attended his funeral, expressed similarly approving sentiments in a speech at the graveside. After commenting on Watriama's military record and his 'aristocratic' blood, Hughes described him as 'a fine man and an old friend whose life's ambition was to see the Union Jack fly over his native Islands'.[4]

White Australia, then, had clearly found room for Watriama and, indeed, it was in warning of a threat to White Australia that he had first come to public prominence. Shortly before his death in June 1907 his father, Yiewene, had written designating him his heir as 'Chief and King of the Loyalty Islands' and enjoining him to seek British rule for the group; but Watriama was slow to advertise this patrimony.[5] It seems that it was not until 1910 that he first approached the Australian Government, urging the transfer of the Loyalty Islands from French to British control, and that he was referred to the British foreign office.[6] At any rate, in January 1911 he directed such a request to the foreign office, signing himself 'king of the Loyalty Islands'.[7] Earlier, in 1910, in a gesture that suggests a burgeoning but incomplete sense of royal self-assurance, he had written to Atlee Hunt, the secretary of Department of External Affairs, congratulating him on the award of a CMG, but on that occasion he had only signed himself 'W.J. Watriama, Loyalty Islands'.[8] Then, in February 1911, prompted by the importation of Japanese labourers into New Caledonia, he took both his cause and his claim fully into the public domain. On 28 February the *Sydney Morning Herald* reported at length an interview with him in which he claimed that the Japanese (of whom 1,015 had entered New Caledonia in 1910) were spies rather than miners and that they represented 'a danger not only to his people, but to Australia' for they aimed 'to establish strong bases [in New Caledonia], and bide their time for further aggression'. If Watriama was sincere, and there is

---

3 *The Australian National Review*, 23 Jan. 1925, p. 18.
4 *SMH*, 8 Jan. 1925.
5 Yeiwene to Watriama, 19 April 1907; Watriama to [British Govt.?], 30 July 1907, copies in my possession by courtesy of Edna Watriama (Sydney, 1984).
6 *SMH*, 28 Feb. 1911.
7 Watriama to Sir Edward Grey (Foreign Secretary), 17 Jan. 1911, in British Consulate, Noumea, General Correspondence 1914–1920, on microfilm WP 162, National Library of Australia (NLA).
8 Watriama to Hunt, 29 June 1910, NLA, Atlee Hunt papers, MSS 52/2331.

no reason to believe otherwise, and besides, other *Herald* contributors agreed with him about the Japanese threat, it was an act becoming of an Australian patriot for him to offer his 'Kingdom' to Britain in order to impede the advance of Japan.[9] The *Herald* report also dealt with Watriama personally. It described him as ' a coloured gentleman of independent means', who had come to Sydney 21 years before. 'He is now a well-set young man of 32 years, decidedly good-looking, cultured and well-educated' and, it went on, he had travelled, knew a number of languages, was intensely religious, and 'had figured prominently as an honorary official during ... the recent Chapman-Alexander [revivalist] mission in Sydney.'[10]

It also recounted Watriama's own story of his life. According to this, he was the son and heir of Yiewene Dokucas Naisiline, who he claimed had recently died, leaving him a considerable fortune. Meanwhile the administration of his 'kingdom' was said to be in the hands of the regent, his alleged brother, Henry Naisiline who, assisted by Watriama's agent in the Loyalty Islands, regularly forwarded despatches to him in Sydney. As for his being in Australia, Watriama claimed that it was due to a quarrel he had had with his alleged father. He said that in 1890, at the age of 11, he had disagreed with Yiewene's decision to allow France to establish a protectorate over the Loyaltys, and had gone into exile rather than submit to the new regime. Arrived in Sydney, he had become a gardener at Paddington and later a coachman, his income being supplemented by gifts from his mother. He further averred that during the Paris Exhibition of 1900 he had visited France, at the invitation of President Emile Loubet, to discuss French rule in the Loyaltys and that he had refused to soften his opposition to that regime.[11]

Honest, hardworking, hopeful in adversity, resolutely principled, Watriama was, by his own account, the very model of the storybook prince down on his luck. But that account, like most romances, unfortunately, contains little that is true, apart from the fact that he had come from the Loyaltys to Australia at an early age. For instance, Watriama had his dates badly wrong. It was not in 1890 but in 1880, 27 years since France had annexed the Loyaltys, and when Watriama was no more than one-year old, that Yiewene Naisiline had agreed to cooperate with the French administration. Again, far from being recently dead in 1911, Yiewene did not die until 1916. As for Yiewene's position, he was not 'king' of the Loyaltys. No such office had ever existed. Rather, in 1880 he had succeeded

---

9 *SMH*, 28 Feb. 1911, 8 Mar. 1911, David Campbell Purcell, 'Japanese Expansion in the South Pacific, 1890–1935', PhD thesis, University of Pennsylvania, 1967, p. 263.
10 Dr J. Wilbur Chapman and Mr Charles M. Alexander were a team of American evangelists who conducted a campaign in Sydney in 1909. *The Australian Christian World: Chapman-Alexander Mission, Special Daily Issue*, no. 1–19, 27 May 1909 – 22 June 1909; *Showers of Blessings: being the 'Australian Christian World' souvenir of the Chapman-Alexander mission in Sydney*, 1909. They also came in 1912.
11 *SMH*, 28 Feb. 1911. For a similar report see the Melbourne *Argus*, 14 Aug. 1912.

his father, Nidoish, as principal chief of the Si Gwahma people of Mare. Even so, the Si Gwahma were but one of the Mare tribes (although, admittedly, the dominant one since the 1870s), while Mare was but one of the three islands in the Loyalty group. Yiewene was succeeded as chief of Si Gwahma in 1916 by his son Henry Naisiline I.[12]

Also fictitious were Watriama's claims to have visited France and to have met the president. So, too, was his claim to be a member of the Naisiline family, let alone Yiewene's heir. Nevertheless, the British and Australian governments and the Australian press never felt sufficiently concerned about Watriama's claims to bother investigating them with seriousness.[13] Not so their French counterparts. French records contain detailed information, gathered in 1911, on Watriama's pedigree while the New Caledonia press gave considerable space to exposing him as an impostor and never spoke of him except to revile him. As in the 1980s, any challenge to the legitimacy of French rule in New Caledonia was not to be taken lightly. According to French records, the chief among which is a letter from Henry Naisiline, Watriama came from a family who were servants of the Naisilines. This is supported by a genealogy prepared by a Catholic missionary, Francois Beaulieu, who had been on Mare since 1866. The story told in these writings is that Watriama's grandfather, Heutr, had shifted to Mare from Anarewedr on the island of Lifu with his two young sons in the 1840s, and had attached himself to the Naisiline chief Yiewene Zeiwewhatr, who died in 1848. Yiewene's mother, Thanaket, had come from Anarewedr. Through her, with the approval of Bula, the chief of the village, other Anarewedr were drawn from Lifu to Mare. There they became, and remained, retainers to the Naisilines, but were not accepted as being members of the Si Gwahma tribe.[14] Henry Naisiline also denounced Watriama in a letter published in the New Caledonia journal *La France Australe*:

---

12 K.R. Howe, 'The Fortunes of Naisilines', in Deryck Scarr (ed.), *More Pacific Islands Portraits*, Canberra, 1979; K.R. Howe, *The Loyalty Islands: a history of culture contacts, 1840–1900*, Honolulu, 1977.
13 In 1914, reporting Watriama's first deportation from New Caledonia, the *SMH* printed a brief factual report from Noumea denying Watriama's claim to royal blood. Even so, the Australian press never showed any subsequent inclination to dispute his claim:

> On arrival [in Noumea] he was interrogated by Governor Brunet as to his identity. He said he was born at Ete, Mare Island, 35 years ago. His parents came from Lifou as vassals to Jeuvene, and old king of Mare. His parents were not of royal blood, and he was employed as a domestic to the Italian consul here. He left for Sydney 25 years ago. He was not invited by the President of the Republic as a guest at the French exhibition in 1903. The accounts about him in the Australian press were all inventions he said. *SMH*, 2 May 1914.

In fact, the Paris exhibition was in 1900.
14 When Heutr left Lifu another man, named Leduwhatr, also shifted from Anarewedre to Mare. According to Fr Beaulieu, their subservient status on Mare was indicated by the name *la-kodraru* (literally 'the way of the food') applied to the gift of food they made on occasion to Yiewene to acknowledge his authority. *La-kodraru* was given by outsiders, those who were not in any way members of Yiewene's 'family'. Information contained in personal letter from Fr M.J. Dubois SM, 5 June 1984.

9. W.J. Watriama (c. 1880–1925): Pretender and patriot, (or 'a blackman's defence of White Australia')

> This person, far from being the issue of the loins of Jupiter and of royal race is descended from people who were servants to my family, and even in that social situation they did not perform higher tasks.
>
> The family, originally from Lifu, was given to my grandfather by the grandfather [and namesake] of chief Bula and, according to well-informed people, belonged to our household staff.
>
> Far, then, from being the Regent or charge d'affaires of Watriama, I consider myself to be not only his chief, as recognised by the French government, but as his master in every meaning of the word.[15]

Of Heutr's two sons, one, Sio, became teacher for the London Missionary Society (LMS) and died of leprosy at Pede on Mare about 1910. The other, Waupo, married a Mare woman named Wakanude. They lived at Tuo, near the main Si Gwahma village of Netche, and had three children: a son, Gortcho (who was to die in Australia, possibly as a labourer in Queensland), a daughter, Wanate (who died about 1909), and Watriama.[16]

By his own account Watriama was born in 1879 or 1880, but in the estimation of Henry Naisiline he was born about five years earlier.[17] In the absence of any clear evidence it is impossible to resolve the question but the earlier date does have the advantage of not leaving one to puzzle over how an 11-year-old child from the Pacific islands managed to survive in Sydney. On the other hand, it is possible that, however young Watriama was when he arrived in Sydney, he would have been looked after by Rev. John Jones of the LMS. After being expelled from Mare in 1887 for encouraging his Protestant flock, who were mostly members of Si Gwahma, to oppose the French regime, Jones had settled in Sydney. Moreover, in 1890 he had corresponded with his former colleague, Stephen Creagh, who was still on Mare, about the possibility of getting a Mare boy to come and live with him and his wife in Sydney.[18] Whether he ever obtained one is, again, unknown, but it may be assumed that he would have been available to assist Watriama if asked to do so.

---

15 *La France Australe*, 21 April 1911.
16 H. Naisiline to Delegue de l'Administration, 13 April 1911, Archives Nationales, Section Outre-Mer, Corton 180 (I am grateful to Kerry Howe for this material); F. Beaulieu, 'Le Roi des Loyalty, Watriama'. Fr Dubois gave me a copy of Fr Beaulieu's notes. It is material he had used in his own work. M.J. Dubois, 'Geographic mythique et traditionelle de Mare', Memoire pour le Diploma de l'EPHE 5e section Paris, 1968, pp. 310–311; M-J Dubois, 'Les Chefferies de Mare', These de Doctorat d'Etat en lettres, Paris 1971–1972, p. 729.
17 While no document exists that states the exact year of his birth, Watriama was consistent on the point. Calculations based on statements about his age in newspapers, on military enlistment papers and on his marriage and death certificates all indicate a birth date of 1879 or 1880. Within his family his birthday was celebrated on 31 Aug. Personal letter from Edna Watriama, 30 Jan. 1984.
18 Creagh to Jones, 5 Nov. 1890, Mitchell Library, Rev. John Jones Papers, A401, p. 257. For an account of Jones's involvement in affairs on Mare, see Howe, *Loyalty Islands*, pp. 75–78.

Henry Naisiline's unpublished letter, which is much fuller than the published one, also contains details on Watriama's personal history. Watriama, he says, left Mare about 1886 or 1887 to go to Noumea. There he worked for a time as a household servant for the Italian consul, Lackerstein, before joining the crew of the Societe le Nickel vessel *Heros*, from which he deserted at Sydney in 1891.[19] Naisiline met him there in 1900. On that occasion Watriama came aboard his ship, the *Armand Behic*, and, as he did with other Loyalty Islands sailors, invited him ashore to discuss plans for bringing the Loyaltys under British control. Dutifully, Naisiline declined to oblige him.[20]

Whether over the next decade Watriama maintained an interest in Loyalty Islands affairs or had any further contact with the group is unknown. If he did, no record of it has yet been found. Then, in February 1911 he propelled himself suddenly into prominence, setting out on a campaign he was to wage for the next ten years. Provoked by the threat to Australian security which he saw in the Japanese influx into New Caledonia, and wishing to impede their movement further afield, he began to campaign for the British annexation of the one part of that country that he could presume to represent, namely the Loyalty Islands. Presumably to add authority to his advocacy and to attract the attention of the press and the public to his cause, he also began styling himself the 'King of the Loyaltys'. In 1911, he wrote once to the British foreign office and twice to the Australian prime minister, Andrew Fisher (1908–1913), about transferring the Loyaltys to British control.[21]

Despite his self-conferred title, it is not clear if Watriama ever received replies to these letters. Yet, it is unlikely that they were dismissed out of hand, as the work of a mere crank, for Watriama's concern accorded with a distrust of Japanese militarism that had been gathering strength and respectability in Australia since Japan's victory over Russia in 1905. This distrust may conveniently be illustrated from the *Lone Hand*, an offshoot of the Sydney *Bulletin* and, like its parent, an avowed organ of Australian nationalism. Beginning monthly publication in 1907, *Lone Hand* was a literary journal that also gave considerable space to discussions of the presumed need for under-populated Australia to defend itself against the crowding hordes of Asia.[22]

The Chinese, *Lone Hand* writers agree, could be kept out by strict immigration regulations, but the more aggressive Japanese were the real problem and would have to be stopped by force of arms. In 1908 *Lone Hand* published a

---

19 There is no mention of Watriama in the published list of reported ships deserters. Jim Melton, *Ships' Deserters, 1852–1900*, Sydney, 1986.
20 Naisiline to Delegue, 13 April 1911, Archives Nationales, section Outre-Mer, Carton 180.
21 See ref 6; index of correspondence regarding petition for annexation of Loyalty Islands, National Archives of Australia (NAA), CRS A 70/2.
22 Kit Taylor, *A History with Indexes of the Lone Hand, the Australian monthly*, [Sydney], 1977. The only run of this serial, listed as complete in the NLA, lacks the issues for Dec. 1917 and Feb. 1918.

four-part article titled 'The Asiatic Menace' on that theme and also began serial publication, in 11 parts, of a novel about Australia's need and duty to resist the expansion of Asia. 'For Australia', the novel concludes, 'is the precious front buckle in the white girdle of power and progress encircling the globe'.[23] In 1910 *Lone Hand* fiction sounded a more urgent note with a short story about an attempted Japanese invasion of Australia and, in 1911, there were five stories on that topic.[24] In most of these stories the invasion is repelled by dashing deeds of Australian bravery but in one, 'The Dead Finish', the seriousness of the Japanese threat is underlined by the defeat of a party of Australian defenders. It concludes:

> The last stand of Captain Barnes' squadron was ended. Rude hands tore down the flag, raising in its stead a small ensign whose red emblem mocked the newly risen sun. Japan's sun had triumphed again. But the world's sun looking down on Australia saw only still, white faces, triumphant in defeat, unconquerable in life or death.[25]

In the absence of an observed Japanese movement towards Australia, defence commentators, however, had to discuss the threat in more general terms than did the fiction writers. Even if real, the threat was still remote. Thus, in December 1910, in an article titled 'The Pacific—a Japanese pond', and pointing to the Japanese presence in Hawai'i, *Lone Hand* could offer no more precise a warning than the following:

> Ours may be a white Australia, all right, but it is set in a remarkably brown Pacific. And the touch of pitch will defile the whitest Australia ever reared on a base that neglects the means of national self-preservation— Defence, Defence and more Defence—while there is yet time.[26]

It was Watriama's achievement in 1911 to introduce a new note of immediacy to discussions of the presumed threat, and to make such warnings seem even more pertinent than they might have been before. Following the interview with him in February, the *Sydney Morning Herald*, although conceding that 'it does seem

---

23 Louis Essen, 'The Asiatic Menace', Sept. – Dec. 1908; Charles H. Kirmes, Oct. 1908 – Aug. 1909, quotation from Aug. 1909, p. 445. See also, Arthur H. Adams, 'Mud Pies: a fable for Australians', in which the Wattle children—Percy, Adelaide, Queenie, Sydney, Victor and Tassie—defend their backyard against coloured children who wish to come in and play there (July 1911, pp. 240–247).
24 Aldridge Evelyn, 'The Deliverer', July 1910, pp. 211–218; J.H.M. Abbott, 'The Raid on Sydney', Jan. 1911, pp. 232 –238: Boyd Cable, 'First Blood', May 1911, pp. 31–37, and 'An Episode', Sept. 1911, pp. 416–422; William Gerard, 'The Dead Finish', July 1911, pp. 217–223; Lawerence Zeal, 'The Command of the Air', Mar. 1911, pp. 404–411.
25 William Gerard, 'The Dead Finish: how the lost squadron was wiped out', July 1911, p. 223.
26 'The Pacific—a Japanese pond', Dec. 1910, p. 161.

as if the Australians were a bit hysterical about [the Japanese threat]', published a further report on the Japanese influx into New Caledonia and its possible implications for Australia.[27]

But *Lone Hand* took up the matter more emphatically. In March 1911 the Sydney *Sun* had published a seven-part report warning of the Japanese danger by a recent visitor to New Caledonia. In June *Lone Hand* republished this as a single article titled 'New Caledonia: a menace to white Australia'. And, in July, it published a survey titled 'White, Yellow and Brown: the present situation of White Australia in a Pacific that is rapidly becoming browner', and in which France was accused of acting irresponsibly:

> France in New Caledonia is not playing the white man's game ... — importing thousands of Japanese and so making New Caledonia a Japanese outpost from which to conquer the French colony first, and probably give it a jumping off place for an Australian invasion afterwards.[28]

Later in the year the issue was also raised in the federal parliament, twice. In November, in the Senate, a questioner was assured that the government would keep the matter of the Japanese in New Caledonia 'under notice'. But that did not satisfy E.S. Carr MHR.

In a speech in December he maintained that New Caledonia had a place on a Japanese scheme to dominate Australia and the Pacific. Accordingly, he urged the government to

> See whether, through diplomatic channels, Great Britain and France cannot arrange to bring New Caledonia, and all the New Hebrides, under the purview of the Commonwealth, and thus enable us to thwart what is undoubtedly the intention of that power which, of all powers, is likely to be the enemy of Australia in the future.[29]

Given the expansionist inclinations of the government of the day, that was not an unreasonable suggestion, but, given the difficulties that constantly confounded Australia's standing bid for Vanuatu, it was scarcely a practicable one.[30]

---

27 *SMH*, 8 Mar. 1911.
28 Sun, 6, 7, 8, 9, 10, 11, 13 Mar. 1911; A.K.Shearston-May, 'New Caledonia; a menace to White Australia', June 1911, pp. 117–122; Randolf Bedford, 'White, Yellow and Brown', July 1911, pp. 224– 228.
29 Commonwealth of Australia, *Parliamentary Debates* (Senate), 24 Nov. 1911, pp. 3, 136; (Representatives), 19 Dec. 1911, pp. 4, 742–743.
30 Roger C. Thompson, *Australian Imperialism in the Pacific: the expansionist era, 1820–1920*, Melbourne, 1980, pp. 178–202; Margot Simington, 'Australia's Political and Economic Relations with New Caledonia, 1853–1945', PhD thesis, University of New South Wales, 1978, pp. 264–271. Thompson seems to have been unaware of Australian anxieties about the Japanese presence in New Caledonia, while Simington deals with the issue in an unduly cursory manner. See also D.C. Sissons, 'Attitudes to Japan and Defence, 1890–1923',

9. W.J. Watriama (c. 1880–1925): Pretender and patriot, (or 'a blackman's defence of White Australia')

In 1912 Watriama continued his campaign. He not only called on Fisher when the prime minister was visiting Sydney, but also travelled to Melbourne to call on the minister of foreign affairs, Josiah Thomas, and the minister of defence, George Pearce, to discuss with each of them the possibility of Australia taking over the Loyaltys. He seems to have received sympathetic hearings. Fisher, he reported as saying that 'the Commonwealth would like to hold all the islands from Fiji down'. Following his Melbourne visit, the possibility of Australian annexation of the Loyaltys was also discussed in the federal parliament. In reply to a question, Thomas stated that

> The Loyalty Islands are of comparatively small importance, but the island of New Caledonia is large and valuable. There can be no doubt that its inclusion in the British Empire would be in many ways to the advantage of Australia. [Therefore] the Government will give the matter every consideration should a favourable opportunity present itself.

While not discouraging, such a reply was, however, from Watriam's point of view, so circumspect as to suggest indifference. He measured the importance of the Loyaltys in the urgent, immediately pressing terms of national security. They would be a valuable advanced defence post against, as he told the Melbourne *Argus*, an impending Japanese threat to the security of Australia:

> These Japanese … are not only workers, they are trained soldiers [veterans of the Russo-Japanese war] and … they look beyond New Caledonia to Australia. At all events, New Caledonia is overrun with them.

> If Australia is not going to take my country … then I am sorry to say that my country will be in the hands of the Japanese, and it will not be very long either. And my feeling is not only to my own country and my own people, but also to Australia. I would like to warn Australians that the danger is greater and nearer than they imagine.[31]

And some Australians did heed the warning. In September 1913 a deputation from the Australian Native's Association recalled Watriama's plea when it, too, petitioned the minister of external affairs, by then P.M. Glynn, for British annexation of New Caledonia. But, again to little avail. The question of New Caledonia, Glynn indicated, was subordinate to the longer running and, from the Australian point of view, ostensibly more winnable argument about control of Vanuatu. It would be discussed should Britain and France enter into

---

MA thesis, University of Melbourne 1956. Sissons deals at length with the Japanese 'threat' (pp. 21–75), but does not mention New Caledonia. He does, however, touch on (pp. 68–70) the *Lone Hand* 'invasion literature', discussed above.
31 *SMH*, 13 Aug. 1912; *Argus*, 14 Aug., 7 (quoted), 12 Nov. 1912; Commonwealth of Australia, *Parliamentary Debates*, 19 Nov. 1912, p. 5, 598; Thompson, *Australian Imperialism*, p. 194.

negotiations over their respective claims to Vanuatu.[32] But, as it happened, that contest for exclusive control was never to be resolved in favour of one power or the other. New Caledonia remained overshadowed by Vanuatu as an object of Australian Government concern.

Still, Watriama persisted. Although in Australia he had succeeded in arousing a modest but temporary interest in New Caledonia, but had won no support for the cause of Loyalty Islands annexation, and little enough for that of New Caledonia, he was not deterred from trying his luck further afield when the chance arose. In October 1916, and again in August 1917,[33] as a soldier on leave in England, he visited the Colonial Office to plead for direct British, if not Australian, annexation of the Loyaltys. Predictably, he again received polite and blandly encouraging audiences, but nothing more.

In contrast, French responses to Watriama's campaign were no less predictable but certainly more clear-cut, especially when, on two occasions, he attempted to return to his homeland. In April 1914, with a companion named Watt, he sailed from Sydney aboard the steamer *Dumbea*. On arriving in Noumea he was treated like a dangerous enemy. The French authorities, said the British consul, feared that he might incite a rebellion. Accordingly, although he was allowed ashore he was kept under police surveillance. He was forbidden to proceed to the Loyaltys and he was prevented from having any contacts with Kanaks in Noumea. Finally, he was expelled, being ordered by the governor to leave on the *Dumbea* when it returned to Sydney. The newspaper *La France Australe* rejoiced at these measures. In 1911 it had been strenuously critical of Watriama, seeing him as representing a recrudescence of the anti-French spirit fanned by Jones on Mare in the 1880s. Now, it magnified the seriousness of his campaign by presenting him to its readers as the agent of an even more powerful anti-French conspiracy. This, it claimed, was organised by the Presbyterians of Australia, who were already firmly established as irritants of French settler sensibilities

---

32 *Argus*, 11 Sept. 1913; *SMH*, 11 Sept. 1913. The *Argus* recalled that 'last year Watriama, King of the Loyalty Islands, visited Australia'. The *SMH*, also referring to his 1912 visit to Melbourne, commented that

> King Watriama also drew attention to the number of Japanese in the islands. They were ostensibly working in the nickel mines. He got his son to work as a mess boy in one of their camps. This boy who could speak English, French and the native tongue, had a smattering of Japanese. He stated that every evening after meals the Japanese would sit around a table and bring out plans of the eastern part of Australia which they had prepared.

As if to suggest that fears of invasion were not fanciful, the *Argus* of 31 Oct. 1913 reported that at Easter 1913 a party of Japanese had been found surveying at Prospect near Sydney.

33 Unidentified newspaper clipping, copy in my possession by courtesy of Miss Edna Watriama; resume of letter from Watriama to W.M. Hughes, 15 Aug. 1917, NAA, CRS A 70/2.

through their persistent criticisms of French activity in neighbouring Vanuatu. Indeed, 'Presbyterian' had become a term of abuse indiscriminately applied to British Protestants and their followers.[34]

Besides being reviled as a Presbyterian agent in 1914—and in 1980 in a speech given to the Noumea Rotary Club, and in 1985 in an article in the local historical journal—Watriama was also so labelled in 1920, when he made a second attempt to return home. On this occasion he travelled in the *Noorebar*, which he had encouraged a Sydney businessman named Cowlishaw to charter by offering him the prospect of obtaining a cargo of copra from the Loyaltys. In fact the Loyaltys produced little copra and it is extremely unlikely that the *Noorebar* would have been able to obtain cargo there. But the matter was never put to the test for, although the governor received Cowlishaw and the captain of the vessel cordially when they arrived at Noumea, his mood changed abruptly when he learned that Watriama was aboard the vessel. He then retracted the permission he had given for the *Noorebar* to go to the Loyaltys. Irrespective of Cowlishaw's intentions, the governor informed the British consul that he believed Watriama planned on 'stirring up the natives of the Loyalty Islands to a "rising" against the French Government'. And that was something he was not prepared to risk, especially as 78 kanaks had recently been tried for a revolt in another part of the colony. As for Watriama, he was threatened with arrest if he dared step ashore, and once again expelled from New Caledonia. He was aboard the *Noorebar* when it sailed for Sydney to the accompaniment of venomous abuse in the local press. Under the heading of 'A Black Pretender', *La Messager de la Nouvelle Caledonie* denounced Watriama as 'This grimy example of Australian civilisation indoctrinated by ignorant Presbyterians [who], from hearing himself called king of the Islands has perhaps finished by believing it'. As for his companions on the *Noorebar*, they were, it continued, blackguards and filibusters engaged in a kind of Jameson raid, 'because the real object of the voyage … was to take possession of the Loyalty Islands in the name of the figurehead Watriama'.

> We hope [it continued] that our administration will show these buccaneers that France still counts a little in the world and [that] it will not fail to make the necessary representations to the Government of Australia, where Watriama and his accomplices have evidently found support and encouragement.[35]

---

34   *La France Australe*, 27 April 1914, 28 April 1914; *SMH*, 2 May 1914; T. Johnston to Governor General, 1 April 1920, NAA, CRS A1, item 20/8469; Numa Daly, 'L'Aventure extraordinaire de Watriama, Roi des Iles Loyalty', *Société d'Etudes Historiques de la Nouvelle Caledonie*, no. 64 (1985), pp. 17–33.
35   Johnston to Governor General, 1 April 1920, enclosing report from *La Messager de la Nouvelle Caledonie*, 31 Mar. 1920; Lew Priday, 'Watriama, the Man who Wanted Britain to Take Over the Loyalties', *Pacific Islands Monthly*, Sept. 1966, p. 86.

What might have been evident to a hostile commentator in New Caledonia is, however, not verified by the information available on Watriama's Australian career. Rather, it appears that he had no accomplices (Cowlishaw was a commercial adventurer) and that he was given no firm support by politicians, by the press or by any of the Protestant churches. If Watriama received encouragement in Australia it was from the generous publicity his claims received in newspaper reports and the polite hearing he was given by a few dignitaries. Expressions of approval from these sources were directed to him personally, as a citizen, and to the broadly patriotic nature of his aims rather than to the details of his demands. His claim to the Loyaltys, for instance, tended to be overshadowed by the larger issue of New Caledonia. But in either case, what he sought, or encouraged Australia to seek, was at least consonant with the expansionist inclination of the Australian Government which, under Fisher, looked covetously to the Pacific, particularly Vanuatu.[36] Indeed, if there was difference between Australian policy and what Watriama wanted it was less one of principle than of degree, detail and timing. Thus, the Sydney *Daily Telegraph* summed up the position with regard to New Caledonia in 1913, printing that, although it would be desirable for Australia to acquire New Caledonia, it was not necessary to do so for 'so long as France remains in possession we ... [know] a friendly and white nation is our neighbour.'[37]

As for Watriama's standing as a citizen, this was established, as the press noted, by his record as a soldier. He was already a member of the St George's Rifles, a civilian volunteer unit, when he enlisted for service in South Africa.[38] He embarked from Sydney in March 1901 with the 2nd New South Wales Mounted Rifles and returned in June 1902.[39] No details of his war service are available, but he apparently considered it to have been unbecomingly prosaic for a king for, in talking of it to the *Sydney Morning Herald* reporter in 1911, he found it necessary to improve upon the truth, albeit modestly. Thus, he did not, as he claimed, attain the rank of corporal and there is no evidence that his valour earned him the personal congratulations of Lord Methuen.[40] Nevertheless, Watriama'a experience in South Africa was to stand him in good stead when Australians next went to war in 1914. Watriama, who at that time gave his occupation as gardener and whose address since about 1907 had been the Methodist Mission

---

36 Thompson, *Australian Imperialism*, p. 194.
37 Quoted in Thompson, *Australian Imperialism*, p. 201.
38 *Sun*, 6 Jan. 1925.
39 P.L. Murray, *Records of Australian Contingents to the War in South Africa, 1899–1902*, Melbourne, 1911, p. 121. Watriama's military number was 2955.
40 *SMH*, 28 Feb. 1911.

headquarters in Castlereigh St, Sydney, was among the first to enlist.[41] In August he left with the Expeditionary Force to occupy German New Guinea, and soon found himself in the role of instructor. As the *Sun* explained:

> It was imperative that [the] force should get away quickly, and so it happened that many of the volunteers in it knew little of the business of a soldier. As Colonel Heritage could tell you if he wished to, some of them hardly knew one end of their rifle from the other. They had to be taught as the *Berrima*, the troopship, was taking them to their destination. Watriama was no new chum soldier. He had already fought in the Boer war. So his services were valuable. That they were given voluntarily was all the more to his credit. It was a strange sight to see this black man surrounded by perhaps half a dozen eager Australians while he demonstrated to them the use of a rifle, how to use it, how to take it to pieces, how to put it together again, and how to sight it.[42]

A participant history of the occupation described him as being 'a favourite with all members of the expedition.' It also records that at Namatanai on New Ireland it was he who captured Dr Braunert, the leader of a party of Germans who had administered a notable thrashing to William Cox, the head of the Methodist mission. Later he took part in the occupation of Bougainville.[43]

Then, in March 1915, with New Guinea secure, Watriama came back to Sydney and in December he enlisted in the First Australian Imperial Force. In March 1916 he married Ethel May Tipping, the daughter of a grocer, at Wesley Church in Melbourne, and in June sailed for Europe.[44] Again his colour, and his claim, attracted favourable attention. Describing the embarkation parade one newspaper reported under the heading 'A King in Exile':

> 'Look at the black man', said somebody pointing to one of the soldiers marching with the machine guns. The dark face was that of a king in exile, the ex-monarch, in fact, of the Loyalty Islands, a little well-named group somewhere in the waste of the Pacific. Formerly a soldier in South Africa, and recently returned from sharing in the conquest of German New Guinea, he was on his way to enter the vast struggle in Europe on behalf of a civilisation removed by thousands of years from his own.[45]

---

41 Governor General to Colonial Secretary, 26 May 1911, copy in British Consulate, Noumea, General Correspondence 1914–1920, on microfilm WP 162, NLA; Nominal Roll Australian Imperial Force, 18 Infantry Battalion, 1st to 18th reinforcement, p. 104, Australian War Memorial.
42 *Sun*, 25 Mar. 1917; *Lone Hand*, Jan. 1918, p. 67. Watriama's military number was 671.
43 L.C. Reeves, *Australians in Action In New Guinea*, Sydney, 1915, pp. 59–60, 90. For the Cox incident see S.S. Mackenzie, *The Australians at Rabaul*, Sydney, 1927, pp. 120–126.
44 Personal communication from Chris Cunneen, Australian Dictionary of Biography; nominal roll, as for reference 39.
45 Unidentified newspaper clipping, copy in my possession by courtesy of Miss E. Watriama.

A member of the 13th reinforcement of the 18th Infantry Battalion, he reached Europe in time for the battle of the Somme and was wounded at Pozieres.[46] He was again wounded in 1917, as the *Sun* duly reported ('"King" Watriama Wounded in France') and, on returning to Australia at the end of the year, began helping, as the *Bulletin* noted, 'in recruiting work'.[47]

With such a record (supplemented by his dignified bearing and his church associations) it is, then, scarcely to be wondered at that Watriama should attain a social position that would ensure tolerance of and even sympathy for, his foibles.[48] Thus, in reporting his wounding in 1917, the *Sun* commented

> As to whether his claim to the sovereignty of the Loyalty Islands was a good one or not no one seemed to know. It is doubtful if anyone cared.[49]

That this was, indeed, the case, at least as far as the Sydney newspapers were concerned, is suggested by the assessments they published following his death in 1925. In these his claim to the 'kingship' of the Loyaltys was merely noted, but his military service was summarised and his possession of strong pro-British ideals was affirmed, and it was agreed that the action for which he would be most remembered involved a demonstration of patriotism that occurred during the Anzac Day Commemoration in Sydney in 1921.[50]

This incident arose as a response to a presumed 'anti-returned soldier policy at the Town Hall', where the municipal council was lead by the allegedly 'socialist' lord mayor, Alderman W.H. Lambert, who was also president of the Australian Labor Party.[51] Suspicions that there was such a policy had been aroused among members of the Returned Sailors and Soldiers Imperial League of Australia (of which Watriama was a founder of the Northbridge branch) by council decisions regarding the use of the Town Hall. In February 1921 the council had declined to hire the hall to the League for 'a meeting to devise the means for the housing and exhibition of war trophies captured by the A.I.F.' It had also declined, until it obtained legal opinion on its obligations under the *Returned Soldiers and Sailors Act*, to grant the League free use of the Town Hall for a memorial service on the approaching Anzac Day. Such permission was in fact given on 10 March,

---

46 *Lone Hand*, Jan. 1918, p. 67. Watriama's military number was 5148.
47 *Sun*, 25 Mar. 1917; *Bulletin*, 13 Dec. 1917.
48 Miss J. Wagschall, a former neighbour of Watriama, remembered him as a 'fine looking man'. She had lived at 11 Namoi Rd, Northbridge since 1921. Interview May 1984.
49 *Sun*, 25 Mar. 1917.
50 *Evening News*, 6 Jan. 1925, *Daily Telegraph*, 7 Jan. 1925; *SMH*, 7 Jan. 1925; *Sun*, 6 Jan. 1925; *Australian National Review*, 23 Jan. 1925.
51 Lambert was regarded with hostility in some 'right wing' quarters. See the two, four-page pamphlets by A.B. Berry, *Infamous Iron Hand and Baily, Lambert and Co: secrets exposed*. Copies in Mitchell Library. ,Yet he did not belong to the 'left wing' of the Australian Labor Party. *Age*, 4 April 1921.

9. W.J. Watriama (c. 1880–1925): Pretender and patriot, (or 'a blackman's defence of White Australia')

but not before patriotic sensibilities had been bruised in many quarters.[52] They were further bruised a few weeks later when the Union Jack was trampled on in Melbourne by trade unionists protesting at the recent killing of railway men by British soldiers at Mallow in Ireland. The anti- British tone of the protest was denounced in the *Sydney Morning Herald* of 24 April as an expression of 'disloyalty' and of a 'bogus Australianism', that needed to be curbed.[53] Many of the people coming to the Town Hall the next day for the Anzac service were said to be inclined to agree when they found the outside of the hall bereft of flags. 'Wherever the eye turned it looked on bare flagpoles', reported the *Herald*. But, it continued,

> When the service was over thousands of eyes turned to the clock tower. There a lonely Union Jack, diminutive enough, but looking even smaller from that pinnacle of the chief civic hall, fluttered and coiled itself into picturesque folds in the sunshine and the breeze. One of the diggers had climbed up the stairs into the tower and placed it there.

Shortly before the service began, S. Henley of the Diggers Vigilance Society had stepped onto the platform inside the hall with a small Union Jack in his hand and had won the cheers of the crowd by announcing that 'we intend to fly this flag, no matter how'. But, he added, they were having trouble in getting the flag to the top of the building. Then

> Out of the black mass in the gallery on the right rose a khaki figure. He volunteered to host the Empire symbol. Again the crowd cheered.

Then, another Digger, an elderly man, stepped forward

> 'I think it is a disgrace,' he said in a stentorian voice, 'to our dead boys who were as true [trade] unionists as ever lived. They have fought for their country and today they are lying in honoured graves. I say emphatically that we will have the flag up.

---

52 *Proceedings of the Municipal Council of the City of Sydney, during the year 1921*, pp. 71, 82, 103; Town Clerk to RSSIL, 10 Mar. 1921, and associated documents in Town Clerk's Department, Registered Papers no 470/21.
53 *Age*, 4 April 1921; *Evening News*, 25 April 1921; *SMH*, 24 April 1921; Patrick O'Farrell, *Catholic Church and Community; an Australian history*, Sydney, 1985, p. 344. There had also been a 'flag incident' in Martin Place a few months before. *Evening News*, 19 Dec. 1917. Among some nationalities of Labor or 'socialist' sympathies, there was a strong preference for displaying the Australian flag instead of the Union Jack. Dispute about what should be regarded as the proper flag of Australia was fostered by the fact that no particular flag was officially held to be the national flag until the commonwealth Blue Ensign was adopted as such in 1951. Department of the Special Minister of State, *The Australian Flag*, Canberra, 1982.

Then to the accompaniment of more cheers, 'with the flag in his hand, and with a heavy support of protesting Diggers,' Henley left the platform and raced for the tower to carry out the plan. Later, other ex-servicemen hoisted both the Union Jack and the Australian flag on the poles flanking the tower.[54]

According to his obituarists, Watriama figured prominently in these proceedings. Indeed, they credit him with having climbed the flagpole in the tower and put the flag in place, although the *Herald* obituary erroneously has him replacing the Australian flag with the Union Jack.[55] There is, however, a serious weakness in the evidence regarding the incident. The *Evening News*, on the very day of the event, reported that it was an ex-sergeant, R.K. ('Dick') Watkins, who had hoisted the flag.[56] In the absence of further details, Watriama's exact role in the affair must, therefore, be open to conjecture. Possibly it was less conspicuous than that with which he was posthumously credited and, if he did climb a flagpole, the external design of the Town Hall makes it more likely that he had climbed one of the sides rather than the one atop the tower. Nevertheless, there can be little doubt that he was closely involved with that dramatic outburst of vexillolatry in 1921.

As for the omission that prompted the outburst, it seems likely that it was the result of oversight rather than a socialist-inspired disloyalty to the British Empire. The inside of the hall had been appropriately decorated and, according to a report from the town clerk, the absence of flags on the outside had been 'entirely due to forgetfulness on the part of the officer accustomed to put them up.'

Nevertheless, the action of Henley, Watkins and Watriama, and their comrades, was sufficient to induce the council to ensure that such a lapse would not occur again. In May it resolved that both the Union Jack and the Commonwealth flag would, thenceforth, be flown daily at the Town Hall and that, on Anzac Day, the hall would be 'be flagged in gala style'.[57] Indeed, if the tributes paid to Watriama in 1925 are any indication, it would have been imprudent for the council to have resolved otherwise.

Following the war Watriama settled down to family life and to working as a house painter. With the aid of a war service loan he bought a house in the Sydney suburb of Northbridge, where he was a founder of the local branch of

---

54 *SMH*, 26 April 1921.
55 *SMH*, 7 Jan. 1925; *Sun*, 6 Jan. 1925; *Evening News*, 6 Jan. 1925; *Australian National Review*, 23 Jan. 1925; *Daily Telegraph*, 7 Jan. 1925.
56 *Evening News*, 25 April 1921; *Sun*, 25 April 1921; *The Daily Telegraph* account of the incident (26 April 1921) is much more dramatic than that of the *SMH*.
57 Proceedings of the Municipal Council of the City of Sydney during the year 1921, pp. 167, 182–183; *Daily Telegraph*, 27, 28 April 1921.

the RSSIL.⁵⁸ Apart from his abortive visit to Noumea in 1920, he did not pursue his Loyalty Islands campaign with his former vigour. Yet, he did not abandon his claim and he continued quietly to proclaim his interest in the group by naming his house 'Netche' after the chiefly village on Mare.⁵⁹ Meanwhile he was making but a modest living and, towards the end of 1925, at the onset of his final illness, the RSSIL organised a benefit function for him. As a mark of respect for him the Northbridge Methodists trustees, albeit almost reluctantly, allowed this to be held in the church hall, on condition that the permission was not taken as a precedent and provided that 'screaming farce' was prohibited.⁶⁰ Later, 'in view of her present circumstances', the RSSIL granted his widow £5 from the Widows Relief Account.⁶¹

Watriama died of cancer on 5 January 1925, leaving his wife to bring up their two children. Both children, a son and a daughter, later served in the Australian forces in World War II.⁶² Although they were following a strong precedent in so doing it is worthy of note that they were serving a country to which their father had never formally belonged. For Watriama had never been naturalised.⁶³ Why this was so is not known. It is, however, consistent with the possibility that he retained a sense of prior allegiance to the Loyaltys. If so, it was a disposition that was entirely proper for one who claimed to be king of the group. Whether he ever truly believed his claim to be valid, however, cannot be known. What is clearer is that he was moved to promulgate it by what he saw as a threat to Australia—to White Australia—and that Australia respected him despite his claim, if not for it.

Watriama was not an important figure in the affairs of his time. The paucity of his achievements, such as they were, and despite the publicity he attracted, precludes the attribution of any such status. Nowhere did he exercise a decisive influence. Nevertheless, in hindsight, he is not without significance as an historical 'marker' or reference point, for his career can be related to important

---

58   Death certificate, by courtesy Australian Dictionary of Biography; Ethel Watriama to W.M. Hughes, 2 Sept. 1925. Hughes papers, NLA, MS 1538/30/136; obituaries, reference 54.
59   The house still stands at 4 Namoi Road. D.H.Lawrence, who was in Australia from May to Aug. 1922, commented extensively on the practice of naming houses in his novel *Kangaroo*. Watriama's signature, with the note 'King of the Loyalty Islands, June 28, 1918' is written on a section of a toast held in the Mitchell Library, ML Doc 2244.
60   Northbridge trust minutes, trustee meeting 22 Oct. 1924. Held by Uniting Church of Australia, Church Records and Historical Society, Sydney.
61   *The Australian Home*, 26 Jan. 1925. This journal, which already incorporated *The Property Owner*, also incorporated from this issue *The Soldier*, 'the official journal of the RSSIL and kindred associations.
62   The daughter, Edna, was ten when her father died and the son, Merlyn, was seven. Edna studied singing at the Conservatorium of Music in Sydney. During the war she was an A.C.W. in the W.A.A.F. (no. 106775). Merlyn (NX 4144) served in the Middle East with the 2/1 Battalion, A.I.F., and was taken prisoner-of-war in Crete. Merlyn's son, Mervyn, became a professional golfer in northern New South Wales. W.J. Watriama's wife, Ethel, died in Sydney on 28 Feb. 1962. Personal communication from Edna and Merlyn Watriama; Edna Watriama to W.M. Hughes, 5 Jan. 1948, Hughes Papers, NLA, MS 1538/1/9398-401.
63   Ethel M. Watriama to W.M. Hughes, 2 Sept. 1925, Hughes Papers, NLA, MS 1538/30/136.

issues in the development of Australian society and to perceptions of Australia's place in the world. Thus, in the history of an Australia that has become an ethnic and cultural melting pot, he is notable in being probably the first black man who can be shown to have attained an apparently thorough and unequivocal degree of acceptance in white Australian society.[64] Besides that, Watriama also had meaning for an Australia that was being increasingly affronted by the continued presence and oppressive policies of France in the Pacific, although the latter have lessened somewhat since the 1980s.[65] Personal, quixotic and unsuccessful though he was in his efforts to reduce France's holdings in the Pacific, he was contributing to a tradition that has had fitful expression in Australia—and among France's Pacific island subjects—for more than a century. If he is to be remembered for telling lies for the sake of his cause it should be conceded that they were, at least, 'white' ones. Yet, since the issue of France's place in the Pacific was being fought more strenuously and for higher stakes in the later twentieth century than ever before, and since the political status of New Caledonia ('Kanaky') is still under review in the twenty-first century, it may be that Watriama deserves to be seen not merely as a pretender or as a patriot or as a prevaricator but as a prophet, albeit a minor one. Certainly, 'prophet' is a title that becomes him better than 'king'.[66]

---

64 'W.J. Watriama', in *Australian Dictionary of Biography*, Melbourne, 1990, vol. 12.
65 Robert Aldrich, *France and the South Pacific since 1940*, London, 1993, pp. 240–284.
66 The preliminary version of this essay was published in French in 1996 in *Mwa Vee: revue culturelle kanak*, no.14, pp.12-33.

10. Lucy Evelyn Cheesman (1881–1969): Traveller, writer, scientist

Evelyn Cheesman, as she was normally known, was an unlikely example of that not uncommon species the naturalist–adventurer. She was a slightly built woman with limited financial means and scant formal training. Such apparent disadvantages, though, were offset, as the record shows, by invincible self reliance and minimal regard for personal comfort. She was an entomologist who made six arduous and extensive solo expeditions to various Pacific islands between 1924 and 1955 to collect insects, and who recounted her experiences in seven books which gratified the capacity for risk-free wonderment of a large popular audience of vicarious vagrants. In New Guinea in 1939 the apparent oddity of the behaviour her work required led local people to describe her as 'the woman who walks'.[1] Substantively, though, as a front-line naturalist—a harvester of specimens for the more laboratory-bound academic systematisers and analysts—she belongs as part of a long and continuing scientific tradition. She was one of those who performed the vital but ancillary role, which is largely taken for granted, of a supplier of raw material.

The custom of scientific collecting may conveniently (if contestably) be taken as having a definitive beginning with Joseph Banks. A botanist, and later president of the Royal Society, he led a team of gatherers, observers and recorders aboard the *Endeavour* on James Cook's first great exploratory voyage through the Pacific in 1769–1770. The object of their industry in this new world, which was gradually being opened up to European scrutiny after more than two centuries of desultory maritime probing, was to advance the limits of knowledge about the natural universe, and to discover what useful—and exploitable—resources it might contain. Science, like religion, was not an exclusive category. Like politics and trade, those other protean and ubiquitous axes of social interaction, it also shared permeable and overlapping borders with further species of activity. Botany, for instance, was an adjunct of pharmacology while entomology, a later noetic development, could have important applications in the control of plant and animal pests. On Cook's second voyage the work of scientific enquiry was directed by Johann Reinhold Forster, a broadly educated German who was well acquainted with the method for classifying and relating biological specimens that had been devised by Carl Linnaeus. That taxonomy, involving describing, naming and grouping particular items, was a potent means of discerning order within the diversity of the natural world. By enriching intellectual curiosity

---

1 Evelyn, Cheesman, *Six-Legged Snakes in New Guinea: a collecting expedition to two unexplored islands*, London, 1949, p. 265; and, *Things Worth While*, London, 1958, p. 259.

with the goal of uncovering obscure—but possibly useful—meanings and linkages through careful observation, it also provided an inexhaustible impetus for purposeful pursuit, often in out-of-the-way places.[2]

Sometimes this might be carried out by teams of scientists and be organised by institutions. Examples abound. For instance, as Cheesman herself relates in a survey titled 'Naturalists' Expeditions in the Pacific', there was the one despatched by the United States National Museum in 1873 to investigate the fauna of coral islands in the eastern Pacific; and the two sent to the then Dutch New Guinea (later the would-be nation of West Papua) by the British Ornithologists' Union between 1909 and 1913.[3] But also, and always, there were individuals. Some of these were amateurs, like Rev. J.-B. Poncelet, who financed his mission station at Turiboiru in southern Bougainville by capturing butterflies and moths for sale to, among others, Lord Rothschild for his museum at Tring in England.[4] Some were primarily gentlemen wanderers: such as David Douglas, who died in Hawai'i in 1834 while collecting for the Royal Horticultural Society; and Charles Woodford, who had hunted insects in the Solomon Islands before becoming Resident Commissioner there in 1896.[5] Others were somewhat more scholarly, although not necessarily by profession. One of the most notable of these enquiring adventurers, and in his *modus operandi* the model for Cheesman, was Alfred Russel Wallace, the begetter of zoogeography, the science of relating animals to their habitats. Belonging among the great nineteenth century contributors to understanding of the natural world, Wallace, a railway surveyor by profession, worked independently. He collected assiduously during 14 years in the field, he helped finance his expeditions by selling specimens to the British Museum, and he published extensively on his travels and findings.

In 1856, during an eight-year expedition focusing on the Malay archipelago, Wallace visited New Guinea. In the course of his travels he observed a sharp discontinuity of faunal types on either side of what became known as Wallace's Line. On the western side, on islands known (in the light of plate tectonics) to lie on the Sunda shelf of south-east Asia, the assemblage of animals is predominantly Asian. On the eastern side of the line, which follows a trench of deep water that runs up from Timor to the Philippines, are New Guinea and

---

2   Edward Duyker, *Nature's Argonaut: Daniel Solander, 1733–1782*, Melbourne, 1998; Michael E. Hoare (ed.), *The 'Resolution' Journal of Johann Reinhold Forster, 1772–1775*, London, 1982, vol. 1, pp. 20–54; Bernard Smith, *European Vision and the South Pacific*, Sydney, 1984 (2nd edn), pp. 1–107; and, *Imagining the Pacific: in the wake of the Cook voyages*, Melbourne, 1992, pp. 41-50.
3   Evelyn Cheesman, 'Naturalists' Expeditions in the Pacific', in Charles Barrett (ed.), *The Pacific: ocean of islands*, Melbourne, [1950], pp. 55–65.
4   Patrick O'Reilly and J.M. Sédès, *Jaunes, Noirs et Blancs: trois années de guerre aux Iles Salomon*, Paris, 1949, Pl.X; Robert Stuart, *Nuts to You: an autobiography*, Sydney, 1977, pp. 62–63; *Missions des Iles*, no. 89 (Mars 1959), pp. 57–58.
5   Ann Lindsay Mitchell and Syd House, *David Douglas: explorer and botanist*, London, 1999, pp. 167, 177; Ian Heath, 'Charles Woodford: adventurer, naturalist, administrator', in Deryck Scarr (ed.), *More Pacific Islands Portraits*, Canberra, 1978, pp. 194–201.

northern Australia, which sit upon the Sahul shelf. There, and extending into the adjacent Melanesian groups of Solomons, Vanuatu and New Caledonia, the fauna is mainly Australia-related. This latter region, formally designated Papuasia, is one of the five great faunal areas into which Wallace divided the world in his masterwork, *The Geographical Distribution of Plants and Animals*, published in 1876.[6]

It was there, on the eastern side of the line, that Cheesman did most of her collecting. As for the islands further to the east, the great distances across the Pacific were filters that relatively few plants or animals could pass.[7] There, as in the Galapagos, to Charles Darwin's amazement in 1835, evolution moved spectacularly. It bred great variety from a small base of initial colonisers that derived mainly from Papuasia.

By her own account, Cheesman's interest in understanding the processes of nature sprang from her upbringing in England, in the depths of 'the country … those carefree happy days soaking in wild life'. At first 'imbibing unconsciously from the unscientific country lore', she happily progressed to 'intelligently assimilating' its contents.[8] She was born on 8 October 1881 at Court Lodge farm, near the village of Westwell, 6 kilometres from the town of Ashford in the county of Kent. Her paternal grandfather, who appears to have been a prosperous businessman, had bought the property and built a new house on it from the ruins of a twelfth century monastery that had once stood there. Her father, Robert (1842–1915), lived the life of a country gentleman. The management of the farm and the mill was entrusted to a bailiff. Her mother, Florence Maud née Tassell (1855–1944), belonged to one of the old families of the county.[9] She was descended from William Spong (1719–1787) whose family had shifted from Yorkshire to Kent in 1652. His grandson, likewise called William (1790–1839), of Cobtree Farm, Boxley, and who was to become Florence's grandfather, was the original for Charles Dickens' fictional Old Wardle of *Pickwick Papers* (1833).[10]

Five children were born to Florence and Robert Cheesman. All of them had a second name beginning with 'E', except for the youngest who was simply Eric. Evelyn (she always used her second name) was the third-born among two girls and three boys. There was also a large and hospitable extended family scattered within easy distance of Court Lodge to compensate for a lack of closeness between parents and children, on which Cheesman comments:

---

6   For Wallace, see Penny van Oosterzee, *Where Worlds Collide: the Wallace Line* (Melbourne, 1997); Peter Raby, *Alfred Russel Wallace* (London, 2002).
7   Andrew Mitchell, *A Fragile Paradise: nature and man in the Pacific*, London, 1989, p. 24.
8   Evelyn Cheesman, *Things Worth While*, London, 1958, p. 25.
9   Ibid., pp. 7–24.
10 Information passed on by Niel Gunson (Canberra), who obtained it from Bryan Tassell (Faversham, Kent), a Cheesman relative.

> Our parents were wrapped up in each other; my father who was thirteen years older than my mother remained devoted until the last minutes of his life. But the children were incidental ... . Never can I recall any suggestion of even encouragement for our futures. It was as though the responsibility of parenthood had never entered their heads.[11]

Still, freedom from restraint within a congenial environment seems to have encouraged in their offspring rewarding habits of curiosity, creativity and self-reliance, qualities which some of them took to the distant reaches of the Empire. Thus, the eldest child, Robert Ernest, had a notable career as a soldier, explorer, author and naturalist, and as a diplomat in Iraq, Arabia and Ethiopia; Edith painted watercolours in Mesopotamia; and Percy travelled widely, laying submarine cables. Only Eric, who became a doctor, seems to have resisted the siren call of the horizon.[12]

In their earliest years the Cheesman children were supervised by a nurse, and their first lessons were provided by a daily governess. Thanks to the generosity of relatives who paid the fees, for the family fortunes appear to have been declining, the children were later sent away to boarding school. The boys went to the elite Merchant Tailors' School while the two girls attended one in Brighton run by the Misses Collingwood, daughters of a clergyman. There the pair acquired a solid grounding in French and German, something they shared with their mother. 'In the holidays', wrote Evelyn, 'Mother and I used to read Schiller and Goethe for pleasure'.[13]

In due course, the girls themselves became governesses. In this capacity, Edith went to Surrey and Evelyn to the Midlands village of Gumley. Although her charge was only 'a small boy', her chances for personal recreation were limited. Still, she recalled her years there with pleasure, 'for the opportunities [they offered] to continue the study of botany and for the hours snatched at night watching badgers and foxes'. A stimulating hiatus was brought to these soothing rustic avocations in 1904, when her pupil was sent away to a preparatory school, prior to going to Eton. At the same time Evelyn was enabled, through family connections, to accept a temporary appointment at a girls high school in Germany. Eighteen months later she returned to Gumley 'to teach Geoffrey's sister for a few years', and to plan her next move. That was, to become a veterinarian. She was already studying animal anatomy from a two-volume work that she had bought in Germany. But to no avail. Twice she applied for admisssion to the Royal Veterinary College and twice she was rejected, on the grounds that the

---

11 Cheesman, *Things Worth While*, p. 28.
12 Ibid., p. 8; *Obituaries from 'The Times', 1961–1970*, London, 1971, pp. 136–137; Florence Cheesman, *Mesopotamia ... Water-colours*, London, 1922; Percy Cheesman, *Around the Map on a Cable Ship*, London, 1933; information from Niel Gunson.
13 Cheesman, *Things Worth While*, p. 30.

course was not open to women. Disappointed, but not despairing, in 1912 she attempted to position herself more advantageously for any change of policy. To that end, she took employment as a canine nurse in a dog's hospital and health care service run by Alfred Joseph Sewell, veterinary surgeon to King Edward VII.[14]

With the outbreak of war in 1914 Cheesman's knowledge of French and German brought a marked change of activity: intelligence work in the Admiralty. When the war ended in 1918, she then made what proved to be portentous decision (one again shaped by personal contacts). Although her old ambition was still strong, at the request of Professor Maxwell Lefroy of the Royal College of Science she accepted an anticipated temporary position at London Zoo. It was, she was told, 'work that a woman can do and no special knowledge is needed'; that is, taking charge of the Insect House. This had become very rundown during the war; specimen stocks needed to be re-established and new collectors obtained; aquaria demonstrating pond life needed to be replenished; exhibits needed to be labelled and displays refurbished; and regular supplies of flowering plants needed to be obtained to feed the insects. Such became her involvement in this work, which soon extended to presenting talks on insect life (an activity that later led to publishing and broadcasting) that, when the veterinary ban was eventually lifted, she did not re-apply to enter the college.

Thus, she was still at the zoo in 1923 when Lefroy drew her attention to a proposed excursion to the Pacific islands. Joining it would offer her the fulfilment of 'an unattainable dream', the chance to travel and 'to study tropical insects', as a member of the St George Expedition. This was a private venture, organised by a body called Scientific Research Expeditions Ltd. The plan was for a round-the-world cruise catering for a group of fare-paying passengers, travelling mainly for pleasure, and a party of scientists who would have free passage, with the opportunity to collect specimens in remote places. The shareholders, some of whom were passengers, hoped (vainly, as it proved) to receive dividends from a film to be made about the voyage and from publication royalties.[15]

In pursuit of these varied aims, the *St George*, a barquentine-rigged vessel of 694 tons, with auxiliary steam power, left Dartmouth on 9 April 1924. There were eight scientists on board, led by James Hornell, a marine biologist with a strong secondary interest in indigenous material cultures. Recently retired as director of fisheries in Madras, he would later return to the Pacific to report on fish stocks in Fiji, but the main result of his acquaintance with the region was the monumental monograph *Canoes of Oceania*, which he published with A.C. Haddon in 1936–1937. Other members of the group, some of whom also achieved

---

14   Ibid., pp. 29–68.
15   Ibid., pp. 57–84.

scholarly distinction, were P.H. Johnston (herpetologist), Cyril Crossland (marine biologist—corals), H.J. Kelsall (ornithologist), L.J. Chubb (geologist), L.A.M. Riley (botanist), and C.L. Collenette (lepidopterist and coleopterist).[16]

After passing through the Panama Canal, the *St George* visited the Galapagos Islands (24 July – 4 August), then returned to Panama for a month before reaching the Marquesas (1 January – 4 February 1925), Tuamotus (7–14 February), and Tahiti (16 February – 19 March). At all of these landfalls Cheesman endeavoured to collect, often helped by an obliging crewman. But all was not well. Already, at the Galapagos, where she was struck by the limited variety of species unleavened by significant adaptations, strains were appearing among the travellers due to their different interests. A disproportionate amount of time, Cheesman felt, was spent at sea. 'Our visits [on land] were far too short for entomological collecting, but the passengers were bored after a few days sightseeing' while, on board, some objected to the smell of drying lizard skins, corals and seaweed. 'The aims of tourists and scientists cannot tally'. Besides, the expedition was proving to be under-financed, and the ship itself was too big to be easily manoeuvred inshore.[17]

At the Marquesas Cheesman spent a day ashore on each of Hiva-oa and Fatu Hiva and two days on Nukuhiva. On the latter, the island to which Herman Melville had deserted in 1842, she made a rarely attempted solo climb up to a rocky interior plateau, almost at the expense of her life. Sliding on some dry grass, she fell rapidly to the brink of 'a perpendicular wall looking down to a small stream thirty feet below', but managed to avoid dropping over by holding on to two fistfuls of bracken. Her rucksack, she surmised, had probably slowed her fall.[18]

Next, the *St George* called at Napuka and Fakarava in the Tuamotus. Again, Cheesman's pickings were scarce. Napuka, for instance, yielded only one variety of ant, lizard and gecko, but five species of land crabs. From these atolls the *St George* proceeded to Tahiti, where Cheesman promptly parted company with it. She was enabled to do so through the generosity of her brother Percy. Having heard rumours that the expedition was financially troubled and was liable to leave the scientists stranded somewhere, he had forwarded her £100 to ensure her independence, which she had come acutely to value. Henceforth she would

---

16   Ibid., p. 86; A.J.A. Douglas and P.H. Johnson, *The South Seas of To-day: being an account of the cruise of the yacht St. George to the South Pacific*, London, 1926, pp. 5–11; Cheesman, 'Naturalists' Expeditions', p. 62; Evelyn Cheesman, *Islands Near the Sun: off the beaten track in the far, fair Society Islands*, London, 1927, p. 86; C.L. Collenette, *Sea-Girt Jungles: the experiences of a naturalist with the 'St. George' expedition*, London, n.d., p. xi; James Hornell, *Water Transport: origins and early evolution*, Cambridge, 1946, p. viii; and, *Report on the Fisheries of Fiji*, Suva, 1940, p. vii.
17   Cheesman, *Things Worth While*, p. 99; and, 'Naturalists' Expeditions', p. 62.
18   Ibid., pp. 18–19.

always go solo. Apart from the particular problems of the *St George* expedition, experience had already revealed, she wrote, that 'working alone was the sole method of reaching desirable [collecting] sites'.[19]

Matching action to intent, she had embarked on her first solo expedition even before the *St George* sailed from Papeete on 19 March, en route for home via Rurutu, Rapa, Easter Island and Panama. Funds received at Tahiti enabled the return voyage to continue, but in a more direct manner than earlier envisaged—and into bankruptcy proceedings.[20] The intrepid entomologist, meanwhile, had made a series of arduous trips into the mountainous interior of Tahiti, as well as brief visits to Raiatea, Huahine and Borabora aboard an ill-found inter-island schooner, the *Temehani*. The collecting was satisfactory, but at the cost of much difficult and dangerous climbing and some painful mishaps. When, about September, she returned to England it was with a modest but adequately representative 'bag' of about 500 specimens, including a new species of short-horned grasshopper.[21] For Cheesman, the significance of the trip, though, was not to be measured by numbers. Not only had it shown her the advantages of operating alone, but she was also poised to comprehend that the insects she had been collecting had not originated predominantly in Australia, but had migrated from Melanesia. That is, that they were mostly 'Papuan'. It was this—unexpected—realisation that would determine her future collecting sites. Henceforth, she would concentrate on the more richly endowed areas that lay nearer to the eastern edge of the Wallace Line.

Probably, Cheesman's Polynesian experiences also strengthened her innate self-reliance for, when she learned that a certain zoo official with whom she 'had never seen eye to eye' was still in office, she decided not to return to the Insect House. Resigning, she took an unpaid position at the British Museum, living frugally off her modest royalties from 'potboilers' (her term) about insect behaviour, and writing scholarly papers on insect taxonomy. On the strength of the latter she hoped to establish her scientific credentials sufficiently for her to qualify for a grant-in-aid to assist with a further collecting venture.[22] The first three of these papers, describing new species, appeared in the *Annals and Magazine of Natural History* in 1926. These were followed by three more in 1927. The same year *Islands in the Sun*, her book on the *St George* expedition, was published. Another three scientific papers appeared in 1928.

---

19 Ibid., p. 125.
20 Douglas and Johnson, pp. 173–175, 202; Don Collinson, *The Chronicles of Dartmouth: an historical yearly log, 1854–1954*, Dartmouth, 2000, pp. 171–174.
21 Cheesman, *Things Worth While*, pp. 132–146; and, *Islands Near the Sun*, pp. 229–232.
22 Cheesman, *Things Worth While*, pp. 146–148. Her early 'potboilers' were *Everyday Doings of Insects* and *The Great Little Insect*, both published in London in 1924.

Her industry was rewarded. In 1928, fortified with a grant of £300 and the remains of a small legacy, Cheesman set off on a solo collecting expedition to the New Hebrides (since 1980, Vanuatu). Sceptics suggested she might last six months; she stayed for two years. Her reason for choosing Vanuatu was uncomplicated. Its fauna represented a clear gap in the national collection. 'We needed information about New Hebrides insects badly, to link up our knowledge of those inhabiting other groups of islands and Australia'.[23]

Indeed, little systematic research of any kind had been carried out there. Anthropologists had shown the way. W.H.R. Rivers visited the New Hebrides in 1908 and 1914, and Felix Speiser from Switzerland (an admirer of the writings of the missionary ethnologist Robert Codrington, who had lived in the Banks Islands) worked in the northern islands in 1910–1911. Subsequently, several promising young scholars were despatched there from Cambridge University. Rivers, who died in 1922, sent John Layard to Malekula (1914–1915). Later, after World War I, his former colleague Alfred Haddon, who was also a confidant of Speiser, assigned Bernard Deacon to Malekula (1926–1927), T.T. Barnard to Efate (1927) and C.B. Humphries to the southern islands (1926). The University of Oxford, in contrast to its rival, promoted enquiries into natural history. In 1933 John Baker, a zoologist who had visited Santo in 1922 and 1927, returned there with his wife Zita and several colleagues. These were Tom Harrisson, a biologist; Jock Marshall, a one-armed Australian ornithologist, who would come again in 1937; and, Terence Bird. The Bakers and Bird left in February 1934, but Harrisson and Marshall stayed on for a few months more. For all these researchers, judging from the published accounts of their experiences, the physical discomforts and deprivations involved in following their interests seem to have been a source less of complaint than of a fortifying sense of 'adventure'— and of high mutual respect.[24] Cheesman wrote an admiring tribute to Deacon who died of blackwater fever on 27 March 1927; and the raffish Harrisson later spoke of 'the plucky Miss Cheesman'.[25]

Concerning her own expedition, Cheesman lightly dismissed well-meant advice, including that of the archbishop of Canterbury, that she should not venture into such an 'uncivilised place'; and later rejoiced that her assured indifference to their strictures had been vindicated. She had read widely in the writing on the New Hebrides, much of it coloured by Presbyterian piety:

---

23 Cheesman, *Things Worth While*, p. 148, and *Backwaters of the Savage South Seas*, London, 1933, p. 13.
24 These researchers and their works may be identified further in Patrick O'Reilly, *Hébridais: répertoire bio-bibliographique des Nouvelles-Hébridais*, Paris, 1957.
25 Bernard Deacon, *Malekula: a vanishing people in the New Hebrides*, London, 1934, pp. xxvii–xxix; Tom Harrisson, *Savage Civilisation*, London, 1937, p. 396. Judith M. Heimann, *The Most Offending Soul Alive: Tom Harrisson and his remarkable life*, London, 2002.

from all this literature [I] had built up preconceptions of holy missionaries sacrificing their lives for ideals; of hard, unscrupulous traders; [of] unchristian settlers hostile to work which was obviously sponsored by the almighty; [of] native people with only animal instincts.

But experience taught otherwise:

All these images proved to be completely false in every particular. In my two years spent in the group I formed an utterly different conception of the conditions of living and realised the erroneous impressions which had been disseminated throughout the world.[26]

She found the down-at-heel 'capital' on the island of Efate distinctly less charming—and far less hospitable—than the villages. Thus, after three days in Port Vila, which she reached at the end of January 1929, she re-joined the Burns Philp vessel *Makambo*, which was going northwards to Malekula, to escape the hateful place. Her plan was 'to build a hut' in some coastal locality to use as a base for collecting expeditions. Instead, she was gratified to be given the use of a house normally occupied by Rev. Fred Paton of the Presbyterian mission at Ounua at South West Bay. For 12 months, assisted by five 'boys' led by one Tarlis, who was recommended by a planter named Charles Dillensenger, that was the point from which she ranged about the island, with trips also to Santo and to Vanua Lava, in the Banks group.[27]

While regular collecting trips, which might last for a week at a time, induced Cheesman to become acquainted with local people and their customs, her interest in such matters was stolidly pragmatic. It did not generate descriptions or explanations of any depth. Thus, she learned the local pidgin English (*Bislama*), she became conversant with the *tambu* or spiritual forces that regulated much of island life, and was familiar with the 'neutral zones' which eased the way for people of hostile villages to reach their gardens. She touched on such topics in books describing her experiences—*Backwaters of the Savage South Seas* (1933), *Camping Adventures on Cannibal Islands* (1949), *Who Stand Alone* (1965) and in an autobiography, *Things Worthwhile* (1958)—and she gathered artefacts for the Cambridge museum, but she eschewed any pretensions to ethnology. 'My interest in them', she wrote, 'was not academic. I simply wanted to get into the interior for collecting'. Similarly *ad hoc* was her ready acceptance of the island people as they were. Acquiescing in the anthropological orthodoxy of the day, she thought that they were at a lower stage of social development than Europeans, but she also believed that they were perfectly adapted to their time and place on some putative evolutionary scale. Her comments are free of criticism and ridicule, and of any wish for her hosts' 'improvement'. If there was

---

26 Cheesman, *Things Worth While*, p. 149.
27 Ibid., pp. 149–153, and *Backwaters*, pp. 24–31, 137, 228.

in this anything of the pervasive colonial assumption that equated 'native' with inherent inferiority, it was not expressed in a condescending way. After all, she was living closely with the islanders, and was dependent on their cooperation in order to do her work. For instance, she matter-of-factly described Tarlis, who guided her on an arduous ascent of Mount Villikus, a specimen-rich peak 16 kilometres from Aunua, as 'a very intelligent fellow'.[28]

Another notable adventure was a visit to Inmaru to see Ringapat, the widely feared chief of the Big Nambas people. The American adventurers Martin and Osa Johnson had visited there in 1918, but only for a few hours, and with a well-armed police escort. More recently, in 1928, a labour recruiter who had kidnapped two Big Nambas youths 12 years before was killed in reprisal at Malua Bay. The attack, though, as Ringapat explained to Cheesman's satisfaction, had not been made without appreciating that the French and British colonial authorities who jointly ruled the 'Condominium' were not going to take action, and it did not betoken any general hostility to Europeans. Indeed, as a sign of cultural convergence, something already seen by his substituting a pig for a human sacrifice in certain initiation rituals, Ringapat gave her a present to take back for King George V. This was a 4-metre-long spear, which was eventually deposited in the British Museum. He later received a gift of water tanks in return.[29]

From densely forested Malekula, Cheesman moved to the more open and solidly missionised southern island of Erromanga. There, in Dillon's Bay, where an Australian named O.S. Martin, the only other European on the island, had a sheep and cattle farm, she once again occupied a vacant Presbyterian mission house. Despite the lighter vegetation there, like that on neighbouring Tanna and Aneityum, which she also visited, her collecting was again profitable and instructive, for the plants of the cooler southern islands were predominantly of Australian origin in contrast to those of the Papuan north. So the insect populations varied accordingly. Here her main helpers, all from a nearby village, were a young man named Mauling and two girls, granddaughters of the chief Waris, who had once been a plantation labourer in Queensland. One important, but hitherto less well documented, piece of information she gained from Waris was the local explanation for the attack on Captain Cook when he attempted to land on Erromanga from the *Resolution* on 4 August 1774, during his second voyage. It was that before going ashore in Polenia Bay, Cook had despatched two boats to an islet (Goat Island) lying off a high bluff he later named Traitor's Head. Cook had directed his men there to cut wood. But, to the Erromangans, Goat Island was a *tambu* place. It was where the spirits putatively lived, and

---
28   Cheesman, *Things Worth While*, pp. 153–155.
29   Ibid., pp. 166–171, and *Backwaters*, pp. 163, 202–207; and, *Camping Adventures on Cannibal Islands*, London, 1949, pp. 44–88.

was never visited. For the first white men the Erromangans had ever seen to have gone near there was reason enough to refuse them water and to resist their landing. In the volley of musket fire that ensued, four people were seen to be hit but only one of them, a chief named Narom, was killed.[30]

Ironically, on shifting to Tanna Cheesman encountered a curious impediment. This was not difficult territory or indigenous resistance, but the pressing concern and hospitality of the British district agent, James Nicoll, and his wife.

> If the island had offered better prospects for collecting, it would have been necessary to circumvent my kind hosts' solicitation for my welfare. It was novel experience to be told that some trip was too strenuous, that I might get over-tired, or wet, or not have enough food or sleep.[31]

Aneityum, where she was assisted as required by an Australian timber miller named P.J. Wilson, offered somewhat better collecting, but by then malaria was beginning to trouble her severely. 'Two years had been rather a long time in these islands, which then had a reputation for being unhealthy'. So she decided to leave, reaching Sydney via Noumea early in 1931.[32]

The cumulative extent of Cheesman's insect harvest from this expedition seems no where to be recorded, but it was apparently sufficient to confirm her professional credibility. The lack of published papers from it in scientific journals suggests that she no longer needed to prove herself as after the *St. George* expedition. Instead, on returning to England, she directed her energies into writing an account of her northern islands experiences, into fitting some of her specimens into the Museum's existing collections and by putting others of them 'into the hands of various specialists'. In the course of these tasks it soon became clear to her that 'if I concentrated on working out coherently the relationship between species and the extent to which each had spread', that 'New Guinea must be my next objective'.[33]

Hence it was that, on Good Friday of 1933, Cheesman arrived at Port Moresby. Her target area was the high rainforest of south-east Papua, accessible by path across the Owen Stanley range from Port Moresby to Buna, via the administrative outpost of Kokoda.

> If I could encamp at different altitudes, this should give me the best opportunity for carrying out the work of observation and collecting,

---

30 Cheesman, *Things Worth While*, pp. 173–180; and, *Camping Adventures*, pp. 145–149; J.C. Beaglehole (ed.), *The Journals of Captain James Cook*, vol. 11, London, 1969, pp. 477–480; H.A. Robertson, *Erromanga, the Martyr Isle*, London, 1902, pp. 13–19.
31 Cheesman, *Things Worth While*, p. 181.
32 Ibid., p. 202.
33 Ibid., p. 204.

devoting what time was necessary in each camp according to whether the site was favourable. Being on or near a patrolled road, I could send away the material to be shipped to London, and be at least within reach of the necessities of existence.

Her plan was to hire carriers and to walk to Kokoda, but this was scotched by the administrator, Sir Hubert Murray. Although he 'had recently boasted that it was safe to be among natives in any part of the Territory [of Papua]', he informed her that this 'did not apply to an unescorted female, but only to miners or prospectors'. Instinctually averse 'to beginning this work under the sheltered wing of officialdom' and confident of her ability to 'manage the native labour', she was chagrined, but undeterred, by the solicitous obstruction. Instead, she travelled in a Tiger Moth aeroplane piloted by the masterly Denny Orme, who was flying to the newly opened Yodda goldfields via Kokoda. There, with her equipment and a substantial quantity of supplies packed into four-gallon kerosine tins, she occupied a thatch-roofed resthouse adjacent to the distinctly more comfortable quarters of the resident magistrate, Charles Karius, himself a noted explorer of New Guinea.[34]

Soon recurrent bouts of malaria became an inconvenience, as they usually did in her Melanesian ventures, but they were never a discouragement. While collecting assiduously around Kokoda, she also had lengthy stays at points higher up in the mountains. Always the immediate task and a functional simplicity prevailed over the conventions of dubious comfort.

> I had no tent; experience of tents under such abnormally moist and hot conditions being that two or three sides had to be open, so what is the use of carrying all that extra weight only to role up the sides? So I carry a couple of fly-sheets; a small one which covers the hammock, and a larger one to roof the whole, with space for the daily collecting equipment.[35]

What in hindsight proved to be a highlight of that time was an arduous trip from Kokoda to Buna. Along a route that would later see some of the hardest fighting of World War II, she took four days to make the 41-kilometre trip, accompanied by four carriers drawn from the local Orakaiva people. The resident magistrate at Buna, who normally travelled with 15 carriers, was astounded by the feat. Cheesman explained her formula:

> From long practice I had become adept in taking the smallest quantity of necessities in the smallest possible space, unless contemplating months in camp in the bush. As for the boys' personal wish to get to Buna in

---

34 Ibid., pp. 205–208, and *The Two Roads of Papua*, London, 1935, pp. 22–35.
35 Cheesman, *Two Roads*, pp. 117–118.

record time, this was because I kept them rather short of tobacco on the road with a promise of a triple ration at the end. This worked well and was repeated on the return [which only took three days].

Similarly, she never had trouble with carriers on her mountain trips, 'because they were always "hungry along tobacco"'.[36]

Then, an outbreak of influenza in the mountain villages above Kokoda brought her sojourn in the area to an end after five months. Rather than than expose her assistants to the risk of infection, therefore, she shifted her operation to Mafalu on the north-western side of the Owen Stanley range. From Kairuku, on the coast above Port Moresby, eight pack mules were employed to get her equipment inland to the camping site, among the Goilala people. She had intended staying there for ten weeks, but benign chance intervened. The patrol officer for the district, Jack Hides, himself soon to be distinguished as an explorer and author, offered her the use of his house at Mondo during an impending long absence. Cheesman was thus able to extend her stay for a further ten weeks. Highlights of that period were two profitable assaults on Mount Taka where, one night between 6.30 pm and one am, she captured 744 moths.[37]

In all, the whole Papua expedition yielded about 42,000 insects. For this quantity, if for no other reason, it was deemed successful by the museum authorities. They seem to have been sympathetic to Cheesman's view, one not universally held, that it was better to collect as abundantly as possible, and to be content with a preliminary rough classification of specimens, leaving the more detailed work for specialists at some later date. The alternative and more myopic view, which was not without its supporters, was to concentrate on particular areas, and build citadels of selective certitude.[38]

Thus, it was in accordance with an officially endorsed approach and within only 18 months of returning to England in May 1934, during which time she wrote a book about her experiences, *The Two Roads of Papua*, and annoyed the *Pacific Islands Monthly* by joining with Jock Marshall in criticising the unkempt appearance of Port Vila to an audience at the Royal Geographical Society, that Cheesman was ready to set out again. This time her gathering was to be directed towards examining the hypothesis that the Asian element in New Guinea flora and fauna was more substantial than commonly believed, and was not due merely to adventitious introductions onto an Australian base. To that end, therefore, towards the end of 1935, travelling via Batavia rather than Sydney,

---

36 Cheesman, *Things Worth While*, pp. 209, 213.
37 Cheesman, *Two Roads*, pp. 158–159, 173, 189, 205, 210–211, 236–238, 254; James Sinclair, *The Outside Man: Jack Hides of Papua*, Melbourne, 1971, pp. 102, 109.
38 Cheesman, *Things Worth While*, p. 148, 'Naturalists' Expeditions', p. 65; *Pacific Islands Monthly* (*PIM*), 1934, May, p. 9.

she headed for the Cyclops mountains in the Dutch-ruled western half of New Guinea. This 48-kilometre-long range, so named by Bougainville in 1768 and lying inland from the tiny settlement of Hollandia (later Jayapura), consisted of the most ancient rocks on the whole island. It was pre-Cambrian and had never been submerged. It might, therefore, be expected to contain a comprehensive range of continental species that could be traced via the Philippines to the Asian mainland. Geologically, New Guinea itself was an amalgam of numerous formations from various periods.[39]

From Hollandia, Cheesman first explored the vast swamps 25 kilometres inland, before establishing a base at Sabron in the Cyclops. Much of her collecting there was done from camps on Mount Lina and around Lake Sentani. The latter was a body of water that had been an arm of the sea until being raised 60 metres by volcanic action, and whose native fish species had adapted to fresh water. Again the harvest was abundant. A paraffin lamp could nightly attract thousands of specimens onto muslin moth screens arranged around it. Of these five or six hundred might on occasion be chosen for preservation, and despatched to the museum. Unfortunately, no figure is available for the total haul but, given those of her other New Guinea expeditions, it is likely to have been at least 40,000. More explicitly gratifying to her, for she tells us so, was the support given to her theories about species distribution in the light of the geological history of the north-west coast. This came from minerologists working for Oil Search Ltd., a consortium formed by the Shell and Standard oil companies, which had been prospecting in New Guinea for nearly a decade. For her part, after ten months, with her work in some way 'complete' and with her funds exhausted, Cheesman was ready to depart. The first step, after despatching her carefully packed specimens via Batavia, was to cross by prau from Hollandia to Vanimo, on the Australian side of the border. By the same means she continued on to Aitape, where she was officially received as a potential disease carrier. Released after two weeks in quarantine, she then faced another problem. The local copra-collecting vessel, *Miawara*, was out of service. In order, therefore, to make her next connection she was forced, in company with the ubiquitous Marshall, whom she had encountered at Aitape, to make a three-day dash by canoe 150 kilometres eastwards to Wewak. From there her route took her again to Port Moresby, to catch the *Macdhui* for Sydney. There, on 21 November 1936, she boarded the liner *Orontes* for London.[40]

Barely 15 months later, having disposed of her collection and having completed the by now customary book, she was back in Dutch New Guinea. This time it

---

39   Cheesman, *Things Worth While*, pp. 236–237, and 'Naturalists' Expeditions', p. 63; *PIM*, 1934, May, p. 9.
40   Cheesman, *Things Worth While*, pp. 238–243, and Evelyn Cheesman, *The Land of the Red Bird*, London, 1938, generally; A.J. Marshall, *The Men and Birds of Paradise: journeys through equitorial New Guinea*, London, 1938, pp. 290–295; *PIM*, 1936, Nov., p. 12, Dec., p. 36.

was primarily to work on Waigeo and Japen, two islands off the western tip of New Guinea, which it had not been practicable to call at on her previous visit. As she explained:

> Transport on islands without much sea traffic is difficult. Thus, if I had landed on Waigeo on the way to the Cyclops Range, I should have been obliged to return to Batavia in order to reach Hollandia. Funds would not permit this. It is trying to be in sight of an objective and yet have to pass it by.[41]

Apart from its place in the agenda of scientific enquiry, Waigeo had long interested her. As a child she had been fascinated by the account of Thomas Forrest who, evading Dutch surveillance, had gone there in 1774 to collect spice plants on behalf of the British East India Company. Besides, Wallace had visited there in 1862. By Cheesman's time it was accessible through a monthly government-subsidised steamer from Macassar. For nearly six months, until July 1938, she collected there, mostly around the fiord-like Mayalibit Bay and the 1,200-metre-high Mt Buffalo Horn (Mt Nok), before moving on to neighbouring Japen, once a centre for the bird-of-paradise trade. This, as she acknowledges appreciatively in her writings, was an enterprise that had been bringing Asian adventurers to eastern New Guinea long before the first certain European sighting of the island by the Portuguese discoverer Don Jorge de Meneses in 1526.[42]

For six months she stayed on Japen, at camps in the central mountains, aided only by two 'camp boys', who were replaced monthly by a pair of their fellows from the foothill villages of Amboari and Montembu. A particular difficulty to be endured here was the monsoonal cyclone, known locally as *Wambrau*, which began in October, but her most bothersome problem was manmade and non-indigenous in origin. That is, financial tangles. Supplies of money and stores that she had ordered from Macassar were being sent to Waigeo well after she had left there. Still, any inconvenience was, presumably, eventually compensated for by the size of the harvest. From Japen alone she collected 100 animal skins and 52,000 insects. All of these, like the 11,000 Waigeo specimens, were despatched to London via Batavia.[43]

With that task completed, there was one other to be essayed. Some years before, Cheesman had promised the director of the South Australian Museum that if she ever got the chance she would obtain for him a collection of insects from the Torricelli Mountains, inland from Vanimo in the north-western corner of Australian New Guinea. The fortuitous arrival of a Hollandia-bound steamer at Serui, the anchorage at Japen, early in December provided an opportunity to

---

41 Cheesman, *Things Worth While*, p. 244.
42 Ibid., pp. 245–249; and, *Six-Legged Snakes in New Guinea*, London, 1949, pp. 31–33, 109–135.
43 Cheesman, *Things Worth While*, p. 276; and, *Six-Legged Snakes*, p. 277.

meet this undertaking. Also on board the steamer were two enigmatic Japanese. They claimed to be tourists with an interest in botany. But the Dutch authorities, already sensitive to any portents of war with Japan, as the American ornithologist S.D. Ripley also attests, not unreasonably suspected them of espionage, and kept them under close watch.[44] Similar fears about Japanese spies, and even of imminent attack from that quarter, were also recorded elsewhere in the southern Pacific about that time.[45]

Meanwhile, Hollandia, which was soon to be destroyed during World War II, and to be renamed Jayapura after western New Guinea was forcibly incorporated into the new nation of Indonesia in 1962, was a modest settlement of about 20 houses. It was embellished only by an 'enormous bungalow' which Richard Archbold, a wealthy American naturalist, had recently built to service elaborate collecting expeditions of his own; Archbold was an heir to the Standard Oil fortune created by his grandfather and John D. Rockefeller. There was also a small naval patrol facility. Spasmodically during the course of two millenia, and busily so in the late 1800s, Hollandia had been used as an occasional camp by bird-of-paradise traders from Asia, but it did not take a more substantial form until 1909–1910 when surveyors marking the political bi-section of the island made it their base. Three Germans were a significant addition to the local expatriate population when they crossed the border in 1914 to avoid Australian rule. Cheesman spent a congenial fortnight there as a guest of the Dutch *controleur* and his wife. She had originally intended to to stay only a week and to cross Humboldt Bay, so named by Dumont d'Urville in 1827, by native prau to Vanimo on the Australian side of the border. But a sudden burst of the *guba* (wind-storm) foiled the attempt. So she decided to walk. Following a long-disused trade route, and with half-a-dozen carriers in attendance, she took four days to cover the 64 kilometres.[46]

Progressively between 1920 and 1922, and countering an enterprise in which members of their own military occupation force—following the example of German settlers—had engaged vigorously, the Australian authorities outlawed the export of plumage from the Mandated Territory. To enforce that rule they established a resthouse and a police post at Vanimo, but these were abandoned after the Dutch issued a complementary regulation outlawing bird hunting in 1931. Subsequently, in 1937, a Catholic mission station had been set up at

---

44 Cheesman, *Things Worth While*, pp. 244–245, 255; and, *Six-Legged Snakes*, pp. 190–191, 194–195, 276; Dillon Ripley, *Trail of the Money Bird: 30,000 miles of adventure with a naturalist*, London, 1949, pp. 303–309.
45 Phyllis Parham Reeve, *On Fiji Soil: memories of an agriculturalist*, Suva, 1989, p. 205; James N. Bade, *Von Luckner: a reassessment. Count Felix von Luckner in New Zealand and the South Pacific, 1917–1919 and 1938*, Frankfurt am Main, 2004, pp. 158–159.
46 Cheesman, *Things Worth While*, pp. 239, 251; and, *Six-Legged Snakes*, pp. 191–194; Gavin Souter, *New Guinea: the Last Unknown*, Sydney, 1963, pp. 198–199; Michael Cookson, 'The Archbold Expeditions to New Guinea: a preliminary survey of archival materials held at the American Museum of Natural History, New York City', *Journal of Pacific History*, vol. 35, no. 3 (2000), pp. 313–318.

Vanimo. Cheesman obtained fresh carriers there for the 128-kilometre walk (ten days) to the government post at Aitape, where she stayed for two weeks before venturing into the mountains to keep her pledge. For a month collecting proceeded well. Then bureaucracy intervened to obstruct it. One afternoon in February 1939 a police-boy arrived at her camp on the flank of Mount Semorra with a cruel radio message. It stated that, since Aitape was not an official port of entry, she should proceed to Rabaul immediately in order to complete entry formalities, and so avoid a heavy fine—or else retrace her steps and leave the way she had come. Considerations of time and money ensured that she chose the latter option, but she was not defeated. En route to the border she travelled via fresh collecting sites in the ranges behind Vanimo, and thus reached her ordained tally. With honour saved, and a total yield for the expedition of 83,000 specimens, Evelyn Cheesman sailed from Batavia in mid-1939. She reached Europe shortly before the outbreak of World War II.[47]

As in the preceding conflict, Cheesman's services were again required. For two years, using her knowledge of German and French, she worked in censorship, before being recruited into the military education service to lecture on the Pacific war. As well as giving 1,020 lectures, illustrated with lantern slides made from her own photographs and sketches, she also wrote extensively on the New Guinea campaigns for Sir John Hammerton's massive familiarity-infused compilation *The Second Great War*.[48]

Then, once the war was over, it was time to plan yet another return to the field. This time her goal was New Caledonia, which she reached in July 1949. There a complicated geological history is 'reflected in the flora and fauna', especially through 'two endemic families of plants and one of birds, the kagu'. Over much of the main island the native forest cover had been burnt off by European settlers trying to establish plantations and farms and had been replaced by tough, thorny scrub. Much of a 'rich legacy of plants, not known from any other part of the world' had, she lamented, 'been obliterated'. Remnants of it survived 'only on the crests of ridges and mountain peaks'. Her chosen collecting site was inland from Pouébo, an anchorage near the north-east end of the island which had been much frequented by the sandalwood traders who had brought European commerce to New Caledonia of the mid-nineteenth century, and from where she 'judged that the [remaining] true forest might be more easily accessible'.

---

47 Cheesman, *Things Worth While*, pp. 251–260; and, *Six-Legged Snakes*, pp. 215–278; Pamela Swadling, *Plumes From Paradise: trade cycles in outer Southeast Asia and their impact on New Guinea and nearby islands until 1920*, Boroko, 1996, pp. 53, 98–99, 105, 132, 205, 212–217, 220–224, 257; *PIM*, Sept., p. 29, Oct. 1959, p. 33.
48 Cheesman, *Things Worth While*, pp. 261–264; and, in Hammerton, 'Allied Operations in New Guinea, 1942', vol. 6, chpt. 249, pp. 2463–2473, 'The Huon Gulf Campaign in New Guinea', vol. 7, chpt. 276, pp. 2753–2765, 'The Allies at Japan's Inner Defences', vol. 8, chpt. 309, pp. 3113–3127, 'Last Landings in the South-West Pacific', vol. 9, chpt. 351, pp. 3587–3602; and 'Japanese Operations in New Guinea', *The Geographical Journal*, vol. 101, no. 3 (Mar. 1943), pp. 97–110.

Besides, the natural history of the area was but little known. This situation she did much to remedy from her camp 600 metres up Mt Titchialit during a spell of about three months. Subsequently she surveyed Lifu in the neighbouring Loyalty Islands for six weeks, before embarking on the eight-hour plane flight from Nouméa to Sydney in January 1950.[49]

On returning to London, Cheesman resumed the routine of classifying specimens at the museum and of broadcasting and writing. Only now it was with an unfamiliar sense of regret, for a severely arthritic hip seemed to rule out more robust avocations. That is, until June 1953, when a surgical operation solved the problem. 'This recovery', she exulted, 'caused a revolution in my plans'. Accordingly, in November 1954, at the age of 73, she began a nine-month return visit to Aneityum, from where malaria had forced her to withdraw prematurely in 1930. She had a house built for herself about five kilometres inland from Alelgauhat village. Named 'Red Crest', it was adjacent to land that had been cleared for logging, a condition that greatly assisted collecting, and was a convenient base camp from which to venture into the mountains with Iorawili, her guide of 25 years before. With a yield of 10,000 insects and 500 plants it was again a fruitful expedition, but which she reluctantly conceded would also be her last, although she would continue to work in other ways. 'We drop down, or get run over, but we never retire', she told an interviewer in 1955. Nor was her withdrawal from collecting as abrupt as she had anticipated. In 1958 sales of her memoir *Things Worth While* financed a three-week trip to the incongruously green and insect-rich enclave of Tarifa on the otherwise sun-browned coast of southern Spain, near Gibraltar.[50]

Cheesman died in London on 15 April 1969. She had published 16 books, half of them on natural history for children and the others on her expeditions, and had collected more than 100,000 insects. While respectfully acknowledging these achievements and reporting on her career, *The Times* obituarist was also concerned to comment admiringly on her character. 'She was kind and friendly', though personally 'austere' and 'single-minded' in her professional devotion. She was 'a frail little woman' but 'full of courage' and 'fearless in tilting against authority', yet notably generous. 'Any money from her tiny income, beyond her humblest needs, was ploughed back in such form as a gift book to a young naturalist or a microscope to a government department'. For Cheesman, science was a *raison d'etre* and the opportunity to pursue it in her own way was its own reward. She was ready to accept help but she never sought sympathy.

---

49   Cheesman, *Things Worth While*, pp. 264–266, 276–279; *PIM*, Aug. 1949, p. 49.
50   Cheesman, *Things Worth While*, pp. 299–317; and, *Time Well Spent*, London, 1960, pp. 190–224; *PIM*, 1955, Sept., p. 21, Oct., p. 21.

Appendix

Evelyn Cheesman: Travels

1924–1925 French Polynesia

Depart Dartmouth, in *St George* (9 April 1924); Panama; Galapagos (9 July–12 August); Coiba; Panama (1–15 November); Marquesas (1 January–4 February 1925); Tuamotu (7–14 February).

Arrive Tahiti (16 February), Cheesman leaves *St George* expedition; stays on Tahiti for a month (?); Raiatea; Borabora ('I spent a month between Raiatea and Borabora); depart Tahiti 'on a French steamer' (April?).

Arrive London (May?).

Specimens collected: 500.

Note: the *St George* sailed from Papeete 13 March, called at Rurutu, Rapa, Easter Island, and Panama, and returned to Dartmouth 18 September 1925.

1929–1931 New Hebrides/Vanuatu

Depart England (late 1928); Sydney; depart Sydney by *Makambo* (19 January 1929); Lord Howe; Norfolk Island; arrive Port Vila (late January); Vila to Malekula (February).

Northern islands (12 months): Malekula, with excursions to Santo and the Banks group.

Southern islands (12 months): Erromanga, Tanna, Aneityum. Depart Vila (December 1930).

Arrive Nouméa; arrive Sydney in *La Perouse* (9 January 1931); depart Sydney in *Moldavia* (23 January); arrive London (February/March).

Specimens collected: 18,000 (*Pacific Islands Monthly* (*PIM*), June 1933).

1933–1934 Papua

Depart London in *Orsova* (February 1933); arrive Sydney (16 March); depart Sydney in *Macdhui* (8 June).

Arrive Port Moresby (15 June); Kokoda (June to November); Yule Island; Mafalu/Mondo (November 1933 – April 1934); depart Port Moresby in *Montoro*.

Arrive Sydney (18 April 1934); depart 'shortly'; arrive England (June?).

Specimens collected: 42,000 (PIM May 1934).

1935–1936 Cyclops Mountains, Dutch New Guinea (West Papua/Irian Jaya)

Depart England (October? 1935); arrive Batavia/Jakarta; depart in inter-island vessel *Rochussen* for Hollandia/Jayapura.

Cyclops Mountains: Mount Nomo, Lake Sentani, Iffar, Sabron ('twelve months were spent in that locality', in 'Naturalists' Expeditions', pp. 63–64; 'has been in the interior of New Guinea for ten months', *PIM*, November, December 1936).

Depart Hollandia by *prau* (mid-September 1936); arrive Aitape (trip took five days); depart Port Moresby in *Macdhui*.

Arrive Sydney (5 November); depart Sydney in *Orontes* (21 November); arrive London (December? 1936).

Specimens collected: total unrecorded, but 1,011 insects were caught in one night at Sabron; 5,000 caught in the month before leaving Hollandia (*The Land of the Red Bird*, pp. 200, 268). Total likely to have been about 40,000.

1938–1939 Waigeu and Japen islands (Dutch New Guinea), Torricelli Range (Mandated Territory, Australian)

Depart England (early 1938); arrive Batavia; depart Makassar (later, Ujung Pandang, south Sulawesi) for Waigeu in monthly K.P.M. steamer.

On Waigeu (February to July); on Japen (July to December).

Arrive Hollandia from Saonek, Japen (December); walk to Vanimo (took five days); walk to Sissano (arrive 24 December); canoe to Molol (arrive 26 December); walk to Aitape ('it was a ten days' journey from Vanimo to Aitape').

At Aitape for two weeks (January 1939); in Torricelli Mountains for a month (January/February); Vanimo, and inland at Krissa (March/April); Vanimo to Hollandia by *prau*; Hollandia (stays ten days); Makassar; depart Batavia (August?), 'I was lucky in securing the last berth on the last cargo boat to leave Batavia for Europe, although war did not break out until later').

Arrive England ('I returned on the last Dutch cargo boat in December 1939').

Specimens collected: a. 63,000 for British Museum—11,000 from Waigeu, 52,000 from Japen; b. 20,000 for South Australian Museum—10,000 from Torricellis, 10,000 from Vanimo and Krissa. (*Six-Legged Snakes*, pp. 276–277; *Things Worth While*, pp. 255–256).

1949–1950 New Caledonia

Depart London; arrive/depart Sydney (July 1949); Nouméa (two weeks); Pouebo; River Tandi; Lifu (December); depart Nouméa for Sydney (January 1950); arrive/depart Sydney; arrive London.

1954–1955 Aneityum

Depart London; arrive/depart Sydney; Nouméa to Aneityum in six-weekly steamer *le Polynésien* (November 1954); on Aneityum (November/December 1954 – August 1955; shift into own house—'Red Crest'—inland from Anelgauhat, 13 March); Vila; Nouméa (September, three weeks); Sydney (late September); arrive London (October 1955).

Specimens collected: 10,000. (*PIM*, September 1955).

1958 Tarifa, Spain

Depart London by air (21 May 1958); return London (mid June).

Specimens collected: total unrecorded. One day collected 'over one hundred insects'; 'it had been a fully occupied three weeks'. (*Time Well Spent*, pp. 209, 224).

L.E. Cheesman: Scholarly publications

Scientific

1926

'Two new species of Veliidae from the southeast Pacific', *Annals and Magazine of Natural History* (*AMNH*), vol. 18, no. 106, pp. 363–367.

'Two new species of Coreidae from the southeast Pacific', *AMNH*, vol. 18, no. 106, pp. 368–370.

(With D. Aubertin), 'Diptera in French Oceania', *Entomologist*, vol. 62, no. 795, pp. 172–176.

1927

'A new species of Miridae from the southeast Pacific', *AMNH*, vol. 19, no. 109, pp. 94–95.

'A new species of Reduviidae from the southeast Pacific', *AMNH*, vol. 19, no. 109, pp. 95–97.

'A contribution towards the insect fauna of French Polynesia', Part I, *Transactions of the Entomological Society, London*, vol. 75, no. 1, pp. 147–161.

1928

'A new species of Sphegidae from Colombia', *AMNH*, vol. 2, no. 7, pp. 102–104.

'A contribution towards the insect fauna of French Oceania', Part 11, *AMNH*, vol. 1, no. 2, pp. 169–194.

(With R.C.L. Perkins), 'Apoidea, Specoidea an Vespoidea', in *Insects of Samoa andother Terrestrial Arthropoidea*, Part 5, *Hymenoptera*, London, Fasc.1, pp. 1–32.

1929

'Hymenoptera collected on the *St George* expedition in Central America and the West Indies', *Transactions of the Entomological Society*, London, vol. 77, no. 2, pp. 141–154.

1932

'Ichneumonoidea', in G. Grande (et al.), *Hymenoptera1—Resultats scientifiques duvoyage aux Indes Orientales Neerlandaisess de LL.AA.RR. le Prince et la PrincessLeopold de Belgique*. In *Memoires Museum Royale d'Histoire Naturelle de Belgique*, hors série 4, no. 5, pp. 53–59.

1935

'A new genus of Reduviide (Hem.) from Papua', *Stylops*, vol. 4, no. 2, pp. 47–48.

1936

'Hymenoptera of the New Hebrides and Banks Islands', *Transactions of the RoyalEntomological Society*, London, vol. 85, no. 7, pp. 169–195.

1945

'The Fauna of New Guinea', *South-eastern Nat[uralist?]*, vol. 49, pp. 35–46.

1948

'Bees of New Guinea and the New Hebrides', *AMNH*, 12th Ser., vol. 1, no. 5, pp. 318–335.

1951

'A collection of Polistes from Papuasia in the British Museum', *ANMH*, 12th Ser., vol. 4, no. 46, pp. 982–993.

'Old Mountains of New Guinea', *Nature*, vol. 169, p. 597.

'Oriental Origin of the Papuasian Insect Fauna', *Proceedings of the Royal Entomological Society London*, vol. 16, p. 43.

1952

'Ropalidia of Papuasia', *ANMH*, 12th Ser., vol. 5, no. 49, pp. 1–26.

1953

'Parasitic Hymenoptera of New Caledonia and Lifu Island, Loyalty Islands', *AMNH*, 12th Ser., vol. 6, no. 68, pp. 625–636.

'Bees of New Caledonia', *ANMH*, 12th Ser., vol. 6, no. 69, pp. 713–716.

1954

'A new species of Odynerus, subgen. Rhygchium (Eumeniae), from the Loyalty Islands', *AMNH*, 12th Ser., vol. 7, no. 77, pp. 385–390.

1955

'Two new species of Sphecoidea (Hymenoptera) of New Caledonia and Lifu Island, Loyalty Islands', *ANMH*, 12th Ser., vol. 8, no. 86, pp. 81–84.

1958

[D.E. Kimmins, 'Miss L.E. Cheesman's expedition to the New Hebrides, 1955. Orders Odonata, Neuroptera and Trichoptera', *Bulletin of the British Museum (NaturalHistory)*, vol. 6, no. 9, pp. 237–250.

[1962]

[J.D. Bradley, *Microlepidoptera from the New Hebrides. Records and descriptions ofMicrolepidoptera collected on the Island of Aneityum by Miss Evelyn Cheesman*', pp. 247–271. In series *Bulletin of the Natural History Museum*.]

[D.E. Kimmins, *Miss L.E. Cheesman's Expeditions to New Guinea: Trichoptera. Bulletin: Entomology*, London, vol. 2, no. 1.]

[NOTE: there is no *Biological Abstracts* author index in Auckland vol. 31–33 (1957–1959), so those years/volumes have not yet been searched.]

Geographical/descriptive

1933

'The Island of Malekula', *The Geographical Journal*, vol. 81, pp. 193–210.

1938

'The Cyclops Mountains of Dutch New Guinea', *The Geographical Journal*, vol. 91, pp. 21–30.

1940

'Two Unexplored Islands off Dutch New Guinea: Waigeu and Japen', *The Geographical Journal*, vol. 95, pp. 208–217.

1941

'The Mountainous Country at the Boundary North of New Guinea', *The Geographical Journal*, vol. 98, pp. 169–188.

1943

'The Island of New Guinea', *Nature*, vol. 152, no. 3845, July, pp. 41–43.

'Japanese Operations in New Guinea', *The Geographical Journal*, vol. 101, pp. 97–110.

1958

'When a Name is Tabu', *The Listener*, 27 February, p. 356.

11. Donald Gilbert Kennedy (1898–1967): An outsider in the Colonial Service

When Donald Gilbert Kennedy, last a resident of Bayly's Beach in northern New Zealand, died in 1976, his passing attracted little attention. True, there was a small item in the *New Zealand Herald*, 'War Hero Dies, aged 77'.[1] But in the oceanic archipelagoes of Tuvalu, Solomons and Fiji where he had lived most of his life and where his name had once resonated, his demise went unnoticed. Even the Sydney-based *Pacific Islands Monthly*, which had followed his career from 1935 to 1954, missed it. Reasons for such an oversight are easy to find: Kennedy's colonial heyday was well behind him, the places in which he had worked were far distant and he had left behind in them few fond memories. Yet, variously, as teacher, technician, administrator, philanderer, soldier and scholar, he had exerted a marked influence on those peoples among whom he sojourned for half a century. It remains, therefore, ironic that, while he has earned a place in their folklore and is mentioned in their history books, his death did not register in any of the local news reports. This essay is an attempt to explain why it should have done so. It is a memorial—if not a salute—to a man of remarkable talents; one whose flaws of character—however they may be judged—sustained the temperament of the adventurer. It also chronicles a pro-consular career notable both for its geographical span and for the range of activity and experience that it embraced.[2]

Kennedy's abilities as a leader and as a man of extraordinary practicality earned him respect, but his readiness to bully and to dominate begot fear rather than affection among his subordinates. To his colleagues in the Colonial Service he was a prickly individualist, a loner, companionable on occasions, but devious, 'always on the defensive and at times openly aggressive'. One of them, H.E. Maude, later a distinguished academic, who first met him in the Gilbert and Ellice Islands colony in the 1930s, and who once saw him fell an 'insolent native' (Kennedy's term) with one punch, considered that

> He felt, with good reason, that he was the most capable man in the government service and yet had to watch others, lackadaisical juniors like myself, arriving late on the scene and yet moving up the rungs of

---

1 *NZ Herald*, 17 July 1976.
2 For a fuller 'life' of Kennedy, see Mike Butcher, '... *when the long trick's over': Donald Kennedy in the Pacific* (Kennington, Vic., 2012).

promotion to the top when he had the utmost difficulty in obtaining a transfer from the Education Department to the bottom of the administrative ladder.

No wonder he detested me (and I fancy just about everyone else). I have never held it against him. It was particularly noticeable after the war when I feel he came to realize that he would probably always be an outsider in a service which was essentially composed (in the top ranks) of British public school and university types with similar backgrounds. He had commenced drinking in the '20s to alleviate his isolation and intellectual loneliness, but he then took to it on a more or less regular basis, and this affected his mental powers, his liver and general mental fitness ... . In the end it meant that he could only be given odd jobs where his handicap would hopefully do the least harm.[3]

Another who worked with him, but in wartime, when the faults of peacetime may become virtues, presented him more enthusiastically. In his mid-40s, tall and strongly built, he was 'a determined man ... with a strong personality ... one of those to whom command came naturally, a full-blooded dominant man'.[4]

Both these descriptions recognise in Kennedy a profound self-sufficiency and resourcefulness. These were qualities that, for all that they may have been fostered by isolation also assisted him to cope with it. On the other hand they did not dispose him to acquiesce to the constraints of domesticity, although he had opportunities to do so. On his death he was survived by each of his three wives, his seven children by them, the son of one other liaison, and by a woman who had borne him a daughter who died in infancy.

Kennedy was of Scottish ancestry, a member of a family with putative links to the lairds of Culzean Castle near Ayr, although his immediate origins were more humble. His paternal grandfather, George, was a soldier who was stationed in Ireland from 1868 to 1871, and subsequently in India, where he took his discharge. He then settled in New Zealand in 1884, taking up land at Springhills near Invercargill. Kennedy's father, Robert, who was born in Ireland in 1869, accompanied his parents. After an unsuccessful spell as a farmer he made a living as a railway ganger, a nightwatchman, an apiarist and a builder. In 1897 Robert married Isabelle Chisholm and the following year Donald, the first of their three children, was born. The family shifted northwards to Oamaru in 1904. There Donald attended local public schools: Tokarahi primary from 1904 to 1910 and, from 1911 to 1915, Waitaki Boys High School.[5] At that point, under

---

3   Harry Maude to Mike Butcher, 9 Feb. 1989. Copy in my possession. Interview with H.E. Maude.
4   Eric Feldt, *The Coast Watchers*, Melbourne, 1946, p. 107.
5   These details derive mainly from Mike Butcher, 'Notes on the military career of George Kennedy' and 'Interview with Ray and Flora Kennedy, 20 Nov. 1988', and Ray Kennedy to Butcher, 10 Oct. 1988. I am

its celebrated rector—and apologist of Empire—Frank Milner, Waitaki was on the threshold of becoming for nearly three decades the outstanding school in the country, and one that attracted pupils from far afield. (One such, was J.W. Davidson, the academic founder of Pacific history).[6] While Kennedy was not distinguished at Waitaki, Milner did commend him for the 'persistence and intelligence' of his work, for 'his quiet earnestness and self-reliance' and for having 'the right disciplinary fibre'. For his part, Kennedy apparently enjoyed his schooldays sufficiently for him to seek a career in teaching.

During 1916 and 1917 he was a probationer at Kaikorai school in Dunedin and also completed the first part of an arts degree in French, Latin and History at Otago University, as well as serving in the territorial army. He never completed the degree. In March 1918 he enlisted for army service and was still in training, newly commissioned as a second lieutenant, when peace was declared in November. During 1919 he taught at the Native College at Otaki, where he acquired a knowledge of Maori and, during 1920, he was at Dannevirke High School, where he was esteemed as a boxing instructor. The following year he intended to give up teaching and study law, but marriage in December 1920 to Nellie Chapman of Waipawa put an end to that scheme. Instead, in 1921, he turned his life in a new direction by joining the colonial service, as an assistant master at the Boys Grammar School in Suva, Fiji.[7] After a year in Fiji he went as headmaster to the Banaban School on Ocean Island in the Gilbert and Ellice Islands Colony. Then, in mid-1923, with his wife and infant daughter, he went to the Ellice Islands to found and direct a new school. Jealous of their Micronesian neighbours, who had a government school, King George V, opened at Bairiki, Tarawa (in the Gilberts) in 1922, the Polynesians of the Ellice (Tuvalu since 1975) had demanded a similar amenity. At first their school occupied the site of a defunct mission school on Papaelise islet near Funafuti but in May 1924 it was transferred to Elisefou on the island of Vaitupu, where food and land were more plentiful.[8]

---

indebted to Mike Butcher for copies of these and other relevant documents.

6 'James Wightman Davidson', in John Ritchie (ed.), *Australian Dictionary of Biography*, vol. 13, Melbourne, 1993, p. 579; 'Frank Milner', in Claudia Orange (ed.), *Dictionary of New Zealand Biography*, vol. 3, Wellington, 1996, pp. 343–344.

7 Details of Kennedy's career up to 1921, plus Milner's letter, are in his 'Application for Appointment to the Colonial Service', National Archives of Fiji (hereinafter NAF), CSO MP765/21. Other sources include an interview with Nellie Kennedy, 20 Feb. 1986; University of Otago to Laracy, 15 May 1986; *Who's Who in New Zealand*, Wellington, 1941, p. 204.

8 Hugh Laracy (ed.), *Tuvalu: a history*, Suva, 1983, pp. 135–137; Barrie Macdonald, *Cinderellas of the Empire: towards a history of Kiribati and Tuvalu*, Canberra, 1982, pp. 135–137; Klaus-Friedrich Koch, *Logs in the Current of the Sea: Neli Lifuka's story of Kioa and the Vaitupu colonists*, Canberra, 1978, pp. 5–6; Arthur Grimble, *Return to the Islands*, London, 1957, p. 151; Frank Pasefika, *The Autobiography of Frank Pasefika*, Suva, 1990, pp. 14–21; *Fiji and Western Pacific High Commission Civil List, 1942*, Suva, 1942. Hereafter, references to Western Pacific High Commission rendered WPHC.

For eight years Kennedy directed the Ellice Islands school. For much of that time, as the only *palagi* (European) official in the group, he also acted as the administrative officer. Indeed, that appointment became fulltime in April 1932, when he took up residence on Funafuti, but it was not formally confirmed until July 1934, whereupon he was also made Native Lands Commissioner. By that time he had not only made a notable impact on the group but was himself ineluctably 'at home' in the Pacific. His wife, though, was less pleased with the isolation and hardships of her position. When a second child was due in 1925 the family returned to New Zealand for the delivery. In 1927, for the birth of the third, Nellie again went back with the children, only this time she set up house in Oamaru, and stayed there, except for a brief return trip in 1932. After a separation scarcely relieved by letters and radio messages and by visits from Kennedy during periods of leave in 1929, 1934 and 1938, the couple were divorced in 1944.[9]

Meanwhile, left largely to his own devices, Kennedy had flourished, seizing opportunities for personal achievement. His school satisfied parents who wished their sons to be taught to speak and read English correctly and to write it in a clear hand, and to be competent in arithmetic. Concomitant with what was, in the circumstances, a high academic standard were firm discipline, stiff regimentalism and the inculcation of a sense of public duty. The Vaitupu school was organised on the English 'public school' model, but with Kennedy's lofty Arnold/Milner-like figure besmirched with more than a trace of Dickens' ignoble Squeers. There were prefects, the pupils were divided into 'houses' that competed academically, at garden work, and at sport; and there was military drill and a large corpus of rules. Breaching any of the latter, Frank Pasefika, himself later a senior administrator, recalled, might mean being punished with 'half a dozen thrashes with a cricket bat, which gave you a bruised backside for several days'. Kennedy, he added, 'was difficult to like'. Another former student has recorded similar comments

> Mr Kennedy was a very tough man. In his teaching he was all right, but outside the classroom he was a hard man. ... [Once, he] took a cricket bat and beat me with it so hard I fell to the ground ... . If a boy walked slowly, Mr. Kennedy called him and boxed him. That's how we learned discipline. Punishment for going to the village without permission was a dozen with the cricket bat.

---

9 Interview with Nellie Kennedy, 20 Feb. 1986; Laracy, *Tuvalu*, pp. 137–138; Macdonald, pp. 139–140; Colin Amodeo (ed.), *The Waterlily Diary of Jack Atkinson*, Christchurch, 2001, pp. 64–66.

Meeting Kennedy outside the classroom, boys were expected to cease what they were doing, stand to attention, and salute him. So, too, even, were 'station labourers and others' who encountered him.[10]

Despite the severity of the regime, though, many of the men who had been Kennedy's pupils looked back to it with nostalgia. They were glad of the opportunity the school offered to acquire a *palangi* education on its own terms, one unalloyed by the distracting 'cultural' sensitivities that would come to influence schooling in the postcolonial era. Some of them also relished the chance he gave them to train as radio operators. When on leave in New Zealand in 1925 Kennedy had collected information on and components for building himself a radio transmitter and, in November 1926, he sent out his first message, to a radio enthusiast in New Zealand. He thereby inaugurated more regular contacts with the world beyond Tuvalu than those hitherto offered by mail deliveries at intervals of several months. Considerable ingenuity was required to create the equipment, as Telavi Fati of Namumea later explained:

> At school on Vaitupu I was selected as one of the 'wireless boys' by Mr Kennedy. We spent much time making batteries. As we had no lead we had to go hunting for empty corned beef and biscuit tins. We would light a fire and throw all our empty cans into it so that the lead could be melted into the ground. When the fire was out and the ashes were cool we would collect the lead.
>
> Next thing we would go hunting for empty beer bottles to use as battery containers. We cut them evenly, using a piece of steel wire about a metre long and looped just to fit a bottle. The wire was placed in a fire. Beside the fire we had a basin of water, a small crow-bar and a piece of wood. When the end of the wire was really red we would take it out and put the loop around the bottle for a short while, pulling it tight with the aid of the crowbar. Next we would dip the bottle into the basin of water, then take it out and give it a light tap with the piece of wood, cutting it to the required size.
>
> To make plates for the battery we started with two plates made of brick and with passages carved on them, through which liquid lead could run. These plates were tied together and boiling lead was poured into the passages. When it had cooled a lead plate would be removed from the mould.
>
> Separators made of pua tree were used to keep the plate erect in the bottle …

---

10   Koch, pp. 6–7; Pasefika, pp. 20–21.

> To put the battery together the wooden pieces were first put in position and then the plate was fitted. Next, on each side of the plate, the bottle was loaded with crushed glass made from the unused sections of the bottle. Finally, the bottle was filled with sulphuric acid. The battery was then ready for charging from a generator ...
>
> A 6 volt battery was charged from a 6 volt generator. The charging system was made from a bicycle turned up-side-down and fixed to a piece of board. The generator was fixed to one end of the board and attached by a belt to the back wheel of the bicycle, which did not have a tyre. The fork of the front wheel was taken off and the steering bar was fixed to the board to balance the machine. Charging was done by one or two boys working the pedals with their hands. This would be done for two hours daily to keep up the power in a 6 volt battery.[11]

Besides his radio work, Kennedy also employed his practical bent in building a schooner, the *Namolimi*; but after returning without Nellie and the children in January 1930 he put an increasing effort into ethnographic study. From early 1928 he had been in contact with H.D. Skinner, an authority on Polynesian material culture, and who, as an officer of the Polynesian Society, encouraged correspondents from remote parts of the Pacific to write for the society's journal. Kennedy's writings were notably welcomed by Peter Buck.[12] When he went to New Zealand in 1929 Kennedy donated a large quantity of Tuvalu artefacts to the Otago Museum. But it was as the author of *Field Notes on the Culture of Vaitupu, Ellice Islands*, published in 12 parts in the journal between 1929 and 1932 and as a book in 1931, that he made his main contribution to knowledge. That work contains an exhaustive description of fishing techniques, canoes and houses, and records various customary practices and traditional beliefs. On the other hand, but consonant with Kennedy's misanthropic tendencies, it ignores the islanders as a functioning community. Maude, who was himself encouraged into scholarly publishing by Kennedy, commented: 'the book is a superb study in material culture but on social organisation is a nonstarter. He told me that this was because the ancestral culture was dead and forgotten and only the technology remained; but this was not the case.'[13]

By 1932, when he transferred to the administrative service, Kennedy was not only ready for a change but his school was running well. He had an able subordinate, Melitiana of Nukulaelae, to succeed him, and he could still exercise

---

11 Quoted in Laracy, *Tuvalu*, pp. 138–139.
12 M.P.K. Sorrenson (ed.), *Na To Hoa Aroha, From Your Dear Friend: the correspondence between Sir Apirana ngata and Sir Peter Buck, 1925–1950*, Auckland, 1987, vol. 2, p. 268.
13 Kennedy to Skinner, 15 May, 28 July, 8 Aug., 1 Oct. 1928, 1 May 1929, H.D. Skinner papers, Otago Museum; Maude to Butcher, 9 Feb. 1989; Laracy, *Tuvalu*, p. 137; M.P.K. Sorrenson, *Manifest Duty: the Polynesian Society over 100 years*, Auckland, 1992, p. 84; Susan Woodburn, *Where Our Hearts Still Lie: Harry and Honor Maude in the Pacific Islands*, Adelaide, 2003, p. 71.

some supervision from Funafuti. Indeed, the school continued to operate effectively during World War II, when Tuvalu was occupied by US forces. Because of that continuity, in the period of postwar reconstruction the Vaitupu school was the main recruiting ground for educated indigenous staff for the whole of the Gilbert and Ellice Islands colony. The school in Kiribati had been disrupted by the Japanese occupation. Subsequently, the over-representation of Tuvaluans in administrative positions in Tarawa during the final years of colonial rule aroused resentment among the more numerous Gilbertese, and contributed to the political severing of Tuvalu from Kiribati before each became independent in 1976 and 1978, respectively.

As an administrative officer, and especially as Native Lands Commissioner, investigating tenure systems and garden productivity, Kennedy travelled regularly through the group. His most significant achievement, begun on Vaitupu in 1926, though, was setting up a bulk purchasing and selling cooperative, the *fusi*, for handling trade matters. It was widely imitated elsewhere (Maude did so in Kiribati in 1931), but the founding and failure of similar institutions was to become a conspicuously sad tale throughout the Pacific islands. In such company the *fusi* of Tuvalu has the rare distinction of having operated continuously and profitably since its inception.[14]

Deservedly, professional achievement also brought some personal reward. In May 1938 Kennedy left Tuvalu on a Carnegie Travelling Scholarship to study for a year at Oxford University for a Diploma in Anthropology. That completed, he returned to the colony in August 1939, and was appointed to Ocean Island. A year later he was transferred from the Gilbert and Ellice to the British Solomon Islands Protectorate.[15]

The appointment was a recognition of his abilities, though it was scarcely generous. After 19 years in the colonial service, Kennedy was a district officer with an annual salary of £660 a year. That was only £30 a year more than was received, for example, by his colleague Charles Bengough, BA (Oxon.), 13 years his junior, and with only seven years' service. Yet, if he was disappointed, it did not show in his performance of his duties. For the first 15 months he was based at the protectorate headquarters of Tulagi. There the main task entrusted him by the Resident Commissioner, W.S. Marchant, was to introduce a form of local government to the people of Nggela and Savo, to counter the apathy and passive resistance which had come to mark their attitude towards the administration. Assisted by two young Nggela men, John Manebona and Stanley Piluniuna, and often by Sgt-Major Sitiveni Sipolo, the senior NCO of the armed constabulary, Kennedy toured the villages of his district, explaining the scheme and setting up

---

14   Laracy, *Tuvalu*, pp. 136–137; Macdonald, pp. 134–137, 142, 246–247; Woodburn, p. 87.
15   *Fiji and WPHC Civil List*, Suva, 1942.

a system of sub-district councils and courts that came to be known in the Pijin lingua franca as *Masini Rulu* ('Marchant's system of rule'). Five years later that name would be echoed in the widespread and disruptive nationalist movement *Maasina Ruru* (or 'Rule'); literally, 'brotherhood rule'. In October 1941, though, when Kennedy was assigned the additional district of Ysabel, it signified merely a promising experiment in administrative devolution, but one soon to be aborted in the wake of the Japanese attack on Pearl Harbour on 7 December. A week after that event Kennedy was commissioned in the British Solomon Islands Protectorate (BSIP) Defence Force. Early in 1942, as a consequence of the re-deployment of numerous other officials in anticipation of a Japanese advance on the Solomons, his district was further extended to cover the north-western half of the Solomons, from Nggela to the Shortland Islands.[16]

When appointed to Ysabel, Kennedy did not immediately take up fixed residence there, but undertook extensive patrolling of his enlarged domain in the auxiliary vessel *Waiai*. The threat of war soon added urgency to his agenda. During January 1942 he was engaged with the evacuation of Europeans and Chinese, and with the repatriation of indigenous labourers (mostly Malaitan) from the plantation-covered Russell Islands. Arriving at southern Ysabel on the 20th of that month, he transferred his headquarters—together with his precious teleradio—from the government station at Tataba to a camp in the mountain village of Mahaga overlooking Thousand Ships Bay. Among other preparations for the impending war, he also organised an intelligence-gathering network of local informants and messengers who would assist him in his military role of coastwatcher. To the same end he sent the local doctor, George Bogese, on a three-week tour of the island to warn people against helping the Japanese. Then, following a minor dispute with Bogese, who was much like himself in being intelligent, libidinous and domineering, Kennedy abruptly expelled the doctor to Savo Island, and instructed Soro the headman there to shoot him if he caused any disturbance. That was in early March. At base the trouble stemmed from a personality clash, with Kennedy translating his dislike into distrust. Despite having been a teacher, he shared the common colonial disdain of the 'educated native'. He construed Bogese's lack of servility as disloyalty. For his part, Bogese regarded his treatment as 'unjust and unfair' but allowed that it 'was due to the general excitement of the time'. Such an explanation is too impersonal to be complete; but, and to Bogese's further disadvantage, the times were becoming increasingly out of joint.[17]

---

16   D.G. Kennedy, 'Marching Rule in the British Solomon Islands Protectorate: a memorandum on the origins of the term', MS copy in my possession; *Fiji and WPHC Civil List*, 1942; *WPHC Gazette*, Suva, 1942 and 1943.
17   Donald Kennedy, 'District Officer's Report on Coastwatching in the Central and Northwestern Districts of the British Solomon Islands Protectorate', 20 Nov. 1943, WPHC archives, BSIP 4, C5; Laracy, 'George Bogese: "just a bloody traitor"'?, in Geoffrey M. White (ed.), *Remembering the Pacific War*, Honolulu, 1991, pp. 59–75; affidavit of George Bogese, 5 July 1945, WPHC archives, BSIP 4, FS66.

Meanwhile, from Savo, Kennedy patrolled north to the Shortland Islands, reaching there in early April. En route, he stopped at Simbo to investigate reports of looting by villagers and, as he had already done at Nggela, to punish the perpetrators. Notable among these was the Methodist pastor Belshazzar Gina. A more detatched consideration of the evidence suggests that besides maintaining a semblance of normal order Kennedy was concerned, at least in the case of the wily Gina, whom another official described as a 'black Elmer Gantry', to assert his continuing authority in an unambiguous way. Begetting compliance through fear was a precarious tactic. It did not have an unlimited shelf life and it sat uneasily with an expectation of loyalty to the Allied cause, but it was generally effective. Gina subsequently served as a scout.[18]

Continuing his tour, Kennedy fortuitously departed the Shortlands just ahead of the advancing Japanese, but they did capture two members of a three-man medical party he had placed there on 10 April to deal with an outbreak of dysentery and influenza. He then returned to Ysabel. There he arranged for supplies of food and fuel to be collected from evacuated plantations and stored at Mahaga. Next he went to Rennell Island where he set up a secondary base at Kangava Bay, and recruited six men who would serve as his machine gun corps for the next 14 months, as well as a 17-year-old woman, Magiko Sogo, to be his mistress.

Kennedy was thus established at Mahanga as comfortably as he could manage by the end of April. But his respite was brief. During the first two days of May, Japanese aircraft raided the Protectorate headquarters of Tulagi and a seaplane base was established on northern Ysabel at Rekata Bay. When, on 3 May, Japanese forces occupied Tulagi, Kennedy and his followers were left firmly behind enemy lines. That, of course, was the place for coastwatchers to be, observing enemy movements and reporting them by teleradio to bases further south, but to do this effectively they needed the support of the local people. After the disaffected Bogese was apprehended by the Japanese on Savo on 9 May and was induced by threats to lead them to Mahanga, it was time for Kennedy to go elsewhere.

For two months, accompanied by five north Ysabel policemen and the six Rennellese, he patrolled Ysabel and the New Georgia–Vella Lavella area. Eventually, on 8 July, he established new headquarters on the channel between New Georgia and Vangunu, at Seghe, the site of a plantation owned by Harold

---

18   Kennedy to Metcalfe, 20 July 1942, WPHC archives, BSIP 21/X/1; Gill to Clemens, 4 July 1944, BSIP 21/X/5; George C. Carter, *Yours in His Service: a reflection on the life of Reverend Belshazzar Gina of Solomon Islands*, Honiara, 1990, pp. 58–63; George C. Carter, *Ti è Varanè: stories about people of courage from Solomon Islands*, Auckland, 1981, pp. 113–120.

Markham, an Australian veteran of World War I. Seghe was a brilliant choice. As Kennedy later reported, it was 'a valuable strategic harbour' with 'military possibilities unknown to the enemy':

> it had not, in pre-war days, been visited by the Japanese fishing craft which did much survey work around many of the islands. Furthermore, the Admiralty Charts, which would, presumably, be the only source of Hydrographic information available to the enemy, showed Seghe Channel as being obstructed by 'foul ground' at either end and noted that the area was only 'partially examined'.

Kennedy, however, had explored the channel several times. He knew that, far from being blocked, it possessed 'an abundance of natural reef protection around navigable deep-water channels'. Though secluded, it offered relatively easy access to the Japanese shipping routes in the Slot (between New Georgia and Ysabel) and Blanche Channel and would be 'extremely difficult to approach by surprise'.[19]

Also fortunate was the timing of the shift to Seghe. Kennedy was ensconced there when, on 7 August 1942, US forces invaded the Solomons, capturing Tulagi and a nearly completed airfield on Guadalcanal. Seghe, just 240 kilometres, or 40 minutes' flying-time away, was on the flight path of the Japanese aircraft sent south from Rabaul over the next six months in a monumentally desperate and bloody effort to dislodge the Americans. Consequently, Kennedy's regular teleradio reports on Japanese military movements and activities made a vital contribution to the early warning system that helped the Americans resist that assault. Within the first few weeks, according to General Roy Geiger, the air force commander on Guadalcanal, his reports had 'resulted in the destruction of more than forty enemy aircraft'.[20]

John Lundstrom, the historian of the air war for Guadalcanal, offers some more explicit details:

> Coastwatch alerts punctuated the morning of 21 October [1942]. Finally, at 1040 CACTUS received notice from Kennedy on New Georgia that 10 minutes before some thirty-five enemy planes in three groups had passed over … in the ensuing action Ota Toshio (34 kills), the top Imperial Navy ace, was shot down and killed.

---

19 Kennedy 'Report on Coastwatching'. This report is a valuable chronicle of 'Kennedy's war'. So, too, is James W. Boutilier, 'Kennedy's "Army": Solomon Islanders at war, 1942–1943', in Geoffrey M. White and Lamont Lindstrom (eds), *The Pacific Theatre: island representations of World War II*, Honolulu, 1989, pp. 329–352. See, also, William Bennett, 'Behind Japanese Lines in the Western Solomons', in [G.M. White et al], *The Big Death: Solomon Islanders remember World War II*, Suva, 1988, pp. 133–148.
20 Geiger, quoted in Kennedy 'Report on Coastwatching'.

Again,

> At 1050 on 23 [October 1942] CACTUS radar and the invaluable Kennedy on New Georgia simultaneously announced enemy planes. Bauer scrambled twenty eight F47s and four P-39s, the last of which barely got off when Condition RED sounded at 1114.

In that action the Japanese lost six fighters and one bomber, while one US F47 was heavily damaged.[21]

Similarly, aided by a force of indigenous scouts, Kennedy reported on seaborne traffic and on troop movements, and also rescued downed American airmen. Much of the Japanese activity emanated from Viru Harbour, only 14 kilometres from Seghe, which the Japanese occupied in October 1942. The following are typical messages from Seghe:

> One barge passed Vakabo island heading SE through Marovo Lagoon about midnight ninth. [sent at 0355 on tenth, month unknown].

> Scout reports about thirty Japs at Sombiro Gatukai have wireless in village church which is larger of two isolated houses in clearing on hill. Japs live in other village houses. Fifteen at Penjuku all moved to camp about one mile to south in garden clearing on low hill near shore. Sombiro endangers Dumbo. Can it be wiped out please. [sent at 1345, 28 May 1943].

> Capt. J.E. Swett USMC, shot down off Lingutu Entrance a.m. eleventh now here. Unhurt. Am sending over in about half hour. [sent at 1955 on twelfth, month unknown].[22]

Kennedy was better placed to call for American assistance than coastwatchers located further to the north, and possibly encouraged by that, especially once Catalina seaplanes began landing at Seghe Channel in December 1942, he adopted a singularly aggressive stance towards the Japanese. Not content with passively observing, he went beyond his intelligence role to engaging them actively. Certainly, it was a modus operandi well suited to his temperament. But he also rationalised it on the ground that it helped him retain the confidence and cooperation of the of the islanders, on which he—like all coastwatchers—depended: 'these people realised that while I was able to fight and able to lead them and to win in the little skirmishes we had ... they were on the right side'.

---

21 John B. Lundstrom, *The First Team and the Guadalcanal Campaign: naval fighter combat from August to November 1942*, Annapolis, 1994, pp. 334–336.
22 Kennedy, radio messages, Mar. 1942 – June 1943, copies in my possession by courtesy of Mary White (born Macfarlane, subsequently Campbell, Kennedy and White). Original documents, coded and uncoded, in University of Auckland library.

It was not that he recklessly went looking for the Japanese but, rather, that he aimed at the total annihilation of all who penetrated what he called his 'forbidden zone'. Enemy patrols and barges that strayed too close to Seghe were wiped out. In the best known of these incidents, on 19 May 1943 Kennedy's force, aboard the former Seventh Day Adventist mission schooner *Dadavata*, destroyed a party of a dozen Japanese who were passing through the Marovo Lagoon. Braving machine gun and grenade attack, the *Dadavata* rammed their whale boat, and its occupants were shot in the water.[23]

While aiming to secure indigenous morale and loyalty through military success, Kennedy also employed intimidation for the same purpose. The standard punishment for anyone he suspected of disloyalty or insubordination was to be lashed across a 44-gallon fuel drum and flogged. There were several notable cases of this, among numerous others, the one involving Belshazzar Gina being typical. Well-educated, self-assured and a cousin Bogese, he was always mistrusted by Kennedy. Thus, in March 1942, Kennedy accused Gina of encouraging looting in the township of Gizo, and took reprisals by burning houses on Simbo. Gina denied the charge but he was convicted of having stolen a rifle. His biographer, however, suggests that this may also have been a means of recruiting him to Kennedy's service. Kennedy refrained from punishing Gina physically on that occasion, but took him back with him to Ysabel and, in April or May (the sources are contradictory), entrusted him with a mission to Ranongga to retrieve two abandoned European vessels, one of which was the *Dadavata*. Gina managed this successfully, but was disappointed when Kennedy showed no appreciation of his efforts. 'He just [took] me as an ignorant person', Gina later recalled, but eventually he also conceded that Kennedy 'was the right man at the right time'.

Following the move to Seghe the relationship between the two men, the dissolute disciplinarian and the *evolué* native, became even more ambiguous. Gina was entrusted with several important scouting missions. In October he reported on the Japanese occupation of Gizo and Viru, and provided information which assisted the Americans to launch air strikes against their positions, but he still failed to rise in Kennedy's esteem. Soon afterwards, he descended even further.

In January 1943 Gina was sent on a reconnaissance mission to Viru. By his own account, recorded by his son in 1977, he displayed considerable courage in this, and earned Kennedy's praise. Kennedy's account of the episode, recorded in 1969, is rather different. According to him, Gina reported the location of approximately nine unguarded barges on the opposite side of the harbour from the Japanese camp, and Kennedy set out to destroy them. He and his 'army' had almost reached the barges when Ishmael Ngatu, the chief of Patutiva village,

---

23   Boutilier, pp. 332, 345–346; [Harold Cooper], *Among Those Present: the official story of the Pacific Islands at war*, London, 1946 (reprinted Honiara, 1962), pp. 43–53; *Fiji Times and Herald*, 2 Sept. 1943.

sent word that they were running into a trap, that not only had Gina not been to Viru but that the barges were well protected. Consequently, the attack was aborted and Gina was severely flogged for his alleged treachery. He was then kept under house arrest at Seghe until September, when he accompanied Kennedy to Guadalcanal. There, away from the battle lines, the colonial authorities were apparently inclined to judge him by his abilities rather than by his alleged misdemeanours. Instead of being punished further, Gina was co-opted into the administrative service—and began a new career as a government official.[24]

Ironies and ambiguities similarly attend other well-known instances of Kennedy's harsh rule. On 18 May 1943 Kato Ragoso, the first indigenous pastor of the Seventh Day Adventist mission and a man of considerable influence, was at Nono, visiting refugees from Viru, when he learned of ten Japanese who had trespassed into the Marovo Lagoon in a whaleboat. His immediate thought was to warn his family. By 4am he was with them at Telina, not far from where the Japanese were camped, when Kennedy arrived in the *Dadavata*. Apparently annoyed that Ragoso had left it to his scouts to tell him about the Japanese (though he had scarcely had time to do otherwise) Kennedy took the opportunity to assert his own authority by punishing the pastor for a presumed lack of cooperation. He arrested him, and took him to Seghe, where he was given a beating from which, although he lived until 1976, he never properly recovered.[25] Meanwhile, from Telina, Kennedy went in search of the Japanese. On the evening of 19 May he caught up with them in the vicinity of Vangunu. Besides the Japanese, the only other casualty in that encounter was Kennedy himself. He received a slight wound to the right thigh; 'just missing the family jewels', he would later joke. It came, though, from a bullet fired not by the Japanese, as was generally believed until the actual perpetrator confessed in 1987, but from the engine room by his own lieutenant, Bill Bennett. Some time before, Bennett and his uncle, Joel Biskera, had been put over the 44-gallon drum and flogged by Kennedy for failing to 'find him a girl'. So, in the confusion of the skirmish, and with Kennedy drunk, it was time for a vengeful victim to settle a personal score. But for the awkward angle of fire, Bennett would have killed him. Instead, Kennedy remained to fight, although with the Japanese patrols coming closer from early June—and with the Americans preparing to advance northwards—his task at Seghe was nearing completion.[26]

---

24 Boutilier, pp. 336, 340, 343–345; Carter, *Gina*, pp. 61–74.
25 'Pastor Rangoso's own account of his beating and imprisonment', SDA archives, Cooranbong, NSW. I am grateful to Dr Dennis Steley for a copy of this document. Boutilier, pp. 345–347. For other accounts, see Eileen Lantry, *King of the Cannibal Islands: the story of Kata Rangoso*, Boise, 1988; Eric Ware, *No Devil Strings: the story of Kata Rangoso*, Mountainview, 1970, pp. 74–78; Reuben Hare, *Fuzzy-Wuzzy Tales*, Washington, pp. 37–46.
26 Interview with Mary White, 10 May 1992; Bennett, interview with Peter Crowe, 12 July 1987, transcript in my possession. Bennett said, 'I denied to Hugh Laracy that I was ever lashed on the drum, but I was. I was intimidated and humiliated by that punishment ... I am looking after the engine room. I have a Springfield .303 [rifle]. I look out the porthole. Kennedy is still there, and I fire at him'. In light of Bennett's action and

The Rennellese were flown out soon after the 'Battle of Marovo'. They numbered five of the six members of Kennedy's 'machine gun corps' (one, Timothy Togaka, having died from a beating at Kennedy's hands), and Magiko, who was pregnant to him. She subsequently gave birth to a girl named Catalina (who died in 1945).[27] Meanwhile, two companies of US marines landed at Seghe on 22 June 1943 and had captured the Japanese positions at Viru Harbour and Wickham Anchorage. The main force arrived on 30 June and proceeded to convert Markham's plantation into an airfield. The same day, further north, operations aimed at Munda began with landings at Rendova and on Zanana Beach in New Georgia.

With these developments Kennedy's war, for which he was awarded the DSO and the Navy Cross (US), was clearly over. He was redundant, and felt a sense of deflation that, taken with the effects of alcoholism, strain and loneliness, led his superiors to fear for his mental health. He was clearly in a run-down state when he left the Solomons on 13 September for vacation leave in New Zealand. But he recovered quickly. In November he wrote a valuable, if somewhat sanitised, report on his coast-watching career. In it he generously acknowledged 'the very great amount of help received from the native communities', not least from his scouts, whose exploits included rescuing 22 US pilots, capturing 20 Japanese pilots and two sailors and killing 'about 120' soldiers.[28] Then, in February 1944, refreshed if not reformed (he still drank heavily), he resumed his administrative career in the Solomons as acting district commissioner, central, based in the new capital of Honiara on Guadalcanal. From there he was soon called upon to investigate the stirrings of a political movement in Nggela which harked back to Marchant's experiment in local government of 1941. Kennedy recommended conceding the petitioners more autonomy, but that advice was not accepted. Within a year the discontent on Ngella had merged with the more powerful stream of nationalist resistance flowing from Malaita in the independently named 'Maasina Rule' movement, which lasted until 1952. By then, Kennedy had moved on.[29]

In July 1944 he returned to New Zealand. There he married a vivacious young war widow named Mary Campbell, whom he had first met in London in 1938. He also found time to complete a book, *Te Ngangana a te Tuvalu: a handbook*

Kennedy's provocations the 'disloyalty' of Bogese and Gina becomes rather more contestable than has been commonly realised. For a less nuanced view, but an otherwise good treatment of 'Kennedy's war', see Walter Lord, *Lonely Vigil: coastwatchers of the Solomons* (New York, 1977), pp. 201–230. See, also, D.C. Horton, *Fire Over the Islands: coast watchers of the Solomons* (Sydney, 1970); and, *New Georgia: pattern for victory* (London, 1971), pp. 32–44.
27 Boutilier, pp. 343, 350.
28 Kennedy, 'Report on Coastwatching'; Medical officer to High Commissioner, 28 Oct. 1944, WPHC archives, BSIP 4, FC2.
29 Kennedy, 'Marching Rule'; Hugh Laracy (ed.), *Pacific Protest: the Maasina Rule movement, Solomon Islands, 1944–1952*, Suva, 1983.

on the language of Tuvalu, which she typed for him. Then, in December, after hospital treatment for alcoholism, he was appointed to Fiji. But his enjoyment of the comfortable routines of a headquarters position did not last long.[30] In August 1945, 'by reason of his long experience' in the Gilbert and Ellice Islands and 'at the request of the Banabans themselves', he was assigned to arrange for the resettlement of the Banaban people of Ocean Island, who had been deported by the Japanese to Nauru, Tarawa and Kosrae in July 1943. Kennedy left for Kosrae in the Carolines in late September 1945 to collect his charges from a camp at Lele Harbour. Then, on 9 December, he left Tarawa aboard the phosphate vessel *Triona* with 1,003 migrants (703 Banabans, plus 300 of their Gilbertese relatives), all destined for a new life on Rabi in Fiji.[31]

Although Maude had bought Rabi for the Banabans in 1942 as a prospective second home, on account of the damage inflicted on Ocean Island by phosphate mining, the resettlement was an unhappy venture. The migrants were suspicious (justifiably so) that the colonial government, in collusion with the mining company, intended not only to keep them on Rabi permanently but to extinguish their residual rights on Ocean Island. More immediately, they were discomforted by the climate, cooler and much wetter than what they were used to; dismayed by the lack of preparations made to receive them; disconcerted by having to resort to subsistence agriculture, an art they had lost; frustrated by road making; and insulted by being pushed into plantation work, and being shown how to cut copra by Solomon Islanders, whom they considered their inferiors. Most of the Banabans were accommodated in tents at Nuku. About 40 of them died during the first six months. The only solid house on the island was occupied by Kennedy and his new wife, and it alone had electricity, hot water and a septic tank.[32]

There Kennedy made it his primary task as 'Banaban adviser' to draw up a constitution for a new society. The members of this were 'formally constituted as an association of families linked by Banaban identity, which elected a council and the management of a cooperative society'. While the scheme was accepted by the new settlers it did little to ameliorate their plight. For this they found it convenient to blame Kennedy and, although he was not the cause of their difficulties, a robust pragmatism diluted his sympathy for them, and did nothing to deflect their growing hostility. He was disappointed by 'people

---

30   Interview with Mary White, 10 May 1992; Donald Gilbert Kennedy, *Te Ngangana a te Tuvalu: a handbook on the language of the Ellice Islands*, Sydney, 1945, pp. 82; Richard Frost, *Enigmatic Proconsul: Sir Philip Mitchell and the twilight of empire*, London, 1992, p. 171.
31   H.E. Maude, memorandum on 'The future of the Banaban population of Ocean Island', 2 Sept. 1946, FNA, CSO F37/269; Albert Ellis, *Mid-Pacific Outposts*, Auckland, p. 238; Woodburn, pp. 198–201.
32   Pearl Binder, *Treasure Islands: the trials of the Banabans*, Sydney, 1978, pp. 93–110; Martin G. Silverman, *Disconcerting Issue: meaning and struggle in a resettled Pacific community*, Chicago, 1971, pp. 145–148, 160–162; WPHC to Colonial Secretary, Fiji, 29 June 1942, 26 Oct., 5, 10, Dec. 1945, and Kennedy, 'Progress report on Banaban settlement scheme, 23 Oct. 1945 to 28 Jan. 1946', FNA , CSO F37/269.

almost wilfully blind to their wonderful opportunities and tending ever more strongly to hark back to old suspicions and complaints'. In contrast, their leader, Rotan Tito, Kennedy's ally before being relegated to 'agitator', shared their grievances, and even condoned challenges to his authority, such as the unsanctioned slaughtering of cattle. By the end of May Kennedy was predicting a breakdown of order on the island, and had even called for police assistance. His appeal prompted two official investigations, but no show of colonial force. Instead, three months later, to mollify the Banabans with an act of expedient irenicism, but ignoring their main—and enduringly troublesome—concerns, their first adviser was removed from his position, and replaced by another.[33]

For Kennedy it was an ignominious end not only to an unusual venture, but also to his career. Strongly self-reliant, he had never cultivated the friendship or admiration of his colleagues or superiors, any more than he had the affection of his subordinates. If he had their respect it was hard-earned and often grudgingly given, and his truculent character, womanising, and over-indulgence in whisky made it difficult to sustain. Already in late 1943, when he was 'of a seniority at which prospects loom ahead for those who are both fit and competent' it had been suggested that he be 'retired from the Service'. And so it soon came to pass. From 31 September 1946 he was granted vacation leave and, on 25 April 1947, he retired as 'District Officer, BSIP'. It was a lowly rank on which to finish after 26 years of service. Even so, he was still under 50 years of age, and his future prospects looked to be not uncomfortable.[34]

From Fiji he had gone with Mary to live on 'Glen Aros' station, an old-established farming property she had inherited from her parents in the prosperous Hawke's Bay district of New Zealand. The life of a country gentleman beckoned. There Kennedy interested himself in animal genetics, and took to cattle breeding with such aplomb that in 1950 his bull Emperor of Glen Aros won the 'champion of champions' award at the local agricultural show. That was also a swansong. Shortly afterwards he was carried from Glen Aros in a drunken coma, and never returned. He and Mary were divorced in 1952. Meanwhile, according to her recollection, early in 1951 he visited New Guinea to advise on an Australian scheme to set up a military intelligence network there. Again the bottle prevailed. The mission was aborted, and the report was never written.[35]

---

33 Maude, memorandum on 'The future of the Banaban population of Ocean Island: with special relation to their lands and funds', 2 Sept. 1946, FNA, CSO F37/269; Silverman, pp. 163–167; Maslyn Williams and Barrie Macdonald, *The Phosphateers: a history of the British Phosphate Commissioners and the Christmas Island Phosphate Commission*, Melbourne, 1985, p. 365; Robert Langdon, 'Harry Maude: shy proconsul, dedicated Pacific historian', in Niel Gunson (ed.), *The Changing Pacific: essays in honour of H.E. Maude*, Melbourne, 1978, pp. 12–14; interview with Mary White.
34 Fragment of letter by Assistant High Commissioner, [1943], WPHC archives, BSIP, FC 2; *WPHC Gazette*, Suva, 1949.
35 Interview with Mary White; White to Laracy, private communication, 19 May 1986; *Pacific Islands Monthly*, Jan. 1950, p. 24. The proposal for a security intelligence service apparently came to nothing. An

Faced now with the problem of what to do next, and where to go. Kennedy sought refuge among some of his former subjects, on the island of Kioa in Fiji. En route from Tarawa to Rabi with the Banabans in 1945 he had visited Vaitupu, and had advised the people there to consider resettlement in order to avoid overpopulation. The idea was well received. In June 1946, therefore, he and Maude, bought the island of Kioa in Fiji on their behalf. Between 1947 and 1963 a total of 217 people shifted there from Vaitupu. About half that number had already come when Kennedy arrived in September 1951. He was invited to stay on as adviser to the fledgling community, and forthwith initiated an ambitious development program involving clearing bush, planting coconuts, grazing cattle and making a road. Not unreasonably, some of the settlers began to fear that Kennedy was aiming to develop Kioa as an estate for himself so, a year later, they expelled him from the island. But he continued to haunt them.[36]

In 1953 he notified the Kioans that he had purchased the small island of Waya, near Kadavu, for himself, and invited any of them who so wished to join him there. Four families, numbering about 16 people, accepted. Among them was a couple named Paka and Samo and their granddaughter Emeline. Their daughter, Mainalupe, had been Kennedy's housekeeper on Vaitupu and, in 1936, he had produced a son named Donald Lipine Kennedy by her. Subsequently, Mainalupe married a man named Kaisami, and they begot Emeline. Aged 11 when she shifted to Waya, Emeline became Kennedy's common-law wife soon after she turned 16 in 1958, and in 1959 gave him a son named Archie Bairn Kennedy. After the last of the Kioans returned to Kioa in 1963, those three had Waya largely to themselves for a decade. In 1973 declining health led Kennedy to sell his island, marry Emeline and return to New Zealand. He died three years later, aged 77. He had fathered eight children by five different women, produced a useful corpus of scholarly writing, and he had left his name deeply embedded in the folklore no less than in the colonial history of the several island groups through which he ranged during the course of 50 years.[37]

Kennedy's was a career energetically pursued and was not without its successes, yet was scarcely calculated to edify in staid, conventional ways. Within the

---

extensive search yielded only a Department of Defence file titled 'The security of key points in Australia and its territories against subversive activity and sabotage'. Generated by memorandum SS.634 of 16 Nov. 1949 from the Chiefs of Staff Committee, it contains reports from various states and government departments but holds nothing relating to Papua New Guines or to Kennedy. National Archives of Australia, A816, file:14/30 3/132.

36   Koch, pp. 45–50, 61–62, 89; G.M. White, 'Kioa: an Ellice community in Fiji', PhD thesis, Anthropology, University of Oregon, 1965, pp. 1–14.

37   Koch, pp. 61–62; White, p. 14. Interviews with Nellie Kennedy, Mary White, Emeline Kennedy, and other family members. Other writings of Kennedy are 'The Polynesian Outliers of Melanesia', *Transactions of the Fiji Society of Science and Industry*, vol. 3, no. 1 (1945), pp. 28–44; 'This is the Solomon Islands', in R.W. Robson and Judy Tudor (eds), *Where the Trade Winds Blow*, Sydney, 1946, pp. 168–170; 'Land Tenure in the Ellice Islands', *Journal of the Polynesian Society*, vol. 64, no. 4 (1953), pp. 348–358. See, also, *Pacific Islands Monthly*, Jan., Feb. 1944, Feb. 1945.

colonial administrative service he became an embarrassingly disreputable figure, one readily dismissed as having brought discredit on it. For instance, one of his former colleagues, Colin Allan, who later became Governor of the Solomon Islands, thought that it would be preferable to leave Kennedy's story unwritten rather than have some of the details of his personal behaviour offered to a general readership. To do that, though, would be wilfully to reduce the quality of understanding attainable in regard to various significant events in which he was involved. Besides, given the way his character coloured his career, it would be to countenance a more than usually specious distinction between public and private matters. A balanced assessment of the man requires an uninhibited consideration of the tangled threads of merit and demerit that animated him. In any case, those closest to him saw no problem. His second wife wrote that:

> He was an extraordinary character—utterly charming, with a great presence and a tremendous sense of humour, extremely erudite and interesting with it. A very clear thinking and brilliant brain, but almost paranoiac. If he thought his authority or pride were touched in any way he became violent. And, of course, being an alcoholic didn't help. His years of isolation in the G.&E. made it difficult for him to adjust to civilised living where his authority could be questioned.[38]

Such comments, even allowing for the mellowing effect of time, betray a sympathetic recognition of complexity rather than any disdain. They suggest that the drama of Kennedy's life, the ambiguity of his personality and the strong responses he elicited might supply the ingredients of an entertaining story for the cinema screen. Possibly it could be told with due panache by his stepson Martin Campbell, director of the James Bond adventure *Golden Eye*.[39]

---

38 Mary White, personal communication, 19 May 1986; interview with Sir Colin Allan. Himself a New Zealander, Allan was a generation younger than Kennedy and was academically well qualified.
39 *Sunday Star-Times*, 3 July 1994; *NZ Listener*, 9 Dec. 1995.

12. George Bogese (1904–1959): 'Just a bloody traitor'?

Although World War II, especially the battle for Guadalcanal, brought the Solomon Islands to international prominence, few of the Islanders emerged from the war with significantly enhanced reputations. Of those who did, probably only three became well known outside the group. Of these, two, Jacob Vouza and Bill Bennett, have been honoured as heroes for their service on the side of the victorious Allies: Vouza for an act of bravery in refusing to tell his Japanese captors about American defence positions and then providing useful information to the US marines; Bennett for sustained bravery while serving behind Japanese lines with the coast watcher and guerrilla leader Donald Kennedy.[1] Other Solomon Islanders, who also served the Allies faithfully, though less dramatically, were left in obscurity.[2] But it is in the nature of things for honours to be acquired selectively and sparingly—and somewhat fortuitously George Bogese, the third of the trio, discovered that those who do not find favour with the victors are distinctly vulnerable. Not all Solomon Islanders, especially in the areas that were longest under Japanese occupation, as in parts of Choiseul and Australian-ruled Bougainville, were immovably staunch supporters of the Allies. Indeed, some of them were subjected to summary punishment for 'disloyalty'. But only two individuals, John McDonald from the Shortland Islands and Geoge Bogese from Santa Isabel, were subjected to the indignity of a trial and the ignominy of a conviction.[3] And of these two it was the fate of Bogese, partly because of a close, if hostile, involvement with the well-publicised heroics of Kennedy and Bennett, to become the more notorious.

In Bill Bennett's crisply stated opinion, Bogese was 'just a bloody traitor', and as such deserved nothing but reprobation and lasting ill repute. Bennett had

---

[1] James Boutilier, 'Kennedy's Army: Solomon Islanders at war, 1942–1943', in G. White and L. Lindstrom (eds), *The Pacific Theatre: Island representations of World War II*, Honolulu, 1989; [Harold Cooper], *Among Those Present: the official story of the Pacific Islands at war*, London, 1946, pp. 15–16, 28–29, 47–53; Eric Feldt, *The Coast Watchers*, Melbourne, 1946, pp. 110–111, 150; *Government Monthly*, vol. 1, no. 27 (March 1984); D.C. Horton, *Fire Over the Islands: the coast watchers of the Solomon Islands*, Sydney, 1970, pp. 49–50, 72, 94–96, 149; Hector MacQuarrie, *Vouza and the Solomon Islands*, Sydney, 1946; *Pacific Islands Monthly* (*PIM*), May 1984, p. 73; *Solomon Star*, 23 March 1984, 21 January 1988; *Toktok*, 22 March 1984.

[2] In response to a request by Bill Bennett at the 1987 'Pacific Recollections of World War II' conference in Honiara, a list of all Solomon Islanders recorded as serving in the war was published in Hugh Laracy and Geoffrey White (eds), *Taem Blong Faet: World War II in Melanesia*, special issue of *'O'O: A Journal of Solomon Islands Studies*, vol. 4 (1988), pp. 117–237.

[3] Unfortunately the court records for the trials of Bogese and McDonald appear to have been lost. The trials were held in Honiara in 1947 before Sir Claude Seton, the chief justice of Fiji, sitting as a judicial commissioner of the Western Pacific High Commission. The records are not in Honiara, the High Court archives (the court was not set up until later in 1947), or in the Solomon Islands National Archives; nor are they in the Fiji National Archives, where Fiji judicial records for that period have been deposited, evidence given at the preliminary inquiries for both hearings is in the Solomon Islands National Archives, BSIP CJ 1945.

some not unreasonable grounds for his view.⁴ Unlike Vouza, Bogese had chosen not to risk his life by resisting the Japanese after he had been captured by them. Moreover, he was involved in an incident in which Bennett received severe burns from exploding petrol. Besides, in 1946 a court found him guilty on a charge of assisting the enemy and sentenced him to four years imprisonment. From a position more detached than Bennett's however, and at a remove of more than half a century, during which time Solomon Islanders have outgrown their subordination to foreign rule, Bogese's actions seem more understandable, and possibly less reprehensible, than they were to his contemporary critics.

Most of the Solomons group had been a British protectorate since the 1890s, but the government had brought few benefits to the Islanders, as many people from Bogese's home island of Ysabel complained during the Chair and Rule movement of the 1930s; and as others from the southern islands were to complain during the Maasina Rule movement of the 1940s.⁵ Solomon Islanders, then, in their own estimation owed the colonial government little. As an institution it was not remote from them yet it was threatening and was represented among them only by a few sparsely scattered officials with extensive powers whose primary tasks were to collect the annual head tax and to discourage breaches of the peace. If the Islanders in 1940 had feelings of gratitude and affection for Europeans, they were for missionaries rather than for the government. Even so they generally remained loyal during the war, although this is easily explained. Whatever their grievances against their colonial 'masters', the Islanders did not find in the Japanese an appealing alternative to the existing regime ('better the devil you know'!). And the Japanese, given that they were on the defensive during most of their occupation of the Solomons, had little chance to make themselves agreeable. Besides, the missionaries backed the officials in urging the Islanders to support Britain and its Allies. In Bogese's case, however, there were additional and acutely personal strains on his loyalty: he was captured at a time when it seemed as if the British had abandoned the Protectorate to the Japanese and, although he was in government employment, there was ill-feeling between him and his superior, Kennedy. Vouza, in contrast, was captured after the American forces had arrived to challenge the Japanese and was, moreover, encouraged to resist by the memory that years before, as a policeman, he had once failed notably in his duty. In being captured he accepted a chance to make reparation for that embarrassing lapse.⁶ Bogese had no such spur to heroism.

---

4   This is a comment Bennett commonly made whenever the subject of Bogese was raised in conversation.
5   Judith A. Bennett, *Wealth of the Solomons: a history of a Pacific archipelago, 1800–1978*, Honolulu, 1987, pp. 259–263, 286–299; David Hilliard, *God's Gentlemen: a history of the Melanesian Mission, 1849–1942*, St. Lucia, 1978, pp. 282–285; Hugh Laracy (ed.), *Pacific Protest: the Maasina Rule movement, Solomon Islands, 1944–1952*, Suva, 1983.
6   Judith A. Bennett, 'Cross-Cultural Influences on Village Relocation on the Weather Coast of Guadalcanal, Solomon Islands, c.1870–1953', MA thesis, University of Hawai'i, 1974, p. 174; Cooper 1946, p. 29; Hugh and Eugenie Laracy, 'Custom, Conjugality and Colonial Rule in the Solomon Islands', *Oceania*, vol. 51, no. 2 (1980),

12. George Bogese (1904–1959): 'Just a bloody traitor'?

Bogese's problems began in May 1942 on the island of Savo. He was there, on Kennedy's orders, in his capacity as native medical practitioner conducting a medical survey. On 5 May he encountered two Japanese survivors from the destroyer *Kitsutsuki* that had been sunk the day before, during the Japanese occupation of the protectorate headquarters at Tulagi. They were suffering from wounds and burns. After getting approval from Leif Schroeder, a former trader working as an allied coast watcher who sent some food down from his bush hideaway for the Japanese, Bogese dressed their wounds. Three days later a Catholic missionary, Desmond Scanlon from Visale on Guadalcanal, visited Savo and gave food and clothing to the pair. He also advised Bogese and others to look after them properly, 'otherwise there will be a row with the Japanese authorities,' and, before leaving, wrote his name and address on a piece of paper, which he gave to the Japanese. For his part Bogese—as he later recounted in an affidavit—attempted to conceal his occupation and identity from the Japanese, but the deception was soon revealed. On 9 May two barges carrying 50 soldiers and guided by a man named Tolia arrived at Savo, near Panuel village where Bogese was living, to collect their compatriots. When they had landed, one of the soldiers addressed the watching villagers in English: 'The rule of Great Britain is finished. You are now under the Japanese military rule. Anybody who disobeys Japanese orders must be shot. We proclaim martial law. All natives must cooperate with the Japanese.' The party then proceeded to the village where Tolia identified Bogese: 'This is Dr George we talk along you before.' The Japanese who had spoken on the beach then said to Bogese: 'My name is Sima. I was in Fiji for nine years. I know the names of all the native Medical Practitioners who were trained in Suva. You must be one of them. You must tell me the truth, and you must cooperate with the Japanese, or you will be shot … You must come with us to Tulagi … . All Native Medical Practitioners must work for the Japanese Government.'

'I was,' admitted Bogese, 'frightened to disobey,' and he proceeded to work for a new 'master' as an interpreter. On 11 May, Sima (who was probably the man more commonly known as Ishimoto) had him write a notice in the Nggela language urging the people of that island to return to their home and not to hide in the bush.[7] On 12 May, Bogese went with Sima to the village of Voloa on Nggela to recruit men to help unload a ship at Tulagi. On 13 May, he and one of

---

p. 140; H.C. Moorhouse, 'Report of Commissioner Appointed by the Secretary of State for the Colonies to Enquire into the Circumstances in which Murders took Place in 1927 of Government Officials on Guadalcanal and Malaita', *Great Britain Parliamentary Papers, 1928–1929*, C3248, pp. 6–8.

7 In a taped interview, Bogese's daughter Margaret pronounced the name as 'Shima' (Kolotevo, interview for 'Olgetta Meri', Solomon Islands Broadcasting commission, 1971). But he seems to be the same man known to Bishop Aubin, and most others who have occasion to mention the English-speaking Japanese familiar with the Solomons, as Ishimoto. Jean-Marie Aubin, 'Journal de Guerre', 3 July 1942, box 'War', Archives of the Catholic Archdiocese of Honiara. Feldt (1946) describes him as 'A Japanese who had lived in the Solomons, and had also been a barber in Fiji, [and] was the head of the Native Department', p. 111. He was also known as Yoshimoto.

those men, Kuini Gee, were directed by Sima to translate from English to Nggela another notice 'To all the Island People,' informing them: 'The Japanese Army came to protect the Natives. You must return to your villages and do your work in peace and remain calm. You must give information to the Japanese Military Authorities.'[8]

On 15 May he had to translate a similar message into the Bugotu language of the southern Ysabel for distribution among his own people: 'Will you return to your respective villages and perform your ordinary occupations and be safe. The Japanese army respect all people in these islands, they didn't come to [do] you any harm or to burn your houses and destroy your property, they came to protect all your people in these islands.'[9] The Bugotu version, however, as Bennett later pointed out, contained an instruction not included in the English original: 'If any natives know of any Europeans hidden around the Islands, who possess rifles, ammunition, etc, they are to report them immediately to the Japanese authorities in Tulagi.'[10]

Meanwhile Bogese had also been told that he was to go to Rabaul, where the chief medical officer of the Japanese wished to ask him about tropical diseases. Before leaving he was taken with two barge loads of Japanese, about 50 soldiers, to Kolare on Ysabel to visit his wife and children, whom he had not seen since 27 February, when he was sent to Savo.[11]

From that point events took a more dramatic turn, although the truth about Bogese's activities becomes more difficult to ascertain. On the afternoon of 17 May, with Bogese and his wife and family aboard, the Japanese set off in search of Kennedy's vessel, the *Wai-ai*, which was hidden with camouflage not far away from Sigana. According to Bogese he had not told the Japanese where the vessel was. Rather, he claimed it had already been spotted by a Japanese aircraft. Nor, he said, had he told them where Kennedy was hiding. According to a Kolare man named Jasper Rutu, however, Bogese had asked him where the *Wai-ai* was hidden; and Rutu, for fear of the Japanese, had told him. Rutu also said that Bogese had instructed him to lead the Japanese to Kennedy's base at Mahaga, in an attack planned for 4 pm on 17 May; and had further advised him that a vessel, the *Joan*, hidden in the mangroves by a departed trader, should be found and handed over to the Japanese. According to another witness, Joseph Supa, Bogese's wife's cousin, who went with them on the barge and who had helped hide the *Wai-ai*, 'from the time we left Kolare, Bogese stood with the Japanese on the stern, at the place where they steered'. Bogese's father-in-law, Maaki Hathavu, meanwhile, on his own initiative sent a message to Kennedy, warning

---

8 Bogese, affidavit, 5 July 1954. BSIP 4 FS 66. In this document Bogese presents an account of his life up to 1944.
9 Yoshimoto, notice, 15 May 1942, BSIP 4 FS 66.
10 Bennett, statement, 4 May 1945, BSIP 4 FS 66.
11 Bogese, affidavit, 5 July 1945, BSIP 4 FS 66.

him of the intended attack. The unfortunate Bennett, however, received no such warning.¹² According to him he was on the *Wai-ai* when he saw the barges approaching, 'and I saw George Bogese talking to the Japanese and pointing to the *Wai-ai*.' Then, to prevent the ship falling into Japanese hands, Bennett ordered his crew to pour petrol about, but the Japanese saved him the bother of igniting it: 'After Bogese pointed out the *Wai-ai*, somebody on board the Barge shouted, but receiving no reply from the *Wai-ai*, the Barge immediately opened fire, the second shot hitting a store of benzene aboard and setting fire to the *Wai-ai*. I dived overboard when the vessel caught fire and managed to swim ashore, but was badly burned.'¹³

In the light of these testimonies it is clear that Bogese was working closely with the Japanese on 17 May. In his defence, however, Bogese denied that he had been a willing participant and, while not denying the facts reported by prosecution witnesses, offered explanations calculated to minimise his responsibility. Thus, regarding the proposed attack on Kennedy's post, Bogese claims that it was only after the Japanese told him they had already detected it by radio direction-finding, and threatened to shoot him if he did not help them locate it, that he told Rutu to lead them to Mahaga. Besides, he said, he did not think Kennedy was there at the time. As for the attack on the *Wai-ai*, he said that:

> an aircraft had already spotted the vessel … . The Japs told me that they had found a ship. I said I knew nothing of a ship. The Japs then said I should ask somebody to say exactly where the ship was, that the aeroplane had spotted one. I asked Rutu. I admit this. I asked Rutu and Rutu said at Sigana … [on the way there] I was sitting on the stern of the ship. Supa and Gee were forward. As soon as we arrived at Sigana, I pointed out and we came to the harbour. We could not find the ship. I asked Supa where the ship was, and he said it was somewhere here. Then we heard a bang, saw the ship burning and the crew diving overboard.

With that the Japanese turned for Tulagi. The attack on Mahaga had been called off shortly before they left Kolare, in response to a message that there was a ship waiting at Tulagi to take Bogese and Kuini Gee to Rabaul. The pair left in it on 18 May, arrived in Rabaul two days later, and for the next two months worked in the native hospital there. In that time Bogese had one brief discussion with the Japanese doctors, about tropical diseases.

Then, on 1 August, after repeated requests, he and Kuini were returned to Tulagi. He was immediately given leave briefly to visit his family at Voloa on Nggela where they were staying. Although tempted to stay there with them he did not dare, he said, for fear 'of Mr. Kennedy, from the Japanese having captured

---

12   Statements collected at preliminary inquiry, BSIP CJ 1945.
13   Bennett, statement, 4 December 1945, BSIP 4 FS 66.

me at Savo and the burning of the ship *Wai-ai*. And the fear of the Japanese coming round looking for me!' On 5 August, therefore, accompanied by his wife and children, he returned to Tulagi. He was there when the Americans invaded two days later. Although he told them what he knew about the Japanese forces on the island, he was shortly afterward sent to Australia for internment at the insistence of British officials. There he and his family remained, at Tatura in Victoria, until October 1945, when he was returned to the Solomons to face charges of having collaborated with the enemy.[14]

It was sad for a man who, in his educational attainments, in his high competence in the English language, and through widespread recognition of his professional abilities, was one of the outstanding Solomon Islanders of his generation—and probably the best known. He was 41 years old at that time. He had known and enjoyed success. But he had also felt the hurt of rejection, commonly experienced by educated Islanders in colonial society, and that well before the events in which, as he put 'I lost my profession and my reputation ... and everything that was important to me.'[15] Although concern for his personal survival prompted actions for which Bogese was to be tried, his behaviour between May and August 1942—and his sense of injustice at what it cost him—cannot properly be understood in isolation from his prewar history.

Bogese was born at Vulavu in Ysabel in 1904, the son of Margaret Semo and Philip U'U, and was baptised into the Church of England by the missionary doctor Henry Welchman. He attended a village school until the age of ten, then went to the Melanesian Mission School at Norfolk Island from 1914 to 1917. After that he returned to Ysabel where he became a teacher. In 1922 he joined the government service. He worked first as a clerk, one of the first Solomon Islanders to do so, for five years. Then, in 1928, on the recommendation of J.C. Barley, district officer at Gizo, he became the first Solomon Islander to be sent to study medicine at the Central Medical School in Fiji.

He completed the course in 1930, winning the Barker Gold Medal for attainment, and returned to the Solomons in 1931 as a native medical practitioner.[16] In this capacity—visiting villages, inspecting labourers on plantations, holding clinics at government stations—'Dr George', as he was called, travelled widely throughout the Solomons, becoming well known to brown and white residents alike. Well known, but not always well liked, and persistently suspected of misbehaviour.

---

14 Statement of Bogese, BSIP CJ 1945; other accounts of these events, but consistent with Bogese's statement, are in Bogese's affidavit and in various letters filed in BSIP FS 66.
15 Bogese to Western Pacific High Commission (WPHC), 4 August 1944, BSIP 4 FS 66.
16 Bogese, affidavit, 5 July 1945, BSIP 4 FS 66; Margaret W. Guthrie, *Misi Uti: Dr. D.W. Hoodless and the development of medical education in the South Pacific*, Suva, 1979, p. 28.

Bogese's professional competence seems never to have been questioned. In 1934 his district officer said he was 'keen and efficient, and takes a thorough interest in his work', an opinion endorsed by the senior medical officer.[17] But objections against his character, especially rumours reported by missionaries of sexual misconduct with his female patients, flourished. They were not totally unfounded, although they were taken more seriously by the authorities than they would have been if he were a white man. Thus in 1934 he was found guilty on a charge of adultery and fined £4. On more serious charges, however, he was acquitted. In 1936, on Malaita, a preliminary investigation cleared him of a charge of rape, but did commit him for trial on a charge of incest with his daughter by Anna Kovaga, the first of his three wives. On that charge, too, he was acquitted (but only after the girl had been medically examined), as he also was acquitted on a lesser charge of indecent assault against the same girl.[18] It was a decision that must surely have brought acute relief to a man who already had another daughter by his second wife, a Fijian named Anna Seini, and who was to have ten children by his third and current wife, Susanna Riko, daughter of Maaki Hathevu of Kolare.[19]

Regardless of alleged sexual delinquencies, Bogese was guilty of another 'failing' which was even more reprehensible in colonial society. He did not regard himself as being inferior to Europeans. One official wrote 'Owing to his unfortunate manner he is not liked by the white residents of the District, with whom he is in frequent contact through their labour.' Another identified the 'fault' succinctly, 'he is very self-confident.'[20] Evidence of this, although as a trait rather than a fault, was given in 1939 when Bogese complained to his superiors about what he saw as 'the unfair treatment accorded to us, whether native officers or ordinary natives, by some European Officers on many matters,' and had the temerity to ask 'is this treatment due to the rules [being] set aside for the natives … or due to carelessness?'[21] Many of the Solomon Islanders were, in fact, concerned about the matter yet few of the European residents would have disagreed with Kennedy's opinion about the kind of person who would openly ask such a question, or how he ought to be treated:

> Bogese is a person of a type well known to all who have had to deal with the educated native at loose, without adequate social control, in a primitive community. The type is characterised by limitless presumption combined with that kind of humility, which has been aptly described

---
17 Miller to Senior Medical Officer (SMO), 8 October 1934; Crichlow to Secretary to Government, 25 October 1934. BSIP I/III, F 58/3.
18 Acting Resident Commissioner to WHPC, 11 August 1936, BSIP I/II: Bengough to SMO, 31 July 1936, BSIP I/III. F 58/3: Bogese, affidavit, 5 July 1945, BSIP 4, FS 66.
19 Nelson Basily, personal communication.
20 Miller to SMO, 8 October 1934; Crichlow to Secretary to Government, 25 October 1834. BSIP I/III, F 58/3.
21 Bogese to acting SMO, 23 May 1939, BSIP I/III, F 58/3.

as arrogant. In the course of some 24 years service in the Pacific Islands I have had more than a little experience of this sort of native. I strongly deprecate any suspicion of harshness or impatient treatment of unsophisticated natives in any environment, and have found that the less one raises one's voice the more cooperation one receives from them. But I have found, to the contrary, that abruptness and direct speech is the only method of achieving satisfactory official relations with those of the Bogese type.[22]

Given the clarity of Kennedy's views and the vigour with which he customarily acted, it is hardly surprising that in late 1941, amid the stress of encroaching war, when Bogese and Kennedy were both appointed to Ysabel, the two should fall out badly. Unfortunately for the historian, their mutual hostility means that neither is to be fully relied on as a witness concerning the other. The trouble began in January over food stocks when, contrary to Kennedy's orders, Bogese gave rice from government stores to patients at the local hospital. He said he did so because they needed it; Kennedy maintained that the patients were young women who were not ill but whom Bogese was merely encouraging to stay at the hospital. Another dispute occurred later that month, after Bogese supervised the carrying the supplies from the government post at Tataba inland to Mahaga. Kennedy accused him of stealing some of the supplies; Bogese claimed that far from stealing, he had given some of his own food to the carriers, and that Kennedy had rebuked him for this, saying, 'You think you are a big chief, to share the food. You are only trying to show off.' Whatever the truth of these matters, one thing at least is clear, Kennedy distrusted Bogese. Moreover, he cites alleged difficulties in recruiting carriers for the shift from Tataba to Mahaga as leading him to suspect that Bogese was influencing the people of southern Ysabel not to cooperate with the government.

To test this theory Kennedy sent Bogese on a tour of the island in February to do medical work and to advise the people to avoid the Japanese when they came, and then sent a patrol after him to check on the instructions he was issuing. Predictably, Bogese claims to have done as he was told, but Kennedy remained unconvinced of his loyalty. After three weeks he recalled Bogese from his tour and, without offering any explanation, took him to Savo. There he left him in the charge of the headman Johnson Soro, with orders not to leave the island and with the warning 'be very careful, or you will be shot, or whipped, the same as the others.' It was the last time the two met.[23] Kennedy went on to become a hero

---

22   Kennedy, note on Bogese, 20 January 1945, BSIP 4, FS 66.
23   Kennedy, report on coast watching, 20 November 1943, BSIP 4, C5; Bogese to WHPC, 8 August 1943, 4 August 1944; Kennedy, note on Bogese, 20 January 1945; Bogese, affidavit, 5 July 1945, BSIP 4, FS 66.

while, just over two months later, Bogese was in Japanese hands. By September 1942, through another sudden change of fate, if not of fortune, he was interned in Australia with his wife and three children.

It was not a fate he accepted easily. Over the next three years Bogese wrote a number of letters—consistently fluent, logically resourceful, and occasionally disingenuous—urging his innocence. He blamed Kennedy for his woes, stating that his appointment to Savo was due to 'persecution and ill treatment' of him by Kennedy 'for purely personal reasons,' and arguing that had he not been sent there he would not have fallen in with the Japanese, and so could not have been forced to cooperate with them. He also compared his case with that of others and pleaded unfair treatment: there had been rumours about him, but there had also been rumours—and even complaints—about Kennedy in regard to brutality and improper dealings with women, and Kennedy had never been punished. Then there was the case of Catholic missionaries of Visale: Father Scanlon had introduced himself to the Japanese, and Father Aloysius Brugmans had accompanied a Japanese patrol to Lungga for two days in July, yet they had not been treated as collaborators. And, he asked with plaintive rhetoric, though not unreasonably, how could he, 'a poor defenceless native,' be expected not to cooperate.[24] As he put it to John Curtin, the Australian prime minister:

> It is well known all over the world how the Japanese committed atrocities in the Solomons, New Guinea, the Philippines, or Netherlands East Indies. Civilians were murdered in masses, captured soldier, both European or natives were ill treated, murdered or forced to do this and that, air pilots were executed as in the case of nine pilots at Rabaul. Filipino citizens were burned to death for disobeying them, etc.etc. How could I, being a defenceless native, resist such a horde of Japanese who proclaimed martial law and death sentences in the Solomons?[25]

Unbeknown to Bogese, he was not alone in pleading his case. In October 1945 the Anglican bishop, although admitting to a personal dislike of Bogese, wrote to the Resident Commissioner expounding excuses for his actions and asking that no charges be laid against him:

> Bogese is a Solomon Islander who perhaps prematurely was 'educated above his station.' ... But it is unreasonable to think that Bogese may well have thought that through a Japanese regime here, the Solomon Islander might get a better crack of the whip. After all there has been a British administration in these Islands for 50 years now ... are you proud, or even satisfied with what has been done for the people here

---

24   Bogese to WHPC, 8 August 1943, 15 November 1943, BSIP 4, FS 66.
25   Bogese to Curtin, 22 March 1945, BSIP 4, FS 6. Other Australians learned about Bogese through *PIM*, April 1945, p. 25; May 1945, p. 34.

by the British Raj? Your two predecessors have told me that the great contribution of the British ... has been ... 'security of tenure' and ... the 'Pax Britannica.' Neither of these has been very apparent since December 1941. Is it treason for a native of these islands to think that the progress of his people is bound up with an Asiatic race rather than with the British regime of which after all, he is only a 'protected' subject?

I have no doubt that Bogese will plead that he acted 'under constraint'. If he so pleaded and I were an assessor on the bench ... he would get my vote for 'acquittal.' There were absolutely blood-curdling stories going the rounds in the Solomons in the first half of '42 as to what the Japanese had done on Bougainville to extract information. If Bogese had heard these stories ... I am not surprised if he gave such information as was asked.[26]

The administration, however, was unmoved. There was wide public interest in the affair, not least because of the crucial role played by the coast watchers in the Solomons campaign and because of their dependence on the 'cooperation of the natives' in operating behind enemy lines. Possibly to have threatened their security was, therefore, seen as a particularly serious matter, and one that required nothing less than a formal court hearing.[27] Accordingly, after a preliminary enquiry, five charges were laid against Bogese; to wit, that he did 'with intent to assist the enemy,'

1. try to induce Rutu to lead the Japanese to the coast watch base at Mahaga;

2. induce Nicholas Gee to go with the Japanese to Rabaul;

3. induce Rutu to tell him the where abouts of the *Wai-ai*;

4. assist the Japanese to locate the *Wai-ai*; and

5. 'voluntarily join himself with the enemy Japanese' between 1 May and 8 August 1942.[28]

Unfortunately for Bogese, the bishop was not on the bench when the case was heard. In May 1946 he appeared before the Chief Justice of Fiji, Sir Claude Seton, sitting in Honiara as a judicial commissioner, with two former planters as assessors, J.M. Clift and H.A. Markham. On the first four charges, which related to specific acts and which called for precise evidence to prove that he had freely and materially assisted the Japanese, he was acquitted. But on the fifth, which

---

26   Baddeley to Noel, 5 October 1945, BSIP 4, FS 66.
27   Resident Commissioner to WHPC, 22 October 1945, BSIP 4, FS 66.
28   Order for removal for trial, 11 February 1946, BSIP CJ 1945.

was a more general charge and one where the prosecution was relying on its own perception and not on the testimony of indigenous witnesses who had been intimately involved in the events, it was a different matter. It was held against Bogese that 'after he returned from Rabaul, he brought his wife and family in from a country place and they lived with him in Tulagi in apparently close association with the Japanese.' On this charge he was found guilty and sentenced to four years imprisonment, of which he served three. Released from Rove prison in 1949 he returned to the obscurity of village life.[29] Nor for him would there be an obituary in the *BSIP Newssheet*.

Bogese paid dearly for his association with the Japanese. He lost his job and spent seven years in custody. Moreover, the colonial administration, unforgiving and ever distrustful—as its records abundantly show—would never risk allowing him an opportunity to regain a position of any standing or influence in the Solomon Islands, or to live down the reputation of traitor that he had acquired, if not earned. He had not been represented by a lawyer at his trial, he was refused leave to appeal against his sentence, and from prison he was prevented from contributing to a political discussion then flourishing among his compatriots.[30] In December 1946 he wrote an open letter to the people of southern Ysabel, urging them to cooperate with the government if they wished to prosper and not to join the Maasina Rule nationalist movement. That in his exhortation he also touched on Solomon Islanders' entitlement to the 'Freedoms' listed in the Atlantic Charter of 1940 and to the conditions of life prescribed by the UN Charter was unlikely to make the letter any more acceptable in the eyes of authorities who were already prejudiced against its author, because such claims were also being made by Maasina Rule.[31] If anything, the letter was likely to strengthen rather than dilute the distrust they had for him. Contemplating Bogese's eventual release from prison, one official even saw risks in encouraging him 'to do a certain amount of anthropological work… Bogese as an Assistant Medical Practitioner was always apt to use his position to his own advantage, and might magnify his association with the University [of Sydney] to suit his own ends in some way.'[32]

In a similar vein, following his release, the High Commissioner ordered that '[Bogese] should not be given any form of public employment',[33] while in June 1951 the Resident Commissioner, after meeting Bogese briefly and for the first time during a visit to Ysabel, denounced him as 'one of the nastiest bits of native

---

29 *PIM*, August 1946, p. 2.
30 Bogese to Elkin, 22 July 1946, Elkin Papers P 130, 4/12/135, University of Sydney Archives; Bogese request to appeal, August 1946 BSIP 4, FS 66.
31 Bogese to Secretary to Government, 16 December 1946, enclosing 'Open Letter', BSIP 4, C91. The United Nations, noted Bogese, aimed to promote and encourage respect for human rights and for fundamental freedom for all 'without distinction as to race, sex, language, or religion'.
32 Trench to Elkin, 26 November 1948, BSIP I/III, 58/3.
33 WHPC to Gregory Smith, 7 July 1949, BSIP I/III, 58/3.

composition I have met.'[34] Presumably this was still his belief the following month when H.E. Maude, a former colonial official then living in Sydney, informed him that two Australian professors, A.P. Elkin of Sydney and S.F. Nadel of Canberra, were planning to bring Bogese ('who gave us so many headaches during the war') to Australia to assist them with their anthropological research.[35] The Resident Commissioner declared himself to be 'very apprehensive about the idea' and needed no persuading to accept a recommendation that 'Under no circumstances [should] Bogese be allowed to go to Australia for a year. He is a potential nuisance of the first order, and after a year in Australia he would[36] wreck Ysabel in no time.' Instead Bogese spent 1952 working in the less corrupting atmosphere of Lever's plantation at Yandina.[37] He then returned to Ysabel where, without profit to himself or danger to the government, he found some diversion in completing a Bugotu–English dictionary.[38] He died on Ysabel, after a brief illness, on 18 June 1959, unlamented and unnoticed beyond his own district.[39]

Both as the first Solomon Islands native medical practitioner, and as a reputed traitor, Bogese has a firm claim to a place in Solomon Islands history. But he also has other grounds for that claim. He was the first Solomon Islander to have his writings published in a recognised academic journal. Already in 1940 he had published a brief article, 'Notes on the Santa Cruz Group,' in *The Native Medical Practitioner*, a journal published in Fiji, but during his internment he completed another and more ambitious project. This was an account of the traditional culture of Bugotu.[40] In May 1945 Bogese wrote to A.P. Elkin, professor of anthropology at Sydney University and editor of the journal *Oceania*, introducing himself and describing the project. He had probably become aware of Elkin through the latter's involvement with the Society for the Protection of Natives Races. In July he was to write to him again, enclosing a long affidavit about the events of 1942 and requesting the society's help in obtaining 'an official enquiry into the unfair treatment I received from Mr D.G. Kennedy, and my subsequent deportation and internment.'[41]

Despite his reputation in official circles for self-seeking, there is, however, no reason to suspect Bogese of any duplicity in contacting Elkin. His first letter,

---

34 Gregory-Smith, Ysabel, 9–18 June 1951, BSIP I/III, F 14/3, III.
35 Maude to Gregory-Smith, 18 July 1951, BSIP I/III, 58/3.
36 Gregory-Smith to Davies, 24 July 1951; Davies to Gregory-Smith, 25 July 1951, BSIP I/III, 58/3.
37 Bogese to Capell, 19 January 1952. Elkin Papers, p. 130, 4/2/122.
38 Cited in A. Capell, *A Linguistic Survey of the South-Western Pacific*, Nouméa, 1962, pp. 179–180, but apparently lost subsequently.
39 Basily, personal communication, 16 October 1987.
40 George Bogese, 'Notes on the Santa Cruz Group', *Native Medical Practitioner*, vol. 3 (1941), pp. 538–543.
41 Bogese to Elkin, 22 July 1946, Elkin papers P 130, 4/2/122; Tigger Wise, *The Self-Made Anthropologist*, Sydney, 1985.

and it was followed by seven others before his request for assistance, was one such as any editor of an anthropological journal would welcome, and does not suggest that he was seeking to ingratiate himself for personal advantage:

> I am a native of Solomon Islands and a Native Medical Practitioner by profession. I understand that you have some interest in natives' welfare and all that I wish to inform you [is] that at present I am writing, in very simple English, Anthropological work about my own District, BUGOTU, Santa Isabel, and S.I. The subjects dealt with are: short history, feasts and marriages, diseases and treatment of herbs and their methods, fishing house and canoe building, children's play and a tale of Mogo tribe (now extinct), Bugotu vocabulary in English, etc. If you think that this will be any use in your department, please kindly inform me. After the war you may publish it if possible.[42]

The work was eventually published in two parts in *Oceania* in 1948.[43] With its appearance Bogese, the 'educated native' rejected by the colonial régime for his lack of docility towards his 'masters', and punished for being reluctant to risk his life for them, at last earned himself a measure of notability unsullied by scandal. At the same time he provided a legacy of knowledge for his people and set a precedent that other Solomon Islanders could honourably follow. And as time passed and more information on the war has come to light, even his unfortunate involvement with the Japanese can be seen in a more honourable light. At a conference in Honiara in 1987, numerous Solomon Islands war veterans publicly expressed misgivings at the readiness with which they had given their youthful loyalty to the Allies, and admitted to some bitterness at how little it had benefited them. Could he have been there, Bogese would surely have smiled knowingly. He too had learned not to expect generosity from colonial rule, but well before they had. The most ironic and surprising revelation of the conference, however, came from Bennett who admitted that, while serving with Kennedy he, like Bogese, had come to hate him. So much so that during a skirmish with the Japanese in September 1943 he had taken advantage of the confusion to try to kill Kennedy, although only succeeded in wounding him. Yet Bennett finished the war a hero.[44]

Such admissions indicate the complexity and subjectivity of the notion of loyalty, and of how it is to be assessed. Loyalty to whom? To what? Why? At what cost? They also contribute to the rehabilitation of Bogese's reputation. He was no hero but he was more than 'just a bloody traitor.' Indeed, without stretching ingenuity too far it may be suggested that latter day Solomon Islanders

---

42 Bogese to Elkin, 20 March 1946, Elkin papers P 130, 4/2/122.
43 George Bogese, 'Santa Isabel, Solomon Islands', *Oceania*, vol. 18 (1948), pp. 208–232, 327–357.
44 This discussion is based on a large body of evidence in Laracy and White (1988), and in Geoffrey White et al. (eds), *The Big Death: Solomon Islanders remember World War II* (Suva, 1988).

might usefully find in Bogese a source of national pride. He was intelligent, self-assured, and pragmatic. And it was for displaying such qualities that he, more than other Solomon Islanders, attracted opprobrium that reflected above all else the unwholesome fears, insecurities, and pretensions in the colonial regime—as in all colonial regimes—from which Solomon Islands became independent in 1978.

13. Hector MacQuarrie (1889–1973): Traveller, writer, friend of Vouza

Hector is an honoured name. It was borne by the valiant defender of Troy who was slain by the Greek invader Achilles about 1,200 BC, and who is commemorated in the rousing marching song *British Grenadiers*:

> Some talk of Alexander, and some of Hercules,
> Of Hector and Lysander, and such great names as these.

Subsequently, it has become not uncommon among Scots surnamed MacQuarrie (with its orthographical variants). Such is scarcely surprising since a national hero named Hector MacQuarrie, from Ulva, near Iona, fought alongside Robert Bruce at the battle of Bannockburn in 1314 in expelling the English forces from Scotland.[1] While the currency of the name in the latter usage quite properly honours a celebrated clan chieftain, that does not help with distinguishing between particular Hectors MacQuarrie of more recent times. In the present instance, the problem was to identify, and trace the career of a Hector MacQuarrie from New Zealand who had served in World War I (for there were several such), had impaired health and who subsequently wrote a clutch of books, three of them relating to the Pacific.[2]

Resembling somewhat in style the works of P.G Wodehouse, these were characteristically racy, anecdotal, first-person-singular narratives in which the author offered accounts of his adventures and experiences, mostly in out-of-the-way places. They include an irritatingly enigmatic volume titled *Vouza and the Solomon Islands*.[3] His best known work, this book has little to say about Jacob Vouza (c. 1900–1984) and is scarcely informative about the Solomons, but, for its time, it was seductively titled and was widely read. It is an ephemeral piece, more a literary indulgence than a report that holds value as a source of solid historical information. But, given its own history and that of its author, it is significant as a stimulus to continuing enquiry into the Pacific past and into the literature pertaining to it (as if such were required!). In that regard MacQuarrie himself provides little of factual substance. He operates within the familiar literary genre of light nonfiction, in which he drops a few tantalising clues about himself personally, but not much precise information, and offers but

---

1 Charles MacKinnon, *The Scottish Highlanders: a personal view*, London, 1984, p. 215.
2 He is not to be confused, for instance, with, Hector Jarvie McQuarrie, born in Glasgow in 1893, and who enlisted in the New Zealand Expeditionary Force in 1914; or with Captain Hector McQuarrie who arrived in New Zealand on the *Favourite* in 1876! Note: Margaret Edgcumbe helped greatly in the research of Mc/MacQuarrie family history.
3 Hector MacQuarrie, *Vouza and the Solomon Islands*, London, 1945, Sydney, 1946, New York 1948.

meagre detail about time, place and other people. In 1934 his compatriot Robin Hyde referred to him as the 'well known New Zealand writer and traveller', but, unlike her, he has not found a firm place in the literary or historical consciousness of later generations.[4] He is not often cited in footnotes, and exists primarily as a bibliographical fact. But a reader may still be drawn by a title, and remain puzzled, and cheated, by the content.

Vouza and the Solomon Islands was first published in London in 1945, then in Sydney in 1946 and in New York in 1948. That is, it was published at a time when the Solomon Islands were still in the news as the site of one of the bitterest and most strategically significant campaigns of World War II. Also famous was the name of Jacob Vouza, a native Solomon Islander, from Koli village of the island of Guadalcanal, who endured bayoneting and being left for dead by the Japanese for refusing to answer questions about the strength and location of American forces, who had countered Japan's southward advance through the Pacific by landing at Guadalcanal on 8 August 1942.[5] Despite the title, though, the book has little to say about the Solomons. Rather it is an episodic memoir about MacQuarrie's brief sojourn in a remote part of the group as a colonial administration officer. The theme of the work is that MacQuarrie had been unfairly dismissed from his position for placing his sympathies for the Islanders ahead of the rulings of his superiors. In fact, a close reading supplemented by archival research shows that the book is also an act of revenge, sharpened by indignation at his colleagues' alleged disregard for his sense of personal and professional dignity. MacQuarrie says in a dedicatory epistle to Vouza, who had been lance-corporal in charge of the small police detachment serving him in the outlying eastern district of Santa Cruz:

> Now that the war is over, perhaps my people in Britain will say, 'We must now do much for the Solomons people. First we must send out a good lawyer, not a servant of the Resident Commissioner, to be the friend of the people when they are accused in court'.[6]

The two incidents that provoked MacQuarrie had occurred 20 years before, during his eight-month sojourn, from December 1924 to July 1925, as acting district officer at Santa Cruz. He had arrived in the Solomons in May 1924. After an uneventful spell on the island of Santa Ysabel and a visit to the atoll of Sikaiana (his scholarly report on which was published two decades later) he

---

4 Robin Hyde, *Journalism*, Auckland,1934, p. 173.
5 Colonial Office, *Among Those Present: the official story of the Islands in the Pacific War*, London, 1946, pp. 24–25; Eric Hammel, *Guadalcanal: Starvation Island*, New York, 1987, pp. 158, 165–166; Hugh Laracy (ed.), *Ples Blong Iumi: Solomon Islands, the past four thousand years*, Suva, 1989, pp. 26–27; Don Richter, *When the Sun Stood Still: the untold story of Sir Jacob Vouza and the Guadalcanalcampaign*, Calabasas, 1992.
6 MacQuarrie, *Vouza*, p. iv.

was transferred to the outlying Eastern District.[7] The first of these incidents concerned a Japanese trocus shell trader named Ito, whom MacQuarrie, holding a then not uncommon view of such nationals, believed to be a military spy. It happened that one evening, while MacQuarrie was chatting in his house with his neighbour, Captain Johnson of the Vanikoro Kauri Timber Company, Ito arrived, uninvited and with brandy-fuelled joviality, to discuss a small matter of business. His intrusion was unwelcome. MacQuarrie was especially dismayed by the fact that Johnson, 'who never failed to embarrass by a display of vast respect for my office' became 'less and less amused', thereby convincing his host that 'unless I now acted with befitting dignity I must prove myself to be quite unworthy to occupy the humblest governmental poop'. Accordingly, Ito was summarily expelled by MacQuarrie, with Johnson commenting that 'the British throne had been seriously undermined by the "the bloody cheek of a bloody Jap"'. From there the matter escalated. Ito wandered down to the native police lines and complained about MacQuarrie. He is reported to have said, in the Gare language of Guadalcanal, '*Tavia taja dou!*', literally 'The master is no good'. The next morning corporal Vouza and two companions laid a complaint about him. They were, wrote MacQuarrie in his book,

> In effect, issuing a challenge which, if ignored, might have endless repercussions not only on the station, but also throughout the vast district where my life amongst the untamed people on parts of Santa Cruz depended on the respect I could command.[8]

Earlier, in a letter to the High Commissioner in Fiji, he had spelled out more fully this dire interpretation of Ito's indiscretion:

> A Japanese trader, living for some time as the only trader throughout a vast and scattered district, and one not completely civilized, entered my police barracks and outraged the sensibilities of my fine loyal police by attacking the authority they respected. After very careful thought, based on my experience in this District [five months!] I stood by my police and sentenced him to six months imprisonment.

Then,

> Without apparent reference to the High Commissioner, without reference to the District court in Santa Cruz, the Resident Commissioner wired to me that I should release the Japanese, and later he informed me that he was permitted to trade as usual.

---

7 Ibid., pp. 8–24; Hector MacQuarrie, 'A Report on the Stewart Islands, Commonly Called 'Sikaiana', Western Pacific High Commission (WPHC) Archives, 4/iv, MP 2804/24; Hector MacQuarrie, 'Sikaiana or Stewart Islands', *Journal of the Polynesian Society*, vol. 61 (1952), pp. 209–222.
8 MacQuarrie, *Vouza*, pp. 81, 82, Chapter VI, 'Ito'.

In reply, in his Observations on those directions, MacQuarrie suggested that he:

> should be permitted to charge the Resident Commissioner with contempt of the High Commissioner's District Court.

Because, as he told the High Commissioner,

> As a Junior officer, with I think the odds against me, I cannot afford to give any quarter. I must therefore set about proving that the Resident Commissioner has little respect for the office of His Majesty's Deputy Commissioner. Incidentally, I am aware that any decision of any judge can be a mistaken one. I complain merely about the procedure in this incident.[9]

The second matter that provoked MacQuarrie concerned three men from the island of Utupua who were charged with murdering a newborn baby. One of them, Sam, had already been found liable in a deposition hearing by MacQuarrie's predecessor, C.E.J. Wilson, and the charge was upheld by the judicial commissioner at Tulagi. Then, in April 1925, the other two, Mobe and Niola, were apprehended and brought before MacQuarrie for depositions. After hearing evidence, and consulting the timber company's medical officer, MacQuarrie concluded,

> that no murder had been committed but that a 'non-viable' foetus had miscarried, perhaps of six months, and that the relations of the mother, Sam, Mobe and Niola, had buried it.[10]

There was still a possibility that they had smothered it (if only to confirm death?) before burying it, but that was of no account. MacQuarrie dismissed the charges, thereby implying that Sam's conviction had been unjustified, and despatched the papers to Tulagi. But to his disquiet he was subsequently informed that the latter decision was upheld, and that the other accused were to be similarly tried. His dissent in this matter was magnified by the fact that he had had come to know and like Mobe and Niola; and also that Vouza believed them to be innocent; and, above all, by his distrust of a markedly disreputable character named Johnny Mamuli from the Reef Islands who had acted as interpreter in Sam's trial.[11]

The upshot of these disputes was that in July 1925 MacQuarrie was posted to Makira District by the Resident Commissioner, R.R. Kane, and, when he refused

---

9 MacQuarrie to Hutson, 26 May 1925, MP 1689/25, WPHC 4/iv.
10 Ibid.; Santa Cruz District: Return of Criminal Cases for the year ended 30 September 1925, MP 769/1926, WPHC 4/iv.
11 Ibid.; MacQuarrie, *Vouza*, Chapter VII, 'Portrait of a Scoundrel', Chapter VIII, 'N'manga's Baby'; Moira Winifred Doherty, 'Post-Lapita developments in the Reef-Santa Cruz islands, southeast Solomon Islands', PhD thesis, University of Auckland, 2007, p. 544.

to accept the transfer, his appointment was terminated and he was directed to leave the Protectorate. His immediate reason for refusing was that he felt a responsibility to protect those he saw as innocent. 'I am not the first "crusader" in the Colonial Service to be shot out'.[12] But that was part of a larger sense of alienation from the Solomons administration itself. As he confessed:

> I might have blustered with a show of force; I could have been brutal; but there is no true power in either. My dismal failure as a D.O. is instantly demonstrated when I admit that I have not the glowing manliness which accepts respect as its due. I wanted to be loved, and that need crowded out even a suspicion of fear and never forbade laughter.[13]

The auguries of the estrangement, though, had appeared on his voyage to Santa Cruz in November 1924.

MacQuarrie had come to the Solomons from Fiji, where he had been private secretary to the governor, Sir Cecil Rodwell, and aide-de-camp, a post he shared with Ratu Sukuna.[14] This was a happy arrangement, but it had to come to an end when Rodwell left Fiji for British Guiana in January 1925, for MacQuarrie was on his personal staff, and did not hold an established position in the colonial administration. Hence, the posting to the Solomons was by way of a favour. But that soon turned sour on the government vessel *Ranadi*, en route from Tulagi to Santa Cruz. MacQuarrie was affronted not to have a cabin and to have to sleep on deck under an awning, together with two respectable fellow passengers, a director of a timber company and his brother, while the Resident Commissioner claimed the comfortable accommodation. There were two cabins, each with two berths, while two more berths could be made up in the dining room. The Resident Commissioner, however, claimed one of the cabins for himself and allocated the other to the wife and young son of the district officer, whom MacQuarrie was to replace, and use of the dining room was restricted to meals for himself and invited guests.[15]

On 26 May 1925 MacQuarrie wrote at length to the High Commissioner.

> I went on board an hour before the time of sailing and I was informed that there was no accommodation for me beyond that offered by the very defective awning on the after deck. Deciding that the laws of hospitality were being attended to and that the Director and his brother were being given the spare state room, I was not disturbed. To my astonishment I found the Director, his brother and the wireless man on the after deck

---

12   MacQuarrie, *Vouza*, p. 217.
13   Ibid., pp. 150–151.
14   Deryck Scarr, *Ratu Sukuna: soldier, statesman, man of Two Worlds*, London, 1980, pp. 41, 62, 74.
15   MacQuarrie, *Vouza*, pp. 25–31, Chapter III 'The *Ranadi*: Vouza'.

and they too, had been informed that there was no accommodation for them beyond stretchers on the after deck beneath the awning. There were no side screens. I thought it rather peculiar that the Director of a Company spending large sums to exploit the Protectorate's resources should be treated in this manner. Later, we were told that we would not dine in then ordinary dining room, but that we would use the mess room of the ship's company.

Just before the ship sailed the Resident Commissioner came on board accompanied by a lady, Mrs Wilson the wife of the officer I was about to relieve on Santa Cruz.

I want at once to dissociate myself from all the foul gossip permeating the slanderous air of the Solomons regarding this fine woman and the Resident Commissioner, but I cannot help thinking that the Resident Commissioner, in permitting a young married woman to travel with him alone with her small son in the Officer's Quarters of the ship might easily add fuel to the fire of gossip already existing. By defying the ordinary conventions, not only in doing this, but in allowing this lady to live with him at the residency unchaperoned, I consider that he showed grave contempt for this lady's fair name and that he brought Government authority into contempt.[16]

Two days later MacQuarrie wrote to Kane himself regarding his actions.

The Jap! You may be able to find fault with my treatment of the case, even the charge, but generally you could not survive your irregular release of him. Have me dismissed from the service and you will have won the first round; you won't win the second. Why are millions being spent on the Singapore base?

I am a Cambridge graduate, you know. We are represented in the Imperial Parliament. Not that I doubt His Excellency's ability to defend his officers—not for a second.

It's beastly having to mention Mrs Wilson. But who is to blame for that? But thank God, never in my life have I allowed myself to think evil of her.

And Wilson, of course you made him a D.O. You know as well as I do that while he is a good fellow, his education and training fit him for the Treasury. Can he survive the charge, that in a serious trial in which the life of a simple native was concerned, he used a convict of alleged

---

16   MacQuarrie to Hutson, 26 May 1925, WPHC 4/iv, MP 1689/25.

weak mind and one who was charged later with assault and battery and convicted, as an interpreter of a language which he only partially understood.

I wouldn't have attacked him in my letter to His Excellency except that I have an idea, perhaps a wrong one, that he advised you in this business.

Then the *Ranadi* business. You will wonder why I did not make a complaint at the time. How could I? Just imagine it. Although I found grave difficulty in not laughing at you when you were very cross about something—the whole ship knew that Mrs Wilson was in tears—and you strafed me saying 'I don't think you understand your position here'. It was so obvious that you did not.

I thought you understood that I am a D.O. merely because I am interested in being one. I thought you understood that I can assume at any time a position in the literary world, through years of hard work, infinitely superior to yours as a Resident Commissioner in the Solomons.

But in my case, how on earth did you think you could get away with the idea of putting a D.O. on the stern of a boat, while there was pleny of accommodation in the proper quarters. And even then a few nice words to Finlayson and myself would have made it all right. His majesty the king would have offered one of the beds in his own state room under such circumstances.

I am hoping to hear that you have resigned and that Wilson has immediately put in an application to be returned to the Treasury. In the event of my hearing that, I will wire officially to you cancelling my letter to His Excellency.

It is not only fair to warn you that there is not a chance in the world of my not winning this fight. Because I am right. My power, therefore, is infinite and invincible.[17]

Later, the Resident Commissioner sent his own commentary on MacQuarrie's complaints to the High Commissioner:

With reference to his treatment whilst travelling on HMCS *Ranadi* I can only remark that his statement that he was not offered the only available accommodation is untrue. There are but two cabins on HMCS *Ranadi* and a dining saloon in which there is a settee which can be used as a berth. I occupied my own cabin and the other was used by Mrs Wilson … . I personally suggested to Capt. MacQuarrie that he should make

---

17 MacQuarrie to Kane, 28 May 1925, MP 1689/25, WPHC 4/iv.

> use of the settee in the saloon but he said he would prefer a stretcher on deck. This did not strike me as unusual as quite a number of people do prefer sleeping on deck owing to the heat of the *Ranadi*'s cabins.
>
> As regards meals, it has always been customary for the Resident Commissioner to have a separate table: a higher messing rate is allowed for the R.C. mess charges are payable to the Master of HMCS *Ranadi* who makes all arrangements for meals.

On two occasions, Kane noted, he had asked MacQuarrie and the Finlayson's to dine with him, but en route he was also unwell and the weather was bad; so that was not often expedient.

Kane continues:

> As regards the accommodation provided for the two Finlayson's and their wireless operator this was in accordance with the terms under which they were granted passages on the *Ranadi*; I having pointed out that other arrangements could be made … .
>
> With regard to the innuendoes made by Capt MacQuarrie as to my relations with Mrs Wilson, I am unaware of any scandal which has been whispered or spread of any scandal. It is true that I am on terms of friendship with Mr and Mrs Wilson, stronger than with other families. I am also on terms of friendship with Mrs Wilson's mother, father and sisters, from whom I have received much hospitality whilst on furlough in Australia.[18]

Alienated from his own *wantoks* and with damaged sensibilities, MacQuarrie (who 20 years later would get a chance to air his grievances) was not surprisingly disposed to identify with the island people; and especially with the solid, reliable Vouza, whom he described in approvingly homoerotic terms.

> You could see that Vouza was a magnificent specimen of humanity … . His build had the grand simplicity of perfection … its warmth and beauty. He wore very little … merely a *lava-lava*. A black sash below his leather belt, with its shining crested buckle, marked his rank.
>
> There was nothing pretty-pretty about Vouza's face … . His mouth was large and generous. Perhaps it was his eyes, a little hard and uncompromising when he was not smiling, which offered a hint that

---

18   Kane to Hutson, 30 September 1925, MP 1689/25, WPHC 4/iv.

hardly more than a generation earlier his forebears were savages who might only live if they were strong and alert. Such was Lance–Corporal Vouza when I first met him on the beach at Pea[u].[19]

Subsequently, in 1937, Vouza retired from the police with the rank of sergeant-major (the highest rank for a Solomon Islander at that time) and, thus, he was to bring a notable level of authority and training to his work as a military scout. For that he was appropriately decorated by Britain and the United States. In 1951 the colonial regime appointed him its advisory council, in 1953 he visited London for the Coronation and, in 1979, he was awarded a knighthood.

Meanwhile, questions remain to be answered about who was this person who left behind a rich and beguiling paper trail in which so much else figures besides Vouza? For MacQuarrie had already experienced a life of marked variety before the Fiji/Solomons stage of his career—and continued to do so. He was born in Auckland in 1889, the seventh of the eight children of John MacQuarrie (ship's carpenter) and his wife Sarah (née McGeachey), who had arrived in New Zealand with their two eldest children on the *Famenoth* in September 1879. Hector was educated first at the local Parnell primary school.[20] Then (1904–1908) he was 'home-schooled' by a private tutor named Philip Ardern who, in 1910, after graduating from Oxford University was appointed to the fledgling Auckland University College, where he distinguished himself as a scholar of Anglo-Saxon and Middle English.[21] Meanwhile, responding to a religious call, and drifting from his familial Presbyterianism into the Anglican orbit, in 1909 Hector enrolled at the theological college of St John the Evangelist. It was a time, however, when the college was fraught with doctrinal disputes and he left the following year, although a severe dose of septic poisoning may also have induced him to do so.[22] Then, in 1911, assisted with funding from various sympathetic fellow parishioners, (notably a widow named Eva Laing), he enrolled at Cambridge University.[23] From there in June 1914 he graduated with a BA (2nd class) in History and Theology.[24]

Whatever his plans might have been at that point is unknown, but his immediate future was shaped by the outbreak of World War I. Hence, in August he enlisted in the 19th Hussars and, in October was commissioned in the Royal Field Artillery with the rank of 2nd lieutenant. Serving in France and Belgium, he suffered

---

19   MacQuarrie, *Vouza*, pp. 28–29.
20   Although 'modernised', the original family home still stands at 30 Bradford St.
21   Keith Sinclair, *A History of the University of Auckland, 1883–1983*, Auckland, 1983, pp. 63,77, 173.
22   Allan K. Davidson, *Selwyn's Legacy: the College of St. John the Evangelist, Te Waimate and Auckland, 1843–1992, a history*, Auckland, 1993, pp. 142, 336. Personal communications from Judith Bright (St. John's College Archives), 20, 22, June 2006.
23   Personal communication from Cathy Wagener (HM's 'grand-niece'), 19 November 2006.
24   Personal communications from Jacqueline Cox (University of Cambridge Archives), 20 June 2006; and from Harmony Lam (Gonville and Caius College Archives), 2 August 2006.

severely from exposure after spending considerable time in an observation post in Ypres, and in mid-1916 was invalided back to Britain. Then, in September of that year, he was despatched to the US to oversee the production of munitions for British forces at factories in Pennsylvania. Next, from November 1917 he was employed by the US Government as a lecturer, travelling from the Atlantic to the Pacific, explaining and justifying America's formal participation in the conflict since 28 February 1917.[25] The ardours of this task again brought on ill-health; so, in May 1918, he embarked for home, reaching Auckland in June.

Two books endure as relics of his American spell. The first, *How to Live at the Front: tips for American soldiers* was published in September 1917, and reprinted three times before the end of the year. It was designed to comfort soldiers and their parents by telling how the day-to-day realities of being under arms did not always mean being in immediate danger. Thus:

> The actual firing of a gun, the actual killing of the enemy is but one part of warfare. Everything else leads up to it and that everything, summed up in the words 'effective management', is most important.
>
> As for saluting: It is merely an exchange of courtesy … there is much in common between ranks. They are all soldiers … brothers in arms, so a greeting is necessary.

In so far as a grim warning was delivered, in the chapter titled 'A Curse of War' readers are advised of the danger of contracting venereal disease when on leave in London or Paris. They are also reminded of their historical kinship with their 'English cousins' and, in conclusion, urged to read the Bible. The second volume, *Over Here: impressions of America by a British officer*, appeared in April 1918. It is a commentary in chronological sequence of MacQuarrie's activities and travels since he arrived in New York in September 1916. Of the American declaration of war he remarks:

> Uncle Sam knows, of course, that like the United States, we are a democracy, a form of government which was never designed for making war outside its own council chamber.

To advance his return to good health and indulge his restlessness, within less than a month of his return to New Zealand MacQuarrie departed on a trip to Tahiti. Unfortunately, his time there, spent mostly cruising about the outer Tuamotu group, was cut short when on 16 November 1918 the *Navua*, a New Zealand-operated vessel coming from San Francisco introduced into Tahiti a share of the postwar influenza epidemic; a phenomenon which caused havoc in

---

25 See, generally, W.G. Lyddon, *British War Missions to the United States, 1914–1918*, London, 1938.

much of Polynesia, most notably in Samoa.[26] Nevertheless, the visit, which lasted six months, was sufficient to generate another book, *Tahiti Days*. Published in New York in 1920, it is largely a description of his travels.

Soon after arriving back in New Zealand on 25 December 1918, MacQuarrie became secretary to the war-blinded politician Clutha McKenzie. But, when the latter lost his seat in the December 1922 election, he was again unemployed. Estimable social connections (via church, university and the military), though, again came to his rescue. So it was that in April 1923 he was appointed to Rodwell's staff in Fiji. In addition he was appointed a lieutenant in the Fiji Defence Force and, in his role as aide-de-camp, was given the honorary rank of captain.[27] Meanwhile in November 1922 he had had the opportunity to become acquainted with the young Queen Salote of Tonga who was visiting New Zealand. Bolstered by this contact and by subsequent briefings, following her celebrated visit to England in 1953 he was able to write with engaging familiarity about Salote and Tonga in *Friendly Queen* (1955).[28]

Meanwhile, the collapse of the brief but portentous Fiji/Solomons venture had brought him back to New Zealand in September 1925. But only to usher in another adventuresome phase of MacQuarrie's life. The first episode was an attempt to build a tourist retreat named 'Pandora' at Spirits Bay on the northern tip of the North Island. There, in 1926, in partnership with Richard ('Dick') Matthews, a great-grandson of the early Anglican missionary Rev. Joseph Matthews (whose brother, Richard Matthews, a lay catechist, arrived on the *Beagle* with Charles Darwin in December 1835),[29] he built *raupo* (reed) huts, a cookhouse, sun-shelters with canvas roofs, rustic bridges and a dance hall with *raupo* walls and roofed with a shipwreck sail. Despite its beautiful site and abundant publicity, difficulties of access and an infestation of bugs, restrained patronage of the resort.[30] So, in 1927, MacQuarrie and the mechanically skilled Matthews sought another project. Their wanderlust was mounting and, through the agency of a friend in Auckland they were pleased to accept a commission from an automobile firm in Sydney (Larke, Hoskins and Co.) to publicise the newly introduced Austin Seven ('Baby Austin') and undertook to drive it up the east coast of Australia. Setting off in August from Sydney, they travelled easily

---

26 Colin Newbury, *Tahiti Nui: change and survival in French Polynesia, 1767–1945*, Honolulu, 1980, p. 270; J.W. Davidson, *Samoa mo Samoa: the emergence of the Independent State of Western Samoa*, Melbourne, 1967, p. 93.
27 *Fiji Times*, 14 April 1923.
28 *Auckland Star*, 8, 9, 11 November 1922; Hector MacQuarrie, *Friendly Queen*, London, 1955, pp. ix–xi, 88, 132, 153, 185; Elizabeth Wood-Ellem, *Queen Salote of Tonga: the story of an era, 1900–1965*, Auckland, 1999, pp. 238–246; Margaret Hixon, *Salote, Queen of Paradise: a biography*, pp. 142–151.
29 James Taylor, *The Voyage of the Beagle: Darwin's extraordinary adventure aboard Fitzroy's famous survey ship*, London, 2008, pp. 64, 67.
30 Personal communication, Malcolm Matthews, 26 August 2006; *The Northlander*, 12 January 1927, 7 March and 4 April 1928, 2 December 1932; Hyde, *Journalism*, p. 173; E.V. Sale, *Historic Trails of the Far North*, Wellington, 1981, p. 66.

to Brisbane, then on less well-developed roads to Cairns (where the narrative of *We and the Baby* begins) and up to Cooktown, where the road finished. From there they drove through the bush, following the telegraph line for the next 960 kilometres to Cape York. They reached there on 31 October, the first motorists to have reached that point. They then crossed over to Thursday Island, where they sold the car; and then went on to Papua, intending to explore the Fly River. But bouts of sunstroke-induced sickness soon sent them southwards. The book of the trip, *We and the Baby*, was first published in Sydney in 1929, then (retitled *Little Wheels*), in London in 1935.

So successful had been the publicity generated by the expedition, that the sponsors suggested another, and even more ambitious one. To wit, to drive a car of the same model around the world. Thus, after leaving Sydney in May 1930 and spending two months motoring around New Zealand, on 12 August they left Wellington in the *Tahiti*, bound for San Francisco via Rarotonga and Pape'ete. Five days later, however, the vessel sprang a fatal leak and sank, but without loss of life. The rescued passengers and crew reached Auckland on the *Tofua* from Samoa on 3 September.[31] MacQuarrie and Matthews, however, had taken abundant photographs of the disaster and within a week these had been crafted into a film for cinema viewing by the pioneering producer Rudall Hayward.[32] The local Austin agent (Seabrook, Fowlds) acted with comparable despatch and, on 9 September, the pair left Wellington for San Francisco in the *Makura* with a replacement vehicle.[33] The journey took them across the United States to New York, then to England, France, Italy, the Middle East, India and to to Singapore, from where they reached Darwin by mid-July; and then, in the *Maunganui*, from Sydney to Auckland, where they arrived on 8 September 1931.[34] As before, newspapers in Australia and New Zealand generously published MacQuarrie's reports of the trip,[35] and these became the basis of the book *Round the World in a Baby Austin* which was published in London in 1933.

With that behind him, MacQuarrie then shifted permanently to England, where he died in 1973.[36] There, with a flat in London and a country cottage at Meadle, near Cambridge, he worked first as a publisher's reader and then, during the 1940s and 1950s, as agent for the Australian publishers Angus and Robertson, but without neglecting his own writing. Socially, he fitted easily into an artistically creative (and extensively homosexual) sub-tribe of expatriate 'colonials'; for instance, Rex Nan Kivell, D'Arcy Cresswell and Hector Bolitho, who was himself

---

31 *NZ Herald*, 4 September 1930; MacQuarrie, *Round the World in a Baby Austin*, London, 1933, pp. 13–63.
32 *NZ Herald*, 9 September 1930. Copies of the films 'The Sinking of the *Tahiti*' (F32965) and 'Around the World in an Austin Seven' (F32964) are in the New Zealand Film Archive, Wellington. *NZ Herald*, 26 May 2007.
33 MacQuarrie, *Round the World*, pp. 63–65.
34 *NZ Herald*, 9 September 1931.
35 *Sydney Morning Herald, Sydney Mail, New Zealand Herald*.
36 Died 2 October 1973 in Deal, County Kent; buried at Deal. *The Times*, 4 October 1973, p. 44.

acquainted with the Pacific.[37] The first notable literary product of this last phase of MacQuarrie's career was *Front to Back* (London 1941), an account of his life in England and of behind-the-lines experience of the approach and impact of World War II. Other works were volumes of children's stories, under the *nom de plume* 'Hector Cameron' and, of course, *Salote* and *Vouza*. Mention of the latter, though, serves as a reminder that MacQuarrie's memorial is not only to be found in tomes on library shelves, but that something of his influence may also have contributed to the political development of the Solomon Islands. For Vouza emerged as a supporter of the anti-colonial nationalist movement, Maasina Rule, which in 1950 prompted the British Protectorate administration to allow for indigenous representation on its Advisory Council, a stepping stone to independence in 1978. Vouza was one of the first four appointed, and served until 1960.[38]

In an analysis of Vouza's career, in 1947 an official, who had known him since 1923, attributed his lack of colonial servility to his encounter with MacQuarrie. Arriving at Santo Cruz, 'impressionistic, idealistic, arty crafty' and 'not in the least practical' the latter was much impressed by Vouza's complete grasp of any situation that arose'. Thus:

> at an important stage in his career Vouza was in close association with a European officer who was dominated by him, and this was at a time when the whole prestige of Government, indeed of the European race, sprang from the dominance of the individual European. [Eventually a situation arose in which] MacQuarrie was honestly convinced that a grave injustice to two Santa Cruz men was contemplated by the Government. There was no truth in this, but MacQuarrie believed otherwise, and his idealism lead him to discuss the matter with Vouza. Probably for the first time in Solomons history a European spoke in derogatory terms of (a) other Europeans and (b) the Government to a native of the Protectorate, and invited comment. MacQuarrie's idealism caused him to refuse to obey the Resident Commissioner's orders, and he was dismissed from the service. ... There is little doubt that Vouza had a sincere affection for MacQuarrie as he served him well at great personal risk to himself. MacQuarrie left the Solomons leaving in Vouza's mind the conviction

---

37 Hector Bolitho, *The Islands of Wonder: Fiji, Samoa, Tonga*, Auckland, 1920; Susan Shortridge (ed.), *Paradise Possessed: the Rex Nan Kivell Collection*, Canberra, 1998, pp. 19, 25: Helen Shaw (ed.), *The Letters of D'Arcy Cresswell*, Christchurch, 1971, pp. 134, 135; Vincent O'Sullivan, *Long Journey to the Border: a life of John Mulgan*, Auckland, 2003, pp. 99, 103, 109, 117; Matt Houlbrook, *Queer London: perils and pleasures in the sexual metropolis, 1918–1957*, Chicago, 2005; *The Times*, 29 May 1935. Creswell and Bolitho are also mentioned in Chris Brickell, *Mates and Lovers: a history of gay New Zealand*, Auckland, 2008, pp. 109, 115–118.

38 Hugh Laracy (ed.), *Pacific Protest: the Maasina Rule movement in the Solomon Islands,1944–1952*, Suva, 1983, pp. 6, 22; Judith A. Bennett, *Wealth of the Solomons: a history of a Pacific archipelago, 1800–1970*, Honolulu, 1987, pp. 305–306; Peter Kenilorea, *Tell It As It Is: autobiography of Rt. Hon. Sir Peter Kenilorea, KBE, PC, Solomon Islands' first Prime Minister*, Taipei, 2008, p. 488.

that he had been dismissed and persecuted by the Government for his attempt to champion the cause of two native men. ... Later MacQuarrie wrote a book dedicated to this incident, and he sent a copy to Vouza.[39]

In the light of the above comments it may not, therefore, be unduly fanciful to suspect that somewhere about the statue of Vouza that stands outside the Central Police Headquarters in the national capital Honiara the ghost of one Captain *Makuari* could well be hovering. Indeed, Sir Peter Kenilorea, the first Prime Minister of Solomon Islands might even be inclined to agree, as suggested by the laudatory recollections of Vouza that he included in his memoir.[40]

Appendix

Books by Hector MacQuarrie

How to Live at the Front: tips for American soldiers, Philadelphia and London, 1917.

Over Here: impressions of America, Philadelphia and London, 1918.

Tahiti Days, New York, 1920.

We and the Baby, Sydney, 1930; (also published as *Little Wheels: the record of a trip across Australia in a Baby Austin*, 1935).

Round the World in a Baby Austin, London, 1933.

Front to Back, London, 1941.

Vouza and the Solomon Islands, Sydney, 1945.

Friendly Queen, London, 1955.

---

39 S.G. Masterman, 'Memorandum [re Vouza]', 16 July 1947, C 173, WPHC 4/iv.
40 Kenilorea, *Tell It As It Is*, pp. 40–41.

14. Patrick O'Reilly (1900–1988): Bibliographer of the Pacific[1]

In 1989 the *Journal de la Société des Océanistes* published a set of four laudatory testimonials in honour of Patrick O'Reilly who had died in Paris on 6 August 1988 at the age of 88. He had been secretary-general of the *Société* from 1944 to 1973. Several years earlier, in 1982, it had also dedicated a double issue of the *Journal* to him.[2] These were both well-deserved tributes. They honoured a man whose scholarly labours—and allegedly 'dictatorial' management style—had helped make the *Société* (from its inception a more academically professional operation than its closest analogue, the Polynesian Society of New Zealand) a major force in the nascent area of systematic Pacific studies; and who, through his assiduity in locating and listing published source materials had, arguably, been one of the two main founders of the post–World War II speciality of Pacific history.[3] He cleared so much of the ground for later researchers. The other one of the pair was J.W. Davidson, a protégé of J.C. Beaglehole and Raymond Firth. From 1951 to 1973, with the considerable resources of The Australian National University behind him, Davidson presided over a uniquely dedicated department of Pacific History. That is, one which was designed to train post-graduate specialists in that field (the flow of whom began to trickle forth in 1957), and which has generated a corpus of monographs that continues to underpin what has become a thriving scholarly enterprise.[4]

Warm as they were, though, the tributes to O'Reilly were anomalously incomplete. The items directly concerned with him were rhetorical effusions, fervently appreciative but vacuously generalised. His life was not chronicled, nor, and this seems especially odd in respect of someone whose bibliographies were invaluable tools within a significant academic discipline, were his own publications listed in the *Journal*. Admittedly, in 1988, the *Société d'Etudes Historiques de la Nouvelle-Calédonie* published an extensive list (234 items) of his Pacific writings.[5] But by not garnering his numerous non-Pacific writings,

---

1   This title echoes the dedication in Colin Newbury, *Tahiti Nui: change and survival in French Polynesia, 1767–1945* (Honolulu: University of Hawai'i, 1980), p. x.
2   *Journal de la Société des Océanistes* (JSO), vol. 38 (1982), pp. 88–89 (1989), pp. 119–127.
3   Sonia Faessel, *Itinéraires Insulaires: le père Patrick O'Reilly, sm*, Nouméa: Le Rocher-à-la Voile, 2002, pp. 71, 81. For a history of the Polynesian Society, founded in 1892, but which came under university auspices only in 1954, see M.P.K. Sorrenson, *Manifest Duty: the Polynesian Society over 100 years* (Auckland: Polynesian Society, 1992).
4   Donald Denoon, 'Pacific Island history at the Australian National University: the place and the people', *Journal of Pacific History*, vol. 31, no. 2 (1996), pp. 202–214. A biography of Davidson is currently being written by Dr Doug Munro (Wellington).
5   Serge Kakou, 'L'Oeuvre du Père O'Reilly', *Société d'Etudes de la Nouvelle-Calédonie*, Bulletin 77 (1988), pp. 7–24.

it could not serve as a definitive memorial to his literary labours. Also, by arranging its contents according to the various islands with which his writings dealt, instead of year by year, it does not present him, as Robert Langdon admiringly observed in 1971, as being 'prodigiously energetic'.[6] That task was eventually accomplished, only in 2002, by the present writer, with a list of 311 items published between 1925 and 1986. This was appended to Sonia Faessel's artfully contrived biography of O'Reilly, a book in which style tends to obscure substance, although with some effort most of the essential information can be distilled from it.[7]

The list, though, is clear. It illustrates not only a steady rate of productivity, but a broad pattern of evolution within O'Reilly's outlook and output. It begins with essays on Catholic local history within France, then moves in the 1930s to solidly researched studies of French religious activity in the Pacific. Most of these were published in the *Revue d'Histoire des Missions*, a journal founded in 1924 by the priest–author J-B. Piolot and the Academician Georges Goyau, both of whom were later associates of O'Reilly. Goyau was a distinguished historian who, mindful of traditional links between Church and society, had a particular concern for reducing the gap in mutual sympathy, and in regard for complementary achievement, that had so markedly alienated Catholicism from French national sentiment since the Revolution of 1789.

From the mid-1930s, items concerning the Solomon Islands, and some showing an ethnographic interest also, begin to appear on the publications list, where they were joined in 1940 and 1942 by books about two of O'Reilly's friends from a Parisian Left Bank literary and bibliophile circle in which he moved. For a decade from the late 1940s, New Caledonia, New Hebrides and Fiji feature prominently in his writings while, from the late 1950s, French Polynesia becomes increasingly conspicuous. All the while he was also producing bibliographies. The first of these, relating to the Marist missions and ranging from the Solomons to Samoa, appeared in 1932. From 1946 to 1963 he published in the *Journal de la Société des Océanistes* annual bibliographies, ranging variously from 30 to 60 pages in length, of writings on the Pacific. During that time he was also working on a volume of bibliography, preceded by an associated dictionary of biography, styled a bio-bibliography, for each of the French territories. These appeared for New Caledonia in 1953 and 1955, New Hebrides in 1957 and 1958, Wallis and Futuna (bibliography only) in 1964, and French Polynesia in 1962 and 1967, the last volume running to over 1,000 pages.

---

6   Robert Langdon, 'Subject Survey: institutional resources', in Australian National Advisory Committee for UNESCO, *Meeting on Studies of Oceanic Cultures*, Canberra, 1971, p. 225.
7   Hugh Laracy, 'Bibliographie des Ecrits du Père O'Reilly', in Faessel, *Itinéraires Insulaires*, pp. 159–179.

'By his works you shall know him'. Not quite. For the question still remains, what else was there to O'Reilly? Where had he come from? Who was this man who was acquainted with and respected by so many of the band of Pacific historians that began emerging in the 1950s? Not least among them John Dunmore who, in his book (1981) on de Surville's expedition, acknowledges 'the encouragement and help over the years [that] has been received from Father O'Reilly of the Société des Océanistes'.[8] This paper is intended to supply an answer.

Patrick O'Reilly (pronounced with a soft 'O', an equal stress on all syllables, and a slight ellision of the 'll's) was, as his name suggests, of Irish ancestry. That forebear was James (subsequently 'Jacques') Farell O'Reilly of Cork, the son of an Irish sea-captain, and who migrated to Le Havre in 1771 (at the age of about 13) in order, so family tradition has it, to escape religious oppression. If so, as the history of Irish migration to France from the late seventeenth century indicates, he was one among many. But that is another, and very long, story.[9] At Le Havre, James found employment with a merchant named Grégoire and demonstrated such an aptitude for business that in 1784 he set up his own firm, O'Reilly et Cie. It prospered, and continued to do so under his son, Philippe-André. Laurent, the latter's son, though, preferred a career as a military officer. In 1891, after service in North Africa, he married Jeanne Gautier, the daughter of a wealthy merchant. Patrick, the second of their four children, was born in the garrison town Saint-Mihiel (Meuse) in northern France on 19 May 1900. But his father's promising career was cut short in 1906 when, rather than submit to the law of Separation of Church and State (passed in 1905), which could oblige soldiers to act contrary to their religious opinions, Laurent resigned his commission and retired to the family estate in Normandy. Still a patriot, though, he returned to the colours when war broke out with Germany in 1914, and was killed three weeks after the outbreak of hostilities.[10]

Meanwhile, after attending boarding schools in Normandy, Patrick came to Paris in November 1918 to study at the Sorbonne, intending to enrol at the Ecole des Chartes. There he stayed at a hostel, the *'Réunion des Etudiants'*, run by the Marist Fathers (Society of Mary) at 104 Rue de Vaugirard, not far from the site (now no. 72) where 95 Carmelite monks were murdered by Revolutionaries on 2 September 1792.[11] But a year later he enlisted for a term

---

8   John Dunmore (ed.), *The Expedition of the 'St Jean-Baptiste' to the Pacific, 1769–1770: from the journals of Jean de Surville and Guillaume* Labé, London, 1981, p. x.
9   Tim Pat Coogan, *Wherever the Green is Worn: the story of the Irish diaspora*, London, 2000, pp. 1–48; James O'Boyle, *The Irish Colleges on the Continent*, Dublin, 1935; John Cornelius O'Callaghan, *History of the Irish Brigades in the Service of France, from the Revolution in Great Britain and Ireland under James II, to the Revolution in France under Louis XVI*, Glasgow, 1870.
10 Family history is recorded in Patrick O'Reilly, *Notices biographiques sur les O'Reilly, descendants normands de Jacques Farell O'Reilly, 1755–1825, Irlandais de Cork* (Paris, 1969); and, *Notices biographiques sur les descendants havrais de Jean Michel Gautier, 1802–1902, originaire de Serrières en Ardeche* (Paris, 1972).
11 J. Verdier, *Les Carmes: les lieux, les martyrs, les souvenirs*, Paris, 1953, pp. 27, 40.

of military service (1920–1922). On completion of that, instead of returning to university, he entered the novitiate of the Marists at La Neylière, near Lyon. He took his vows of membership there in December 1922. Then came six years of study at the Marist seminary at Differt in Belgium, culminating in ordination to the priesthood on 25 February 1928. Apart from his acquaintance with them at '104', O'Reilly's joining the Marists probably derived also from the convergence of two persuasive influences: that of a youthful, romantic attraction towards the tropics, together with an awareness of the missionary work of that congregation, which had initiated the Catholic evangelisation of the islands of the western Pacific in 1837. One of his early school friends, Gilbert Vieillard, about whose life he would later write, became a missionary in Africa.[12] As for O'Reilly himself, health problems seem to have barred him from joining various of his seminary classmates in following the wake of Bishop Pompallier to the Pacific, but his intellectual avocations shaped a complementary career.[13]

In 1931, following three years of school and parish work he was appointed chaplain at '104'. Founded in 1895 to provide assistance and religious guidance for pupils from Marist colleges coming to Paris for higher study, this had quickly became an elite institution with a vigorous intellectual life. Under Alphonse Plazenet, who became director in 1897, it expanded and was soon receiving students from all over France, drawn to study at Saint-Cyr, the Polytechnique, the Faculté de Droit and others of the Grandes Ecoles that constituted the University of Paris. Many of its inmates moved on to notable careers.[14] François Mauriac the Nobel Prize-winning novelist and the philosopher Jean Guitton, both of them later Academicians, and who both retained their close links with the place, had preceded O'Reilly there.[15] In 1963 Guitton became the first layman to address a modern ecumenical council (Vatican II).[16] Among those who came to '104' after O'Reilly, but with whom he became well acquainted, were François Mitterand, student president in 1935 and later president of the Republic (1981–1995), and Edouard Balladur, a minister of economy and finance, and eventually prime minister (1993–1995). Early literary and political writings of Mitterand were published, under O'Reilly's editorship, in *Revue Montalembert*. This was a

---

12 Patrick O'Reilly, *Mon Ami Gilbert l'Africain*, Dijon, 1942.
13 'O'Reilly', personal file, Archivio Padri Maristi, Rome; Patrick O'Reilly, 'Chronique de la Reunion: le père Thoral', *Revue Montalembert* (*RM*), nouvelle serie no. 2 (1962), pp. 144–147. Biographical sources also include Faessel, *Itinéraires Insulaires*, and two useful obituaries in *La Dépeche*, 12 August 1988, and *Le Semeur Tahitien* 28 August 1988.
14 Patrick O'Reilly, 'Les enfances auvergnates d'un anecdotier', 'Le Père Plazenet à la Réunion des Etudiants', and 'Les derniers jours du Père Plazenet', *RM*, no. 263 (1944), pp. 1–11, 13–33, 101–106.
15 *RM*, nouvelle serie, no. 2 (1962), pp. 1, 101–108; no. 4–5 (1963), pp. 325–338.
16 Patrick O'Reilly, 'Portrait de M. Guitton', *RM*, no. 4–5 (1963), pp. 37–40; Xavier Rynne, *The Second Session; the debates and decrees of Vatican Council II*, New York, 1964, p. 291; and, *The Third Session ...*, New York, 1965, p. 83.

monthly journal published at '104' since 1908. In its title it honoured the memory of a nineteenth century proponent of reconciliation between Catholicism and political liberalism in France, a disciple of Lamennais.[17]

Residence at '104' also made it possible for O'Reilly to finish his own academic studies. These had come to centre on the *Institut d'Ethnologie* (within the *Ecole Pratique des Haute Etudes*) and its founder Marcel Mauss, who had been a protégé of Emile Durkheim (his uncle), and both of whom were seminal contributors to advances in the scientific examination of human society. In 1932 O'Reilly obtained his *Licence ès lettres* and the diploma of the *Institut*. While there he also became friendly with another set of people, enthusiasts who shared his Pacific interests. One such was André Ropiteau, whose biography he would later write. Ropiteau had in 1926 embarked on a four-year long voyage around the world in his yacht, in an escapist quest for natural innocence and simplicity. This he found, according to his lights, and the romantic vision of the novelist Pierre Loti, on the island of Maupiti in French Polynesia, where he stayed for two years. Ropiteau was killed in action early in 1940, but he bequeathed his extensive library of writings on Tahiti to O'Reilly, who made it the basis of a notable collection of his own, and the key source for a massive bibliography.[18]

Buoyed by his new professional status, O'Reilly then became involved in the developing field of missiology, a form of applied ethnology. To this end he was among the founders of the quarterly journal *Etudes Missionnaires*, which commenced publication in 1933. Unlike the *Revue d'Histoire des Missions*, which 'is concerned with the past and seeks to integrate mission history with national and world history', *Etudes Missionnaires* was concerned with 'the actual conditions of spreading the Gospel, the diversity of needs and methods, the relations between missionaries and other agents such as governments and philanthropic associations, and the implications of international affairs'.[19] Meanwhile, he had also come to the notice of Paul Rivet, director of the *Musée d'Ethnologie du Trocadéro*, located near the Eiffel Tower.

In March 1934, at Rivet's behest, with the approval of his Marist superiors, and with a grant from the *Centre National de la Recherche Scientifique* to cover costs, he was despatched for a year to Australian New Guinea, to the island

---

17 E.E.Y. Hales, *The Catholic Church in the Modern World: a survey from the French Revolution to the present*, (New York, 1960, pp. 127–129; Jean Lacouture, *Mitterand: une histoire de France*, I, Paris, 1998, pp. 23–36. Francois Mitterand, 'De Quelques Livres: un cours sur Victor Hugo a la Sorbonne', *RM*, no. 231 (1936), pp. 684–686, 692–694; '"Les Anges Noirs": livre d'esperance', *RM*, no. 232 (1936), pp. 54–59; 'Les Géants fragiles', *RM*, no. 245 (1938), pp. 9–12; '"Jusqu'ici et pas plus loin"', *RM*, no. 248 (1938), pp. 144–147.
18 Patrick O'Reilly, *Portrait d'Andre Ropiteau, 1904–1940*, Dijon, 1940; new edition *Vignes, Voyages, Vahines ou le Bonheur de Maupiti*, Paris, 1950); JSO, 1 (1945), pp. 5–7.
19 Patrick O'Reilly, 'Pourquoi ces études'?, *Etudes Missionaires*, no. 1 (1933), pp. 1–3.

of Bougainville, where the Marists were strongly entrenched.[20] The object of the expedition was to collect artefacts for the museum, to record traditions, to describe local customs, and to make a film about them. These ends were all substantially met, especially the first (he collected 4,000 items), but Rivet was deeply chagrined when O'Reilly never produced the doctoral thesis or the major monograph that his harvesting was also expected to yield.[21] Still, he did save much that would otherwise have been lost, as was particularly the case with missionary papers. In 1901 the Marists became the first permanent European residents of Bougainville and, by 1935, their manuscript letters, journals, memoirs and ethnographic notes constituted an unparalled archival record of the history and culture of the island. In the hope of writing a history of the mission, O'Reilly took them all back to France with him. Again the promised book never appeared, but the predation was soon to be justified by events. Bougainville was devastated by heavy fighting during World War II. Had O'Reilly not acted as he did, and so endowed later enquirers with access to unique documents (as he did when my wife Eugénie and I worked with him at '104' for six weeks in 1967), much of the prewar history of Bougainville would not only have remained unknown, it would have been rendered unknowable.[22]

That O'Reilly so disappointed Rivet is probably not unconnected with the fact that, on returning to Paris in October 1935, he was appointed to succeed Plazenet as director of '104'. Here he continued to write articles but the duties of the post and his obligations as a Marist were impediments to accepting additional scholarly responsibilities, especially if, as seems likely, Rivet had been grooming him for a professional position in the new *Musée de l'Homme*, as the *Musée d'Ethnologie du Trocadéro*, which had less socially contextualised displays, was reconstituted in 1937.

The outbreak of World War II in 1939 and the German occupation of Paris in 1940 further distracted him from concentrating on a major project, but it seems, in any case, that by temperament he was more disposed to the busyness of ordering and organising than to the solitary ruminations of the grand synthesiser. Still, O'Reilly did maintain a close association with Rivet. During the war years he put considerable effort into reorganising the Pacific exhibits of the *Musée*, and was involved in discussions, especially with Maurice Leenhardt, a former Protestant missionary in New Caledonia (1902–1926) and, in 1940, Mauss's successor at the *Institut d'Ethnologie*, on the better ordering of Pacific studies in France. In 1936 a group of enthusiasts, organised by two people who

---

20 He was out of France from March 1934 to October 1935, and in Melanesia from June 1934 to July 1935. For Bougainville, see Hugh Laracy, *Marists and Melanesians: a history of Catholic missions in the Solomon Islands* (Canberra: Australian National University, 1976).
21 Faessel, *Itineraires Insulaires*, pp. 45–53, 151.
22 Witness to O'Reilly's 'rescue operation' is given in my contributions to Anthony Regan and Helga Griffin (eds), *Bougainville Before the Conflict*, Canberra, 2005, pp. 123–4, 163.

had had professional experience in the Pacific, Louis Marin and Leon Sasportas, and which included several noted scholars such as Peter Buck, Fritz Sarasin and Felix Speiser formed the *Société des Océanistes*, and established a bulletin to publish its proceedings. Later, in 1939, within his new *Musée de l'Homme*, Rivet organised a less formal association known as the *Groupe d'Etudes Océaniennes*. Clearly such a division of energy and resources was wasteful. O'Reilly and Leenhardt, accordingly, made it their business to amalgamate the two bodies, which occurred at a meeting on 22 December 1944, not long after the liberation of Paris. Like the *Groupe*, the new organisation was an adjunct of the *Musée*, but, in a diplomatic concession to the Marin–Sasportas party, it adopted the name *Société des Océanistes*.[23] Leenhardt was elected president and O'Reilly secretary-general. In this post, he was not only principal editor of the *Journal* from 1946 (volume 2), but also director of the *Société*'s publication series, the first item of which appeared in 1951; and contributed prolifically to both. Indeed, the *Journal* came to be funded largely from the profits made on the sale of his other publications.[24]

Extensive as it was, O'Reilly's work with the *Société des Océanistes* did not limit his religious activity. Indeed, insofar as from its beginning in 1946 to its demise in 1967 he was intimately involved with *Missions des Iles*, a popular journal issued monthly by the Marists to publicise their Pacific missions, the two were complementary. That was especially the case after 1951, when he gave up the directorship of '104', although he continued to reside there. When he was in Paris, that is. For in the post–World War II decades he was to make several return visits to the Pacific. The first of these was to Fiji, New Hebrides and New Caledonia in 1948–1949. Particular fruits of this trip, ones combining his interest in the finer points of book production and typography with an appreciation of the importance of the written word in establishing Christianity in the Pacific—a point later expounded by the historian G.S. Parsonson in a classic article titled 'The Literate Revolution in Polynesia'[25]—were detailed bibliographies that listed and described the imprints of the Catholic mission presses in New Caledonia and Fiji (forerunners of similar works on the Solomon Islands and Samoa). But there was much more. Among other results in an outburst of eclectic fecundity, were comments on current developments, including the first extended published account of the Jonfrum cult, a religious–political movement that was challenging European authority on Tanna in the New Hebrides.[26]

Meanwhile, publications based on other phases of research and rumination were also appearing. These included, in 1948, *Pirogues au Vert-Galant*, an elegantly

---

23 *Bulletin de la Société des Océanistes*, no. I (1937), p. 6; JSO, no. I (1945), p. 1.
24 Faessel, *Itinéraires Insulaires*, p. 154.
25 *The Journal of Pacific History*, vol. 3 (1967), pp. 39–58.
26 Patrick O'Reilly, 'Jonfrum is a new Hebridean *cargo cult*', *Pacific Islands Monthly*, vol. 20, no. 6–7 (January and February 1950), pp. 67–70, 59–65.

written and produced essay on 'souvenirs' of the Pacific to be found in the streets and cemeteries of Paris, which he had explored during the four years of German occupation; and, in 1949, a book on the wartime experiences of his Marist confrères in Japanese-occupied Bougainville, written in collaboration with Jean-Marie Sédès.[27] O'Reilly, as his publication list shows, was a vigorous recruiter of 'collaborators'. Then, in the late 1950s, with his main New Caledonia and New Hebrides work behind him, his attention was drawn increasingly eastwards, and found a new and enduring expression there. In 1959, resuming the mantle of ethnologist, he was commissioned by UNESCO to report on the existence of, and prospects for, museums in the Pacific. No ascertainable material results issued from this undertaking, but it was a happy portent. In 1963 the Singer-Polignac foundation, a philanthropic trust, hired him to design and organise a museum at Tahiti dedicated to the painter Paul Gauguin. Given Gauguin's irreligion and his dissolute ways, it could be seen as an ironical task for a priest to accept, but that France might draw glory from his achievement was a more pertinent—and persuasive—fact to O'Reilly. The museum, located near Pape'ete, where Gauguin had lived in the 1890s, was duly opened in 1965. With that completed, O'Reilly turned his attention to building a museum at La Neylière to commemmorate Jean-Claude Colin, the founder of the Marists. This was extended in 1969 into a mission museum, illustrating the history and work of the Society of Mary in the islands of the Pacific.[28] O'Reilly made his last major visit to the Pacific in 1971, to attend an important UNESCO-sponsored conference on source materials for Pacific studies held at The Australian National University. At the end of it he undertook an extensive tour, visiting many of his haunts of former years; his journal of which has been edited for publication by Jean Guiart.[29]

From a survey of the life and works of O'Reilly a clear theme emerges. That is that for him, through the medium of Pacific studies, being Catholic fused with being French. In writing on the Pacific, O'Reilly was both reporting on and celebrating the French presence there. After all, that presence was a given, and his particular imperative, as it was for the bibliophile Ropiteau, was to ensure—and preserve—its knowability, rather than to engage in criticisms or to indulge in misgivings about it. Monocultural his oeuvre may have been, although he did write on a Marist who had founded seminaries and organised an indigenous development program in New Caledonia, and on indigenous artists and on traditional myths. But that characteristic did not diminish its empirical value; other dimensions of the subject could be studied by others. O'Reilly's task was to record the French imperial/colonial enterprise in the Pacific, not to review

---

27 Patrick O'Reilly, *Pirogues au Vert-Galant: souvenirs océaniens de Paris*, Paris, 1948; Patrick O'Reilly and Jean-Marie Sédès, *Jaunes, Noirs et Blancs: trois années de guerre aux Iles Salomon*, Paris, 1949.
28 Faessel, *Itinéraires Insulaires*, pp. 73–81; Kakou, 'L'Oeuvre du père O'Reilly', p. 7.
29 Patrick O'Reilly, *Carnet de Route Oceanién* (ed. Jean Guiart), Nouméa and Papeéte, 2012.

it. At the same time he was concerned to highlight, as an integral part of it, the participation in and contribution to that enterprise of Catholic missionaries. In them piety combined with patriotism. Moreover, they were additionally estimable because they also extended the range of French achievement well beyond the French Pacific as a politically defined entity.

Consonant with such an outlook, indeed, logically following from it, O'Reilly, a cleric who consorted with admirals, artists, antiquarian booksellers, anthropologists, administrators, restaurateurs, and historians, never obscured the fact that he was a Catholic priest. He was rarely seen without his clerical collar; his regular street dress was a soutane and a round, flat-brimmed Roman hat (which gave him the appearance of an eighteenth century abbé) and he was customarily known as 'Père O'Reilly'. But '104' was not allowed in any way to subvert the Museé de l'Homme. The anthropologist Jean Guiart, a protégé of Leenhardt and later a colleague of O'Reilly, has confessed that in 1945 he and Leenhardt feared that O'Reilly might turn the *Journal de la Société des Océanistes* into a missionary propaganda organ.[30] They need not have worried. For O'Reilly piety and patriotism, *l'eglise* and *la patrie*, were to be linked by mutual respect and acceptance rather than by the scourges of internecine competition, hostility and partisanship, out of which the Marists had been born in 1836, and which remained prevalent until the 1920s.[31]

Finally, regardless of anything else O'Reilly's legacy endures. Indeed, in accord with the Latin maxim *scripta manent, verba volent* ('the written word remains, the spoken word flies away') his guides to source materials should permanently endorse his status as a patron of 'Pacific History'.

---

30   Faessel, *Itinéraires Insulaires*, p. 153.
31   Donal A. Kerr, *Jean-Claude Colin, Marist: a founder in an era of revolution and restoration: the early years, 1790–1836*, Dublin, 2000; Hugh Laracy, 'Saint-Making: the case of Pierre Chanel of Futuna', *New Zealand Journal of History*, vol. 34, no. 1 (2000), pp. 145–161.

Index

References to people, places or other items that are scattered through parts of particular essays are contained within the pages followed by *passim*.

Agassiz, Louis, 71
Allan, Sir Colin, 228
Allen, Ernest Frederick Hughes, ix, x, 127-39 *passim*
Allen, Ernest Tanumafili 'Joe', 130-1
Allen family, 134-8
Allen, Frederick Kenneth, 127
Ancell, Captain E., 98
Apitz, Anders, 100
Ardern, Professor Philip, 251
Ashe, Otto, 100
Aube, Captain, 81
Aubert, Rev. Mother Suzanne, 16
Austen, Jane, 48
Australia, 53-68 *passim*, 87, 97, 234, 253-4
Australian Steam Navigation Company, 114
Aylmer, Reverend William, 39

'Baccarat' or 'Tranby Croft' case, 84
Baddeley, Reverend, W.H., 237-8
Baker, Reverend Shirley Waldemar, 34
Baldwin, Stanley, 110
Banabans on Rabi, 225-7
Banks, Joseph, 187
Bataillon, Reverend Pierre Marie, 4, 7, 9, 12
Beaglehole, Professor J.C., x, 257
Beaulieu, Reverend Francois, 172
Becke, Louis, 47, 128, 130
Belfast, 142-3
Bennett, Bill, 223, 229-30, 241
Bird, Isabella, 44, 69, 75, 83
Bligh, Captain William, 1
Blacklock, William, 131
Bogese, George, xi, 218, 222, 229-42 *passim*
Bolitho, Hector, 254
Bougainville Island, 16, 67, 117-8, 262, 264
Bourdin, Reverend Antoine, 9, 10

Brander, Titaue, 81-2
British Grenadiers, 245
Brodie, Niel, 99
de Brosses, Charles, 61
Brown, Reverend George, 63
Bruce, Robert, 70, 243
Brugmans, Reverend Aloysius, 237
Buck, Sir Peter, 34, 216, 263
Bulletin, 174
Burke's Peerage and Baronetage, 70
Burns, Philp and Co., 135, 137, 139

Cambridge University, 88
Campbell, Elizabeth, 70
Campbell, Martin, 228
Campbell, Mary, 224
Campbell, Walter, 72
Cartland, Barbara, 34
'Chair and Rule' movement, 220
Chalmers, Reverend James, 157
Chambers, L.W., 106
Champagna, Reverend Marcellin, 16
Chanel, Reverend Pierre, ix, x, 1-31 *passim*, 59
Chapman, Reverend, J. P., 63
Charlemagne, 70
Charles Hennings and Co., 117
Cheesman, Lucy Evelyn, ix, x, 187-210 *passim*
China, 82, 88-9, 131
Chiniquy, Reverend Charles, 63
Churchill, William, 105-8 *passim*
Cleghorn, Thomas and Archibald, 46
'Coastwatchers', 238
Cochrane, Admiral Thomas, 127
Coe, Jonas 134
Coe, 'Queen' Emma, 123, 137
Colin, Reverend Jean-Claude, 3, 4, 9, 10, 15, 16, 264
College of St. John the Evangelist, 251
Collingridge, George, 60
Colonial Sugar Refining Co., 116
de Comyn, Counts, 70
Cook, Captain James, x, 1, 2, 61, 187, 196-7
Cook Islands, 136
Cook, Joseph, 119

Cornwall, Frank, 129
Corris, Peter, 110
Coste, Reverend Jean, 15
Couppe, Reverend Louis, 58
Cowlishaw, 179-80
Cox, Reverend William, 181
Craig, Sam, 100
Cremation, 84
Cullen, Reverend Paul, 54
Cumming, Sir Alexander, 70
Cumming-Bruce, Charles, 72
Curtin, John (PM of Australia), 237
Cyr, Reverend Alcyme, 13

Darrach, J., 129
Darwin, Charles, 189
Davidson, Professor J.W., xi, 125, 257
Daws, Professor Gavin, 34
Deakin, Alfred (PM of Australia), 147-8, 157
Deans, John, 38
Deutsche Handels-und Plantagen-Gesellschaft (DHPG), 128
Dickens, Charles, 189
Dillon, Peter, 125-6
Dolling, Mary, 117
Dollinger, August, 118, 122
Douglas, Reverend Francis V., 17
Dumont d'Urville, Captain J.S.C., xi, 7
Dunmore, Professor John, 258
Durkheim, Emile, 261
Dutch New Guinea ('West'/'Jayapura'), 188, 200-2
Dyer, Henry, 82

Edward VII, King, 84
Elkin, Professor A.P., 240
Elloy, Reverend Louis, 81
Epalle, Reverend, Jean-Baptiste, 8, 59

Faessel, Sonia, 258
Faramond, Jean, 8, 9
Farrell, Thomas, 100
Favenc, Ernest, 60
Favre, Reverend Julien, 10
Ferguson, Alexander, 118
Fiji Islands, 63-4, 75, 85-7, 112-3, 128, 145, 213, 234, 247

Firth, Professor Raymond, 257
Fisher, Andrew (PM of Australia), 174, 177
Flynn, Errol, 149
Forster, Johann Reinhold, 187
Fuahea, Reverend Lolesio, 15

Garran, Sir Robert, 125
Gauguin, Paul, 1, 41, 264
Gay, Thomas, 33-48 *passim*
Geiger, General Roy 220
Gibson, Walter Murray, 34
Gilbert and Ellice Islands (Kiribati and Tuvalu) 59, 211
Gina, Belshazzar, 219, 222-3
Glasgow, Senator T.W., 125
Glover, Denis, 38
Glynn, P.M., 177
Godeffroy und Sohn, 113, 128
Godley, Charlotte, 44
Goodenough, Commodore James, 78
Gorai, 'Chief', 118
Gordon, Sir Arthur Hamilton, 78-80, 85, 88
Gordon-Cumming, Alexander 72, 73
Gordon-Cumming, Anne 74
Gordon-Cumming, Constance Frederika, ix, x, 64, 69-92 *passim*
Gordon-Cumming, Francis, 71
Gordon-Cumming, Frederick, 73
Gordon-Cumming, Lady Jane, 77-8
Gordon-Cumming, John, 72, 77
Gordon-Cumming, Roualeyn, 72-3
Gordon-Cumming, Walter, 84
Gordon-Cumming, William, 70-2, 76, 84, 87
Goyau, Georges, 258
Grant, Eleanora and George, 74, 83
Grant, Ulysses S., 82
Green, Reverend James, 81
Gregory, Reverend Abbot, 9
Grey, Sir George, 43, 46, 80
Grimes, Reverend John, 11
Grimshaw, Beatrice Ethel, ix, x, 141-67 *passim*
Grimshaw, Ramsay and Osbourne, 149
Guiart, Professor Jean, 265

Haddon, Professor A.C., 191, 194
Hanner, Ruth Knudsen, 42

Hawai'i, viii, 33-4, 39-52 *passim*, 62, 175
Hay, Ebenezer, 38
Hayes, William 'Bully', 93
Hearst, William Randolph, 104
Henry Cave and Co., 116
Holmes, Col.onel William, 119, 122
Hornell, James, 191
Houghton, Frances S.E., 127
Houghton, Robert, 127
Hughes, W.M., (PM of Australia), 169-70)
Hunt, Atlee, 170

im Thurn, Sir Everard, 145
Ireland and Irish, 53, 66, 142, 144, 259
Ishimotu, 231
Ito, 245

Japan and Japanese, 82-3, 170, 175-7, 202, 218-9, 231, 236-9
Jermyn, Reverend Hugh, 77
John Paul II, Pope, 15
Johnson, Martin and Osa, 196,
Jolliffe, Sarah, 135-6
Jones, Reverend John, 173
'Jonfrum' movement (Vanuatu), 263
Journal of the Polynesian Society, 216

Kalakaua, King David, 46, 83
Kamehameha V, King, 40
Kane, R.R., 246, 248-9
Kenilorea, Sir Peter, (PM of Solomons), 256
Kennedy, Donald Gilbert, ix, 130, 211-28 *passim*, 229-237 *passim*, 240-1
Kioa Island, 227
Kipling, Rudyard, xi, 141, 145, 156
Knudsen family, 33-49 *passim*
Komine, Isohiki, 122
Kronfeld family, 139

La France Australe, 178
Laing, Eva, 251
Laland, Sven, 101
Lamaze, Reverend Armand, 12
Lambert, Alderman W.H., 182
Lambton, R. L., 122
Landseer, Edward, 71
Langdon, Robert, 258

Langham, Reverend Frederick, 63-5, 80
La Perouse, Captain Jean-Francois, 125
Laracy, Eugenie, 262
Leenhardt, Reverend Maurice, 262
Lefroy, Professor Maxwell, 191
Le Menant de Chesnais, Reverend Theophile, 55
Leo XIII, Pope, 60, 63, 80
Leslie, Charles, 99
Leslie, T. G., 97, 102, 108
Lessard, Reverend Gaston, 16
Lever Bros Ltd, 117
Likelike, Queen, 46, 83
Liston, Reverend James, 14
Loades, David, 9
London, Jack, 103-4, 130
Lone Hand, 174-6
Loyalty Islands, ref. New Caledonia
Lundstrom, John, 220-1

Maasina Ruru ('Rule') 218, 224, 230, 239
Macdonalds, 'Lords of the Isles', 74
Macfarlane, Harry and Eliza, 46
MacQuarrie, Hector, ix, 243-56 *passim*
Magellan, Ferdinand, xi
Malietoa, Tanumafili, 57
Malietoa, Sa (family), 134
Malo, David, 34
Marchant, W.S., 217
Markham, Harold, 220, 238
Marryat, Frederick, 127
Marshall Islands, 56
Marzin, Reverend Jean de, 66
Masira, Timoci, 63
Mata'afa, Iosefa, 56
Matanitobua of Namosi, 66
Matthews, Richard, 253
Maude, H.E., 211-2, 216-7, 225, 240
Maudsley, Alfred, 78-9, 86
Maugham, Somerset, 41
McArthur and Co., 95
McDonald, Reverend James, 55
McHardy, Reverend Emmet, 16
McHutcheson, John and William, 39, 46
McKenzie, Clutha, 253
McKillop, Reverend Mary, 16
McLean, Alexander, 104-7

McLiver, Finlay, 117, 128
Mecredy, R.J, 144
Meitala, 6
Melanesians, character of, 150-2
Melville, Herman, 1
Meredith, Mary and Thomas, 134
Michener, James A., 141
Middleton, Dorothy, 69, 144
Middleton, Lord and Lady, 76
Milner, Frank, 213
Missionary organisations:
    Divine Word (Catholic), 149
    London Missionary Society, xii, 56, 64, 81, 138, 173
    Marist (Catholic), 1, 3, 54, 259, 263
    Melanesian Mission, 234
    Methodist, 63, 65
    Presbyterian, 194-5
    Seventh Day Adventist, 223
    Sacred Heart (Catholic), 59
Missions des Iles, 263
Mitterand, Francois, 260
Moors, H.J., 136
Moran, Reverend Patrick, ix, 15, 53-68 *passim*
Morgan, J.P and Co., 110
Morrison, George Ernest, 71
Mouton, Octave, 117, 123-4
Mulekupa (of Mono), 109
Munro, Doug, 128
Murchison, Robert, 71
Murray, Professor Gilbert, 147
Murray, Sir Hubert, 147, 149, 154, 157, 198
Murray, Reverend William Hill, 89
Musumusu, 6, 17

Naisiline, Henry, 172-4
Naiseline, Yiewene Dokucas, 171
Nelson, O.F., 138
New Caledonia, 169-86 *passim*, 203-4, 262, 264
New Guinea, 54, 118-24, 149, 197-9, 201-3
New Guineans, 153-4
New Hebrideans, 151-3
New York, 107, 110
New Zealand, 2, 4, 7-9, 14-17, 35-40, 55, 86-7

Nicolet, Reverend Claude, 10-12
Nielson, Lars, 97
Ni'ihau, 33-52 *passim*
Niue Island, 132
Niuliki, 'King', 1-17 *passim*
Norfolk Island, 234
North, Marianne, 69, 87

O'Farrell, Professor Patrick, 66
O'Haran, Reverend Denis, 56
Olsen, Anders, 100
O'Reilly, Reverend Pierre, ix, 257-65 *passim*
Osborn, L.W., 106
Osbourne, Lloyd, 57

Pacific Islands Monthly, 211
'Pandora', 253
Papua, 141-67 *passim*
Parkinson, Phoebe, 137
Parsonson, Professor G.S., 263
Paterson, A.B. 'Banjo', 127
Paton, Reverend Fred, 195
Patteson, Reverend John Coleridge, 2-3
Paton, Reverend Fred, 195
Pearce, George, 177
Penny, Reverend Alfred, 95-6
Piolet, Reverend J-B, 258
Polynesians, character of, 150
Pomare IV, Queen, 81
Pomare, V, King, 81
Pompallier, Reverend Jean-Baptiste, 4-8 *passim*, 260
Poncelet, Reverend J-B, 188
Pond, E.B., 103
Proctor, James Toutant, 93

Quiros, Pedro Fernandez de, 60-2, 67-8

Ragosa, Kato, 223
Revue Montalambert, 280
Rodwell, Sir Cecil, 247, 253
Rhodes, Henry, 45
Rhodes, W.B., 38
Rieu, Reverend Ernest, 13
Richardson, Sir George, 138
Rivet, Paul, 261-2

Index

Robinson family, ix, x, 33-52 *passim*
Robinson, Sir Hercules, 78
Ropiteau, Andre, 261
Rorique brothers, 93
Rougier, Reverend Emile, 65-6
Rouillac, Reverend Pierre, 59, 61
Rozier, Reverend Claude, 15
'104' Rue de Vaugirard, 259-65 *passim*

Salote, Queen, 139, 253
Salvado, Reverend Rosendo, 80
Samoa, 2, 56-8, 65, 81, 105, 127-39 *passim*
Samoa Shipping and Trading Co., 131, 135, 139
San Francisco, xi, 80, 103, 139
Scarr, Deryck, xi,
Saunders, Charles, 71
Scanlon, Reverend Desmond, 231, 237
Schwartz, W., 96
Sea Wolf, 104
Selwyn, Reverend George, 43-4
Sergison, Amelia, 74
Seton, Sir Claude, 238
Ships:
  AEI (*submarine*) 120, *Aimable Josephine* 7, *Albatross* 129, *Albert* 97, 105, *Allier* 7, *Anadyr* 78, *Au Revoir* 64, *Bessie* 39, 46, *Berrima* 181, *Beagle* 96, 253, *Bedford* 107, *Berrima* 119-21, *Blenheim* 35-7, *Borealis* 113-4, *Brisbane* 78, *Buka* 118, *Candia* 75, *Constitution* 94, *Corsair* 39, *Coulnakyle* 116-7, *Dadavata* 222, *Dawn* 133, 137, *Diamond* 98, *Douro* 99-101, 105, 108-9, *Dumbea* 178, *Eastern* 122, *Eclipse* 59, *Endeavour* 187, *Excelsior* 103, *Famenoth* 251, *Federal* 118, *General Grant* 107, *Ghost* 104, *Golden Gate* 100, *Gungha* 115, *Haapai* 115, *Hindoo* 77, *Hinemoa* 80, *Hopeful* 102, *Hudson* 4, *Ida* 95, *Iriquois* 95, *James Hamilton Lewis* 104, *Jeanette* 133, 138, *Jeanne d'Arc* 59,
  Jessie Miller 36-8, *John Hunt* 116, *John Williams* 64, *Kawau* 130-1, *Kitsutsuki* 231, *La Carbine* 117, *Lahloo* 117, *Laura* 133, 135, 137, *Lorengau* 121, *Louisa Craig* 134, *Ly-ee Moon* 114, *Macdhui* 200, *Makambo* 195, *Makura* 254, *Manu Tagi* 129, *Maori* 131-3, *Maroma* 82, *Mary Anderson* 95, *Matunga* 123, *Matupi* 121, *Maunganui* 254, *Meg Merrilies* 117, *Meklong* 121-2, *Merrimack* 94, *Miantonomah* 94, *Miawara* 200, *Mindini* 109, *Monantha* 117, *Monitor* 94, *Montana* 83, *Namolini* 216, *Niue* 123, *Offley* 39, *Orantes* 200, *Othello* 77, *Paloma* 82, *Pearl* 78, *Pera* 75, *Percy Edwards* 103-4, *Piscataqua* 95, *Porpoise* 130, *Princess Louise* 100, 105, 115, *Rainbow Warrior* 14, 93, *Ranadi* 247, 249-50, *Resolution* 196, *Richmond* 37-8, *Ripple* 118, *Rob Roy* 133, 137-8, *Royalist* 130-1, *Samoa* 133, 138, *Sandfly* 115, *Sea Breeze* 112-4, *Seignelay* 81-2, *Senta* 121, *Siar* 121, *Sisters* 36-8, *Sophia Sutherland* 103-10 *passim*, *Stanley* 114, *Star* 121, *St. George* 192-3, *Sumatra* 121, *Susquehana* 94, *Tahiti* 254, *Takobur* 123, *Tauranga* 65, *Titus* 106, *Tofua* 254, *Upolu* 13-1, *Van oon Stratten* 123, *Venture* 114, *Wai-ai* 232-4, 238, *William Hamilton* 7, *Zephyr* 96
Shipman, Captain H., 96
Shirriffs, Williamina, 46
Simmons, Reverend Ernest, x
Sinclair family, ix, 33-52 *passim*, 82
Singh, Rajah Sir Deo Nareien, 75
Skinner, H.D., 216
Societe des Oceanistes, 257, 263
Society of Mary, ref. Marists
Sogo, Magiko, 219, 224

Solomon Islands, 3, 59, 96-9, 105-6, 114, 117, 125, 133, 217-24, 243-256 *passim*
Sorensen, Niels Peter, ix, 93-110 *passim*, 115, 117
Stevenson, Robert Louis, 57, 130
St George Expedition, 191-3, 195, 197
Strasburg, John, ix, 111-26 *passim*
Stuart, Captain Leslie, 65
Sturdee, Captain A.C.D., 130
Sydney, xi, 116, 131
Sydney Morning Herald, 64

Tahiti, 45, 252-3, 261
Tamasese, 56
Taylor, James, 113
The Times, 141
Thomas, Josiah, 177
Thomson, Sir Basil, 145-6
Tipping, Ethel May, 181
Tokelau Islands, 132-4
Tonga, 128, 155
Torot, Reverend Peter, 16
Torres, Pedro de, 62
Towns, Robert, 112
Tryon, Admiral George, 100-1
Tupua lineage, 56, 81
Turner, Reverend George, 81
Tuvalu (Ellice Islands), 130, 133-4, 137, 213-7, 224-5, 227

Union Steam Ship Co., 145

Vanikoro Kauri Timber Co., 245
Vanuatu (New Hebrides), 60, 96, 176-9 *passim*, 194-5 (researchers), 199, 204
Veuster, Reverend Damien de, 16
Viard, Reverend Philip, 8
Victoria, Queen, 84
Vidal, Reverend Julien, 63-6
Von Holt, Ida, 40
Vouza and the Solomon Islands, 243-4
Vouza, Sir Jacob, 229-30, 244-56 *passim*

Wade, Reverend Thomas, 67
Wallace, Alfred Russel, 188-9, 193, 201
Wallen, Frederick, 137
Wallis and Futuna islands, 1-17 *passim*, 56
Watriama, William Jacob, x, 169-86 *passim*
Watson, Lt.Col. W.R., 122
Webber, John, 2
Welchman, Reverend Henry, 234
Whibley, J.G., 137
Whitaker, Frederick, 80
'White Women's Protection Ordinance' (1926), 154
Wilde, Oscar, 48
William McArthur and Co., 129
Williams, Reverend John, 2
Woodford, Charles M., 105-6, 108-9, 188
World War I, 1, 119, 136-7, 161, 169, 181-2, 243, 251, 259
World War II, x, 11, 198, 217-24, 229, 262
Worrall, Henry, 63, 65
Wright, Hamilton, 96